John McGahern and the Imagination of Tradition

John McGahern and the Imagination of Tradition

STANLEY VAN DER ZIEL

CORK UNIVERSITY PRESS

First published in 2016 by
Cork University Press
Youngline Industrial Estate
Pouladuff Road, Togher
Cork, Ireland

British Library Cataloguing in Publication Data
A CIP record for this book is available from the British Library.

ISBN: 978-1-78205-164-0

Printed in Malta by Gutenberg Press
Print origination & design by Carrigboy Typesetting Services, www.carrigboy.com

www.corkuniversitypress.com

For Jana, Sonia and Vincent

‘I don’t think that you can be a writer without being a reader first’

John McGahern

Contents

Preface

John McGahern has traditionally been regarded as the foremost 'chronicler' (that word appears often in criticism of his work) of the lives of farmers, teachers, schoolboys and policemen in the Irish midlands in the twentieth century. So consistent and so true are his treatments of life in rural Leitrim and Roscommon — the isolated counties in the north-west midlands of Ireland where he had grown up and to which he returned to make his permanent home on a secluded lakeside farm in the early 1970s — that he has often been described as a writer of purely local or national interest, one who is noteworthy principally for the painstaking accuracy of his depictions of a recognisable culture at a specific moment in history. To a critic like Eamon Maher, for example, McGahern is distinguished by 'his unique ability to capture in a poetic way the lives of rural families in the west of Ireland in the forties and fifties. For people who wish to get an insight into this close-knit, religious and sometimes violent race, there is no better reference than the writings of McGahern.'[1] This is well put, and it is certainly not my intention in this book to suggest that the geography and the social and cultural milieu in which McGahern lived and worked did not inform his work. To suggest that any writer exists in an ahistorical bubble would be reckless. At the same time, this book does not seek to add to the considerable amount of existing literature devoted to placing McGahern's fiction in its social or historical contexts. It shall be taken as read that McGahern's environment supplied the direct inspiration for the settings, characters and story materials of much of his fiction, and that his novels and stories operate both as critiques and validations of the culture from which they sprung. Nor will it aim, as certain other recent critics have attempted, to link the plots of his novels and stories to events that may have happened in his life, making use of *Memoir* as a kind of guidebook to navigate the autobiographical landscape of the fiction. Instead, I here propose a more purely literary or literary-historical approach to McGahern's fiction. The aim of *John McGahern and the Imagination of Tradition* is to elucidate how McGahern's imagination was informed by his extensive reading of and thinking about classic literature — or to put it another way, how the writer's imagination is simultaneously highly individual and deeply 'traditional'.

This book is the result of more than a decade of reading and thinking about the work of John McGahern. I have during that period accrued many professional and intellectual debts.

I wish to acknowledge receipt of a Government of Ireland Postdoctoral Fellowship from the Irish Research Council for the Humanities and Social Sciences in 2011–12.

I continue to be grateful to Declan Kiberd and John Brannigan, who supervised the PhD dissertation on the fiction of John McGahern for which much of the research which eventually made its way into the present volume was first carried out. With their very different styles of supervision, their unfailing scholarly integrity and their lucid insights into different aspects of my work, they have both been constant presences behind all my subsequent scholarly endeavours. Derek Hand took over those formal duties when he agreed to act as my post-doc mentor at St Patrick's College, Drumcondra; for his reading of and commentary on the manuscript as it evolved, and for inexhaustible moral support during the difficult times, I am very grateful. I owe as great a debt to Denis Sampson, whose friendship and whose conversation about all things McGahern, as well as on many other topics both literary and esoteric, has been indispensable ever since our first meeting in 2005. Eamon Maher, too, has provided intellectual and practical support stretching back over many years, especially during the earlier stages of the research.

Other friends, teachers and colleagues who have in their different ways been helpful or supportive at various stages include: Adam Bargroff, Neil Belton, Ron Callan, Niall Carson, Thomond Coogan, David Coughlan, the late John Devitt, Brian Donnelly, Noreen Doody, Alan Graham, Michael J. Griffin, John Kenny, David Malcolm, P.J. Mathews, Frank McGuinness, Joe Morris, Raymond Mullen, Christopher Murray, Tony Murray, Kate Murray-Browne, Mark Nixon, Avril Patterson, Anthony Roche, Richard Robinson and Frank Shovlin. I am particularly grateful to Graham Price and Tom Walker, who both read the manuscript at an early stage, and whose insights into my weaknesses and oversights have greatly improved the final text. My gratitude extends also to Fergus Fahey at the James Hardiman Library, National University of Ireland, Galway, whose generosity with ideas, time and resources has been invaluable; and to Catriona Clutterbuck for providing me with copies of her notes taken during McGahern's seminars on modern writing at University College, Dublin, in 1999. Maria O'Donovan and Mike Collins at Cork University Press have been unfailing with practical help and guidance on all manner of issues.

Thanks also to Madeline McGahern, to Monica, Paddy and Paula Gilligan, and other members of the extended McGahern family who have been generous with their time to share memories and answer questions on various topics related to McGahern's reading and writing.

My greatest debt, as always, is to my wife Jana, who has been extraordinarily patient and supportive throughout the long process of writing this book, and whose conversation has 'lightened and deepened' much of my thinking. I have been very fortunate to have been able to draw on her experience and expertise as a scholar throughout all the stages of the composition and production of this book. The book is dedicated, with love and gratitude, to her, to our newborn son Vincent, and to our daughter Sonia, a little girl who is fascinated with the little penguins on the spines of many of dada's books.

Beckett. Excerpts from *Nohow On*, copyright © 1983 by Samuel Beckett. Excerpts from *Play* and *Rough for Theatre I* from THE COLLECTED SHORTER PLAYS by Samuel Beckett, copyright © 1982 by the Estate of Samuel Beckett. Excerpts from *Proust* from POEMS, SHORT FICTION, CRITICISM (VOL IV), copyright © 2006 by the Estate of Samuel Beckett. Excerpts from *Three Novels* by Samuel Beckett, English translation copyright © 1955 by the Estate of Patrick Bowles and the Estate of Samuel Beckett. Excerpts from *Waiting for Godot*, copyright © 1954 by Grove Press, Inc.; copyright © renewed 1982 by Samuel Beckett. Excerpts from *Watt* by Samuel Beckett, English translation copyright © 1953 the Estate of Samuel Beckett. Used in the US/Canada by permission of Grove/Atlantic, Inc. Any third party use of this material, outside of this publication, is prohibited. Reprinted in all other territories by permission of Faber & Faber Ltd, Editions de Minuit and Rosica Colin Ltd.

Lines from three poems by Patrick Kavanagh are reprinted from *Collected Poems*, edited by Antoinette Quinn (Allen Lane, 2004), and the quotation from Patrick Kavanagh's 'From Monaghan to the Grand Canal' is reprinted from *A Poet's Country: selected prose*, edited by Antoinette Quinn (Lilliput Press, 2003), by kind permission of the Trustees of the Estate of the late Katherine B. Kavanagh, through the Jonathan Williams Literary Agency.

Quotations from poems by W.B. Yeats are reprinted with the permission of Scribner, a Division of Simon & Schuster, Inc., from THE COLLECTED WORKS OF W.B. YEATS, VOLUME I: THE POEMS, REVISED by W. B. Yeats, edited by Richard J. Finneran. Copyright © 1928 by The Macmillan Company, renewed 1956 by Georgie Yeats. Copyright © 1933 by The Macmillan Company, renewed 1961 by Bertha Georgie Yeats. Copyright © 1940 by Georgie Yeats, renewed 1968 by Bertha Georgie Yeats, Michael Butler Yeats, and Anne Yeats. All rights reserved. Quotations from plays by W.B. Yeats are reprinted with the permission of Scribner, a Division of Simon & Schuster, Inc., from THE COLLECTED PLAYS OF W.B. YEATS, REVISED EDITION by W.B. Yeats. Copyright © 1934, 1952 by The Macmillan Company. Copyrights renewed © 1962 by Bertha Georgie Yeats and 1980 by Anne Yeats. All rights reserved.

All reasonable efforts have been made to contact certain other copyright holders. The author and the publisher will be happy to include further acknowledgements in future editions of this book.

Part of chapter two was previously published as 'McGahern, Austen and the Aesthetics of Good Manners', *Essays in Criticism*, vol. 63, no. 2 (2013), pp. 203–22; reused by permission of Oxford University Press.

Abbreviations

Page references to books by John McGahern are included in the main text in parentheses using the following abbreviations. All in-text references are to the first (hardcover) editions published by Faber & Faber. Unless otherwise stated, references to short stories are to the collections in which they first appeared. References to *The Leavetaking* are to the original edition.

AW	*Amongst Women* (1990)
B	*The Barracks* (1963)
CE	*Creatures of the Earth: new and selected stories* (2006)
CS	*Collected Stories* (1992)
D	*The Dark* (1965)
GT	*Getting Through* (1978)
HG	*High Ground* (1985)
L	*The Leavetaking* (1974)
Lrev	*The Leavetaking*, revised 2nd edn (1984)
LW	*Love of the World: essays*, ed. Stanley van der Ziel (2009)
M	*Memoir* (2005)
N	*Nightlines* (1970)
P	*The Pornographer* (1979)
PD	*The Power of Darkness* (1991)
TRS	*That They May Face the Rising Sun* (2002)

Introduction

> I came to write through reading. It is such an obvious path that I hesitate to state it, but so much confusion now surrounds the artistic act that the simple and the obvious may be in need of statement. I think reading and writing are as close as they are separate. In my case, I came to read through pure luck. I had great good fortune when I was ten or eleven. I was given the run of a library. I believe it changed my life and without it I would never have become a writer.
>
> 'The Solitary Reader' (*LW*, p. 87)

Every writer, John McGahern knew, is also a reader. When during the last two decades of his life he began to construct a version of his younger self in a series of talks and essays and eventually in *Memoir*, he stressed again and again the relationship between reading and writing. It is striking that in the much-cited autobiographical sketch of his formative years first published in the early 1990s, he casts his life in the shape of a portrait of the artist as a 'solitary reader' rather than an apprentice poet.[1] McGahern was clear from the beginning of his career about his dislike of what he would later describe as the worship of the 'romantic vision of the artist ... the artist as hero, the artist as God' which originated in the nineteenth century and which continued into the age of Joyce and Proust and their biographers.[2] As early as in a letter to Michael McLaverty written in June 1961, eighteen months before the publication of *The Barracks*, he remarked that 'I could not keep a diary of things or work, it would seem too self-conscious, a kind of beautization of the role of [the] artist.'[3]

It is no surprise, therefore, that unlike other important twentieth-century novelists, such as Joyce or Proust, J.M. Coetzee or John Banville, McGahern only rarely chose artists or writers as the subject of his novels and stories. The spectacle of a successful professional writer at work, as McGahern knew very well, is not a very dramatic thing to behold. The handful of writers we do encounter on the pages of his books — Maloney and the nameless title character of *The Pornographer*, or Eva Lindberg in 'The Beginning of an Idea' painfully aware of the difference between *writing* and *trying to write* (*GT*, p. 19) — are never successful ones. Much more often, readers are cast as potentially heroic figures in key scenes in his novels and stories. One of these, Mrs Waldron in 'Creatures of the Earth', recalls the merriment with which her husband had once greeted the announcement of a colleague that he would give up reading and concentrate on mountain climbing instead. To the Waldrons, the thought of giving up reading would be like giving up life itself, because without the pleasure and knowledge that reading brings she would consider her life to be 'spiritually idle' (*CE*, p. 322).[4]

Reading, writing and tradition

McGahern's identity as a writer is inseparable from that of the reader he had first become in his teens. In a speech given on 8 November 2003 to mark the conferral of an honorary doctorate from his alma mater, St Patrick's College, Drumcondra, where he had trained to be a teacher between 1953 and 1956, McGahern dutifully emphasised the importance of education. He proceeded by elaborating on how exactly he had come to understand the importance of a period in his life that had been largely spent reading classic works of poetry and prose not actually on the curriculum. Higher education, especially in the humanities, was finally important to McGahern because it offered a sense of tradition: 'Without knowledge we can have no sense of tradition, which must be continually renewed; and tradition is civilization' (*LW*, p. 116). The phrase after the semicolon was a direct quote from the American novelist and teacher of literature John Williams, to whose novels McGahern had recently written two new introductions.[5] Just as importantly, the first half of the same sentence explains how McGahern understood the term 'tradition', and suggests a critical approach through which his fiction might be understood. McGahern was clear in his conviction that no writer exists in isolation. If a writer is to be an important and original artist, he or she must first be a careful and responsive reader aware of the shape of the tradition in which their work exists. In an unpublished manuscript draft of an essay about reading and writing, McGahern quotes Ruskin's remark that 'Books are a society of friends.'[6] Writing, for McGahern, was a form of dialogue with all the great authors who had come before. He was fond of repeating W.H. Auden's epigrammatic description of the writer's relationship to his forebears: 'breaking bread with the dead'. That epigram had become common currency in the McGahern household in Leitrim; it is also invoked in an early draft of one of McGahern's essays, in which he writes that 'To continually break bread with such company is almost as necessary for our spiritual lives as plain bread is for our daily sustenance.'[7] To write without reading is an act of barbarism, as it breaks the continuity of the tradition. It may even be, in its refusal to break bread, a form of bad manners! McGahern suggested as much when he said in an interview that 'There are basic structures that one leans on, whether in speech or in meeting people. One could say that there are manners of the intellect as well as social manners, and that not to have read certain books is almost as ill-mannered as not being able to greet somebody coming into a room.'[8] He was perhaps somewhat hyperbolic for rhetorical effect on that occasion, but the basic idea nonetheless expressed an important conviction at the heart of his artistic identity.

This does not imply, of course, that a writer like McGahern was merely derivative of the successful literary examples of the past. On the contrary, McGahern's admiration for writers who honoured or developed or even established traditions (as he recognised W.B. Yeats had done)[9] was unstinting precisely because the idea of 'tradition' signified not stagnancy but the potential for progression and growth. That argument is itself of course deeply traditional. The suggestion in McGahern's honorary-doctorate acceptance speech that tradition 'must be continually renewed' clearly invokes T.S. Eliot's seminal 'Tradition and the Individual Talent', an essay he almost certainly first read when he was a student at St Patrick's College in the 1950s. Eliot's argument proposes a sense of literary continuity that is much more complex than mere imitation. Eliot argues that while there is a general tendency in literary criticism to 'dwell with satisfaction upon [a writer's] difference from his predecessors . . . we shall often find that not only the best, but the most individual parts of his work may be those in which the dead poets, his ancestors, assert their immortality most vigorously'. What makes a writer 'traditional' is not a 'blind or timid adherence' to the successes of previous generations. Tradition does not live by endless repetition of what is greatest in the literature of the past. Such a limited idea of tradition should be discouraged. Instead, Eliot argues that a sense of tradition cannot be simply 'inherited', but that only by 'great labour' can the individual talent become part of the tradition.

Eliot's argument in its entirety underlies McGahern's understanding of the importance of tradition. His comment about the continual renewal of the tradition specifically invokes the section in which Eliot argues that not only are the most original parts of a writer's work also usually the most deeply indebted to tradition, but that

> No poet, no artist of any art, has his complete meaning alone...what happens when a new work of art is created is something that happens simultaneously to all the works of art which preceded it. The existing monuments form an ideal order among themselves, which is modified by the introduction of the new (the really new) work of art among them.[10]

A truly 'traditional' writer is one who is compelled to write with a constant feeling for the traditions of the past, but who simultaneously uses the lessons from the past to shape a body of work that is so startlingly unique and individual that it forces future writers to take renewed stock of the shape and the values of the tradition. The work of such a traditional writer, in the words of Jorge Luis Borges, another author whose essays on literature McGahern much admired, 'modifies our conception of the past, as it will modify the future'.[11] It is clear that McGahern thought of literature as 'traditional' in this sense not just in his old age at the beginning of the twenty-first century but from the beginning of his career. All his life, writing and tradition were for him vital, living things. So when as early as 1968 McGahern came to consider the work of some of his near-contemporaries, he chose to regard them not only as individual talents but also, as he wrote in a letter, as representatives of 'different traditions in their continuance'.[12] He was equally conscious of his own position in a number of traditions, and often wrote with one eye firmly fixed on the achievements of some of his most illustrious predecessors.

McGahern certainly did not passively inherit the traditions in which he worked; his sense of tradition was obtained, as Eliot stipulated, 'by great labour'.[13] This book is concerned with how his years of reading went into the formation of a literary imagination that was at once wholly individual and deeply traditional. From his first published novel onward, McGahern developed a recognisable voice and style. Like that of all important original writers, his style was firmly rooted in a deep and subtle appreciation of the richness of the Irish, the English and the wider European literary tradition. McGahern's earliest introduction to the Western tradition as a boy copying and memorising speeches from Shakespeare's plays and lines of eighteenth- and nineteenth-century verse in the schoolrooms of rural Leitrim and Roscommon, and the way in which memories of that early schooling lingered ever after, are more than once invoked in the fiction of his maturity. Guard Casey in *The Barracks*, involuntarily remembering and automatically reciting a line from Robert Browning during a conversation, as is his wont, remarks about that habit to Elizabeth that 'we used to have to fairly sweat to learn the lines out of the auld school-books and you find them all the time, even the ones you forgot, comin' back and back. It's a terror, isn't it?' (*B*, p. 207)[14] The same debt is acknowledged through the voice of the mother in *The Leavetaking* when she tells the nun at the school where she teaches that 'What gives me most pleasure still from my own schooling are the poems I learned by heart then; constantly I find them passing through my mind, not unlike old friends or stray strands of music, while I hardly remember anything else with pleasure from the same schooling' (*L*, p. 37).

With its aurally striking repetition of the word 'pleasure', the latter passage pays silent homage to W.H. Auden, who, in an aphorism McGahern liked to quote in lectures and at public readings, had written that 'Pleasure is by no means an infallible critical guide, but it is the least fallible.'[15] The importance of pleasure as the preferred guiding principle in all matters literary is stressed particularly in 'The Solitary Reader', in which Auden's remark is quoted (*LW*, p. 90). Pleasure is associated in that essay with McGahern's introduction at the age of ten or eleven to two Protestant gentlemen, a father and son called Willie and Andy Moroney. The Moroneys gave the young McGahern free access to their nineteenth-century library, from which he would take and return books by the dozen in an old oilcloth shopping bag. At the Moroneys, he recalled, he would read without guidance and 'for nothing but pleasure, the way a boy nowadays might watch endless television dramas' (*LW*, p. 89), thus living out Auden's dream. The crucial part played in McGahern's intellectual development by the Moroneys' laissez-faire approach to literature has been much remarked upon, as has the fact that tributes to their example of tolerance and learning were subsequently worked into short stories such as 'The Conversion of William Kirkwood' and 'Oldfashioned' (both from *High Ground*). As critics such as James Whyte and Belinda McKeon have pointed out, the portrait in the latter story of the liberal and artistic attitudes of the Protestant Sinclairs who live at the old rectory and who give the protagonist his first book, a volume on natural history (*HG*, p. 49), is clearly a tribute to the inhabitants of the house in which the future novelist had first read about the Rocky Mountains.[16] It is equally tempting to think that the boy Willie who provides Elizabeth with library books in *The Barracks*, written twenty years earlier, may already have been named in memory of old Willie Moroney (although another possible namesake is suggested elsewhere in this book).[17]

There may be a danger, however, of overemphasising the importance of pleasure at the expense of all other criteria of literary value. To suggest that McGahern thought it the only valid way of approaching literary works would suggest a lack of discipline or conscious, intelligent critical awareness. For that reason, it is important to recognise how 'The Solitary Reader',

Memoir and certain other works of fiction and non-fiction pay equal homage to an important model for rigour, discipline and learning which entered the author's life around the same time in his early teens. In 'The Solitary Reader', McGahern remarks that he had had the 'great good fortune' (*LW*, p. 87) of being introduced to not just one but two significant influences almost simultaneously during that formative period. He was always conscious of the fact that his admittance, shortly after his introduction to the Moroneys, to the newly opened Presentation Brothers Secondary School in Carrick-on-Shannon, which he began attending in 1948, was no less of a stroke of good fortune at a time when education beyond primary level was not universally available, especially in the remoter regions of rural Ireland. It was for this reason that he would on several occasions in his later life make a comic occasion of the coincidence by which one of the brothers not just once but twice discussed the continuance of his education with his father in the incongruous setting of the potato field (*LW*, pp. 104, 107); it was one of his myths of origin as a writer.

At the Presentation Brothers both the type of literature and the intensity with which it was studied could not have been more different either from that at the local primary school where his mother taught or from his private reading at the Moroneys with which it was contemporaneous. Their educational model was the English grammar-school tradition, which emphasised such classical disciplines as grammar, syntax, rhetoric and prosody. The nature of the different kinds of initiations to books and reading the young McGahern underwent at the Presentation Brothers and the Moroneys, respectively, perfectly complemented one another, and both were of lasting value to the budding professional writer. There may have been tales from Ovid and Homer in the Moroneys' library, and no doubt they were a source of pleasure, but the teenage McGahern would have been more systematically instructed in the language and literature of Roman antiquity by the brothers. There is in McGahern's recollections of the Moroneys in 'The Solitary Reader' a niggling sense that his reading would perhaps have benefited from at least *some* guidance (*LW*, p. 90). The truth was that, of course, his school life with the brothers provided exactly such guidance and structure to counterbalance the complete anarchic freedom he experienced in that other setting. There is evidence to suggest that McGahern, for all his later vocal agreement with Auden's pleasure principle, enjoyed the methodical approach of the Presentation Brothers. A later work like 'Crossing the Line', from *High Ground*, mildly satirises the type of adult who professes to have literary interests but whose spectrum of tastes and values has never managed to move beyond the appreciation of the Latin poems he had once translated as a schoolboy.[18] This is not to say, however, that Horace and Virgil did not continue to offer him pleasure and enlightenment (as they do to the boy in *The Dark* who so joyfully recites Horatian odes as he pedals his bicycle home through the boglands of Roscommon (*D*, p. 124)), even after he had moved to Dublin and discovered the different insights which twentieth-century literature has to offer.

McGahern always remembered how he liked Latin as a subject when he was a schoolboy. He grew so fond of Horace, in fact, that he once 'attempted to smuggle some of his thought into my Irish essay' only to be good-humouredly corrected by his teacher for his use of a 'pagan opinion' (*LW*, p. 106). Systematic instruction in Latin grammar and vocabulary, and in the related classical arts of prosody and rhetoric, deepened his understanding of other things that were already rooted in his life. As he later remarked in *Memoir*, the Ordinary of the Mass, which he knew by heart and which he would sometimes chant aloud in moments of joyful solitude, began during his schooldays 'to take on meaning through Caesar and Virgil and Cicero and Horace' (*M*, p. 169). And if McGahern fundamentally believed, like Auden, that the measure of good literature should be that it gives pleasure, then this is not to say that he could not also appreciate the formal lessons about grammar and literary form and genre that were so thoroughly treated by the brothers. Those lessons, indeed, stood him in good stead in his later career as a poet who worked in prose. Michael C. Prusse has drawn attention in a couple of meticulously researched articles to McGahern's use of poetic devices such as repetition, and specifically of the chiasmic construction favoured by many classical poets. There are many examples in McGahern's fiction of chiasmus (that is, of an *x*-structure). The concluding lines of the published 'episodes' from *The End or the Beginning of Love*, the youthful first novel which McGahern withdrew from publication with Faber & Faber in 1961, are of particular interest because they draw explicit attention to this poetic technique. They document the father's fascination with a pattern he discerns in the words of advice he offers his son:

> Over and over again Francie heard him mutter the same words as if they held some hidden poetry or magic:
>
> 'Think what you say, but don't say what you think. Think, say; say, think. Think what you say, but don't say what you think.'[19]

The command of the classical arts of rhetoric and prosody underlying a stylistic habit such as this originated not only in McGahern's love for the prose style of the Bible, as Prusse astutely suggests;[20] it went back also to the Presentation Brothers' Latin classes in Carrick-on-Shannon.

It is only fitting, therefore, that McGahern should once more 'smuggle' Horace into his prose thirty years after leaving Carrick-on-Shannon, when he came to write his moving tribute to the Presentation Brothers and their tradition of learning in 'Oldfashioned'. An early, much-cited passage in that story introduces a striking simile which imagines schoolboys moving through the landscape 'like uncertain flocks of birds on bicycles' to learn Latin, English, geography and mathematics (*HG*, p. 37). That image is not indebted to the indigenous example of Gaelic poetry, but rather to the Latin poetic tradition which owed its survival in the consciousness of rural Ireland through the nineteenth century to the culture of 'hedge schools and the poor scholar' which is invoked in the same paragraph (*HG*, p. 37). McGahern's simile constitutes a loose rendering, in soaring elegant English prose which wittily acknowledges the freewheeling realities of the mid-twentieth century, of an idea from 'Non usitata', the last poem in Book II of Horace's *Odes*, in which the poet is transformed by his poetic powers into a soaring bird.[21]

The way in which traces of this and other examples of his wide reading found their way into his fiction was as immensely subtle as it was purposeful. McGahern was not interested in repeating favourite lines from poems in his novels and stories simply as a form of highbrow literary ornament. Such a habit could only lead to the sentimentalising of literature, a temptation against which the mother in *The Leavetaking* speaks out when she encounters it in others (*L*, p. 38). Instead, he was interested above all in the *ideas* he found in his predecessors: in the metaphysical, social and moral ideas surrounding the nature of human life as it is lived in solitude or in company,[22] and particularly in the myriad ideas and theories surrounding the nature and the purpose of writing. This is perhaps not how most readers initially think of McGahern, but literary or academic professionals who came to know him closer invariably soon recognised this aspect of his personality. Christopher Murray, a lecturer at University College, Dublin, during McGahern's time as writer in residence there in 1977–78, later recalled how he was 'immensely impressed' when the novelist first arrived because he was 'a complete professional, a teacher to his fingertips, but one who knew literature inside out and had thought deeply about its nature and purposes'.[23]

This book will read McGahern as a self-aware novelist of ideas. It is clear from his fiction no less than it is from his occasional literary essays and reviews that McGahern had, ever since he first discovered the pleasures of reading in his early teens, developed into a knowledgeable and a very skilled and independent-minded critical reader who was always ready to read the literary values of the past against the grain in order to shed new light on well-worn tenets and ideas. He learned this lesson well in the stifling intellectual climate of 1950s Ireland, where even the rare opportunity of pursuing a third-level education was no guarantee of being encouraged to think for oneself. Through his discovery of a new and exciting way of reading books during that time, he came upon the realisation, as he recalls in 'The Solitary Reader', that 'We have to discard all the tenets that we have been told until we have succeeded in thinking them out for ourselves' (*LW*, p. 90). For the mature McGahern, that thinking out for oneself of the accepted tenets of literary criticism most often took the form of original fiction writing. McGahern's major subject, as a fiction writer no less than as a book reviewer or as a teacher of literature, was the history and the nature of literature itself. His fiction continually reimagines and rewrites — often ironically — the very traditions within which it operates; because sometimes, it seems, the most subtle and incisive acts of literary criticism are those written in the form not of formal critical books or articles but of original works of fiction. The purpose of this book, therefore, is not simply to identify quotes from and allusions to classic books and authors. Instead, it will isolate some of the major ideas McGahern took from his most eminent predecessors, and demonstrate how his fictional oeuvre can be read as a sustained critical commentary on the various literary traditions within which it operates. In a way, then, this book is a potted history of literary and aesthetic ideas reflected through the eyes of one particular individual 'solitary reader' who happened to become a writer.

The chapters that follow will look in detail at the main ideas McGahern borrowed and adapted from some of the Irish, English and European authors whom he most admired, and whose stamp can be most consistently discerned on central aspects of his own thinking about the nature and purposes of literature. The 'tradition' presented in a book such as this is necessarily limited. The inclusions and omissions of writers may seem like an idiosyncratic, highly selective and ultimately rather fraught act of canon formation, one which unjustifiably foregrounds minor Irish figures such as Forrest Reid or Tomás Ó Criomhthain over more established names from other continents and centuries. But the tradition upon which any individual writer calls never exactly corresponds with the established canon or 'Great Tradition' of important and representative writers which has solidified in university departments since the late nineteenth century. The writers foregrounded in this book reflect a selection from the tradition which McGahern 'created' for himself — in the sense in which Borges says all writers do.[24] It reflects the writers to whom McGahern had for a variety of reasons been exposed early on in the schoolrooms of Leitrim and Roscommon, and later in the educational institutions, bookshops, libraries and theatres of Dublin, and who remained important to him all his life as he plotted the trajectory of his career as a novelist.

The book is divided thematically as much as it is chronologically. The chapter headings contain adjectives which roughly correspond with the periodisation one expects to find in a literary history. The opening sections of each of the chapters do indeed provide an overview of allusions in McGahern's fiction to works from the genre (for example, the realist novel), movement (such as Romanticism) or period (the post-war decades) under scrutiny. It is not my intention, however, for the chapters to take the form of extended collections of notes. For this reason, the bulk of each chapter develops an argument about McGahern's adoption and adaptation of one or more central ideas, tropes or themes, the origins of which may be traced to an author or a group of authors in that period. Just as importantly, the range of allusions in each of the chapters is not confined exclusively to the literature of a single period. Many ideas are freely transmitted, developed, revised and revisited by successive generations, and so different periods cannot be hermetically sealed. The dominant *ideas* McGahern took from various movements or periods form the structural backbone of the chapters. Accordingly, each chapter makes reference to relevant aspects in the work of authors from different historical eras. The emphasis, as much as possible, is on how McGahern read those authors, rather than on their conventional place in literary history. Writers such as Shakespeare, Yeats, Proust and Beckett appear in many of the chapters, because McGahern found in those authors versions of many areas of literary thought. Thus, Proust is a major subject twice in the book, once (in chapter five) as a modernist innovator of traditional ways of thinking about time, memory and the autonomy of the individual subject, but also (in chapter three) as a belated exponent of a Wordsworthian tradition of visionary Romanticism. Yeats is significant as the founder of an indigenous modern Irish tradition, as a poet who can validate familiar north-west-of-Ireland places and place names, and as a deep thinker about this life and the next (all subjects discussed in chapter six); he was also a champion of abandoned social and cultural values that may be rediscovered in the literature of the eighteenth century (discussed in chapter two), and many more things beside. Equally, the subject of the main part of chapter one is the self-conscious theatricality, derived from the Shakespearean trope that 'All the world's a stage', which runs through McGahern's fiction. The emphasis of that chapter may be mainly on Shakespeare, but it is also attentive to McGahern's uses of a wider post-Shakespearean theatrical tradition which includes writers as diverse as Synge, Beckett and Eugene O'Neill.

'books that act as mirrors'

For McGahern, literature was a way of seeing and knowing the world. In an interview from the 1980s, McGahern quoted the eminent Shakespearean scholar A.C. Bradley, who had said that 'About the best poetry . . . there floats an atmosphere of infinite suggestion. The poet speaks to us of one thing, but in this one thing there seems to lurk the secret of all.'[25] That same point was also emphasised in a number of linked key passages about the nature of reading — and by extension that of writing — which appear in works of fiction and non-fiction spanning the length of McGahern's career.

Elizabeth Reegan, the central consciousness of his first novel *The Barracks*, is McGahern's original 'solitary reader'. Her memories of discovering 'real books' for the first time under the influence of the well-read but ill-mannered Halliday (*B*, p. 87) anticipate the points McGahern would make in his own voice nearly three decades later in the central paragraphs of 'The Solitary Reader'. In an argument that is more than a little reminiscent of Auden's analysis of the growth of the reader in *The Dyer's Hand*, McGahern proposes in that essay how

> A time comes when the way we read has to change drastically or stop . . . This change is linked with our growing consciousness, consciousness that we will not live forever and that all human life is essentially in the same fix. We have to discard all the tenets that we have been told until we have succeeded in thinking them out for ourselves. We find that we are no longer reading books for the story and that all stories are more or less the same story; and we begin to come on certain books that act like mirrors. What they reflect is something dangerously close to our own life and the society in which we live.
>
> A new, painful excitement enters the way we read. We search out these books, and these books only, the books that act as mirrors. The quality of the writing becomes more important than the quality of the material out of which the pattern or story is shaped. (*LW*, p. 90)[26]

The bookish ghost of Elizabeth Reegan is revived a final time in the late story 'Creatures of the Earth', in which another middle-aged woman gives much thought to the deeper significance of reading. Mrs Waldron knows that reading is not a 'passive' activity, and that to truly read a work of literature takes as much exertion as the mountain climbing on which her late husband's colleague had decided to concentrate instead (*CE*, p. 322). In this conviction she echoes the concerns of the author. McGahern was himself a great advocate of slow, patient and conscientious approaches to novels and poems,[27] who knew that only after looking at books long and hard — as one might in a mirror — can they conceivably begin to 'answer back' (*CE*, p. 326). Mrs Reegan and Mrs Waldron are the two heroic readers who bookend McGahern's career as a writer of fiction. They both recognise, as McGahern does in his essays, that all 'real books' (*B*, p. 87), in the hands of a receptive reader, have the potential to 'lighten[ ] and deepen[ ] life, [give] recognition and pleasure' (*CE*, p. 323).

One of the great paradoxes McGahern savours in the key passage about reading in *The Barracks* is how Elizabeth Reegan finally succeeds in discovering her own 'uniqueness' through her immersion in the lives of fictional characters in favourite novels (*B*, p. 87). Obviously, the female protagonists of *The Barracks* and 'Creatures of the Earth' both know that they are not *literally* characters in a novel by Jane Austen (an author whose significance in the latter story will be discussed in chapter two). They certainly do recognise, though, how the ideas and preoccupations they find in novels like *Mansfield Park* or *Emma* can come to reflect and illuminate their own most private nature and beliefs. Elizabeth Reegan is helped on her way to expressing that knowledge by Halliday. She remembers how, when she had exclaimed that the books she had been reading '[a]re real! They're not stories even. They're about my life', Halliday's immediate reaction had been to point out that this is not 'exactly' true because the lives they depict are 'not yours'. Of course, Elizabeth knows this already. Halliday's initial interpretation of Elizabeth's response is literal-minded, patronising and ultimately deeply unhelpful. He somewhat redeems himself, though, when he continues to offer a more subtle way of understanding and articulating the importance of 'real' books which Elizabeth had only been able to intuit by proposing that 'You *feel and see them with your own life*, so much that it becomes real as your own' (*B*, p. 87, emphasis added).

Clearly this is a lesson that has been well internalised. Years later when she looks back on her early life with Halliday from her vantage point in the barracks she recognises how 'she was *seeing* [his words] now *with her own life*' (*B*, p. 86, emphasis added). That turn of phrase suggests how it is not just true that books function as mirrors in which one might see one's own life reflected in new and illuminating ways, but that in a very similar process one can also use one's own life as one might use a great novel to elucidate the significance of the words or the worlds of another. Elizabeth often uses the present state of her own life as a mirror. Just before her death near the end of the novel, again, an admission of selfish ulterior motives made to her by Halliday many years in the past 'appeared in terms of her own relationship with Reegan' (*B*, p. 210). The same thing also happens on occasion in later McGahern novels. In the original edition of *The Leavetaking*, Patrick Moran deliberately uses his own life in his attempts to *read* the story of that of his beloved when he says that 'I try to animate [her words] by turning them into my own life, I garland them with memory, embellish them with what I know' (*L*, pp. 120–1).

These are among the central ideas that underpin McGahern's entire artistic endeavour. Usually he confined his remarks to the nature of reading, leaving unspoken or undeveloped the implication that something similar must by analogy also be true for writing. In an exception to that rule, the short essay 'Playing with Words' (written in the mid-1980s but unpublished during his lifetime) contains a rare explicit suggestion of how the same principles which define mature reading should also be applied to the way a mature novelist approaches the act of writing: 'As in reading, when we become conscious that we are no longer reading romances or fables or adventure but versions of our own life, so it suddenly came to me that while I seemed to be playing with words in reality I was playing with my own life' (*LW*, p. 9). Reading and writing are closely related activities: both are ways of playing with one's own life, and both can 'act as mirrors' (*LW*, p. 90). With its emphasis on a metaphorical mirror through which internal and external realities can be made to correspond, that key passage in 'The Solitary Reader' might even be read as a natural and obvious development of McGahern's comments on the nature of artistic creation in his early poetic manifesto 'The Image', originally published in 1968, in which he had suggested that the artist can only look on the realities of his own life and times by 'purely *reflect[ing]* on our situation through this created world of ours, this Medusa's mirror' (*LW*, p. 5, emphasis added). Thus, the idea of 'books that act as mirrors' which McGahern would develop in a more reader-friendly form in 'The Solitary Reader' in 1991 is already latent in the dense, opaque prose of his first essay about writing.

It is easy to see, in light of this, why McGahern so disliked it when critics resorted to what he described in an exasperated early letter to his friend Patrick Swift, the painter who co-edited the literary magazine *X* in which McGahern made his print debut in April 1961, as 'the autobiography stunt!'[28] Beginning with his unpublished review of a 1968 biography of Eugene O'Neill, McGahern's occasional literary criticism regularly returned over the course of the next four decades to restating his conviction that knowing what happened to an author in his youth is immaterial to an appreciation of his or her writing. He made this position unambiguously clear for the final time in an interview with Eamon Maher conducted shortly after the publication of *Memoir*. There he repeated almost verbatim a comment he had previously made in his 1990 review of John Halperin's academic study of *Novelists in Their Youth* (see *LW*, p. 353) when he maintained that it was not only futile but actually counterproductive to look for the historical or biographical elements in a work of art, because 'Often it seems to me that the effect of much biographical criticism is to return fiction to the original confusion out of which clarity was won.'[29]

Flying in the face of such cautions, a critic like Dermot McCarthy is primarily interested in tracing McGahern's plots back to the incidents and accidents of the author's life. In that pursuit he leans heavily on *Memoir*, which he treats very much as a factual account of that early life. McCarthy is defiant in his insistence that McGahern's art is above all a form of therapy that endlessly repeats the personal traumas of childhood, and that '[McGahern's] claim "that personal therapy has no place in art" now seems contradicted by what the memoir shows about the fiction'.[30] It is undoubtedly true that many events described in McGahern's fiction rely on memories of lived experience. Still, this kind of reading of his fiction finally tells us very little about the way in which those raw experiences were transformed into great and universal works of art. This most narrowly biographical approach to McGahern's fiction sheds very little light on how, in the words of the narrator of the early story 'Wheels', that early life would be consciously cast again and again 'in the shape of a story' (*N*, p. 22) — or rather how it could be turned into a succession of different narratives, all drawing on the same basic set of broadly autobiographical story materials, by putting into practice the lessons he had learned in his parallel life as a reader. A comment McGahern made when he introduced Seamus Heaney to an American audience at Colgate University, upstate New York, in the early 1980s is telling in this respect. On that occasion he cannily chose to invoke the etymological root of the word 'poet' when he remarked: 'When I think of Mr Heaney's verse I turn as ever to an older word for the poet and that is maker, literally one who makes, *out of nothing*.'[31] The last phrase is specifically calculated to denigrate the importance of materials drawn from life. McGahern well knew that Heaney's poems rely on story materials which might be broadly termed autobiographical as much as his own fiction does. Yet his Colgate University speech consciously privileges the effort of shaping and creating over the intrinsic importance of those materials drawn from life to such an extent that the latter are wilfully reduced to a state of almost total irrelevance.

Literary examples are crucial presences in all of McGahern's reimaginings of his early life. Much more interesting than the question of how incidents from the author's life may make up the source material for the plots of his fiction is the opposite tendency: that by which things in a supposed non-fictional account like *Memoir* may sometimes actually be the result of McGahern's total immersion in the literary tradition. Often in a novelist like McGahern, textual or literary truths are allowed to override historical or biographical ones. Good fiction is rarely a straightforward record of autobiographical fact, but some 'facts' in the memoirs of great novelists can easily be inspired not by what has happened to the subject but by their immersion in works of literature. In the letter to Patrick Swift in which he decried 'the autobiography stunt', McGahern emphasised that 'the books I liked' were as important a feature of the 'autobiographical' landscape of his youth which is reimagined in his fiction as any aspect of local character or geography, or any instance of personal suffering or joy.[32] Critics keen to mine McGahern's fiction for plain autobiographical facts should beware, therefore, of how those facts are liable to have been shaped or created in the mind of the solitary reader.

Even in a supposedly truthful account of the author's early life like *Memoir*, things that sound like they are based in fact can have eerie literary analogues, and some things that are presented as simple autobiographical truth may actually be more indebted to McGahern's reading of 'certain books that act like mirrors' (*LW*, p. 90) than to childhood events. Sometimes the things we read about in books can come to seem much more real than things that have actually happened. What is more, these two forms of experience often cannot be fully separated by conscious intellectual effort.[33] McGahern's appreciation of the complex interplay between lived and read experience is illustrated by the Proustian sentence in 'The Solitary Reader' which proposes that 'There are no days more full in childhood than those days that were not lived at all, the days lost in a favourite book' (*LW*, pp. 89–90).[34] A case in point is the episode in *Memoir* which details the extraordinarily violent and traumatic circumstances of the young boy's first haircut:

> I had a head of curls like a girl. My father decided to remove them in spite of my frightened protests, made worse by my mother's and grandmother's obvious distress ... The chair was set down on the newspaper and it did not take long to remove the curls. Exultant, he brought me back into the living room, where my outraged cries must have added to the distress of the two women. He carried the curls in the folds of the newspaper. 'Weep not for me, O women of Jerusalem, but for yourselves and for your children,' he quoted triumphantly. (*M*, pp. 9–10)

This episode may be presented as simple autobiographical truth, but as the author immediately acknowledges it is at best a truth inflected by the 'religious imagery ... [which was] part of the air we breathed' (*M*, p. 10). That last remark is particularly revealing, since it demonstrates McGahern's consciousness of the way literary texts inform the way we perceive reality. When, more than sixty years after the event, the mature novelist draws attention to his father's habit for introducing biblical quotation into everyday situations (the verse quoted in *Memoir* is from Luke 23:28), and when he remarks that the curls on a sheet of newspaper 'came to resemble for me John the Baptist's severed head borne into the room on a silver plate' (*M*, p. 10), he is really also making a more general point about how memories of the past can over time be easily confused or conflated with powerful images from favourite works of literature. Thus, the writing of a historical narrative such as *Memoir* becomes, in the words of Linda Hutcheon, a complex 'form of cross-referencing that operates within (and does not deny) its unavoidable discursive context'.[35]

The Gospel of Luke is not the only intertext at work in the haircut episode of *Memoir*. In an additional 'remarkable parallel' the dramatic incident in its entirety also repeats a key scene in the formative years of young William Morel in chapter one of D.H. Lawrence's *Sons and Lovers*.[36] The latter parallel is so remarkable, in fact, that it raises the question whether McGahern's memory of his first haircut is indeed a memory of an early confrontation with his father, or whether it is consciously or unconsciously indebted to his subsequent reading of Lawrence. The appropriation of a plot element from *Sons and Lovers* may be part of a postmodern game which challenges the reader to make precisely this connection; the explicit reference in the relevant passage of *Memoir* to the father's habit for quotation may point to this. On the other hand, McGahern's reading of *Sons and Lovers* may have been so fully 'lived' (in the sense in which that word is used in 'The Solitary Reader') that over the intervening decades a scene from that novel took on all the vividity and veracity of a real memory. A memorable incident from Lawrence's novel may have become part of McGahern's consciousness, and the fictitiously factual experience he remembered would be no less real for its origins in a novel. Or to put it in those suggestive, resonant words of Halliday in *The Barracks*, McGahern may have *felt* the experiences of the young Morel 'with [his] own life, so much that it bec[ame] real as [his] own' (*B*, p. 87).

Then again, some things that look like they must have their origins in fiction or been made up for literary effect can be as real as anything. In what may be read as a gentle warning to over-zealous critics to tread sensitively in their hunt for literary analogies, McGahern suggests as much when Robert Booth, a minor character in *That They May Face the Rising Sun*, remarks that Bill Evans, the dishevelled, slow-moving figure carrying two buckets around the lake, 'looks like something out of a Russian novel', only to be corrected by Ruttledge that 'He's all ours, completely home-grown and mad alive' (*TRS*, p. 155). Of course, despite Ruttledge's intervention on the side of historical or biographical veracity, Robert Booth is not wrong, and the connection he makes is far from gratuitous. Bill Evans *is* like a serf in a novel by Tolstoy, and reading him as one allows an outsider like Robert Booth to understand a portion of his hardship. This is not as eccentric a strategy as it may seem. The rest of the lakesiders, many of whom have known him all his life, resort to the same need for literary analogy in their efforts to understand Bill Evans' lot when they compare one type of cruelty often inflicted on him by his keeper during trips to the creamery with Christ's journey to Calvary (*TRS*, p. 13).

If the haircut episode in *Memoir* demonstrates how fictional scenes may silently and spontaneously displace real memories, then McGahern and his characters alike also often consciously use their knowledge of classic texts to cast light on — or to 'mirror' — first-hand experiences. Beside Robert Booth, other characters in *That They May Face the Rising Sun* and elsewhere also repeatedly deepen their appreciation of their own situation by calling on literary analogies. For these characters, as, according to one theorist of the autobiographical genre, for many writers who had grown up amongst books, literature is not a distraction *from* but an indispensable 'source of self-definition'.[37] After saving the hay into the big new shed, Mary in *That They May Face the Rising Sun* wonders aloud what Jamesie's 'poor old father', who had lived with the young married couple for many years in the small downstairs bedroom of the farm of which he had once been lord and master, 'would make out of the shed now if he ran and put his nose to the window?' Jamesie, Mary and Ruttledge, the three characters who are present in the hayshed, respond in very different ways to that reminder of human mortality and social and generational mutability. Jamesie concludes simply that 'He'd think the world had gone mad', and gets on with his work, while Mary offers a follow-up thought to her husband's easy dismissal which suggests the next generation will soon be talking about *them* in the same careless way after they, too, will be dead and buried in the local churchyard. Ruttledge's response essentially rings the same cautionary note as the latter observation. But his remark that 'We may all be the father at the window yet' (*TRS*, pp. 122–3) is also an attempt to 'lighten[ ] and deepen[ ]' his own understanding and that of the others of the inevitable and universal process of marginalisation experienced by the old, the feeble and the dead through borrowing a well-known image from a favourite play. Declan Kiberd has suggested that Ruttledge's 'richly ambiguous sentence' must refer to the way in which the past keeps returning to haunt the present as it does at the denouement of J.M. Synge's *The Playboy of the Western World*, a play quoted by the same characters earlier in the novel.[38] The same sentence is equally evocative, though, of the apparition of the 'dead, living, murdered man' at the lit-up window of the ghostly house in W.B. Yeats' *Purgatory*,[39] a play that had, as some of the chapters that follow shall demonstrate, a more lasting and profound influence on McGahern's imagination than that of Synge. Madness, change and eternal recurrence, and the stories the living tell about dead precursors who are presumed to be cognisant of contemporary changes brought to bear on their old haunts — these are the subjects of Mary, Jamesie and Ruttledge's exchange in the hay shed; they are also among the central themes of *Purgatory*. All of these are introduced into the novel with a uniquely complex resonance owing to their life in that play, in a way not available through any *un*literary statement that Ruttledge could have offered in its stead.

Sons and Lovers, again, was one of the novels which served the purpose of a mirror 'reflect[ing]... something dangerously close to our own life' (*LW*, p. 90) for the young McGahern when he was discovering his own powers as a novelist during his twenties. The coincidence by which an early childhood experience apparently echoes that of William Morel's unfortunate haircut may be so close that it cannot but raise suspicions about the strict autobiographical veracity of that passage in *Memoir*. It is much more clear to see how there are other elements of *Sons and Lovers* which served to consciously 'lighten[ ] and deepen[ ]' all-too-raw memories of painful experiences when McGahern came to reimagine them into fiction in his early novels. John Cronin has recognised how the process of 'maturing from agonized adolescence to full sexual experience, from intense and inevitably tragic involvement with the doomed mother to a full physical relationship with a lover' that is depicted in *The Leavetaking* cannot but conjure memories of both *Sons and Lovers* and Joyce's *A Portrait of the Artist as a Young Man*. As Cronin points out, the 'fervid and painful exchanges between the dying woman and the son, who is agonizingly aware of her terminal illness but unable to admit its reality lest his world collapse about him' in that same novel recall 'the well-nigh unbearable poignancy of the closing section of *Sons and Lovers*'.[40] It may have been necessary for McGahern as a novelist to find such literary examples for a very practical reason. Since his own mother had died when he was only ten years old, it was all the more imperative for him to find a mature model for reflecting the emotions connected with the traumatic experience which was to be his chosen subject in a number of works.

Many key character traits of the father figures in his novels, too, are as much literary echoes of Lawrence as they are immediate attempts to capture the erratic tempers of his own father, whose innermost personality was destined to remain a mystery to his novelist–son all his life.[41] Chapter four of *Sons and Lovers* provides an analogy for the cruel habit of the children in *Memoir* and *The Dark* for shutting out their father behind a wall of silence when he wants the companionship of conversation and play. The young Mahoneys' refusal to play cards with their father in chapter two of *The Dark* (*D*, pp. 15–16) is more than a little reminiscent of this passage from Lawrence's novel:

> He was shut out from all family affairs. No one told him anything... as soon as the father came in, everything stopped. He was like the scotch in the smooth, happy machinery of the home. And he was always aware of this fall of silence on his entry, the shutting off of life, the unwelcome... He would dearly have liked the children to talk to him, but they could not... And that was all. Conversation was impossible between the father and any other member of the family. He was an outsider.[42]

The same chapter from *Sons and Lovers* also contains a likely model for the 'savage need to do' (*D*, p. 50) which characterises the restless personalities of Mahoney in *The Dark* and Moran in *Amongst Women*. Both of those characters are happiest when they are mending things, like Walter Morel who 'only... entered again into the life of his own people... when he worked, and was happy at work'.[43] The momentary proximity of fathers and sons at work which that sentence from *Sons and Lovers* suggests finds particular resonance in *Amongst Women* when Moran experiences a rare spell of 'high good humour' after working in the fields with Michael (*AW*, p. 47).

McGahern first read Lawrence soon after leaving the paternal home. His name is consistently invoked in McGahern's several accounts of his first discovery of twentieth-century literature after arriving in Dublin from the provinces.[44] The timing of McGahern's discovery of one of the great psychologists of the fraught interactions between fathers and sons could not have been more fortuitous, as it coincided with his first real opportunity for gaining a distancing perspective on living with his own troubled father. While there is little reason to doubt, therefore, that the narrative kernel both of the Mahoney children's strategy for revenge and of their father's personality trait of demanding constant activity can probably be traced in some form to the author's first-hand experiences of life in the barracks, it is equally clear to see how the budding novelist's rational understanding of these things must have been enhanced when he first encountered Lawrence's clear and even-handed analyses of the same things in chapter four of *Sons and Lovers*. In his assimilation of Lawrence we can clearly see at work a process which operates more generally throughout McGahern's fiction: that in which the basic outlines of biographical events are fused with apposite, illuminating literary allusions which are just as deeply grafted in the author's consciousness.

Tradition and the well-mannered talent

With its many echoes of, and allusions to, other literary works and ideas, then, McGahern's fiction is deeply intertextual; that is to say that it exists in a complex and 'endlessly interwoven relationship' of parallels, connections and affinities with many other texts, not all of which are explicitly acknowledged.[45] However, despite increased attention in recent years to McGahern's use of sophisticated themes and techniques, the extent to which allusions to other books and authors are woven into the texture of his prose is still often overlooked. At least some of that critical oversight must be attributed to the way McGahern chose to present himself as a writer. In the astute words of one long-time admirer, he was 'a shrewd, intelligent individual possessed of an intellectual sophistication he prefers to conceal behind the easy-going demeanour of a countryman jovially ill at ease in the big city'.[46] This is not to say, of course, that McGahern played the fool in public. To do so would be a form of intellectual dishonesty — a serious charge for an author who in his first novel had drawn attention to the falsity of saying prayers without religious belief, which 'sounded as dishonest as something intended to be overheard' (*B*, p. 123) — and so when he was confronted with even a hint of such an accusation he was liable to vehement protest. When a reviewer of *Memoir* suggested how the structure of that book appeared to be designed 'to reinforce the carefully maintained pose of naïve, rural unsophisticate', he was promptly rebuked in a long letter in which McGahern emphasised that 'The myth of Farmer John is not my doing. Over the years many TV crews have been here who wanted me to play the farmer. This I always refused. I was a writer who happened to live on a farm.'[47]

It is nonetheless undeniable that McGahern often consciously downplayed precisely the 'writerly' side of his personality which many other writers are liable to exaggerate. His friend John Banville is fond of repeating a comic anecdote which summed up the contrasting personalities of the two foremost Irish prose writers at the turn of the twenty-first century:

> John McGahern and I used to have fun with something someone had said of me — or perhaps I had been foolish enough to say it of myself — to the effect that in my fiction and my literary journalism I was trying to open a window on the world. Yes, McGahern said, with a basilisk look, and while you're trying to open it, I suppose I'm trying to slam it shut. It was a nice image, the two of us struggling at the sash, me pulling and him pushing. Thus do one's pretensions turn to comedy.[48]

McGahern's response was not intended to promote an isolationist view of Irish writing. Instead, he was riffing on the way he knew he had been all too often represented by reviewers and literary critics. Banville knew as well as anybody what McGahern was doing. He was aware both of McGahern's intimate connection with the European tradition and of the total intellectual confidence which allowed his friend not to slavishly pursue the approval of the literary establishment by playing the role of international man of letters. Ultimately, the comedy of Banville's anecdote is directed not so much against McGahern's apparent naivety as it is against the most common type of misreading of his literary aims. Banville's dig is as squarely aimed at his own need for maintaining a self-consciously cosmopolitan artistic mask, an attitude which McGahern would no doubt have characterised with a colloquial west-of-Ireland expression that was a particular favourite of his: 'highfalutin'.

McGahern habitually strikes the same pose in his fiction. On the face of it, his prose appears deceptively free of learned literary references, quotations and allusions — so much so that in 1985 Colm Tóibín could describe him as something of an enigma: 'a most unliterary writer [who] talks incessantly about books'.[49] Despite the breadth and depth of his reading in the literatures of Europe, and despite his acute awareness of the literary traditions that underpin any responsible artistic endeavour, McGahern's books only rarely invoke other authors by name. On a first or casual reading, they almost never appear overly laden with allusions or quotations, or to be otherwise overtly 'literary'. This is the result of a deliberate artistic choice. There was no reason why a good book should not also be an enjoyable book, or why it should be enjoyable only to highly trained professional readers. McGahern occasionally invoked this very notion of hidden or obscured literary influence or debt. When he remarked in a 1994 review of Ingmar Bergman's autobiographical novel *Sunday's Children* that 'Chekhov and Martin Luther are the only writers mentioned in the text, once each and in passing. But so careful is the work that I doubt if it is as casual as it appears' (*LW*, p. 387), that comment was no doubt intended as a warning to critics of his own fiction as much as it was the highest form of compliment to a fellow practitioner who had followed Ovid's counsel to use art to conceal art.[50]

McGahern's penchant for writing a brand of understated yet highly referential prose, as well as the unassuming stance that made him so popular with audiences at public talks and readings, are both functions of his most essential and private personality. His resistance to prominently placing literary references in his fiction was part of his lifelong pursuit of the 'good manners of the mind' (an idea he borrowed from Chekhov).[51] If not listening to one's predecessors was a form of bad manners, then dropping their famous names into the conversation at every convenient turn for the purposes of intellectual self-aggrandisement or the belittlement of others would be infinitely worse. His remark about *Sunday's Children* could just as easily be made — as indeed it has been — about McGahern's own fictional oeuvre in its entirety.[52] He would for that reason perhaps have been quietly gratified — though never so much as to violate the delicate good manners of the mind, and certainly not in public! — to see how he was remembered by one former student who recalled his manner in the classroom on the letters page of the Colgate University alumni magazine shortly after his death. That recollection perceptively linked McGahern's classroom demeanour to the well-mannered personality that had also written the unshowily brilliant novels:

> In 1972, I took his course on Irish literature . . . McGahern, a visiting professor, taught as he wrote. Soft-spoken, eloquent, understated. He drew little attention to himself the way his writing drew little attention to itself. One student asked McGahern why he had not assigned any of his own novels. He paused, then quietly said, 'I'd be embarrassed.' Not by the novels, I assume, but by the presumption that his students should be forced to pay for and read what their professor had written.[53]

That recollection is testament to the great tact for which McGahern perpetually strove in his dealings with others. The same kind of tact which should, as far as McGahern was concerned, rule the relationship between a novelist and his readers is also briefly a subject in *Amongst Women*. The description in his penultimate novel of Rose's 'tact' (a prominent subject in the fiction of the second half of his career, as chapter two will discuss) might be read as an idealised self-portrait of McGahern's own artistic identity, or a statement of intent: 'Rose's tact was so masterful that she resembled certain people who are so deeply read that they can play with all ideas without ever listing books' (*AW*, p. 34). If this sketch of the fictional Rose is an idealised portrait of the supremely tactful 'solitary reader' to which McGahern aspired in his own dealings as a human being and as a writer, then that portrait was based on the very real example of one of his earliest guides to literary tastes and literary etiquette. McGahern echoed that same sentence from *Amongst Women* in a 2006 letter in which he referred to Jimmy Swift, who had been an early influence in Dublin in the 1950s, as 'one of the most deeply read men I ever knew, and you could never tell that he had read anything unless it came naturally into play. To do otherwise he would have viewed as bad manners, the bad manners of the mind.'[54]

Even his approach to the various positions as writer in residence or visiting professor which he held at a number of Irish, British and North American universities from the late 1960s, and which could so easily be the breeding ground for writerly arrogance, was testament to his natural reticence. Students and academic colleagues who worked with him not only remember his knowledge and professionalism but also his great charm and self-effacing modesty. The 'Soft-spoken, eloquent, understated... embarrassed' young Irish novelist who first turned up in Colgate University in 1969 would be recognisable to students in that and other institutions up to the 2000s. The headnote on the syllabus for the seminar series on modern writing which he taught at the English Department at University College, Dublin, in 1999 is revealing in this respect. It provided students with a brief biographical note for the novelist, but it also prepared them for a teaching method which reflected McGahern's modest and unprepossessing nature as well as his wide reading:

> Mr McGahern does not wish to offer formal lectures on his own books, preferring to outline his literary and aesthetic principles in the study of other writers whose work he greatly admires. However, students should feel free in every class to ask him questions about his own works and to make links between them and the subject under discussion.[55]

That brief note not only gives an indication of how McGahern saw his work as part of a larger tradition; it also suggests the novelist's reluctance to discuss the great aesthetic intricacies and intellectual depth which he knew his work possessed. It is the aim of this book to elucidate how aesthetic principles and ideas McGahern found in the writers he admired are reflected in his own fiction.

CHAPTER I

Shakespearean Antics

> 'Do you think Shakespeare's all he's bumped up to be?' he asked. He'd heard that I'd gone two years to Secondary School, and he believed that he and me could speak as one educated man to another: he was sometimes called the *Professor*, and baited mercilessly...
>
> 'Hearts of Oak and Bellies of Brass' (*N*, p. 54)

A simpleton called Tipperary in McGahern's early story 'Hearts of Oak and Bellies of Brass' has become obsessed, after failing the exams which would have qualified him as a teacher, with the question of whether 'Shakespeare's all he's bumped up to be' (*N*, p. 54). His inquiries about the merits of Shakespeare and Shaw soon become one of the story's refrains. Questioning the value and relevance of those canonical playwrights has taken over the young man's life, as the repetition of the question has been transformed into an act of penance or punishment, a purgatorial task. The narrator — who, judging from his incorrect use of the objective case of the personal pronoun ('he and *me*') is perhaps not as educated as his interlocutor believes him to be — is unable to assuage Tipperary's uncertainty about Shakespeare's greatness and the foundations of his reputation. 'I told him that I didn't know if Shakespeare was all that he was bumped up to be, but people said so, and it was people who did all the bumping up or bumping down', he explains through the detachment that indirect speech offers (*N*, p. 54). Even Ingolsby, the pompous retired lecturer of English in 'Strandhill, the Sea', the story which follows 'Hearts of Oak' in *Nightlines*, may seek to show off his intellectual superiority by asking the other guests in the boarding house, 'What's your opinion of Shakespeare's validity for the modern world?' (*N*, p. 68) It is notable, however, that when none of the others deign to respond he does not himself volunteer an answer to that question — one that sounds like a cliché lifted straight out of a hundred different exams every bit as much as Tipperary's does.

In contrast with these minor characters from *Nightlines*, McGahern had already acknowledged the pervasiveness of Shakespeare in the popular imagination in his first two novels, and Shakespeare's influence would remain a constant in his work for the rest of his career. His plays are prominent among the texts regularly 'quoted in support out of some forgotten schoolbook' (*N*, p. 48) — as the narrator of 'Hearts of Oak and Bellies of Brass' puts it — by characters and narrators. (One example of a faint Shakespearean echo in the same story comes earlier in the same exchange when Keegan accuses the narrator's appearance in his work clothes of being a 'disgrace to the livin' daylight' (*N*, p. 48), recalling Ross' description of the darkness that falls over Scotland after Duncan's murder: 'the day's shame' that causes the sky to darken 'When living light should kiss it'.[1]) In early works like the *Nightlines* stories, *The Barracks* and *The Dark*, Shakespeare is often explicitly linked with the school curriculum. His plays are repeatedly connected with the anxiety which this association inevitably casts over the enjoyment of classic authors.[2] Guard Casey's memory of a clownish drunk professor reciting *Twelfth Night* in a pub on Abbey Street (*B*, p. 76) confirms Shakespeare's ties with the educational system, but it also deliberately undercuts the seriousness of the Shakespearean legacy.

For McGahern, as for many Irish writers, Shakespeare remains one of the supreme artists, one who 'casts different shadows depending on where and when he is read'.[3] His legacy is nonetheless problematic, partly because of the intellectual paralysis which the pressures of school exams invariably bring. Only by freeing the plays from the fear associated with these pressures through reimagining them in a contemporary guise can they be allowed again to provide renewed meaning and pleasure. The first sections of this chapter trace some of the echoes from Shakespeare's plays which can be found throughout McGahern's work. The latter half of the chapter will discuss McGahern's development of a playful sense of theatricality in his fiction. It will show how that self-conscious theatricality is steeped in his absorption of one of Shakespeare's major recurring tropes — even as he also looked to other, more recent dramatic variations on the same idea when it came to conceiving his own specific versions of it in his novels. The Shakespearean trope that 'All the world's a stage' is perpetually reimagined by a long succession of McGahern's heroes. Many of these take Shakespeare's edict to be literal truth. They believe it describes the hidden reality of their own existence, and allow their literal-minded devotion to an idea only half understood to take over their lives. The chapter is not concerned with McGahern's work for the stage. He wrote only one stage play, a version of Tolstoy's melodrama *The Power of Darkness* rendered into Irish vernacular speech to which he intermittently returned between 1972 and 2005. McGahern's version of *The Power of Darkness* certainly has a number of Shakespearean elements — such as the inclusion of the truth-telling family retainer, Paddy, who, devoid of his senses when all moral and worldly certainties are dissolving for the central characters at the end of the play, is 'drunk but he makes more sense than most of the sobers' (*PD*, p. 51) like the Shakespearean fools and madmen in *Hamlet* and *King Lear* — but it does not self-consciously engage with the *idea* of theatricality or the world-as-stage.[4] To do so would perhaps not be appropriate to the spirit of the Tolstoy original. Those sorts of meta-theatrical concerns are instead reserved for the characters in McGahern's novels and short stories, who are much more self-consciously 'dramatic' than the dramatis personae he adapted from Tolstoy's play.

'lines out of the auld school-books . . . comin' back and back' (*B*, p. 207)

Shakespeare is central among the poets whose work McGahern was 'grateful' to have learned by heart as a schoolboy.[5] There is evidence in his fiction and elsewhere that McGahern's relationship with Shakespeare did not end after he graduated with a BA in English from University College, Dublin, in 1958. He recalled the excitement of seeing John Gielgud and Marlon Brando in the 1953 film adaptation of *Julius Caesar* at a Dublin cinema in various works of non-fictional prose during the latter part of his career (*LW*, p. 91; *M*, p. 242). Half a century after first studying *Macbeth* and *Henry IV* at the Presentation Brothers Secondary School in Carrick-on-Shannon, and *Hamlet* and *King Lear* at university, McGahern still listed Shakespeare's plays among his three desert-island books in an interview with Paul Clements.[6] It is not surprising therefore that versions of generic Shakespearean tropes as well as specific quotations from and references to individual plays can be found in most of his books.

McGahern overtly set out his Shakespearean stall from the very beginning of his career. The opening chapters of *The Barracks* contain a number of allusions to Shakespeare's plays. The most obvious one comes at the beginning of chapter three, when Elizabeth remembers how the alcoholic but good-natured Guard Mullins had once quoted to her a line from *Twelfth Night*, which had in turn been suggested to him by a fellow-drinker in a Dublin pub:

> Elizabeth . . . Can you answer me this, 'lizabeth? *Who are they to say that we shall have no more cakes and ale?* That's what you might call a question,

> Elizabeth! A professor told me that, one Saturday night before an All Ireland Final, in Mooney's of Abbey Street, and he was drunk as I was! (*B*, p. 76)[7]

The insertion of the quote suggests that Mullins may be a modern-day incarnation of Shakespeare's great comic drunkard Sir Toby Belch. This would cast Elizabeth — whose feelings towards the alcoholic policeman are compassionate nearly to the point of being motherly rather than vindictive — as a sort of anti-Malvolio. The passage in which Elizabeth recalls that meeting with Mullins is part of an extended moral lesson which is present throughout McGahern's work.[8] Interestingly, that lesson is cast on more than just that one occasion in an implied contrast with pompous Shakespearean patricians. Elsewhere in the same novel, Elizabeth's system of values is cast as an ironic revision of *Hamlet*'s Polonius, as her thoughts about money initially repeat but then deviate from his stern advice to Laertes to 'Neither a borrower nor a lender be,/ For loan oft loses both itself and friend'.[9] This type of sensible but boring advice is fully at home with the outlook of those male members of a security-conscious older generation whose obsessions are regularly disparaged by the young protagonists of McGahern's fiction. In contrast with Polonius and his modern followers, however, Elizabeth is not at all concerned with the loss of money, only with that of friends, as 'She hated to either borrow or lend, she'd give money but not lend, she felt any relationship based and bound by money more loathsome than rotten flesh' (*B*, p. 156).

The *setting* of Guard Mullins' encounter with a Shakespeare-quoting professor is ironic, too. It transports the re enactment of a scene from a work from the Western theatrical canon across the street from the main stage of the Irish National Theatre to the unofficial stage of the public house. Thus, it dramatises Shakespeare's virtual banishment from the Abbey Theatre during the first half of the twentieth century.[10] (In a similarly tongue-in-cheek reimagining of the nationalist pieties of the Abbey's repertoire, it is no coincidence that the two tramps in the later story 'Doorways', who could so easily be figures in a tragical comedy by Beckett, Yeats or Synge, should live out their pointless lives on, of all places, Abbey Street, perhaps suggesting that the stylised poverty so routinely depicted on its stage has its mirror image in real but largely unacknowledged hardships just outside the building.) The irony is no doubt intentional. It signals the concern of McGahern and other members of the generation who came to prominence around the same time in the 1960s with reinstating Shakespeare as a viable cultural example after his marginalisation from the mainstream of Irish culture during the decades immediately following independence. For writers like McGahern, Heaney and Friel, Shakespeare was not simply the foremost icon of British cultural hegemony and oppression but a vital part of a cultural tradition which, by rights of their education in the English language and literature, belonged as much to them as it did to their English contemporaries.[11]

Shakespearean echoes in McGahern's fiction serve a number of purposes. Often, authority can be borrowed from a canonical text. In *That They May Face the Rising Sun*, Jamesie deflates one of *Macbeth*'s great poetic antitheses (the witches' 'Fair is foul, and foul is fair' which serves as an emblem of moral equivocation throughout that play) when, at the end of recounting Johnny's history as star-crossed lover, he concludes simply: 'Right or wrong, fair or foul, what does it matter?' (*TRS*, p. 5)[12] In the revised text of 'Oldfashioned' which first appeared in the *Collected Stories*, the father dramatically seals his objection to Colonel Sinclair's suggestion that his son might go to Sandhurst and become a British army officer with a misquotation from the same play. 'He can't. That's the end and the be-all' (*CS*, p. 260), he tells the colonel, implying that to join the forces of the old enemy would be a kind of death. The irony is that the subject of Macbeth's 'be-all and the end-all' soliloquy is doubt, not certainty, so that the father's apparently sure-footed statement in fact contains the seeds of its own denial.[13]

On other occasions, brief allusions may serve as a form of shorthand to introduce important themes, such as sex and death. When the morbid narrator of *The Pornographer* alludes, for example, to the proximity of 'The womb and the grave (*P*, p. 30), McGahern is borrowing a familiar Renaissance trope which appears in Shakespeare and Donne. When he elaborates on that idea by remarking how 'The christening party becomes the funeral, the shudder that makes us flesh becomes the shudder that makes us meat' (*P*, p. 30), the first part of that thought clearly inverts Hamlet's misgivings about the inappropriate timing of the queen's second marriage — even as the immediate source for the final thought is probably the *Hamlet*-esque image of the obstetrician-turned-gravedigger in *Waiting for Godot* rather than *Hamlet* itself.[14] The two Beckettian railway porters discussing the legal and theological ramifications of suicide by drowning in the opening scene of 'Wheels' (*N*, p. 11), meanwhile, just as clearly recall the gravedigger–clowns discussing Ophelia's death in Act 5, Scene 1 of *Hamlet*. One of the central concerns in *That They May Face the Rising Sun* is the pursuit of local news, which is, as one critic has proposed, 'a currency far more negotiable than any money and far more eagerly sought'.[15] That this was probably intended by McGahern becomes clear from a pun on

Shylock's demand for a 'pound of flesh' in *The Merchant of Venice*, which occurs when Patrick Ryan recalls how years ago a local boy had been stopped on the road by inquisitive neighbours who would not let him continue on his way 'until they had extracted every word of flesh' (*TRS*, p. 45).[16] A pun on the same line appears in *The Pornographer*, a novel in which the failed poet Maloney is repeatedly associated with ironic snippets of Shakespeare.[17] When the titular writer of pornography describes his painful contribution to Maloney's magazine as his 'pound of flesh' (*P*, p. 163), that pun encapsulates both smut (the naked flesh of pornography) and, through the invocation of the fate of Shylock, penance. On one occasion a Shakespearean allusion is even deployed to signal a character's total lack of introspection. The narrator's remark in 'Oldfashioned' that the sergeant 'was not a man to look in any abstraction on the sparrow's fall' (*HG*, p. 46) slyly juxtaposes that character's prosaic and practical temperament with the depth and inwardness of one of Hamlet's soliloquies.[18]

The purpose of some other Shakespearean echoes and allusions can be less clearly defined. Some quotations are simply a spontaneous, involuntary function of memory. Shards of half-remembered schoolroom poetry occasionally appear playfully, and without fulfilling a definite thematic agenda in the minds of characters and narrators as they might in that of the author. The workings of the mental process through which this happens are explained in a meta-narrative passage in chapter one of *The Barracks*, in which precisely this happens to Guard Casey. When the four guards are talking about Christ, Casey is reminded through a process of association of the rebel ballad 'Kelly, the Boy from Killann': 'There was immediate feeling of blasphemy. The song connected up with Jesus Christ, though Casey had meant no harm, he said it just because it happened into his head' (*B*, pp. 30–1). Like that of Guard Casey, the mind of a novelist like McGahern was filled with quotations going back to his early schooling, and many of the most memorable spins on lines he learnt at school originated in Shakespeare's plays. As Denis Sampson suggests, 'The memorable poetry of Shakespeare's vision may have stayed with McGahern, more vivid even than the great characters of the tragedies'.[19] That poetry found its way into his fiction even when it did not serve a definite thematic or dramatic purpose. Elizabeth's memory of Mullins' farewell gesture as she cycled away from the barracks to the town one frosty winter's morning is fused with another memory, that of a line from *King Lear*. When she reflects on how 'She saw him close his fist and stiffen the arm as he waved for the last time: to have courage, and calling on God to stand up for all sorts of bastards' (*B*, p. 76), the memory from her own past is inflected with an echo of Gloucester's villainous son Edmund: 'Now gods stand up for bastards!'[20] There is of course no suggestion here that Mullins plans to depose an illegitimate brother, or even to betray a colleague;[21] the benevolent Mullins is more Falstaff or Sir Toby Belch than Edmund. Instead, through focalising the narrative through Elizabeth's consciousness here and on other occasions, McGahern shows how the literary imagination works by repeating lines and phrases from memory — and how those memories are often set off by the slightest lexical trigger, in a process similar to that described by Locke as the 'association of ideas'.[22] In this case, Elizabeth is perhaps drawn into the echo by the connection that exists in her mind between Mullins and Shakespearean drama owing to the anecdote he had on an earlier occasion told her about the Shakespeare-quoting professor on Abbey Street.

On some occasions those associations can extend beyond the purely aural joys of remembered lines of poetry to private circumstances in the life of a character or the author with which they are only tangentially connected. In *That They May Face the Rising Sun*, Ruttledge is forced to prepare Johnny's body for the wake because Patrick Ryan, the old actor who was meant to perform that task, arrives at the house late. When the Ruttledges discuss Patrick Ryan's late 'entrance' on their way home afterwards, a private process of association triggers a quote from *Hamlet* in Ruttledge:

> 'What was it like preparing the body?' Kate asked . . . ' . . . Did you ever see anything like that entrance?'
>
> Ruttledge shook in silent laughter . . . 'Sergeant Death appeared and found he had arrived too late.' (*TRS*, p. 279)

The unusual combination of death and lateness, with the additional reference to a theatrical 'entrance', must account for triggering Ruttledge's recollection of the dying Hamlet's reference to 'this fell sergeant, Death'.[23] The personal significance of that same line to McGahern is probably less casual. The line is likely to be quickly forgotten or passed over altogether by most readers of *Hamlet*, but it would have struck McGahern's ear because of the personal resonance it possessed for a writer whose difficult father held that rank in the Irish police force, and whose novels feature many major and minor characters who hold the same rank. The personal significance behind his recollection of that line from *Hamlet* once more suggests that, as the introduction of this book proposed, McGahern could often read the images and incidents of his own past through those he encountered in works of literature.

McGahern's *Lear*

Of all of Shakespeare's plays, McGahern seems to have been fascinated most with *King Lear*. Versions of its language and themes regularly recur in his fiction as well as, occasionally, in his non-fiction. Of the latter, two examples stand out. He peppered an *Irish Independent* article about political malaise and electoral apathy ahead of the 1989 Irish general election with a joke about Lear wailing in his prison cell (*LW*, p. 121). In an aside in a 1986 book review he compared a plot element from one of Leonardo Sciascia's short stories to the abrupt disappearance of the Fool from *King Lear* (*LW*, p. 317).

McGahern's engagement with *King Lear* in his fiction is more sustained, and more serious in its intent. The emphasis on nothingness which is something of a leitmotif in *The Barracks*, *The Dark* and the early short stories may not be so much Beckettian or existential (as a number of critics have intimated) as they are Shakespearean. In *The End or the Beginning of Love* there is an obvious pun on one of *Lear*'s most famous lines when the narrator describes the fruitless endings of Mahoney's interminable games of solitaire in which 'nothing will fit nothing'.[24] Other allusions to that and similar lines from *King Lear* generally serve to deepen the treatment of more serious concerns. A case in point is the language used to reflect the pain of Elizabeth's childlessness in *The Barracks*. Many of the stepmothers in McGahern's fiction are childless, but only Elizabeth's realisation of the import of that fact is coloured by the language of *King Lear*. Her feeling that 'She was nothing to these children ... she had believed that she could yet have a child of her own, and *that, too, had come to nothing*' (*B*, p. 8, emphasis added) echoes, with cruel irony, the exchange between Lear and his youngest daughter, in which the careless father predicts that 'Nothing will come of nothing.'[25] In 'The Recruiting Officer', the language of Shakespeare's play is enlisted in a critique of the practice of corporal punishment in schools. The narrator's comparison between having to watch the priest 'shake a confession out of [a] boy' and seeing how 'a dog shakes life out of a rat; and having nothing to do' (*N*, p. 152) echoes, on a level that is so subtle as to be almost subliminal, the key lexical elements of Lear's final lament for the injustice of Cordelia's untimely death: 'Why should a dog, a horse, a rat have life,/ And thou no breath at all?'[26] In the implicit comparison with Cordelia's brutal treatment is the condemnation of contemporary practices.

McGahern's most sustained versions of *King Lear* can be found in *Amongst Women* and *The Barracks*. Nowhere in McGahern is that play referenced with greater intensity as in the opening chapter of his first novel. Sergeant Reegan's entrance out of the rain of an inhospitable Roscommon night in the opening chapter of *The Barracks* is constructed in the form of a sustained homage to, or pastiche of, *King Lear* (and so it may be apposite that his name is a homophone of that of one of Lear's wicked daughters). The invocation of a rainy Roscommon night is not just an example of local colour (a literary mode McGahern disliked)[27] or a realist description of a country in which it always rains; it is also a masterful exercise in intertextuality, as two Shakespearean refrains are woven into the prose throughout the first chapter. In the opening paragraph, 'The wind and rain rattling at the window-panes seemed to grow part of the spell of silence and increasing darkness' (*B*, p. 7). Two pages later, Elizabeth and the children 'listened to the rain beat and wind rattle' (*B*, p. 9); and when Reegan finally comes home from patrol, his face is 'chafed red with wind and rain' (*B*, p. 11). Almost subliminally, McGahern introduces into the description of a barracks evening the refrain from Feste's song at the end of *Twelfth Night*:

> With hey-ho, the wind and the rain; . . .
> For the rain it raineth every day.[28]

A version of the same song is also repeated by the Fool in *King Lear*, and it is that later play which McGahern's novel seems to be more deliberately invoking.[29] Lear's Fool sings the song as the royal entourage is about to enter a hovel for shelter from the storm. The first words spoken by Reegan when he enters soaked to the skin into the barracks kitchen are a complaint which explicitly invokes a comparison with Lear's faithful companion on the heath: 'Wet to the bloody skin . . . A terrible night to have to cycle about *like a fool*' (*B*, p. 11, emphasis added).

Another phrase from *King Lear* is even more prominently repeated in the same chapter. Taken together they suggest that the echo of Shakespeare's tragedy is not an accident but a deliberate insertion. Elizabeth wonders why Reegan 'should have to go out at all *on a night like this*' (*B*, p. 10, emphasis added). The same phrase occurs numerous times in the first chapter. The two children are never at ease with each other 'On nights like these' (*B*, p. 38); Casey wonders what would take Superintendent Quirke outside 'on an evenin' like this' (*B*, p. 20); Casey's wife can't sleep on her own 'on these nights' (*B*, p. 11). Mostly, though, the phrase is associated with the foul weather of this particular night. 'A terrible night,' Reegan mutters at the fire after his return home: 'Not fit for a dog to be out in' (*B*, p. 12). He repeats the same assertion in his mimicry of the conversation he has had with Quirke during his patrol: 'And what has you out on a night like this?' (*B*, p. 12) The phrase 'on a night like this' is repeated three times during that short conversation (*B*, pp. 12–13).

It echoes Lear's refrain from the bleak central act of Shakespeare's tragedy, set on the heath on a night in which even 'Things that love night/ Love not such nights as these', and on which even the most fearful nocturnal predators stay out of the weather.[30] That last detail is recalled by the guards' final resurrection of the chapter's *Lear*-like refrain, that which occurs in Casey's summing up of the night's horrendous conditions:

> The devil himself wouldn't venture down . . . on a night like this. I stuffed a few auld coats against the butt of the door but the draughts still go creepin' up the legs of yer britches like wet rats. (*B*, p. 19)

The repeated invocations of the barren psychological landscape of Shakespeare's most brutal tragedy may suggest that perhaps men like Reegan are prone to take themselves a little bit too seriously. The implicit comparison between a bad day at the office dealing with a superior with whom one does not get on particularly well on the one hand, and the fate of Shakespeare's fallen king in the midst of losing everything on the other, is certainly an uneven one, and thus a justified source of irony. But the recurring echo of *King Lear* also prepares the reader for how another, very different, tragedy is about to unfold in the later chapters: that of Elizabeth's struggle with a waning faith and the pain of her long-drawn-out and solitary death. Appropriately enough, Elizabeth eventually vocalises that tragedy surrounding what she herself describes toward the end of chapter three as 'the mind's refusal to endure more torture' in the form of another echo from *King Lear*, as '"No, no, no, no," came on her breath' (*B*, p. 104) straight out of the mouth of the suffering Lear in Edmund and Albany's fateful prison camp in Act 5.[31] One of the novel's early reviewers was clearly struck by McGahern's treatment of the themes of Shakespearean tragedy, its pity and its terror, and his casting of the heroine's inner life into fully fledged soliloquies about life and death (unusually presented in the third person, yet still unmistakably related to those of *Hamlet* or *Macbeth*). In the *Irish Independent*, John D. Sheridan praised *The Barracks* for 'its intensity and pathos . . . the inevitable note of classic tragedy', and for the way 'people and things . . . are merely the background to [Elizabeth's] inner life. She is occupied always with the riddle of existence, the purposes and meaning of life.'[32] Years later, Denis Sampson also remarked on how 'The ambience of *King Lear* is certainly appropriate to this study of suffering and endurance'.[33] Indeed, Elizabeth does at one point explicitly consider her death through the prism of Shakespearean tragedy when she reflects on how all individuals are 'tragic figures in their death', but she also undercuts the underlying idea of that same genre, because to think of death as tragic is 'ridiculously human' and depends very much on the personal involvement of the spectator in the life that is ending (*B*, p. 136). For a modern consciousness like that of Elizabeth, which exists after Arthur Miller's response to the critical reception of *Death of a Salesman*, the sense of tragedy no longer depends, as it had for Sophocles and Shakespeare, on the exalted social position of the man or woman who dies.[34] For Elizabeth, everybody's death is insignificant to most of the 'millions of others' who had once 'jigacted' with them on the world's stage; yet the death of every single person is, to that person him- or herself, 'no joke ... byjesus, the whole world [was] falling when they fell' (*B*, p. 136).[35]

King Lear again asserts itself as an important model during a later phase of McGahern's career, when he redirected his attention to themes of old age and family. In *Amongst Women*, Shakespeare's most mature tragedy makes a significant reappearance on a number of levels. Moran's playful reaction to Rose's comment that, in his old age, his hands are always cold certainly brings to mind a sort of comical pantomime *Lear*: 'As if to turn attention away from the continual coldness of his hands, he pulled on the gloves comically and pretended to grope about the room with them like a blind man' (*AW*, p. 3).[36] On a structural level, too, the various relationships in the Moran household in *Amongst Women* echo the two central family situations of *King Lear*. In this novel about ageing and transition, the old patriarch Moran is Lear and Gloucester rolled into one. Central to the novel are his relationships with his three daughters — two of whom bring into the house unsuitable suitors who represent the modern realities of social and political life which are beyond the old man's grasp — and with his two very different sons, one at home and the other banished. *Amongst Women* and *King Lear* are both turbulent family dramas set in an age of immense social and political change, in a world making the transition from old-fashioned feudalism and chivalry to modern capitalist individualism, from pagan to Christian ways of thinking.[37] Stephen Greenblatt's summary of the plot of Shakespeare's play — 'Lear is a man who has determined to retire from power but who cannot endure dependence. Unwilling to lose his identity as absolute authority both in the state and in the family ... [his] aim seems to be to allay his own anxiety by arousing it in his children'[38] — is not an inaccurate summary of Moran in *Amongst Women*. It is even reminiscent of the rich and complex first sentence of McGahern's novel: 'As he weakened, Moran became afraid of his daughters' (*AW*, p. 1), a sentence loaded with the antithetical themes of Shakespeare's tragedy — to inspire fear or to be feared, filial love versus hatred, and the shifting power dynamic of the parent–child relationship — and with the same potential for the drama of social and familial disintegration.

Nevertheless, the conclusion of *Amongst Women* is a sort of anti-*Lear*. The novel does not end in the unmitigated tragedy foretold by Shakespeare's play, with the favourite daughter dead and the kingdom in turmoil. Rather, some sort of natural order is restored at its conclusion, as Moran's daughters survive their fearsome parent and even in their different ways find they have turned into him (*AW*, p. 183). McGahern's sense, so hard won at the conclusion of *Amongst Women*, that there could be a move away from the tragic family story of a play whose language he would always continue to admire is again intimated by a detail in his last novel. That the reliable, good-natured of the two Ryan brothers in *That They May Face the Rising Sun* should be called Edmund, after Gloucester's twisted illegitimate son, appears to signal a final and deliberate reversal of the strained, 'unnatural' family relations of *King Lear* which were still at work for most of *Amongst Women*.

Tragedy and comedy

Handling the inescapable Shakespearean legacy is not always easy or unproblematic for McGahern's characters. Despite McGahern's love for Shakespeare, works like 'Hearts of Oak and Bellies of Brass' and *The Dark* suggest — often with humour and irony — how possessing a mind saturated by the language of Shakespeare's plays might just as easily ruin your life as save it. The intellectual paralysis of a character unable to satisfactorily answer an exam question about Shakespeare was discussed in the opening section of this chapter. Another danger that may result from overexposure to the plays is demonstrated in *The Dark*, in which *Macbeth*, the play the teenage boy is studying for his school-leaving exams, is one of the main intertexts. Young Mahoney has a tendency to cast himself in the role of Macbeth going to his certain doom. This is achieved in the narrative by the assimilation of the language of the Scottish tyrant's final great soliloquy — the one that begins 'Tomorrow, and tomorrow, and tomorrow,/ Creeps in this petty pace from day to day' — into the young boy's internally focalised narrative.[39]

The words 'nothing' and 'tomorrow' reverberate through some of the chapters straight out of the boy's favourite soliloquy from the final act of the Scottish play. This is most visible in chapter twenty-two, when the narrator–protagonist becomes aware of how the word 'tomorrow' 'started to beat to the mind out of *Macbeth*' with the oppressive weight of a physical object (*D*, p. 140), like the shovels and sledgehammers driving rhythmically on the London building site in 'Hearts of Oak and Bellies of Brass'. The presence of that play, or even that soliloquy, is not confined to that late chapter in which the boy tremulously awaits his exams. Long before his obsession with *Macbeth* is overtly signalled in that later chapter, the imagery of the same soliloquy is already a presence. When young Mahoney questions his religious faith during a sojourn at Father Gerald's presbytery in chapter twelve, his description of life as a 'haphazard flicker between nothingness and nothingness' (*D*, p. 69) is more than a little indebted to Macbeth's comparison of the limited duration of his life with, among other things, a 'brief candle' which will soon be extinguished.[40]

Shakespeare can only be allowed to ruin your life if you allow him to do so. Only a total lack of perspective or proportion would lead one to confuse the 'banality of the whole situation' (*D*, p. 141) of everyday living with the classical fate of the tragic hero. *The Dark* makes repeated reference to the need to put events into perspective. Even as he is comparing his upcoming exams with Macbeth's inevitable demise, young Mahoney is occasionally aware of the necessity to distance himself from mythical or literary exemplars, whether it is Macbeth in Act 5 or Christ on his way to Calvary. In the end, though, his taste for histrionics still gets the better of him:

> It was impossible not to laugh too, it was too comic, the whole affair exaggerated, I was going to no crucifixion on a mountain between thieves but to a desk in a public building to engage in a writing competition. The whole business had grown out of proportion, though in a way why shouldn't it, I was at the heart of the absurdity and what proportion was there to my life . . . (*D*, p. 141)

In *Autobiographies*, Yeats had suggested that Hamlet might be an appropriate model 'for the poses of youth and childhood to copy', but young Mahoney is lacking in the 'image of heroic self-possession' which Yeats so admired in Shakespeare's tragic hero.[41] He is given over instead to melodramatic hysteria. Like that other over-earnest young man, Stephen Dedalus in Joyce's *A Portrait of the Artist as a Young Man*, young Mahoney is not possessed of the capacity for irony or critical distance from his own situation which is required for normal living.[42] He is, as his father and his cousin Fr Gerald respectively diagnose, prone to 'make a mountain out of a molehill' (*D*, p. 116), to 'take things far too serious, and bottle them up, and brood' (*D*, p. 74). The comedy of disproportionate suffering which comes of taking things too seriously is appropriate in the work of an author who once suggested in an interview that 'if you set out to write tragedy, it would serve you right if it turned into a comedy'.[43] Indeed, in the final chapter of *The Dark* (after the revelation on the university football pitch sets the protagonist free to pursue his unheroic dreams), the tendency to turn ordinary life into Shakespearean tragedy is deliberately cut short. There, the narrator's apparent invocation of Lear's three bloodcurdling howls at the sight of Cordelia's corpse ends in a pathetic, comic deflation of tragic expectations. 'It seemed that the whole world must turn over in the night and *howl* in its boredom,' he reflects on the last page, before adding with dry, self-effacing irony: 'but it did not' (*D*, p. 191, emphasis added).[44] One sign that young Mahoney is maturing at the end of the novel is this final ironic resistance to indulging in yet another grandiose identification with Shakespearean tragic suffering.

The significance ascribed in *The Dark* to dramatic genres is not an isolated instance in McGahern's oeuvre. McGahern had been a student of tragedy and comedy from the beginning of his writing life. As a student at St Patrick's College, Drumcondra, he had been a keen and attentive theatre-goer, and what he had first observed at the Gate, the Abbey and the Pike in the 1950s eventually found its way into his fiction over the decades that followed.[45] As the next section will show, *The Barracks* contains a number of references to tragedy and comedy, but the narrators of a number of other works from the 1960s and 1970s also show that they have internalised some of the theories surrounding the dramatic genres. By 1967 McGahern had read and thought about Bergson's essay on *Laughter*, which argued that if one could 'step aside, look upon life as a disinterested spectator: many a drama will turn into a comedy'.[46] The boy in *The Dark* knows, even if he cannot fully accept that wisdom until the very last page, that the difference between tragedy and comedy consists simply of a contrast in point of view. The same thing has also occurred to the narrator's drinking companion Lightfoot in 'Wheels'. That minor character borrows Horace Walpole's famous aphorism that 'this world is a comedy to those that think, a tragedy to those that feel',[47] and transforms it into the coarse diction of the public house to explain his own outlook on life's fortunes and misfortunes: '"Looked at with the mind, life's a joke; and felt, it's a tragedy and we know cursed nothing," he'd said last night over the pints of Guinness' (*N*, p. 12).

Spins on definitions of classical tragedy are incorporated in a number of McGahern's fictions to describe the lives of narrators or those around them. When he realises that the chain of events of his recent past which originated in a single moment of sexual ecstasy makes up a generically perfect classical tragedy, the narrator of *The Pornographer* remarks that 'The old plays were not wrong: there are single moments of weakness when our whole life can be changed to nightmare, set in a sweet flutter so faint that we are uncertain if it touched us at all in passing; but already we had fallen' (*P*, p. 162). A similar idea occurs to the narrator of 'Bomb Box',[48] who notices that his father, a police sergeant, begins to feel curiously fated, like a helpless pawn whose days are 'willed' (*N*, p. 81), from the day he buys the auction lot containing an old medical dictionary which makes him believe he literally suffers from every disease in the book. Many tragedies are propelled by such self-fulfilling prophesies, and 'Bomb Box' is no different in this respect from *Oedipus Rex* or *Macbeth*. The story may be a farce, with hypochondria taking the place once reserved for hubris, but still the sergeant's decline is introduced by his narrator–son like a classical tragedy, a chain of events set in motion by a single fateful act that appears significant only in retrospect (*N*, p. 72), like that which may befall the tragic hero in a Shakespeare play.

'this great stage of fools'

Running all the way through McGahern's oeuvre there is a sense of theatricality which is deeply Shakespearean in nature. A.C. Bradley, the pre-eminent Shakespeare critic of the early twentieth century, whose *Shakespearean Tragedy* (1904) was a standard text which McGahern had almost certainly read by the time he left University College, Dublin, wrote about Shakespeare's characters as if they were real people.[49] McGahern in turn was to write fictions about characters who believe themselves to be Shakespearean actors. Arguably the most common way in which Shakespeare finds his way into McGahern's novels is in many of the protagonists' self-conscious awareness that they are, like Lear, merely players on 'this great stage of fools'[50] rather than autonomous, free-willed individuals. Many of McGahern's characters know that they go through life constantly playing a part. While the boy in *The Dark* waits for his turn to enter the confessional, for example, he observes how 'All waited for forgiveness, in the listless performance of habit and duty or torturing and turning over their sins and lives' (*D*, p. 39). It may be no accident, therefore, that one of the guards in *The Barracks* is introduced through a line from *Twelfth Night*, a play set during, and named after, a carnival which is, 'like all theatre, a matter of disguise and appearances, of *impersonation*'.[51] That idea introduces a general preoccupation running throughout McGahern's works.

The tendency to turn into Shakespearean actors is shared in the fiction by fathers and sons and elderly bachelors alike, but it is probably most obviously enacted by the father in *The Dark*. Like many of the fathers in McGahern's fiction, the elder Mahoney is a sad figure as well as a domestic tyrant — again, incorporating with skilfully handled pathos the two sides of Lear's conflicting personality — who insists to his children that he, too, went to school when he was a boy. It is clear from his performance in chapter twenty that Shakespeare's plays must have been on the curriculum then:

> Mahoney's violence was turning more on himself. He came reeking with Guinness from the April market. When they'd given him his meal, answered his inquiries about the pigs and milking, and he could find nothing to fault, he let himself slump before the heat of the fire. It seemed he'd doze quietly there. Then suddenly he jumped up, the face red and bloated, dramatic arm outstretched, to do a half-circle swing on the floor and shout, 'I went to school too.'
>
> 'This is my life, and this kitchen in the townland of Cloone is my stage, and I am playing my life out here on,' and he stood, the eyes wild, as if grappling for his lines.
>
> 'And nobody sees me except a crowd of childer,' the voice trailed bitterly, and then burst out again . . . (*D*, p. 128)

In his drunken state Mahoney is transformed into the picture of a particular kind of actor uncertainly speaking his lines, one who is unintentionally comical because of his exaggerated theatrical gestures — the kind of actor, in fact, to whom Shakespeare alludes in that same soliloquy from the final act of *Macbeth* with which young Mahoney has become obsessed, in which the futility of a life 'Signifying nothing' is compared to:

> a poor player
> That struts and frets his hour upon the stage
> And then is heard no more.[52]

This portrayal of old Mahoney's faltering performance may draw not only on McGahern's reading of Shakespeare but equally on one of his other most enduring theatrical memories: that of seeing Eugene O'Neill's *Long Day's Journey into Night* (perhaps more than once) at the Abbey Theatre around the turn of the 1960s.[53] Mahoney's overtly actorly gestures are reminiscent of the 'drunken[ ] . . . childish, bitterly dramatic self-pity' of the retired actor James Tyrone in O'Neill's play.[54] Like Tyrone, Mahoney may have come from a humble Irish background, crippled by an inherited fear of the poorhouse, but like Tyrone also he is more naturally suited to be an actor than a farmer, as he lives out his life in a series of dramatic gestures and curtain calls. Mahoney behaves like an actor throughout the novel, particularly at decisive moments. When he travels to Galway in response to his son's telegram in chapter thirty, for example, he is again cast in a self-consciously theatrical light: 'Mahoney came the next morning, full of a sense of drama. There was an important decision to be made. He'd play in it to the last' (*D*, p. 183).

More than once, Mahoney's theatricality has specifically Shakespearean overtones. If his teenage son is in the habit of grandiosely comparing himself to Macbeth, then Mahoney senior's role of choice is King Lear. *King Lear* is ascertained as an ironic intertext long before his alcohol-fuelled matinee in chapter twenty. When he complains about his fate while gathering potatoes in the rain in chapter four — '"I'll get me death out of this. Such cursed yokes to be saddled with. No help, no help," he turned to the rain instead' (*D*, p. 27) — that powerless gesture unmistakably recalls Lear railing against the forces of nature on the heath. As on many other occasions in the novel on which he complains about the ungrateful children with whom he has been cursed, Mahoney's rhetoric of paternal disappointment in that chapter repeats Lear's self-pitying vitriol about having 'a thankless child!'[55]

Mahoney's bitter complaint in chapter twenty at the way his life has turned out is coloured by memories of the very schooling he insists he has once enjoyed, as it parodies the well-known Shakespearean trope that

> All the world's a stage,
> And all the men and women merely players ...[56]

In Shakespeare, the wide 'imaginative reach' of the comparison between the everyday realities of the world and the artificial realm of the theatre may occasionally be considered a liberating one.[57] The theatrical metaphor promises individuals a possibility of escaping into 'many parts', while the modest cockpit or 'wooden O' that is the theatre, its stage not much larger than a country kitchen, may become capable of accommodating whole kingdoms.[58] (In *Memoir*, McGahern observes the effectiveness of this method of escape from the burdens of reality through forms of play-acting in his own father. Frank McGahern had in his time played many epistemological 'roles' — from 'a devoted member of the Catholic Church' to 'the head of police in rural districts where he was the law ... the sergeant who was dangerous to cross', to the final role of 'Daddy' which alone remained after all other parts had been forcibly relinquished — but his 'happiest role', his son surmised, had been in the IRA during the War of Independence (*M*, pp. 226–7).) For Mahoney in *The Dark*, the idea that his life is a performance acted out on a stage has the opposite effect. He uses the same Shakespearean trope to express his feeling not of expansiveness or escape, but of confinement to a rural kitchen which has more or less the same dimensions as a theatrical stage — the same sense of confinement his son feels when his whole 'world' is reduced to the 'few square inches' of the unopened envelope containing his exam results (*D*, p. 151). In *The Dark*, Shakespeare's famous trope is turned against itself as Mahoney feels, like Lear, that he has 'come/ To this great stage of fools' that is the world, and that he has been ill-treated by it. He believes, like Antonio in *The Merchant of Venice*, that the world is 'A stage where every man must play a part,/ And mine a sad one.'[59] He also appears to feel the need to be observed, like an actor on the stage or a character in one of Beckett's plays, because 'being seen'[60] would at least validate the farce in which he must act. Sadly, though, the only audience to witness his antics are a disappointing 'crowd of childer' (*D*, p. 128). That detail perhaps recalls, as has been suggested, the fate of Yeats' fallen hero in *The Wanderings of Oisin*, who complains that he has in his old age been reduced to being 'a show unto children, alone with remembrance and fear'.[61] A more likely model, however, is again that of James Tyrone in Act 4 of *Long Day's Journey into Night*, whose only audience for his moment of greatest vulnerability and self-revelation consists of his younger son Edmund.[62]

Old Mahoney's confinement on a country-kitchen stage not only inverts a well-known Shakespearean trope; it also slyly recalls one of the central conventions of the post-Revival cultural scene in Ireland, that of the Abbey Theatre's ubiquitous country-kitchen stage set on which much of the Irish National Theatre's output of the post-independence decades was staged. A version of the same conventional Abbey stage set already appeared in the first chapter of *The Barracks*, which, as John Montague has observed, 'seemed as comfortable as the first act of an old Abbey play'.[63] Brian Friel has often been credited with inaugurating modern Irish drama by ironically rewriting the possibilities of the Abbey's stale country-kitchen conventions in his 1964 breakthrough play *Philadelphia, Here I Come!*, which brings new modern sensibilities to a recognisably old-fashioned stage set.[64] McGahern's novel had beaten him to it by a year, though, and may even have confirmed to the young playwright the possibilities for subversion and renewal dormant in those old theatrical pieties.[65] The domestic opening set piece of *The Barracks* cleverly parodies the peasant realism of a Revivalist drama. Its first line in particular — 'Mrs Reegan darned an old woollen sock as the February night came on, her head bent, catching the threads on the needle by the light of the fire, the daylight gone without her noticing' (*B*, p. 7) — knowingly recalls not only the introduction of Emma Bovary in Flaubert's novel,[66] but also such Abbey Theatre scenes as the opening tableau of T.C. Murray's *Autumn Fire* (1924), with its 'homely simplicity… The only uncomely thing to be seen is a woman with drooped head sitting under the window knitting.'[67] When Elizabeth reflects on how her life has changed since returning to rural Ireland from London, where she had been a nurse during the Blitz, she does so in a passage that juxtaposes memory with a painful awareness of the present moment:

> to plague her, a vision of herself in London before the war flashed on her mind, a spring Sunday in London, when the light is grey and gentle as anything on earth. She had come out the great black hospital gates, a red tartan scarf thrown back on her shoulder; and turned right, up the marvellous width of Whitechapel Road, away from the crowds milling into the Lane, for it was the morning. Now she was spitting like any common slut in a barrack kitchen. (*B*, p. 21)

In passages such as this, Elizabeth watches her life unfold from a great distance, dispassionately, as if it were acted out on a stage. The scene that presents itself to her disembodied eye is a picture that captures both the hopes and the disappointments which the Revival offered to subsequent generations of Irish writers and intellectuals. At the beginning of Elizabeth's journey she is filled with the visionary Romanticism of Yeats and Lady Gregory's folklore plays, and appropriately dressed in tartan for the part of a Revivalist stage peasant; yet it is not long before all that is left of the idealism of the early Abbey is the drudgery of the peasant dramas that dominated the national stage between the 1920s and the 1950s, as she has become nothing more than a 'common slut' spitting in the turf fire of a rural kitchen from the Abbey stage.

The Barracks is a highly theatrical novel, filled with allusions to players, footlights, performances and dramatic genres. Elizabeth regularly takes solace from reimagining distasteful or upsetting realities as mere spectacles in a play. Her stay in the Dublin cancer ward is so 'ridiculous' that she can only think of it as a 'fantastic comedy', while the visitors to the other patients are conscious of being watched from the beds as they perform their entrances and exits and the little 'stilted' shows in between (*B*, p. 136). Later, it occurs to her that the provincial gossips in the village whom she cannot stand can simply be declared a 'mess' and 'a shocking comedy' (*B*, p. 162). Even when the priest comes to give her extreme unction she witnesses the whole visit like an uninvolved spectator who is 'detached' and 'could watch' (*B*, pp. 216–18).

Elizabeth and old Mahoney are not the only McGahern characters who observe their own lives from the outside, with great detachment, as if they were watching a play, and who 'turn[ ] over their sins and lives' (*D*, p. 39) as if they belonged to somebody else. During one of his retreats to the outside lavatory, where he takes solace after a confrontation with his father, the boy in *The Dark* also considers that 'The show of your life would be always moving on to the next moment. The best was to dress up and bow to it and smile or just look on' (*D*, p. 116). This sense of becoming an onlooker of your own life is strikingly dramatised in *The Dark* by the use of shifting grammatical perspectives. In the chapters narrated in the second and the third person, in particular, the protagonist–narrator appears increasingly too far removed from the 'show of your life' to feel properly involved in its goings-on. He has become both actor and spectator all at once, in a process psychologists refer to as dissociation: the development in a person's mind of multiple centres of consciousness. In many of McGahern's other works a similar purpose is served by another striking stylistic device: his trademark use of the passive tense, which achieves a similar impression that actions are no more than a type of ritual or performance, something from which any sense of personal agency is eliminated. This happens, for example, on Moran's wedding day in *Amongst Women*, when the central character becomes aware of how 'Distances were walked. Words were said. Rings were exchanged... All seemed a kind of mockery. It was as if nothing at all had happened' (*AW*, p. 45). Those last two phrases may not only contain an echo of the detective Jacques Moran in the second section of Beckett's *Molloy*, as has been argued;[68] they are also reminiscent of Edward Dowden's summary in *Shakspere: a critical study of his mind and art* (a book McGahern had probably read as a student in Dublin in the 1950s) of the cause of Jaques' melancholy in *As You Like It*. Dowden's comment that 'His [Jaques'] whole life is unsubstantial and unreal; *a curiosity of dainty mockery*' may be detected as a presence behind McGahern's description of Moran's feelings in that passage in *Amongst Women*.[69]

The sense of turning into a spectator in a theatre where one's own life is played out in front of one's eyes — Jaques' melancholy in *As You Like It* at the loss of control that comes from being 'merely' a player — is a recurring motif in McGahern's fiction. Similar sensations to that of Moran on his wedding day in *Amongst Women* are experienced by characters in other novels and stories, notably in *The Pornographer*. Words and phrases like 'farce' (which McGahern often said was one of his favourite words) and 'the doomed charade' (*P*, p. 70) are used on a number of occasions in that novel to indicate the narrator's sense of distance from his own life as it unfolds. When Josephine reads one of the pornographic stories he has written, he feels, in a sentence that anticipates the description of Moran on his wedding day in *Amongst Women* a decade later, as if 'I was both taking part in some farce and at the same time watching it from miles far off' (*P*, p. 66). The pornographer's sensation of distance from the immediate reality of a moment of great crisis in his own life, like that of Moran, recalls such Shakespearean theatrical tropes signifying psychological distance as that experienced by the citizens of the besieged city of Amiens in *King John*, who are seen to

> stand securely on their battlements
> As in a theatre, whence they gape and point
> At your industrious scenes and acts of death.[70]

Even Josephine's objection against using a condom is not based on reasons of religious belief but on the fact that 'It turns the whole thing into a kind of farce' (*P*, p. 56), presumably because it eliminates the sense of real involvement and personal risk from the act. For Josephine, it seems, using a condom would make performing the sexual act feel as if she were watching two other people doing it — a substitution of viewing over first-hand experience which one of the characters in *That They May Face the Rising Sun* foresees for that particular activity any time in the near future anyhow (*TRS*, p. 189). It is important that the loss of control is described as a farce, not as a comedy or a tragedy. In farce there is no scope for personal growth, no opportunity for lessons to be learned. Farce, as McGahern would have read in two of his favourite books of non-fiction, by Yeats and Auden respectively, is devoid both of 'character' and 'serious emotion'.[71]

None of this is particular to that later period of McGahern's work. In *The Barracks*, amid the joys of play-acting experienced by the policemen, the Reegan children, too, had already experienced what it is to lose control over the performance of one's own life the moment a force external to the self begins to tinker with the script. When the adults decide whether Una can spend the night with Casey's wife, both girls feel that 'They were simply pawns . . . All the two black-haired girls could do was sit there and wait, coming and going as they were willed' (*B*, pp. 23–4). At such moments the world appears worse than just inattentive and arbitrary, but actively cruel and hostile as impersonal fate becomes personified as a peevish pagan god in possession of a chess set — an image reminiscent of Gloucester's famous description of the uncaring universe in *King Lear*:

> As flies to wanton boys are we to the gods;
> They kill us for their sport.[72]

'actions that a man might play'

A sense of theatre or performance is particularly useful when it comes to moving in the public arena. Some who knew McGahern in his early life remarked how the future author had himself become an adept performer of expected roles during his incarceration with his father in the Cootehall barracks, and how he developed his theatrical gift as a student in the conformist atmosphere of St Patrick's College and later as a primary teacher. His mastery of role playing ensured his survival in environments in which he was ill at ease.[73] *Amongst Women* offers the shrewd observation that 'established forms . . . can be used like weapons when they are mastered' (*AW*, p. 24). That remark comes in a passage which is usually read as either a feminist or a postcolonial commentary on the power of subversion open to those in inherently subordinate positions, but its significance is more universal than that. All the most formal of social interactions have their own established forms, conventions and rituals; if these can be learned and adapted into a self-conscious play script or dramatic mask, even the most rigidly conventional types of situation can be 'mastered' and adapted to one's own ends. Of the planning of Moran's wedding to Rose in *Amongst Women* the narrator remarks how 'As a play it was close to perfect', since it discharges all the social obligations to both families without compromising the couple's own wishes (*AW*, p. 38). In *That They May Face the Rising Sun*, John Quinn's defiance of the priest by publicly parading his many mistresses is performed within the rules of the game of social convention, and is described as a brilliantly subversive 'performance', acted out each time in exactly the same way (*TRS*, p. 33).

In order to really live out one's life in a series of theatrical performances, it is imperative to wear the correct costume. Shakespeare knew the correlation between clothes and social standing, and the power of 'borrowed robes' to suggest a social position not one's own by rights.[74] In McGahern, as in Shakespeare, it is often necessary for people to wear the clothes that suit the part in which they would like to be regarded by those around them, for as the pompous Polonius in *Hamlet* proclaims, 'the apparel oft proclaims the man'.[75] Thus, the scheming Senator Reegan in 'High Ground', whose machinations would not be out of place at a Shakespearean court, ensures that he 'always appeared immaculately dressed. It was as if he understood instinctively that it was only the shortest of short steps from appearance to becoming' (*HG*, p. 94).

In a number of McGahern's works, dramatic costumes hide — or fail to hide — forms of social anxiety experienced by those whose origins are on the social, economic or geographical margins of a culture. Perhaps the most obvious of these is the 'darkie' who lives in Johnny's building in *That They May Face the Rising Sun*, who with his posh English accent and Oxford scarf is stuck in a perpetual postcolonial performance meant to emulate the cultural norm of the metropolis. Far from being convincing, however, the role is so overacted that it strikes those around him as parodic and ridiculous (*TRS*, pp. 260–1). Dressing up is also a recurring motif in *The Dark*, that novel about a theatrical father-and-son pairing living out their lives as if they were King Lear or Macbeth. Young Mahoney feels 'half unreal ... in old clothes in the cornfield' (*D*, p. 162), playing the role of a farmer rather than actually being one. After he wins a university scholarship, his father insists that he will need new clothes to fit that new role, because 'We can't have you looking the part of the ragman' (*D*, p. 153).[76] As far as his father is concerned, the young man will be an imposter in the big city (and he certainly feels like one when he finally arrives in Galway), so he should at least, as one of Shakespeare's comic characters says to the pedant he intends to pass off as a nobleman, be 'clothe[d] ... as becomes you' in that new ill-fitting role.[77] Old Mahoney's provincial fear of appearing like a 'ragman' in the eyes of members of the polite middle classes whose ranks he is so desperate for his son to penetrate is gloriously inverted at the end of McGahern's career by Patrick Ryan in *That They May Face the Rising Sun*. The latter is wise enough to disregard Polonius' advice and instead takes great delight in puzzling the barmaid in a roadside public house by theatrically telling her to let the landlord know that 'the man who wore the ragged jacket called' (*TRS*, p. 51), preferring to be thought of as a romantic figure out of a folk-ballad rather than a mock-respectable man in expensive clothing.[78] Patrick, in common with a character like Petruchio in *The Taming of the Shrew*, is confident that his worth as a man is not diminished by shabby clothes because ''tis the mind that makes the body rich', and 'honour' will shine through even the meanest of habiliments.[79]

The importance of clothing to sustaining a part is also a constant theme in *Memoir*. That book is as full of actors as any of McGahern's novels. It suggests, for example, that while his brother-in-law Con — the real-life original for the Teddy boy Mark in *Amongst Women* — may initially appear like an exciting and colourful character, he is really no more than an ineffectual fool behind an expensive fashionable façade. All surface but very little substance, Con is a man after Polonius' heart who 'with his jewellery and trendy outfits ... appeared like a figure out of pantomime' (*M*, p. 221). Con is only a minor character, though. Probably the greatest user of dramatic costume in *Memoir* — indeed in all of McGahern's work — is that book's version of the author's father.

Memoir consistently characterises Frank McGahern as the man 'who acted out his life in parts and who lived his life, as far as it was possible, in roles' (*M*, p. 226). The role of 'Sergeant McGahern' is probably that which most clearly defined Frank McGahern to his son, who would set many of his novels and stories in rural police barracks, and fill them with vivid details from the rituals surrounding the cleaning, polishing and inspection of boots and tunic buttons. McGahern's idea of his father in *Memoir* is of a supreme actor, the perfection of the role previously played by Reegan and other garda sergeants in many of his novels and short stories. In one passage, McGahern recalls a family legend which relates how his father had turned up to help save the hay on a hot day above Lough Gowna while he was on the run in the IRA:

> without warning, he appeared in the hayfield dressed in a tailored suit, white shirt, tie, new shoes. He took hold of a pitchfork and proceeded to work with his neighbours until nightfall, when he left as suddenly as he came. What amused and interested them was that never once, in spite of the heat, did he remove his jacket or loosen his collar and tie. They were plainly proud of his authority and striking good looks — 'A young lord turning up at a barn dance' — but even more intrigued by his stance and vanity. (*M*, p. 48)

As his son describes him in *Memoir*, Frank McGahern was from an early age careful to play the part he envisaged for himself, always ready to dress for the part in which he wished others to think of him. Clothes can actually become the man and erase the personality that once existed underneath. The beginnings of such a transformation can be seen in a comical moment in 'A Ballad' when the narrator notices how the simple act of putting on a dress suit for a dance 'seemed to have a formalizing effect' on a companion's way of speaking (*HG*, p. 31).

Frank McGahern's novelist–son knew the dangers of turning into the part one had once merely played, to the point where one's own identity is all but erased by the costume and the role. He was also aware that the real danger of so perfectly embodying a theatrical role comes only after one's positively final appearance, when it must be forcibly relinquished forever. When Sergeant Frank McGahern finally retired from the police force, he found himself fresh out of interesting roles to play. 'The sum total of it is I am an X Police Sergeant', he wrote in a letter to his eldest son — a characteristically self-pitying explanation that may have put the recipient in mind of the Fool's witty put-down of King Lear after *his* retirement from public life: 'Dost thou call me fool, boy?' 'All thy other titles thou hast given away; that thou wast born with.'[80] The result, McGahern wrote in *Memoir* almost half a century later, was that 'He was no longer protected by his uniform, and stood as just another man among men' (*M*, p. 226). In his letter, Frank McGahern defines himself by an absence or a lack, not in terms of a new 'role' or a fresh set of 'borrowed robes' which might replace those that had been discarded. The assumption of any type of mask brings with it the danger of erasing the identity it was originally intended to hide or protect. The implications of that loss of dramatic identity clearly made an impression on the growing consciousness of his son, and it became in time a subject in his fiction when thirty years later he came to write of the emptiness felt by Moran after the War of Independence in *Amongst Women*.

The question faced by the father in *Memoir* is that which confronts actors who have enjoyed great successes playing defining roles early in life: how can the self be defined in the aftermath of a truly great performance? This question is posed at length in *That They May Face the Rising Sun*. It should be possible to distinguish the player from the part, and for those who are firmly grounded in reality, like Jamesie and Mary in *That They May Face the Rising Sun*, the actor's own personality will always remain visible through even the most elaborate of theatrical disguises. After all, Jamesie remembers how Patrick Ryan had once stolen the show in an amateur production of J.M. Synge's *The Playboy of the Western World* with his mimicry of the local solicitor, whom he had 'down to a T as — I forget rightly who it was' (*TRS*, p. 5). The hesitation is telling: this one member of the audience, at least, has forgotten vital things about the role but remembers the actor. In the same novel, though, some of the actors themselves have much more difficulty making the transition back from role playing to everyday life. In their different ways, neither Johnny nor Patrick Ryan have ever fully recovered from the experience of acting in *The Playboy of the Western World*; neither has found it as easy as the down-to-earth Jamesie to believe with gentle conviction that 'You are what you are and to hell with the begrudgers' (*TRS*, p. 2). And so Johnny, like Frank McGahern, has found it difficult to return to being his original self once the play run ends and to distinguish the boundaries between art and life, believing, it seems, like Oscar Wilde, that the former informs the latter. It is appropriate, therefore, that ironic echoes of the plot of *The Playboy of the Western World* are incorporated into the account of Johnny's tragic love for Anna Mulvey, who had played Pegeen Mike to his Christy Mahon in Synge's play. It is reported that he followed Anna Mulvey to England in the hope that the romance they had acted out night after night on the stage would become a reality (*TRS*, pp. 5–7), but nobody except Johnny is surprised when she drops him for another man — an eventuality he should really have foreseen, considering how it, too, mirrors Pegeen's eventual refusal of Christy. Even when it is suggested that Johnny had been so smitten with Anna that 'He'd have gone into a blazing house if she asked' (*TRS*, p. 6), that proverbial image ironically recreates Pegeen's final vicious turning on Christy as she burns his leg with a sod of turf.[81]

The only remedy against the emptiness of an old actor's life that has become devoid of interesting parts to play may be to reinvent for oneself the greatest role of all, one that will last an entire lifetime. Play-acting can take the form of the invention of a mask which can be donned regardless of what lies beneath, either to protect the original self from the prying eyes of the world or simply to hide an underlying emptiness. A number of McGahern's characters are engaged in precisely such a construction of their life in the shape of a work of art. Sergeant Reegan in *The Barracks*, for example, suspects that his son Willie, like his namesake Willie Yeats, 'only goes to school to recreate himself' (*B*, p. 17).[82]

The recreation of the self in the form of a dramatic role is a recurring theme in McGahern's final novel. Kate's former boss Robert Booth (who is based on Charles Monteith, the Ulsterman who was McGahern's first editor at Faber & Faber) had once taken refuge at an acting school to eradicate the North-of-Ireland accent which was holding back his career, and has been engaged in a form of perpetual play-acting ever since, as the part he has constructed for himself is so perfect that it has taken the place of the original self and become his whole life (*TRS*, p. 151). Patrick Ryan in the same novel has also managed to construct his whole life as one long theatrical performance. It is related that his 'poor cattle' have been spotted 'about the hill'. When Ruttledge wonders why Patrick Ryan bothers to keep any cattle at all since he is forever away on different construction jobs around the country, the Shah offers a simple explanation: 'For the name. The name of cattle and land. Without the cattle and the land he'd be just another wandering tradesman' (*TRS*, p. 14). The 'name of cattle and land' is a permanent, lifelong role, put in place because it is more interesting than having no specific social role to play. Later, Patrick Ryan himself also explicitly explains the psychological importance of acting. He confides in Ruttledge that 'There are times I don't know who I am from one minute to the next. That's why I always liked the acting. You are someone else and always know what you are doing and why' (*TRS*, p. 203). This contrast between the insecure private and the bravura public faces of the actor is that which W.H. Auden proposes for actors playing Iago in his essay on *Othello* in *The Dyer's Hand*. '[W]hen Iago is with others', Auden suggests, 'he must display every virtuoso trick of dramatic technique for which great actors are praised, perfect control of movement, gesture, expression, diction, melody and timing, and the ability to play every kind of role'. When he is on his own, on the other hand, he must be the opposite and display all the mannerisms of a bad actor, because he is ultimately defined by the 'nothingness' — and the fear of that nothingness — which underlies the mask of the confident actor.[83]

Like Hamlet, many of McGahern's characters know that there are many 'actions that a man might play'.[84] It is important to be aware that you are playing a role — not, like Patrick Ryan, to *become* a role. The conscious assumption of a dramatic persona can be intensely liberating. (As McGahern wrote in the prepublication proofs of *Memoir*, in what was an obvious paraphrase of a famous Wildean aphorism from 'The Critic as Artist': 'masks set us free'.[85]) Guard Casey in *The Barracks*, for example, is 'Naturally timid', but it takes no more than the 'little comic success' of dramatic mimicry to 'release him from the burden of himself' (*B*, p. 23). McGahern well knew that self-conscious theatricality, for all its pitfalls, is capable of offering a release from the seriousness of real-life tragedies. Where father and son in *The Dark* had gone wrong in imagining themselves characters in a Shakespearean tragedy was in taking themselves far too seriously. Nothing can be gained from seeing experiences in a self-pityingly tragic light.

The most 'dramatic' of McGahern's novels are *The Barracks* and *That They May Face the Rising Sun*. Many of the characters in those two novels bookending his career are happiest when they imagine that their world is a stage, and that they are merely players. In contrast with the Mahoneys in *The Dark*, many of McGahern's characters choose to turn themselves not into tragedians but into comedians who live their lives in a series of comic gestures and routines. In order to achieve a state of psychological equilibrium, the greatest personal traumas of many of his characters must not be transformed into fateful versions of Shakespearean tragic suffering. The greatest theatrical triumphs of many characters are their most wildly or grotesquely comical ones. One of the lessons that can be consistently gleaned from the fates of McGahern's theatrical characters is that the greater the levity with which a role is performed, the more effectively it can serve its cathartic purpose. Thus, the Mahoney children in *The Dark* refuse for the most part to see themselves as tragic victims and engage instead in comic mimicry of the tyrant who inflicts their suffering. As an earlier section of this chapter demonstrated, much of the first chapter of *The Barracks* is spent inserting Reegan into a latter-day Shakespearean tragedy through the recurring echoes of *King Lear*. Rather than aiding him in coming to terms with his fate, the tragic connotations only work to intensify rather than abate his sense of injustice and personal and professional frustration. Only in the final pages of *The Barracks*, when he reneges his old role of suffering and engages instead in a carefully staged 'ridiculous parody of an inspection' which turns the frustrating, futile rituals of his daily life into a comic version that may be laughed at, does he finally achieve the freedom which he had so long craved. Reegan's 'ridiculous parody of an inspection' not only defies his much-hated superior Quirke; it also returns to him a measure of control over the 'performance' of duties which are so ingrained in his nature that they have become his life (*B*, p. 230).

On more than one occasion in the same novel is Elizabeth Reegan's kitchen overtly likened to a stage, as Mullins, Casey and Brennan all try to delay their exit into the anonymity of the night by being 'before the footlights to the last' (*B*, p. 174). Many things in *The Barracks* are repeated at least twice (as Karl Marx suggests all history is), first as tragedy and then again in the guise of a comic 'turn' performed by one or more of the guards treading the boards of Elizabeth Reegan's kitchen.[86] Reegan performs the same story about his encounter with Quirke three times in one night, each time more extravagantly theatrical than the last. The first time it is done 'reluctantly' (*B*, p. 12), the second time 'more extravagant, more comic and vicious since the first telling' (*B*, p. 20), until finally in the third telling 'the tones of violence had... taken the resonance of a constant theme repeating itself through the evening' (*B*, p. 27). Immense delight is taken from dramatic mimicry by many of McGahern's characters. In *The Barracks* alone, Reegan's 'savage mimicry' of Quirke both delights and frightens the children (*B*, p. 13), Casey and Elizabeth share his 'marvellously ridiculous and accurate' imitation of a sports commentator (*B*, p. 61), and Casey's clownish parody of 'the tones of a pompous schoolmaster' is a bravura performance enjoyed by all (*B*, pp. 22–3).

The comic 'turns' of the kind performed by the guards in McGahern's first novel were not to be a feature of his fiction again until his last. *That They May Face the Rising Sun* is McGahern's most comprehensive study of the lives of comic actors. Mullins, Casey and Brennan are only 'before the footlights' at night in Elizabeth's kitchen. A number of the characters in McGahern's last novel, on the other hand, really do treat '*all* the world' as their stage. That line from *As You Like It* is revisited a last time in *That They May Face the Rising Sun*. When the semi-omniscient narrator points out that for Jamesie 'all forms of social intercourse were merely different kinds of play' (*TRS*, p. 2), that statement pays overt homage to Jaques' most famous speech in Shakespeare's play. In a book full of all sorts of 'performances' (a word that is used numerous times throughout to describe all sorts of events), Jamesie is not merely playful but often downright theatrical. His exits throughout are often marked by the same gesture, in which 'He paused and turned to bow low' (*TRS*, p. 15) like an actor awaiting an ovation — a gesture which is later replicated by his brother Johnny (*TRS*, p. 261). Even the conversation between Jamesie, Kate and Ruttledge with which the narrative begins is played out again almost verbatim later in the novel. The automated responses of that dialogue are not just a form of 'ritual', as the narrative suggests (*TRS*, p. 3); they also convey the sense of a dramatic dialogue that has been rehearsed and performed in exactly the same way many times over.

No characters in McGahern's fiction are more exuberantly theatrical than Johnny and Patrick Ryan in *That They May Face the Rising Sun*, those two erstwhile stalwarts of the amateur stage. Even now, in old age, when someone utters the words 'Will you listen … for a minute', 'As if out of a deep memory of timing and ensemble playing, both men flung themselves into a comic, exaggerated attitude of listening, a hand cupped behind an ear, and stood as frozen as statues in a public place' (*TRS*, p. 77). These are no longer the self-pitying mock-Shakespearean tragedians who so often took centre stage in the earlier fiction. Theirs, rather, is a brand of exuberant, broad physical comedy. The detail of that description suggests that the importance of the joyous and the playful over the tragic and the solemn was not brought home to McGahern by a purely theoretical text (such as Bakhtin's classic *Rabelais and His World*) but rather by his immersion in examples of the post-Shakespearean theatrical tradition.[87] Johnny and Patrick's theatrical exchanges are clearly conceived as a version of the Shakespearean trope that 'all the men and women [are] merely players'. More precisely, they are an incarnation of a very specific and identifiable version of that trope which McGahern had encountered in one of the seminal plays of his own time. On one level, their 'exaggerated attitude of listening' is simply a vivid characterisation of two original fictional characters. But the same description also contains a clear literary allusion. Patrick and Johnny's pose copies that of Vladimir and Estragon in Beckett's *Waiting for Godot* as they 'listen, grotesquely rigid' to an imaginary sound offstage.[88] The passage, therefore, functions as a commentary on a play about which McGahern had thought much over the course of almost half a century by the time he came to write his final novel. The novel momentarily becomes a commentary on that play and its constant concern with playfulness and dramatic routine, and it makes its point much more potently than McGahern could have done in any formal act of literary criticism. By borrowing one of its stage directions, *That They May Face the Rising Sun* dramatises a suggestion that has sometimes been made about the protagonists of Beckett's play: that they are two out-of-work actors passing the time by compulsively performing the routines of their glory days in the theatre, and that only when they lose themselves in such play are they momentarily able to transcend the cares of the present moment. It is that lesson about the importance of joyous Shakespearean play-acting which he had seen so perfectly interpreted when he first discovered to Beckett's work in 1955 that is also at the heart of so many of McGahern's own subsequent fictions about performance and theatricality.

CHAPTER 2

An Augustan Sensibility

> Now her only interruptions were rare telephone calls — and when her reading brought her face to face with some affection or sharp memory. 'She had done more than she wanted to, less than she ought.' She found herself repeating the sentence long after she had closed the book, seeing elements of her own life and people she knew reflected in it, elements of that life seen and given a moral sweetness that was close to smiling.
>
> 'Creatures of the Earth' (*CE*, p. 322)

Mrs Waldron in 'Creatures of the Earth' is quoting — misquoting, in fact — from chapter twenty of Jane Austen's *Emma*.[1] McGahern spent much of his adult life intermittently rereading Austen's novels. We cannot be certain when he first read them, though it is more than likely that it was in the Moroneys' nineteenth-century library where he was also introduced to Scott, Meredith and Dickens; we do know that he continued to reread them for the remainder of his life. In a 1992 interview McGahern singled out Jane Austen as the novelist he most admired.[2] During his final stay in the Mater Hospital in Dublin, where he died on 30 March 2006, he brought only a single book, and that book was *Mansfield Park*.[3]

McGahern's affinity with Austen's novels slowly developed over many decades. On one of the rare occasions when he discussed Austen's work in an interview, he told Joyce Andrews that he found *Persuasion* 'an extraordinarily difficult book. I didn't understand it until I was twenty-seven or so, and I'm not sure that I do fully yet.'[4] Though critics have often overlooked the influence of Austen and other eighteenth-century Augustan writers on McGahern's thought, Austen's novels certainly formed an important part of the storehouse of phrases, images and characters that made up his literary imagination. Mrs Waldron's affection for *Emma* in 'Creatures of the Earth' (first published in *Granta* magazine in 1994) may not be unique as a tribute to Austen's example among the works belonging to the late phase of McGahern's career. When Maggie 'closes [her] book and hides it beneath the chair cushion' as she hears Peter approach in the opening stage direction of his 1991 stage version of *The Power of Darkness* (*PD*, p. 1), that furtive gesture recalls the well-known anecdotal accounts of Jane Austen's habit for modestly hiding her work under soft furnishings and blotting papers.

This chapter will focus on some of the various late-eighteenth-century Augustan influences in McGahern's fiction. McGahern's eighteenth-century forebears included but were not restricted to Austen's school of late-Augustan thought and style. The novelist whose first two novels had both been under scrutiny by the political and religious establishment of his day was, from the outset, no stranger to the eighteenth-century literary genre par excellence, the satire. His love for that mode of writing is most obvious in *The Pornographer*, which shows the harsh repercussions of social, sexual and religious non-conformity more starkly than any of his other works, and does so in a ferocious humour that is at times Swiftian. In particular, Maloney's idea of wheeling around a baby in a coffin-shaped pram to see if anyone would pay the slightest bit of attention (*P*, pp. 127–8, 249) certainly harks back to the darkly comic genius of 'A Modest Proposal' — a text which is also alluded to in *Amongst Women* when Moran, temporarily taking on some of the tastes and mannerisms of the voracious Anglo-Irish and English landlords against whose tenure he has fought in his younger days, jokes that he is hungry enough to 'tackle a live child' (*AW*, p. 47).[5] It must be added, though, that Maloney's bizarre prop in the former may call on the author's memory of more than one text, in a complex fashion which suggests how McGahern's imagination works like a veritable intertextual web rather than conforming to a model of straightforward linear 'influence'. While Maloney's black humour and his satirical intent are distinctly Swiftian, the image of the coffin-shaped pram may itself be more immediately indebted to the mention of a 'big black hooded perambulator, most funereal thing', in Beckett's *Krapp's Last Tape*, which was one of McGahern's favourite plays. The link with *Krapp's Last Tape* is only strengthened by the fact that that bizarre object appears in the 1979 novel whose narrator becomes obsessed with the figure of a black-haired nurse who cares for an elderly female relative in a Dublin hospital, a character perhaps reminiscent of the 'dark young beauty' who Krapp notices works at the hospital where his mother lies dying, and who is in charge of the 'funereal' perambulator.[6]

The English Augustans of the eighteenth century also offered a number of other things that were singularly useful and attractive to the middle-aged novelist in the second half of his career, as he engaged with the social realities he observed around him after emerging from more than a decade of silent isolation in deepest rural Leitrim as an outspoken public persona, a commentator not only on literary matters but also on Irish society and the recent Irish past. It is interesting that when he was invited by Brian Friel to join the Field Day company when it was formed in 1980, McGahern was in fact in the midst of making an aesthetic move in almost the exact opposite direction: away from the increasing conflation of art with politics that would define Field Day's course over the decade that followed, and towards a depoliticised moral and aesthetic code for living and writing that could draw freely on classic works of English literature.[7] As this chapter will show, after the publication of *The Pornographer* in 1979 the ferocious satire of his earlier work gradually made way for a different set of Augustan preoccupations. In his fifties, McGahern became increasingly attracted to the gentler neoclassical values of other eighteenth-century authors such as Austen, Goldsmith, Burke, Locke and Hume. Over the decades that followed, he found himself drawn to forms of pastoral nostalgia that had been previously unavailable to his work. Simultaneously, he also became increasingly preoccupied with principles of tact, manners and reason whose origins went back to the same group of eighteenth-century English and Scottish writers.

The two short sections that open this chapter will focus on McGahern's adoption, respectively, of the Augustan idealisation of local and particular experience, and of Oliver Goldsmith's *The Deserted Village* as a model for Anglo-Irish nostalgia which might be revived in the context of the rural Irish late twentieth century. The majority of the chapter will be concerned, however, with the presence of Jane Austen in the fiction of the last three decades of his career, proposing how an intellectual or aesthetic affinity with Austen which resulted from decades of careful rereading of her novels may be detected in McGahern's later fiction. It will argue how McGahern was particularly interested in Austen as a novelist of manners, a concept that was to become increasingly central to his art as he entered the sixth decade of his life amid the decline of the Irish countryside in the 1980s.

'little social commonwealth[s]'

One of the things which the later, post-1980 McGahern has in common with the world of Goldsmith, Burke and Austen is the emphasis on the importance of localised culture. When McGahern drew attention in his essay about his native County Leitrim to the importance of 'each single, enclosed locality [where] everything that happens within it is of passionate interest to those who live there' (*LW*, p. 24), he was merely repeating a point Jane Austen had made about similar culturally and imaginatively self-sufficient remote localities in the south of England at the turn of the nineteenth century in novels like *Mansfield Park* and *Persuasion*. Equally, his well-known comment in an interview after the publication of *Amongst Women* that Ireland was not so much made up of twenty-six or thirty-two counties but of thousands of little 'independent republics' called families[8] recalled an eighteenth-century vision of parochial social harmony elevated beyond political ideology. Specifically, it replicated Austen's description in *Persuasion* of each locality as a neighbourly 'little social commonwealth [that] should dictate its own matters of discourse', or the titular hero's vision of his dependent family as the 'little republic to which I gave laws' in Goldsmith's *The Vicar of Wakefield* — the latter a family dynamic very much like that envisaged by the authoritarian Moran in *Amongst Women*.[9] The vitality of the localised allegiance individuals feel to the family, the neighbourhood or the parish instead of a centralised vision of the nation is also the subject of Burke's *Reflections on the Revolution in France*, a book that had been on the English curriculum at University College, Dublin, when McGahern was an undergraduate there between 1956 and 1958.[10] In one of the most-cited passages of that book, Burke argues that:

> To be attached to the subdivision, to love the little platoon we belong to in society, is the first principle (the germ as it were) of public affections ... We begin our public affections in our families ... We pass on to our neighbourhoods, and our habitual provincial connections. These are inns and resting-places. Such divisions of our country as have been formed by habit, and not by a sudden jerk of authority, were so many little images of the great country in which the heart found something which it could fill.[11]

A devotion to the world of the parish and the family characterises all of McGahern's fiction. It is also a recurring theme in the occasional essays from the latter decades of his life.

Like those of Austen or Goldsmith, McGahern's detailed accounts of small, out-of-the-way provincial localities are not intended as documents of merely local interest but profess instead to offer an insight into the whole of human experience. When Jamesie in his last novel boasts that 'I've never, never moved from here and I know the whole world' (*TRS*, p. 7), he is articulating a truth which is not new to the later phase of McGahern's career. The same idea was already expressed with absolute clarity in a 1959 letter to Tony Whelan, written shortly after McGahern returned from London, where he had experimented with writing fiction about the metropolis, and on the threshold of composing the two great Leitrim–Roscommon novels of his early career: 'But it hardly matters where you are! Suffering cannot be better developed in one part of the world than another . . . London may be the meeting place of the world; it seems to me that the meetings are no different in London than in Cootehall.'[12] The sense that to form an understanding of the specific and the local is the only way of approaching the general was an idea McGahern certainly also encountered in his reading of certain twentieth-century novelists, such as Miguel Torga and Joyce (whose remark that 'I always write about Dublin, because if I can get to the heart of Dublin I can get to the heart of all the cities of the world. In the particular is contained the universal' may be discerned as a presence underlying Jamesie's plea for the universal significance of the experiences that may be had in his own parish).[13] The origins of such thinking, however, lie in the literature of the English eighteenth century.

The idea of a universal art is essentially a neoclassical one. The Augustans, more than their Romantic and post-Romantic successors, firmly believed in the importance of restating known and universal truths more than in developing new ones. The obsession with original expressions of familiar ideas is one of the defining traits of the literary culture of the eighteenth century, summed up by Alexander Pope's definition of true wit as that which 'oft was thought, but ne'er so well expressed'.[14] The most apposite expressions of universal truths often sound instantly familiar, as if they have been articulated and received in precisely that way before. This is why truly original thoughts expressed with perfect elegance can sometimes sound like second-hand quotations rather than fresh insights. This happens in McGahern's story 'Parachutes', when the cynical Mulvey 'started to laugh at some private joke. "And nature will have provided her usual hundredfold overkill. For the hundred that fall on stone or pavement one will find its dump and grow up into a proud thistle and produce thousands of fresh new thistledowns."' His fluent and original generalisation of the universal quirks of nature sounds so much like an aphorism coined by an eighteenth-century wit that it is mistaken by his companion Kelly for a quote from the critic and essayist William Hazlitt, only for the first speaker to deflate the promise of a literary echo that hangs in the air: '"Hazlitt's far too refined," Mulvey said. "Just old boring rural Ireland strikes again"' (*HG*, p. 23). It is only fair to recognise, though, that while Kelly may be mistaken in attributing Mulvey's idea to Hazlitt, his association with that author may not be the result of blind guesswork. Perhaps reaching back to a half-forgotten classical education, he is probably calling on a memory of a passage in Hazlitt's 1816 essay 'On Beauty' known to schoolboys of a certain era. In purest neoclassical fashion, Hazlitt there defines a motion as beautiful if it is 'not contradictory to itself, — that is free from sudden jerks and shocks', an idea he illustrates with anecdotal evidence: 'We have, when boys, often watched the glittering down of the thistle, at first scarcely rising above the ground, and then, mingling with the gale, borne into the upper sky with varying fantastic motion. How delightful, how beautiful!'[15] This begs the question: is McGahern having the last laugh at those who, despite their own ignorance of Hazlitt, condemn what they assume is Kelly's ignorance by joining in Mulvey's laughter? Be that as it may, this hidden allusion to a system for ordering and defining aesthetic experiences is certainly appropriate in a story whose characters (as a later chapter will show) are prone to recycling various other ideas and theories from across the nineteenth century.[16]

Augustan pastoral

A tone of nostalgia for the lost world of rural Ireland associated with the author's childhood defines many of McGahern's works from the 1980s and the early 1990s. His screenplay for the 1987 BBC television drama *The Rockingham Shoot*, the essay 'The Solitary Reader' and a number of the stories published in *High Ground* ('Oldfashioned', 'The Conversion of William Kirkwood' and 'Eddie Mac') are all concerned in one way or another with the ambivalent legacy in mid-twentieth-century rural Ireland of the Protestant Big House. As a boy, McGahern had developed his early identity as a 'solitary reader' in one such house when he discovered the joys of classic English and European literature in the Moroneys' library. The nostalgia for eighteenth-century Big House culture evident in these works of pastoral elegy from the 1980s and 1990s is not merely the personal longing of a middle-aged man for his lost youth. It is also an expression of a harmonious cultural ideal that had become associated in McGahern's mind, as it had in W.B. Yeats', with the Irish eighteenth century of Berkeley, Burke, Swift and Goldsmith: 'that one Irish century that escaped from darkness and confusion' (as Yeats wrote in the introduction to his play about Swift) as Irish writers and thinkers participated in the culture of the European Enlightenment.[17]

As happened so often, in later years McGahern began to reread an aspect of his own past through the lens of works of literature that deal with the same concerns. Mannered expressions of melancholy and nostalgia for idyllic pastoral settings are a potent theme of a genre of English poetry produced during the Augustan period in the third quarter of the eighteenth century by authors such as Cowper, Gray and Goldsmith. The mode of pastoral nostalgia which characterises this period of McGahern's career is associated particularly, and self-consciously, with one of the seminal poems of that century: Oliver Goldsmith's *The Deserted Village*. The schoolteacher Reilly who is the central character in *The Rockingham Shoot* is painfully aware of the way in which that poem has the potential to 'act as [a] mirror' (as McGahern put it in 'The Solitary Reader' (*LW*, p. 90)) for things that concern both him and his author in the twentieth century. Reilly can only fully understand the social and economic deterioration of the countryside at the hands of forces like industrialisation, economic malaise and emigration which he witnesses first-hand every day by reading it through a literary representation of the same theme. In an aside during a poetry lesson early in the play, Reilly tells his class that 'Goldsmith called his poem *The Deserted Village* because people were leaving the land and small villages. A thriving happy way of life was being ruined. (*almost to himself*) It is not unlike today.'[18] Reilly, like McGahern, is perfectly attuned to the way *The Deserted Village* effortlessly mixes protest with nostalgia in its description of processes at work in Ireland in both the eighteenth and the twentieth centuries.[19] For if the land fares as 'ill' as Goldsmith's poem famously proclaims, then it also suggests a very compelling argument to explain the cause of those ills. McGahern had probably long been aware of the continuing relevance to contemporary society of Goldsmith's sociopolitical argument. The sense of equivalency he felt existed between the realities so forcefully described by Goldsmith and those he observed first-hand in the countryside of north-west Ireland where he lived was likely deepened early on in his career through his reading of John Montague's 'The Sentimental Prophecy: a study of *The Deserted Village*', an essay originally published alongside an extract from *The Barracks* in *The Dolmen Miscellany of Irish Writing* in 1962. McGahern's later recruitment of Goldsmith as a spokesman against the ruination of a 'thriving happy way of life' in the second half of the twentieth century certainly builds on the critical framework set out in Montague's essay. Montague was among the first to draw explicit attention to the modern or contemporary significance of the poem when he wrote:

> the real motive force of the poem … is not merely that villages, like Auburn, are being dispossessed, but that this dispossession is part of a whole pattern of economic greed which will in time, destroy society … *The Deserted Village* is one of the first statements of a great modern theme, the erosion of traditional values and natural rhythms in a commercial society: the fall of Auburn is the fall of a whole social order.

'The Sentimental Prophesy' draws attention to Goldsmith's rehearsal of 'one of the most Irish themes of all, a forecast of the downfall of Britain through imperial greed'; what Montague leaves unsaid (but what is nevertheless strongly implied) is that the poem's warning carries over beyond that narrow scope to include an equally strong critique of the greed and mismanagement of independent Irish governments after 1922. Through his mouthpiece Reilly in *The Rockingham Shoot*, McGahern makes explicit what Montague's essay had only implied.[20]

The Deserted Village not only takes the remembrance of lost places and the destruction of the countryside as its subject; it is also a poem associated more than almost any other by many members of McGahern's generation with wistful memories of their own schooldays. The pupils of a Master Glynn, who taught him as a young boy in Cootehall, McGahern writes in *Memoir*, 'were still able to quote reams of Goldsmith from his tutelage' years after leaving school (*M*, p. 29). Because of this association with McGahern's schooldays, the section of *The Deserted Village* dealing with the village schoolmaster in particular became a rich source which might be borrowed from and reimagined many times.

The depictions of flawed small-town teachers in 'High Ground', *The Rockingham Shoot* and *Memoir* all fuse aspects of McGahern's memories of his boyhood teachers with traits taken from the schoolmaster in the Goldsmith poem they had once made him learn by heart. In each case, the likeness is highly ironic. McGahern was certainly aware of the simultaneous presence in *The Deserted Village* (identified later by Declan Kiberd, who had been one of McGahern's pupils when he was a schoolteacher in Clontarf in the early 1960s) of haunting 'images of famine, eviction and forced migration' that came out of its author's experience of Irish malaise, 'alongside passages of nostalgia for things past' — what Kiberd describes as 'the more dubiously quotable bits which tend to be anthologized in children's school books'.[21] This 'dubious' sentimentality is a target in McGahern's versions of the poem in his fiction. Master Glynn in *Memoir* and Master Leddy in 'High Ground' are each distinguished by their popularity among their former pupils, even though they have never really taught them anything. The depictions of these characters are ironic twists on one of Goldsmith's most famous couplets about the schoolmaster, whose pupils

> laughed with counterfeited glee,
> At all his jokes, for many a joke had he.[22]

Thus, the plot of 'High Ground' is not just a reimagining of the character of an influential figure from the author's childhood; it is simultaneously also McGahern's prolonged critical commentary on the figure of Goldsmith's schoolmaster — perhaps a belated answer, in the form of a short story, to one of the standard school-leaving-exam questions about that poem. (Reilly in *The Rockingham Shoot*, in fact, guesses that the schoolmaster will be the subject of that year's exam when he revises the poem with his class.[23]) These revisitings in his fiction seek to rectify the rosy picture of the Goldsmithesque schoolmaster as it had been cemented by twentieth-century syllabi. 'High Ground' refuses to romanticise a teacher who is primarily an easy-going, popular village character instead of a dedicated professional educator. Like many of McGahern's stories, 'High Ground' takes place in two narrative times simultaneously, as a narrator remembers key episodes of his past life which may shed light on (as in other stories explicitly concerned with memory such as 'Swallows' or 'The Wine Breath'), or ironically contrast with (as is the case here), the narrative present. 'High Ground' dramatises the inaccuracy that must be at the heart of the villagers' sentimental praise of the schoolmaster's learning and character in *The Deserted Village*, as the narrator contrasts his unquestioning youthful 'infatuation' with Master Leddy with a newly acquired recognition of the naivety of his younger self which allows him, as a well-educated young teacher in the narrative present, to see his old teacher in a stark, unromantic light, for the good-natured but simple-minded alcoholic he really is (*HG*, pp. 99, 102).

Eighteenth-century modes and ideas do not always come mediated through eighteenth-century texts or authors. Another intertext which lent itself readily to McGahern's construction of his own version of nostalgic Augustan pastoral was W.B. Yeats' *Purgatory*, a play that haunted his imagination for decades and to whose various themes and preoccupations he often returned in his fiction. Much of the yearning for an earlier, civilised age that is apparent in his fiction from the 1980s is the product of McGahern's reading of Yeats' reading of the eighteenth century. McGahern's memories of the great houses of rural Roscommon in the vicinity of which he spent his childhood and youth — Rockingham, Strokestown, Woodbrook — eventually not only became associated with the Anglo-Irish ascendancy culture of art, learning and literacy in the same way they had been for the Old Man in *Purgatory*; they also became intimately entangled with his reading of that play itself. Elements of the plot of *Purgatory* assumed the status of local historical reality in his imagination. In a lecture on that play, he made the connection which existed in his mind between the realities depicted in *Purgatory* and those of his own life and times explicit. In what must be regarded as a mixture of frivolous *bon mot* and serious literary and cultural criticism, he remarked that any one of a number of gamekeepers' wives connected to the Rockingham estate whom he had known as a boy 'could have taught the old Man in *Purgatory* to read'.[24]

McGahern's works from the 1980s share with those of the later Yeats a sense that the loss of Ireland's eighteenth-century heritage would equal a loss of connection with a wider European culture. The purpose of the inclusion in 'Oldfashioned' of the list of priceless Continental art treasures lost in the Rockingham fire — 'a rocking chair that could be drawn as a sleigh, beautifully carved leopards asleep on the armrests, one of three made by the great German craftsmen of St Petersburg for Catherine the Great' (*HG*, pp. 50–1) — certainly replicates that of the Old Man's invocation of the burning of the library with its many 'books made fine/By eighteenth-century binding, books/Modern and ancient' in *Purgatory*.[25] Another striking image which appears in two of McGahern's works of that period is even more obviously indebted to his immersion in Yeats' belated nostalgia for the eighteenth century. The 1984 story 'Oldfashioned' and the essay on County Leitrim that was written just a few years later both contain vivid descriptions of the burning of Rockingham House, and of the skeletal remains of the front of the house which survived in the landscape overlooking the lake afterwards as ghostly reminders of a loss of culture or civilisation, 'the magnificent shell and portals, now full of sky and dangerous in high winds' (*HG*, p. 51). That striking emblem in both works almost certainly owes as much to McGahern's memory of seeing *Purgatory* as it does to his memory of an event that had taken place near Grevisk, County Roscommon, on the night of 10 September 1957. That thought is particularly pertinent since on the night of the burning McGahern was most probably in Dublin, where he was working as a teacher at the time. Because he could not have witnessed the burning, the vivid account in 'Oldfashioned' cannot be read simply as a belated fictionalised eyewitness report but as a literary construct that must draw on literary models as much as on first-hand knowledge.[26] Ultimately, McGahern's romanticising of the eighteenth- and nineteenth-century Protestant ascendancy in the Kirkwood stories and in the recollections of the Moroneys in 'The Solitary Reader' were very much for the same reason as his defence of the Catholic Church which became a regular feature of his non-fictional writings from the early 1990s onwards. Both had given him a sense of aesthetic beauty and ceremony in the otherwise barren intellectual landscape of rural, early-independence Leitrim and Roscommon.

'using the imagination on behalf of others'

The most important aspect of eighteenth-century Augustan thought for McGahern, however, is its treatment of manners. Manners are present as a theme from his earliest fiction, but their treatment evolved significantly as his career progressed. In the early fiction the idea of manners had generally been part of a satirical mode, as manners were often equated with outdated social convention, disingenuousness and empty formulae — with aspects of the 'provincial' rather than the 'parochial', in the distinction made by Patrick Kavanagh that has become a staple in Irish literary thought.[27] Often, this took the form of a comedy of manners of the variety he would have found in novelists such as Proust and Austen. Think, for example, of Elizabeth Reegan's description in *The Barracks* of the local branch of the Legion of Mary as 'a kind of legalized gossiping school' (*B*, p. 163), of the comic image of Gillespie gleefully covering his tracks in anticipation of the only-too-predictable visit from an over-inquisitive neighbour in 'Why We're Here' (*N*, pp. 23–4), or of the paragraph in *The Pornographer* (so much more delicately poised in tone than, say, the debates about pregnancy and marriage in the same novel which are more bitterly satirical of bourgeois values) which describes the 'sweet medley of hypocrisy' surrounding the unchangeable ritual of Sunday visiting (*P*, pp. 206–7), a brilliantly polished piece of social comedy that rang true to successive generations of Irish readers which the author liked to include in public readings well into the final decade of his life. The cutting social observations offered in such passages are of course in a broad sense Austenesque, but they do not exploit the full range of meaning about well-mannered behaviour which a careful reader like McGahern might draw from novels such as *Sense and Sensibility*, *Emma* and *Persuasion*.

A vision that encompasses a more comprehensive reading of Austen's complex understanding of what manners really consist of only came into being in the second half of his career, contemporaneously with his adoption of Goldsmith's nostalgia for lost youth and lost places. From the 1980s onward, manners became a central theme in his work, and the Austen novels that he had always privately enjoyed became a model on which he could now draw for the construction of his fictional worlds. This belatedness is perhaps to do with how, during the early part of his career, the lessons that could be learned from Austen remained imprisoned in her Englishness. In an unpublished essay about the Irish writer's relationship to Britain and Europe, McGahern recalls how for young Irish writers coming of age in the early 1960s, most twentieth-century English writing 'seemed to us to be exclusively concerned with social nuance and class and to us it was no use'.[28] It may have taken McGahern a while to clearly separate class (which was not relevant to his experience and did not interest him as a writer of fiction) from manners, which was of the utmost importance to the functioning of any community or group, no matter how classless it considered itself to be.

The Pornographer marks a turning point in McGahern's sensibility, as the 'respect, tact, and deference' which characterise the narrator's relationship with his aunt and uncle exist side by side with harsh and uncompromising satirical and social-critical elements.[29] The process of maturation away from biting social satire and toward a genuinely tactful sensibility which is accomplished in that novel could be said to mirror the maturation of English literary tastes and fashions that took place during the long eighteenth century, between the era of Swift and Pope and that of Austen and Burke. The portrayal of an Irish lack of social graces is so exaggerated in the pornographer's short story 'Mavis and the Colonel Take a Trip on the Shannon' (*P*, pp. 153–61) that that story-within-a-novel reads, in retrospect, like McGahern's deliberate final hurrah, a joyously over-the-top farewell to the genre of aggressive social satire before that mode was largely relinquished in his later fiction. Even *The Pornographer*'s fictional publisher Maloney has to acknowledge that the satire offered in 'Mavis and the Colonel' is not in the 'untranslatable league' (*P*, p. 163) of *The Midnight Court* — a sly reference to the banning under the Censorship of Publications Act of Frank O'Connor's 1945 translation of Brian Merriman's eighteenth-century satirical poem about sexual desire and repression.

Starting from the conclusion of *The Pornographer*, the outlook of McGahern's fiction turned away from social satire, both the comical and the aggressive varieties, in order to observe the minutiae of the social machine at work. From the 1980s his novels and short stories became increasingly preoccupied with simply observing 'the same people living in the same place'; that definition of 'a nation' proposed by Leopold Bloom in *Ulysses* is an equally valid description of the parish.[30] Jane Austen was an infinitely more suitable model for this mode of writing than Brian Merriman. As Declan Kiberd suggests in an essay about *That They May Face the Rising Sun*, McGahern eventually came to share Austen's desire 'to find a mode of expression for her critical attitudes within rather than beyond society'.[31] This shift in outlook away from ferocious Swiftian satire towards the gentler world of manners was a decisive move for the novelist. Its objectives are summarised, in a way, in an aphorism from David Hume's *Enquiry Concerning Human Understanding* that is quoted by the Protestant Colonel Sinclair in 'Oldfashioned'. Hume's remark that 'I never discuss religion because its base is faith — not reason' is upheld as a central tenet of neighbourly good manners by the colonel in an effort to avoid arguments with garrulous townspeople on a night out (*HG*, p. 39).[32] McGahern quoted Hume's resolution in a number of interviews from the same period, probably because he recognised its usefulness in a number of spheres.[33] Firstly, the indispensable practical value it offers to everyday living was not lost on McGahern as the son of an old IRA man who lived only twenty miles from the border with the North for the duration of the 'Troubles'. Moreover, the sense of manners which can be taken from the *Enquiry Concerning Human Understanding* is also a version of the code of conduct McGahern believed the writer must follow. Matters of opinion, faith or taste should be left to each reader's best judgement — a belief that led him on various occasions to invoke Chekhov's letter about '"good manners" of the mind' (*LW*, p. 94), the article of 'literary etiquette' which dictates that the only decent thing an author can do after publishing a book is to 'bow' politely to the reader and not to argue with whatever disagreements he or she may have with its contents.[34]

Ultimately, almost every aspect of living and writing could in some way be connected with manners. McGahern's later work repeatedly reacts against forms of individualism which endanger the social equilibrium. Not all of these are loutish forms of anti-social behaviour. Individual romantic passions could in their own way also suspend social considerations. Thus even the basic generic properties of the love story could in the end be regarded in terms of their intersection with the world of manners and the social order. In a 1997 'Note' on the stories 'My Love, My Umbrella', 'Sierra Leone' and 'Gold Watch', McGahern analysed the behaviour of his male and female protagonists with the observation that

> Like young lovers everywhere they seek happiness through pleasure. Underlying all the stories is the idea that in a sexual attraction of any passion or profundity the possibility of calamity lies close to the promise of happiness. The ethical niceties can be thrust to one side, in the interests of vanity or sensual gratification or through mere carelessness, but suffering quickly restores a very keen appreciation of manners and the moral order.[35]

This same idea that sexual love or lust can become a hazard to 'manners and the moral order' had first been broached by the narrator of *The Pornographer* in the final reckoning of his pleasure-seeking life in the city. In the closing paragraphs of that novel, the narrator comes to realise for the first time how inattentiveness and carelessness ('not attending... thinking any one thing was as worth doing as any other... sleeping with anybody who'd agree') are selfish traits which often result in 'pain and confusion and evil' to others (*P*, p. 251).

In the period that followed the publication of *The Pornographer*, McGahern became increasingly interested in whole communities made up of interrelated lives rather than in isolated individuals. That aesthetic departure is explicitly signalled in retrospect towards the end of *Memoir*, where in referring to 'My own separate life' he adds a crucial qualifying phrase: 'in so far as any life is separate' (*M*, p. 260) — an idea rehearsed, too, by Jamesie in *That They May Face the Rising Sun*, who dismisses Kate's invocation of another character's independence and individuality by observing that 'None of us has a life of our own' (*TRS*, p. 232). This new approach was first given expression in a key story that marks the turning point in McGahern's career as a writer of manners and community, 'Oldfashioned', whose opening pages read like a nineteenth-century novel in miniature, and many of whose themes and motifs (like the incessant enquiry for local news), as well as its tone of graceful quietude, anticipate *That They May Face the Rising Sun*, the great work of his maturity.

For McGahern, books like Austen's novels or Burke's *Reflections on the Revolution in France* might provide the modern writer with a conception of good manners even while living in the midst of a society urgently in need of some. McGahern was well aware that, as he wrote in a set of notes on Yeats' *Purgatory*, '[an] Individual can do little to halt the deterioration of society'.[36] Yet he still believed that civilised conduct could be achieved by rediscovering certain social and cultural values that had been lost with the onset of modernity, when (as the narrator of 'Oldfashioned' dispassionately records) manners 'grew loud, uncertain, coarse' as people lost touch with traditional social structures which had previously enforced standards of behaviour (*HG*, p. 36). He found the same theme in *Purgatory*. In a set of notes, McGahern wrote that Yeats' play dramatised the contrast between the 'Barbarism of the boy, of the new Ireland, against the high morality Yeats associated with poetry' — a reading which echoes Yeats' own argument in his defence of *Purgatory* that the loss of culture which followed the destruction of Ireland's Big Houses was 'Sometimes … the result of poverty, but more often because a new individualistic generation has lost interest in the ancient sanctities.'[37] The deterioration of manners which came with the erosion of the boundaries of old communities in the twentieth century, with the break-up in rural Ireland of those Austenian 'little social commonwealth[s]', was a recurring theme in the second half of McGahern's career. The collapse of manners is a central subject of key works like 'Oldfashioned' and 'Creatures of the Earth', as well as of the different versions of his essay on Tomás Ó Criomhthain's *The Islandman* (eventually revised and extended under the title 'What Is My Language?') (*LW*, p. 272). The mindless individualism of the modernised world, typified in McGahern's work by the antisocial terror wreaked on Achill by Murphy and Heslin in 'Creatures of the Earth', could only result in a restriction of collective freedoms, a development Edmund Burke had warned against when he wrote that 'solitary, unconnected, individual, selfish liberty' can only lead to the collapse of collective '*social* freedom'.[38] 'In this sense the restraints on men,' Burke argued, 'as well as their liberties, are to be reckoned among their rights.'[39] The grown-up son in 'Oldfashioned' thinks like the author of the *Reflections on the Revolution in France* and urges, in a Burkean phrase, against forms of anarchy and antisocial behaviour perpetrated in the name of freedom in twentieth-century Ireland when he says that 'There have to be rules if there's to be any fairness or freedom' (*HG*, p. 55).[40]

A political thinker like Burke argued a vital point which McGahern would always remember. In the end, however, an infinitely more subtle guide to good conduct might be found in a novelist like Jane Austen. Her aesthetic embodied a code of manners which was very close to that which McGahern saw in some of his neighbours in Leitrim. One of the characters in *That They May Face the Rising Sun* protests that there are 'No misters in this part of the world. Nothing but broken-down gentlemen' (*TRS*, p. 2) (a statement that was probably meant to recall Vivian Mercier's famous comment about *Waiting for Godot* that Beckett's tramps are not tramps at all but rather fallen-down gentlemen, 'more shabby-genteel than ragged').[41] That statement points to the fact that many characters in McGahern's later fiction, in particular, are possessed of very graceful manners. McGahern's lakeside-dwellers may live materially modest, 'broken-down' lives, but they still retain — like many of Jane Austen's heroines, and like Moran's tactful, self-effacing Protestant neighbour Rodden in *Amongst Women* (who 'had been taught as a child that any boasting was a symptom of inferiority' (*AW*, p. 164)) the social sensibilities that bespeak good breeding.

On more than one occasion in *That They May Face the Rising Sun* (as in the essay 'What Is My Language?'), the characters gently satirise Synge. Yet McGahern's final novel shares its sense of manners with *The Aran Islands*, Synge's anthropological study of a remote west-of-Ireland culture based on 'courtesy', which is 'singularly attractive' and full of 'grace'.[42] *That They May Face the Rising Sun*, like *The Aran Islands*, is a novel about a community's ability to 'reach[ ] back' at every opportunity 'to an old tradition of courtesy' (*TRS*, p. 48). Concerns with manners and community are a key theme throughout. Many of the lakeside's social guidelines are imparted by Jamesie. His lesson in civility advances from the very first page of the novel. Jamesie's comment in the exchange with the Ruttledges which opens the novel, that nobody goes to Mass except 'To look at the girls. To see the whole performance ... to see all the other hypocrites' (*TRS*, p. 2), for instance, is not just the glib refusal of organised religion which it may at first appear to be; it is also an affirmation of the culture of good neighbourliness. Jamesie's playful response to Ruttledge's concern with the hypocrisy of attending Mass as a non-believer in the Church's teachings echoes Leopold Bloom's motives for that same act in *Ulysses*. Bloom goes not only because it is a 'Nice discreet place to be next some girl', but also to wonder 'Who is my neighbour?'[43] He goes, in other words, to take a genuine interest in the inner lives of those around him, in a reversal of the impoverishment of communal life which modern urban living can so easily bring.

The presence of this delicate social equilibrium is not obvious to everyone, however, and it is at times a source of fierce debate among the characters. Patrick Ryan may complain, like Henry James, that there are no manners to be found in his native country (*TRS*, p. 79), but many of the other characters know better. Kate, an outsider to the community, who can see it with the critical distance and detachment of a novelist, protests immediately against his dismissal of the social skills of the lakesiders by pointing out that 'Some people here have beautiful manners' (*TRS*, p. 79). Only a few pages earlier her husband had already explained his own social code to Patrick Ryan. That code is not so much moral as imaginative. Ruttledge believes that 'The truth isn't always useful', and that it is better to rely on 'Kindness... understanding... sympathy maybe' (*TRS*, pp. 75–6). That idea elaborates on the vital observation of a character from the 1983 story 'Parachutes' that 'Lies are the oil of the social machinery' (*HG*, p. 15). McGahern, like many of his most tactful characters, knew that in the pursuit of harmonious social interaction there are more important things than the truth.

Ruttledge may have added 'imagination' to his little list, because *That They May Face the Rising Sun* constantly rehearses one of the central principles of McGahern's late thought, the striking definition of manners which recurs in a number of the essays and interviews from the last decade of his life:

> good manners, rather than the formula, is in using the imagination on behalf of others. You actually imagine if you were that person how you'd feel, and such a thing, and you adapt your manners to correspond to that.[44]

The idea of 'using the imagination on behalf of others' (a phrase that probably originated in McGahern's reading of George Eliot's *Daniel Deronda*, in which the protagonist 'had the stamp of rarity in a subdued fervour of sympathy, *an activity of imagination on behalf of others*, which did not show itself effusively, but was continually seen in acts of considerateness that struck his companions as moral eccentricity'[45]) is a constant feature of McGahern's late thought. The same phrase occurs in *That They May Face the Rising Sun*, where the Shah 'was intensely aware of every other presence, exercising his imagination on their behalf as well as on his own, seeing himself as he might be seen and as he saw others' (*TRS*, p. 36). Ruttledge's 'understanding' and 'sympathy' are benign but remain vague enough. Relying on the ability to read the needs of others, his sense of manners is that which was regularly articulated by McGahern from the early 1980s. It was first introduced in 'Oldfashioned', where Mrs Sinclair possesses 'the perfect tact that is a kind of mind-reading' (*HG*, p. 48), and repeated, for example, in his 1995 preface to a book of photographs of County Leitrim, where it was posed as a rhetorical question: 'what, after all, is true tact but a kind of mind-reading?' (*LW*, p. 18) The Shah's code of manners, on the other hand, is more sophisticated: it relies on an *active* use of the imagination, a true imaginative sympathy which relies not just on a passive act of reading the joys or sorrows of another, but on actively writing one's own version of the other's hidden inner life — like the eponymous creamery manager in McGahern's short story who, born out of his fear of hurting people, has the ability to 'partly underst[and] them, could put himself in their place' (*CS*, p. 370). Analysed in such a way, manners are an aesthetic attitude as much as a social or moral imperative. One of Oscar Wilde's characters may stress the importance of placing manners before morals, but in McGahern the two are never really fully separate in the first place.[46]

Such a conception of manners is, of course, intimately connected with the art of the novel. It has been said that poems are about oneself, while novels are about other people.[47] 'To use your imagination on behalf of others was not only McGahern's 'favourite description of manners'; he also shrewdly added that it was 'not too far from the notion of art itself'.[48] To do so means becoming a narrator or a novelist, one who enters the consciousness of another in order to imagine what they may fear or desire — and that other always has to be treated with dignity and consideration. In the twentieth century that idea is central in novels by Joyce and Kate O'Brien.[49] (The second half of the sentence describing the Shah's code of manners, after all, echoes Leopold Bloom's articulation of the rudiments of civilised conduct in *Ulysses*, which itself echoes another late-eighteenth-century exponent of the literature of sensibility, Robert Burns' 'To a Louse': 'Still you learn something. See ourselves as others see us.'[50]) Although McGahern probably took the phrase 'imagination on behalf of others' from George Eliot, his sense of manners should be traced back further, to late-eighteenth-century English writers such as Samuel Johnson, Adam Smith and Edmund Burke. All of these formulated roughly equivalent theories about manners and social responsibility which emphasised the use of the imagination. Smith's *Theory of Moral Sentiments*, for example, defined sympathy as 'our putting ourselves in their situation ... and thence conceiving what would be our emotions in this case'.[51] Johnson begins his *Rambler* essay on biography with the observation that:

> All joy or sorrow for the happiness or calamities of others is produced by an act of the imagination that realizes the event however fictitious, or approximates it however remote, by placing us, for a time, in the condition of him whose fortune we contemplate; so that we feel, while the deception lasts, whatever motions would be excited by the same good or evil happening to ourselves.[52]

The eighteenth-century tradition of imaginative sympathy arguably found its most refined utterance in Jane Austen. Her novels are written with a constant awareness of the contrast, vocalised by Mr Knightley in *Emma*, between superficial 'smooth, plausible manners' (being merely 'agreeable') and genuine tact, which requires 'delicacy towards the feelings of other people'.[53] In Austen we repeatedly find the same moral imperative for the use of the imagination on behalf of others that we see in works like 'Oldfashioned', 'The Country Funeral', *That They May Face the Rising Sun* and elsewhere in McGahern. Elizabeth Reegan in *The Barracks*, for example, proves herself a true heir of *Emma*'s Mr Knightley when she displays an acute sensitivity to the distinction between being polite or agreeable on the one hand, and genuinely tactful conduct on the other. When a compliment to Guard Mullins makes him feel awkward and self-conscious, 'She saw the effect of her slight politeness, and wished she'd been silent, it wasn't true courtesy if it made Mullins so uneasy, only a silly, affected fashion of manners' (*B*, p. 203).

In *That They May Face the Rising Sun*, as in *Persuasion* and *Sense and Sensibility*, the characters can be crudely divided into mind readers and egotists: those who effectively use their imagination on behalf of others, and the many others who fail to do so. Colonel Brandon and Elinor Dashwood in *Sense and Sensibility*, for instance, are both characterised as tactful mind readers. The greatest of Austen's users of the imagination on behalf of others, however, is surely Anne Elliot in *Persuasion*, which was McGahern's favourite of Austen's novels.[54] Early in the plot of that novel, when her sister Mary complains that she had not visited her soon enough, Anne replies: 'you must be aware that my wish would be to remain with Lady Russell to the last: and besides what I felt on her account ...'[55] To '[feel] on her account' is an ambiguous phrase: it can mean to have feelings of tenderness or affection for her, but also to feel *on her behalf*. The second reading of that sentence is by far the more interesting one.

Anne's exercising of her imagination on behalf of her friend, who would on that occasion be too polite to ask her directly to stay, is a constant feature of her behaviour. It is possible, of course, that Anne is so mindful of exercising her imagination on behalf of others that this completely exhausts her imaginative faculties and makes her own inner life rather bland. Many readers, after all, have picked up on her transparency as a character compared with Emma Woodhouse or Elizabeth Bennet. Even in this, however, Anne is the perfect novelist, who must herself cease to exist in order for her creation to take on a life of its own. Many artists, as Oscar Wilde knew, are irredeemably boring people because all their genius goes into the life of their imagination.[56] In *That They May Face the Rising Sun*, those who, like the Shah, exercise their imagination on behalf of others are on at least one occasion even explicitly compared to artists. Rare instances when the Shah's tact breaks down are compared by the narrator to a failure of his vision: 'With people he disliked he could be rough. People or places that made him ill at ease or uncomfortable he went to great lengths to avoid. When caught in such situations his manners would turn atrocious, like a clear-sighted person going momentarily blind' (*TRS*, p. 36).

The system of manners operated by John Quinn, *That They May Face the Rising Sun*'s grotesquely drawn villain whose guiding social principles are summarised by Jamesie as 'They'll try anything. "Fuck them. What can they do but refuse?"' (*TRS*, p. 25), is the opposite of the mind reader's tact. If John Quinn uses his faculty to enter the minds of others, it is only to imagine how he can exploit their good nature. For him, manners are something you can *put on* somebody who is weaker than you are (*TRS*, p. 24), not something one should aspire to cultivate for oneself. If selfishness, as Wilde proposed, 'is not living as one wishes to live, it is asking others to live as one wishes to live. And unselfishness is letting other people's lives alone, not interfering with them',[57] then one form of bad manners identified in *That They May Face the Rising Sun* is to 'think the whole world revolves around their whatnot' (*TRS*, p. 128), as Jamesie says about his daughter-in-law Lucy. As Mrs Waldron in 'Creatures of the Earth' recognises in that sentence from chapter twenty of *Emma*, what you want to do and what you ought to do are rarely the same thing, and to negotiate a path between those two extremes, the wishes of the self and the needs of the other, requires imagination and tact. Much of the pathos in *That They May Face the Rising Sun* comes from moments when the imagination refuses to cooperate and make the crucial leap into the mind of another, even if that other is a close relation. This is true for Johnny's failure to think of offering Jamesie his gun and his dogs when he leaves for England after living in his house for years, an omission which upsets his brother no end (*TRS*, p. 6). It is also at the heart of the comedy that springs from Patrick Ryan's boorish behaviour in the hospital, when he decides to shake his brother Edmund awake because he is unable to imagine he may be more desirous of rest than idle chatter with his estranged sibling (*TRS*, p. 48). It is clear, then, that the naming of Edmund Ryan in McGahern's final novel may not after all be solely in honour of *King Lear*, as the previous chapter suggested. It may equally serve as a reminder of *Mansfield Park*'s Edmund Bertram, who is attractive to Fanny Price because of the thoughtful nature which distinguishes the younger of the two Bertram brothers from his careless older sibling.

An important aspect of tact is the knowledge of when to speak and when to be silent. As McGahern pointed out on several occasions, the rudiments of timing are as important to style in prose as they are to tact in manners. Social interaction, in other words, takes the form of a rhythm, the ceaseless ebb and flow of genuinely social conversation.[58] In a novel filled with all kinds of rhythms — the auctioneer's rhythmic incantations at the Monaghan Day fair (*TRS*, pp. 222–4), the rhythms of the seasons as they come and go — it is the most enigmatically rhythmic paragraph which perhaps best demonstrates this principle. Near the end of the novel Jamesie repeats the list of dos and don'ts which make up the rules of social engagement, and sets it to the rhythmic tick-tock of a house filled with clocks:

> All they said was tick-tock. Tick-tock. Pass no heed. Tick-tock. Say no bad. Tick-tock. Turn a blind eye. Tick-tock. Get into no trouble. Tick-tock. Put the hand over. Tick-tock. Don't press too hard. Tick-tock. Ask why not but never why. Cleverer than the wisest that ever tried. (*TRS*, p. 293)

The ticking of the clocks which punctuate the proverbs familiar from the start of the novel (*TRS*, p. 7) turns his words into something simultaneously familiar and strange, a sort of ritual, like a nursery rhyme or magic spell.[59] It is important that, out of all the areas on which he has so expertly discoursed during the course of the novel, the ticking of the clocks should remind Jamesie specifically of a speech about manners. Perhaps the regular rhythms of the clocks are themselves deeply connected with crucial aspects of mannered thought and conduct such as reticence and restraint. As the narrator remarks elsewhere, Jamesie's clocks serve 'as a cool corrective to the excited commentary' of a televised football match (*TRS*, p. 182). They temper the excitement of a solitary speaker. As a reminder of the formal rhythms which are crucial 'to tact in manners — when to be silent, when to speak'[60] — the ticking of Jamesie and Mary's clocks works as an analogy for truly mannered social intercourse, a constant reminder mounted on the Murphys' walls of the importance of good manners. The same detail had already appeared in McGahern's earlier fiction, but to very different effect. Reading *The Dark* through the prism of the later novel, it becomes clear how the 'broken medley' of the collection of clocks all chiming out of sync in Father Gerald's presbytery (*D*, p. 75) is an emblem of disharmony in a society where everybody does as they please, when they please.

Declan Kiberd remembered that for McGahern 'a bore was someone who took away your solitude but offered nothing in its place'.[61] It is striking that the character in *That They May Face the Rising Sun* who most perfectly displays the tact of a novelist is not one of the virtuoso conversationalists but he who is known for his silence and reticence. The Austenian precedents for this are clear. The Shah shares his acute sense of 'when to be silent, when to speak' with Edward Ferrars in *Sense and Sensibility*, who 'did not disturb the wretchedness of her [Elinor's] mind by ill-timed conversation'.[62] Even the caddish Mr Elliot in *Persuasion* first strikes Anne as possessing a 'sensible, discerning mind' precisely because he carries himself gracefully in conversation, with 'His tone, his expressions, his choice of subject, *his knowing where to stop*'.[63] In McGahern's fiction, eloquent silences are consistently preferred over needless talkativeness. The Shah's substitute family — that 'monastic' community of old men in the railway cottages — is described as a utopian society of mind readers: 'They were all silent, withdrawn people who spoke little, but seemed to understand one another perfectly and to get on well together without talking' (*TRS*, p. 38). There are more such eloquently silent acts in the novel, most notably the reaction to John Quinn's brutal sexual transgression at his own wedding. While most of the guests retreat into a self-protective silence that is understandable but not very helpful, the most eloquent gesture of sympathy towards the father of the bride is that of Packie Donnelly, the fiddle player:

> all Packie did was to put his arm round poor Tom's shoulder and hold him tight to show that they understood everything and wanted nothing and that no fault or blame was attached in their minds to him. (*TRS*, p. 29)

(This description of the fiddler's wordless gesture of sympathy may owe something to McGahern's reading of John Butler Yeats' recollection, in one of the letters which McGahern admired all his life, of the powers of imaginative sympathy of his friend York Powell. In the presence of a convalescent, the elder Yeats recalled with admiration, his friend 'had nothing to say, no phrases, only the offering of gifts'.[64])

In stark contrast with this, the inability to maintain silences and not succumb to the need for 'idle speech' is the most unattractive characteristic of the guards in 'Oldfashioned', for whom even the smallest, insignificant occurrences 'were enough to start an endless flow of conjecture and criticism'. What the boy in that story likes best about the Sinclairs' house is that 'There was no idle speech. What words were spoken were direct and towards some definite point' (*HG*, p. 43), a preference for one way of life over another that is expressed in a manner which distinctly recalls Fanny Price's reasons for preferring Mansfield Park over her home in Portsmouth. Fanny abhors 'living in incessant noise... It was the greatest misery of all. At Mansfield, no sounds of contention, no raised voice, no abrupt bursts, no tread of violence was ever heard; all proceeded in a regular course of cheerful orderliness'.[65]

The same contrast in temperament — between those who are needlessly talkative and those who are quiet to the point of almost total self-effacement — also distinguishes two sets of brothers in the fiction of McGahern's later years: Patrick and Edmund Ryan in *That They May Face the Rising Sun*, and 'The Country Funeral's Philly, Fonsie (each gregarious in his own distinct way) and John, the withdrawn, quiet brother who orchestrates their uncle's wake with immaculate tact — which he is able to do because his inner life is as blank as that of Anne Elliot in *Persuasion*: because he has the self-effacing temperament of an author or a narrator. Philly's inability to read potentially embarrassing displays of excessive generosity makes him the target of envy and malicious conjecture at the local pub at the start of the story (*CS*, pp. 375–6). It takes a firm, wordless gesture of their uncle's neighbour Jim Cullen before their departure from Gloria Bog, observed by the other two brothers in the rear-view mirror of the Mercedes, to potentially begin to correct that fault (*CS*, p. 402). Even McGahern's return to communal values at the denouement of *The Pornographer* emphasises the importance of silence and reticence. The protagonist's uncle's insistence on pointing out necessary repairs to the house his nephew has inherited and long neglected is a form of unwished-for interference which can only work to validate the latter's decision to leave his native countryside for the anonymity of Dublin. However, among the traits which ultimately attract him to his uncle's way of life is the fact that the two men can spend time in one another's company looking at the fields and livestock, but that this can be achieved in a mutually agreeable silence in which 'I took pleasure in his pure pleasure, and I didn't have to talk at all' (*P*, p. 242).

Yet despite the definite leaning of preference towards silence in all those passages, the narrative presences in both Austen and McGahern also point out without fail that sometimes it is, of course, necessary to speak. The novelist and the tactful person alike need to know when to speak as well as when to be silent. As the narrator of *That They May Face the Rising Sun* points out at the conclusion of his summary of the native code of manners which relies more on what is left unspoken than on what is actually said, a habit which is singularly attractive but not always very efficient or safe, 'a more confident, forthright manner' may go a long way to avoid unpleasantness and confusion (*TRS*, p. 186). This is true in Austen as well as in McGahern, and both authors repeatedly point this out with gentle humour. In *Persuasion*, for example, the same Mr Elliot is mildly ridiculed later on the same page for his 'absurd practice of never asking a question at an inn, which he had adopted . . . on the principle of its being very ungenteel to be curious', a habit that has directly led to a measure of unnecessary loneliness.[66] In *That They May Face the Rising Sun*, while it may not have occurred to Johnny to offer Jamesie his dogs when he left for England (a definite failure of the imagination), neither had it occurred to Jamesie to simply ask him (*TRS*, p. 6); and the Shah and Frank Dolan may have completed their transaction more efficiently if they had occasionally spoken to one another (*TRS*, p. 131). Similarly, Annie May's ultimatum about marriage to the Shah could not have been more clear or direct, but it is only countered by the Shah's 'negative resourcefulness' (*TRS*, p. 39), a refusal or inability to communicate which cancels every possibility for positive human interaction or happiness. The reference to the Shah's 'negative resourcefulness' clearly echoes Keats' 'negative capability'.[67] Puns on that famous phrase occur on at least two other occasions in McGahern's fiction and non-fiction. A satiric comment in response to the political apathy of the electorate ahead of the 1992 Irish general election in an essay, that 'The supply of negative capability in this country seems to be endless' (*LW*, p. 124), echoes a joke from his own story 'Oldfashioned', written a decade earlier. That story's Colonel Sinclair masks exasperation with humour when he implicitly compares the sergeant (who he knows will try and frustrate his attempts to help the career of the sergeant's son) both to Keats and to the eponymous anti-hero of Herman Melville's 'Bartleby, the Scrivener' when he says: 'He's a survivor and far from being without guile. Like the rest of the country he has a great store of negative capability. He'd much prefer not to' (*HG*, p. 46).[68] The quotes from Keats and Melville in each of those works serve to identify unhelpful, unconstructive varieties of silence.

Not every silence is the same, and not all kinds of silence are tactful or well mannered, or even very desirable. This is why the narrator of 'Like All Other Men' can refer to 'A silence . . . that wasn't silence' when the conversation between the two lovers breaks down in the face of mutual embarrassment and resentment, and a safe way has to be found to navigate back out of the silence

(*HG*, pp. 64–5). It was Samuel Beckett, in his pursuit of silence as an ideal of literary expression, who famously asked what quality exactly his silence would have.[69] But the acute awareness of the existence of different types of silence was already a concern in Jane Austen, where it is invariably inflected with a sense of moral and social awareness. Emma Woodhouse, for example, contrasts the 'manner... of being silent' of three of her gentleman friends.[70] McGahern's awareness of different types of silence, like that of Austen, is inextricably bound up with manners: with the various reasons and intentions, some more attractive than others, which may compel people to hold their tongues. So when Anne Elliot admires Mr Elliot for 'knowing where to stop', she mistakes his devious and self-serving silence designed for ruthless social and financial personal advancement for a delicate sense of feeling, tact and decorum. Similarly, when John Quinn in *That They May Face the Rising Sun* keeps quiet, it is, as in the case of Mr Elliot in *Persuasion*, usually in order to attain some selfish end, to ruthlessly exploit the expectations of people possessed of 'timid, gentle manners' (*TRS*, p. 186). These sly, self-serving silences are the opposite of the tactful taciturnity of the mind reader which both Austen and McGahern admired. As Anne Elliot and so many other characters in the work of both authors discover from bitter experience, however, different types of silence are not always easily distinguished by those at whom they are aimed.

Both Austen and McGahern repeatedly demonstrate how using the imagination on behalf of others is fraught with danger. Using one's own imagination on behalf of another person will always necessarily yield no more than an approximation of their real feelings. That approximation is a necessary one, as nobody can have access to the inner life or the imagination of another, as McGahern well knew. The act of using the imagination on behalf of others must be accomplished with extreme care and sensitivity, because there is always the danger, not merely of mis*reading* the other, but of mis-*writing* them, too — an act that can, if it is intrusive enough, be tantamount to a violation of their person. McGahern alluded to this danger when he spoke about the 'idea' of *The Leavetaking* (which had to do with the self's efforts to understand the other, and not to let her slip away in 'poor reportage' (*Lrev* 5)) in a conversation with Denis Sampson in 1979: 'To interfere with the life of the Other would seem to me like bad manners or discourtesy.'[71] The marvellous comic set piece at the end of 'The Country Funeral' in which Fonsie rewrites his uncle's funeral ceremony because he has not had access to its original context, watching it as he did from the car with rock-and-roll music drowning out the sound (*CS*, pp. 399–401, 405), is on one level a clever rewriting of another little comic triumph. The idea that a mute tableau is open to many different accurate and inaccurate interpretations harks back to the drawing-room scene pivotal to the resolution of the plot in *Sense and Sensibility*. There Marianne's piano playing prevents Mrs Jennings from hearing a conversation between Elinor and Colonel Brandon, making it necessary for her, too, to write her own version of a conventional romance plot in its place.[72] Both Fonsie's and Mrs Jennings' imaginings, of course, prove wildly inaccurate to those who had been involved in the first place, as becomes clear when Fonsie and his brothers, Mrs Jennings and Elinor, each compare notes on a later occasion in the narrative. The inaccuracy, comic as it may be, is only partially to the point. The important thing is that Mrs Jennings at least *tries* to exercise her imagination, even though she often gets it wrong. To occasionally err is inevitable, but it is an unavoidable part of the process of imaginative sympathy — all part of what Austen calls in *Emma* 'the necessary penance of communication'.[73] To simply say that we can never really know what goes on in other people's minds does not mean that we should stop trying to engage with their inner lives. Even though the attempt is always futile, we must constantly strive to use our imaginations on behalf of others. One of Moran's principal failings in *Amongst Women* is that he fails to acknowledge that other people have their own independent inner lives at all. To see the lives of the autonomous individuals who make up his family simply as a 'larger version of himself' (*AW*, p. 22) is a catastrophic imaginative failure — one which he shares with Tommy McHugh in 'Creatures of the Earth', who 'never talked about his wife unless she reflected a part of his own life' (*CE*, p. 324), and which starkly contrasts with 'Rose's tactful and imaginative management of relationships [which] suggests that she is like a character in a novel by Jane Austen'.[74] If Moran cannot recognise that those others exist independently of himself, with their own uniquely complex inner lives, then how could he even begin to consider using his imagination on their behalf?

Austen, tact and style

Not only does the exercise of manners make individuals like Anne Elliot or the Shah, who can achieve that leap of imagination required for truly civilised conduct, into artists of sorts; the reverse is also true. The art of the novelist is itself deeply reliant on a mastery of tact and manners, on an identical understanding of 'when to be silent, when to speak'. A novelist's style, McGahern believed, must possess the same well-mannered characteristics as his or her characters' behaviour. As he explained about writing in an interview, 'The rhythm is the emotional binding of the images. Especially in novel-writing the rhythm is very close to tact in manners — when to be silent, when to speak. Paragraphs and punctuation are part of that.'[75] He often described a novelist's relationship with his characters in social or moral terms, insisting on the author's responsibility to honour his subjects, and above all to refrain from judgement because, as he said in an interview, 'It's very easy to be judgmental, and very difficult to make that act of imaginative sympathy with your characters'.[76] Or as he reformulated that same thought in more universal terms in his 2003 introduction to John Williams' *Augustus*: 'Judgement is easy. Knowledge, since it involves an act of the imagination on behalf of others and their situations in the exigencies of the world, is difficult' (*LW*, p. 217).

A novelist, therefore, should be constantly mindful of maintaining sufficient levels of tact. The narrative voice of McGahern's ideal novel would be one that shares Jamesie's disposition in one of his most grandiloquent Shakespearean moments, during the drive to the cattle mart in Roscommon, when

> A long, slow-running commentary rose out of the avid looking. He praised where he could, but most people were allowed their space without praise or blame in a gesture of hands that assigned his life and theirs to their own parts in this inexhaustible journey. (*TRS*, p. 135)

In one of only two mentions she gets in the essays collected in *Love of the World*, McGahern describes Jane Austen's prose in terms of exactly such tactfulness or well-manneredness, praising its 'delicate sense of timing' (*LW*, p. 199)[77] — that is to say, her sure knowledge of when to explain or comment on the action of the story and when to hold back, allowing everyone their space. The qualities of the well-mannered novelist, therefore, are not so much those of a talker as of a listener — a species whose rarity had already been alluded to in *The Barracks* (long before McGahern's invention of a fully fledged Austenian aesthetic of good manners), where Guard Brennan 'envied Casey and Mullins their flow of talk, their ability to shine in company, and he did not know that those content to listen are rarest of all' (*B*, p. 30). Austen's well-known flights into indirect speech at sensitive moments are part of such delicate tact. It is this kind of considerate timing, imaginatively mindful of the dignity of all the characters, that McGahern shares with Austen in works like *Amongst Women*, 'Creatures of the Earth' and *That They May Face the Rising Sun*, a novel which not only describes a culture whose language 'dealt in avoidances and obfuscations' (*TRS*, p. 186) but which is itself written in a prose constantly mindful of 'honouring', and not judging, its characters.

McGahern's preoccupation with Austenian authorial tact may account for one of the most striking stylistic oddities of *Amongst Women*, one which it shares with *Persuasion*. Both novels contain passages in which, barely noticeable on a casual reading, the omniscient narrator momentarily loses his ability to report the characters' inner lives and has to resort to guessing instead. In *Persuasion* the generally omniscient narrator momentarily tactfully loses her sight when Lady Russell is reunited with Anne, as 'either Anne was improved in plumpness and looks, or Lady Russell fancied her so'.[78] The narrative does not divulge which of these alternative views on Anne's plumpness is correct. McGahern employs an identical narrative strategy in *Amongst Women*. That novel may initially seem to be no more than the 'straightforward ... simple, direct' narrative for which it has often been taken.[79] In its own sly way, though, the style of *Amongst Women* is much more complex than that initial impression would suggest. The omniscient narrator has access to McQuaid's thoughts, feelings and intentions as much as he does to those of Moran. He knows, for example, what McQuaid 'had come intending' to do (*AW*, p. 21), and that he 'felt for ... authority' (*AW*, p. 18). Yet he immediately follows the paragraph in free indirect speech in which Moran 'saw with bitter lucidity that he would marry Rose Brady now' with the decidedly less sure-footed statement that 'McQuaid had either struck true by pure chance or had picked up reliable gossip at the Mohill Fair' (*AW*, p. 22) — the narrator evidently does not know, want to know, or care to tell which. In that passage the narrator shows a degree of restraint from prying into other people's lives which can come only from a highly developed sense of tact, and which goes far beyond the novelist's habitual aversion to judgement.

Equally tactful is the narrative's treatment of Moran's adolescent daughters' budding sexuality in the same novel. Like a delicate Austenian creation, the narrator of *Amongst Women* is able to hide potentially offensive or scandalous material within the folds of the prose. Sometimes the most significant details in a text are those to which the narrator does *not* draw attention. This is especially true if those details are connected with a sensitive or taboo subject like sexuality. McGahern was conscious of the way attitudes to sex are often characterised by a curious mixture of the puritan and the puerile. The existence of such matters is often discreetly hidden even though its existence is common knowledge. One of his favourite sentences — 'There wasn't a haycock safe for a mile around in the month of July' — alludes to the fact that sexual activity in rural communities is always at once discreetly hidden and a source of common amusement,[80] as does the reference in the uncollected story 'The White Boat' to 'the matter which the dresses and ribbons and music and dancing both flaunted and hid'.[81] Probably nowhere before or since in McGahern's fiction, however, do narrative pace and grammar so perfectly replicate the secrecy surrounding sexuality as in two passages about the Moran girls early in *Amongst Women*. When the narrative relates that 'The dishes had been washed and put away … Maggie was going visiting. Another night Moran would have questioned her but not tonight' (*AW*, p. 13), that information seems at first not to warrant too much attention, and so it is easily passed over or soon forgotten about. A few pages later, amid the tension between Moran and McQuaid and their reminiscences of the War of Independence, it is as easy for the reader to fail to take notice of the details of Maggie's re-entry into the house as it is for her father:

> When Maggie returned she found them locked in the strained silence. Beforehand she had combed her hair by the light of the flashlamp, smoothed and rearranged her clothes but even if she hadn't Moran would not have noticed this evening. (*AW*, p. 18)

The narrative's inattention to the precise purpose of Maggie's visit mirrors Moran's blindness and inattention to the private life of his teenage daughters. The sentences describing her entrance and exit raise questions whose answers only exist in suggestion, not exposition (a distinction at the heart of McGahern's definition of good writing). Those questions are: why does Maggie, who is 'eighteen, tall and attractive' (*AW*, p. 8), need to rearrange her hair and clothes before re-entering the house, and what exactly has she been doing under the pretext of 'visiting'? Readers may have their own suspicions about the nature of Maggie's leisure activities, but the narrative voice is too delicate to enter into a discussion of these. Equally unspecified are the details of the young couple's retreat into the house during the haymaking later in *Amongst Women*, where they will engage in an activity whose nature is known to all but spoken of by none (*AW*, pp. 165–6). The tactful silence of the remaining family members in the meadow is mirrored on that occasion by the equally well-mannered reticence of the novel's narrative voice.

The idea that manners were essentially an act of the imagination which he distilled from his reading of Jane Austen and her contemporaries became one of the central preoccupations of McGahern's later work, one which he sought out in many places. In the latter half of his career McGahern was consistently attracted to writers in whom he recognised a delicate sense of tact that might serve as an implicit model for well-mannered conduct. When he introduced

Seamus Heaney at a reading at Colgate University in about 1983–84, for example, he betrayed his own preoccupations more than he illuminated the central themes of Heaney's poetry when he singled out 'his perfect tact[,] reflected with that beautiful image from the Glanmore Sonnets [*sic*] as "a book of manners in the wilderness", spread out on a lawn'.[82] In three book reviews from the early 1990s he praised *The Great Gatsby* for the way its 'tact and moral sensibility are as finely tuned as in any of Turgenev's great novels' (*LW*, p. 390), congratulated the historian Tim Pat Coogan on 'the tact of his anecdotes' (*LW*, p. 366), and singled out one of Mavis Gallant's short stories for its 'wit and feeling and rare tact' (*LW*, p. 377). Even when he reread Primo Levi's account of the horrors of the Holocaust for a series of seminars sometime during the same decade, his attention was arrested by a version of the same theme. One of the sentences he copied out in his reading notes on *If This Is a Man* is that from the final chapter which articulates the hard-won wisdom that 'Part of our existence lies in the feelings of those near to us'[83] — a statement which pre-empts Kate's remark in *That They May Face the Rising Sun* just a few years later that 'None of us has a life of our own' (*TRS*, p. 232). In his own works, only those characters capable of Austenian acts of mind-writing, an activity at once moral and aesthetic, could achieve truly civilised conduct by taking on some of the qualities of a novelist — even as the novelist himself needed to be as tactful and well-mannered as a Jane Austen heroine. 'Oldfashioned', 'The Country Funeral', 'Creatures of the Earth' and *That They May Face the Rising Sun* alike are all works filled with 'broken-down gentlemen' (*TRS*, p. 2), an aristocracy of the mind made up of individuals possessed of the immaculate imaginative tact which enables them to live contentedly in an idealised social harmony far from the busyness and idle chatter of the metropolis, and to know to allow others to do the same without judgement or interference.

CHAPTER 3

A Romantic Imagination

> The island is simply there as a human habitation, a bare foundation of earth on which people live and move. The scenery is there only insofar as it furnishes the necessary frame and sustenance for life ... There are no idle stretches to be filled with contemplation of the daffodil.
>
> 'An tOileánach/The Islandman' [1]

This passage from McGahern's 1987 essay about *The Islandman*, Tomás Ó Criomhthain's autobiography of life on the remote Blasket Islands, at first appears to contain an unambiguous slight against Wordsworth and the poetry of nature worship — specifically against the lyric 'I Wandered Lonely as a Cloud'.[2] The essay implicitly contrasts the leisured idleness of writers who have time to stop and look at a bank of flowers with the epic narrative of Ó Criomhthain. The influence of such an epic style, in which the drama of setting out and returning is played out on the 'bare foundation' of a landscape only described in minimal, sometimes symbolic detail, has been traced by many critics in McGahern's own style — particularly in that of *Amongst Women*, the novel on which he had been working for some time when these comments about *The Islandman* first appeared in print in the mid-1980s.[3] It would be a mistake, however, to read McGahern's comment in 'An tOileánach/The Islandman' as an outright rejection of Romantic principles. In *Amongst Women*, as in much of his other fiction, the epic strain which draws on the example of Ó Criomhthain and others exists side by side with many distinctly Wordsworthian elements. The acerbic remark about the 'idle' contemplation of the daffodil in the essay, then, serves to highlight particular stylistic strengths of writers like Ó Criomhthain or Homer which McGahern sought to emulate. It should not, however, lead readers to the conclusion that daffodils are of no interest to McGahern; nor should it be interpreted as a glib dismissal of Wordsworth's achievement.

Like many of his readers, McGahern first read Wordsworth as a schoolboy, and later at university, where a significant portion of the English curriculum was made up of the poetry of the nineteenth century — that of first- and second-generation Romantics such as Wordsworth, Coleridge, Keats and Byron, as well as of high-Victorians like Hopkins and Matthew Arnold, all authors whose presence can be felt in different places in his fiction.[4] Yet it seems as if his appreciation for the full extent of Wordsworth's importance still remained to be pointed out to him when he took up his first academic appointment as a research fellow at the University of Reading in 1968. Nearly forty years later he recalled a conversation with Donald Gordon, the eminent Yeats scholar who was the professor of English at Reading, who liked his work and had ensured his appointment. When McGahern mentioned that he considered W.B. Yeats to be the greatest poet in English since Shakespeare, Gordon responded simply that: 'You must *paaause* at *Words*-worth.'[5] When he recalled this exchange shortly before his death in 2006, McGahern appeared to take pleasure from repeating Gordon's correction of the foolish opinion of his younger self, comically mimicking it in slow, elongated syllables and exaggerated emphases in a way that suggested how he had subsequently come to agree with the older man's judgement. In a seminar on Patrick Kavanagh at University College, Dublin, in 1999 McGahern showed that he had somewhat adjusted his sense of the shape of literary history since his stint at Reading in the late 1960s when he referred to Wordsworth as the greatest poet before Yeats.[6] The rest of this chapter will show how McGahern spent much of the intervening years internalising details from some of Wordsworth's major poems and thinking about some of the Romantic age's key obsessions. This chapter will show the extent of McGahern's engagement with the legacy of Wordsworth and the tradition he instigated. Throughout, the epithet 'Romantic' and its derivations are used to refer to qualities and ideas which belong specifically to the tradition of Wordsworth (and to an extent that of Coleridge and Keats) rather than to the very different set of attributes belonging to writers like Byron and Shelley which can be described with the same protean adjective.

Wordsworth, childhood and memory

An appreciation of the aims of the English Romantic poets, and of Wordsworth in particular, is important to understanding some of the central aims of McGahern's work. Certain Wordsworthian ideas can be identified in McGahern's own pronunciations about the nature and the function of literature. His conviction, for instance, that there is no essential difference between verse and prose, and that 'Poetry is most recognizable in both practices by its absence', was not just indebted to his reading of Stanislaus Joyce (as he acknowledged in an interview),[7] but owed as much to Wordsworth's well-known comment in the preface to *Lyrical Ballads* that 'there neither is, nor can be, any *essential* difference between the language of prose and metrical composition'. Specifically, McGahern's reference in a 1986 book review to 'those old, useless arguments about the upperosity of verse contra prose' (*LW*, p. 311) recalls, in its tone as well as its subject matter, Wordsworth's exasperation with the way in which 'much confusion has been introduced into criticism by this contradistinction of Poetry and Prose'.[8]

Ideas that originate in the Romanticism of the turn of the nineteenth century underlie some of McGahern's core aesthetic beliefs and practices: those connected with vision and memory, as well as with the recovery of childhood experiences and points of view. It is well known how childhood was invented as a separate and important state by Romantic poets and thinkers such as Rousseau and Wordsworth, and how both of those writers were fundamentally interested in how childhood memories are recovered by mature writers and by the way in which a child perceives the realities of the world differently from an adult. In *The Leavetaking*, the protagonist, Patrick Moran, writes one of Wordsworth's best-known lines on the blackboard for his pupils to copy: 'The child is father of the man' (*L*, p. 35).[9] That idea is writ large almost everywhere in McGahern's fiction. It is particularly relevant in *The Leavetaking* and *Memoir* and in the early short stories from *Nightlines*, in which the influence of the respective protagonists' childhood experiences on the development of the adults they will subsequently become is a constant theme. A novel like *The Leavetaking* is centrally concerned with ways in which the past can shape the present. It contains a number of images explicitly metaphorical of that idea: for instance, on two separate occasions the narrator compares the way in which a day in the past has shaped his life in the present with the way 'the salt and wind shaped the trees the tea lord had planted as shelter against the sea' (*L*, pp. 82, 71). Patrick Moran's belief in the truth of the Wordsworthian statement he writes on the blackboard is demonstrated by his tireless reconstruction in part one of the novel of crucial events from his own early childhood and subsequent life which have finally led to his position in the here and now of the schoolroom in which he teaches. This obsessive quest for discovering a key to self-definition or self-explanation contained within the circumstances of his early life compels him even to imagine the most unimaginable scene of all: that of his own begetting. Like the eponymous hero of Laurence Sterne's *Tristram Shandy* (a book McGahern had read and thought about),[10] or indeed like the Old Man in Yeats' *Purgatory*, the narrator of *The Leavetaking* is forced to reconstruct in disturbing detail the movements of his parents on the night when he was conceived. As he says in the first part of the novel, he must 'turn to memory and images out of my own life to imagine the night that she conceived' (*L*, p. 65). Nor is the bizarre compulsion to imagine his own conception unique to that character. The pornographer describes a night of passion with Josephine with recourse to the same model when he says, 'We were one. It was as if we were, then, those four other people, now gone out of time, who had snatched the two of us into time' (*P*, p. 42).[11]

Both Denis Sampson and Dermot McCarthy have drawn attention to McGahern's debt to Wordsworth as a writer of memory. McCarthy remarks, for example, on the 'palpable sense of the writing itself *becoming* the remembering... the sense of Wordsworthian amazement that the recollecting mind experiences when the past it conjures suddenly *appears* before it'.[12] The importance given to the act of remembering is one of Wordsworth's key themes. The crucial part of 'I Wandered Lonely as a Cloud' is not the description, so gently mocked in 'An tOileánach/The Islandman', of the 'host, of golden daffodils' which the speaker observes during a walk. Infinitely more important is the individual's ability to call on the memory of those same daffodils years later when 'In vacant or in pensive mood,/ They flash upon that inward eye'. Wordsworth's poetry regularly discusses the nature of memory in all its elusive subjectivity, as it works 'both to evoke and to consider' memories of the past.[13] So it is in McGahern's fiction. As the introduction of this book discussed, nothing in McGahern is ever purely remembered. Every detail of his own childhood as it is narrated in *Memoir*, for instance, is imagined by the novelist from the vantage point of later maturity. McGahern drew attention to this fact when he received the *South Bank Show* Award for Literature for *Memoir* in 2006. In his acceptance speech, he remarked self-consciously on the difficulties inherent in the process of writing such a book when he said: 'What an uncertain place the mind is, even as it is searching for certainty.'[14] The obvious inaccuracies in the mnemonic record presented by the narrator of a novel like *The Leavetaking* (out of all of McGahern's novels the one whose story most closely resembles the narrative arc of the early sections of *Memoir*) only serve to alert critics writing in the wake of the publication of the memoir to beware of *all* supposedly remembered details. McGahern intended for even his characters' most treasured memories to be unreliable, and for the reader to be aware of this. For this reason, *The Leavetaking* is a book full of carefully placed misremembrances and misquotations. The mother twice quotes a poem by Gerard Manley Hopkins that '[had] been a thread through her life': once correctly, and once in a bowdlerised version which deviates from the correct words and rhythms but which just as accurately sums up her feelings (*L*, pp. 36–7, 39). (That this is no mistake on McGahern's part is suggested by a typescript bearing McGahern's instructions for the typesetter, which shows that he took especial care over the correct setting of the quote on pages 36–7.[15]) The untrustworthiness of the narrator's memories in that novel is also signalled when he remembers how his mother had told him to 'count between the clap and flash' to tell how far away a thunderstorm is (*L*, p. 27). This is of course the wrong way round. The mother, a practical countrywoman, would not be likely to make such a basic mistake, and nor would McGahern. Again, the mistake is ultimately immaterial. What counts is the essence of the mother–son relationship during that particular period of his early development, the nature of the emotion recollected in tranquillity by Patrick Moran. In both cases the essence of the memory remains intact despite the factual mistakes in the characters' recall of the precise event.

Like many Romantic records of the past — Rousseau's *Confessions*, Wordsworth's *The Prelude* — *Memoir* is primarily concerned not with the reconstruction of fact in the manner of a formal history but with reconstructing the *consciousness* of a younger self — what George Eliot, herself a great admirer of Wordsworth, would describe as the 'recover[y] [of] the experience of... childhood, not merely with a memory of what he did and what happened to him... but with an intimate penetration, a revived consciousness of what he felt then'.[16] Ultimately, the act of remembering itself is of as much interest to a modern, post-Romantic artist like McGahern as the memories his writing conjures. In this he is close to Wordsworth and to Proust, for both 'Tintern Abbey' and *In Search of Lost Time* are more concerned with coming to an understanding of the process of remembering and rendering past impressions into art than they are interested in accurately relating past experiences. McGahern's repeated emphasis on the nature of memory will be discussed in more detail in the chapter on Proust. There are, however, some particularly Wordsworthian elements in the composition of the early pages of *Memoir* which are worth noting here.

The connections made in *Memoir* between landscape and memory, and the conception of memory as a collective process shared between intimates, both have their antecedents in one of Wordsworth's most famous poems. *Memoir*'s opening pages, like the first stanza of 'Tintern Abbey', are set not in a sublime natural wilderness but in a cultured landscape of hedgerows and small farms that might be equally at home in a novel by Jane Austen. Both texts are explorations of the nature of memory, concerned with the emergence of a remembered younger version of the self who had once observed those same scenes in the past. They each also foreground expressions of gratitude to the memories of a variety of female relatives which are treated as more reliable than those of the author (*M*, p. v). *Memoir*, like 'Tintern Abbey', depends on a collaborative sense of memory shared between siblings. Not only does the book begin with McGahern's acknowledgement of the role of his sisters' memories reminiscent of Wordsworth's dependence on the recollections of his sister Dorothy; the sentimental suggestion in the final lines of 'Tintern Abbey' that

> this green pastoral landscape, were to me
> More dear, both for themselves and for thy sake![17]

also has its parallel in McGahern's identification at the conclusion of *Memoir* between the lanes of Leitrim and the mother in whose presence he had first learned to love that place. The remembered landscape is not described in the detail it is for the simple purpose of providing local colour, or even to introduce a socio-economic history of the Irish midlands. Both those things *do* happen of course, but its essential function is to allow the writer to make deeply personal connections with his memories of the past and with the living and the dead with whom those places are associated.

For much the same reason, *Memoir*'s content and structure also have much in common with Patrick Kavanagh's 'In Memory of My Mother'. That poem begins with the thought:

> I do not think of you lying in the wet clay
> Of a Monaghan graveyard; I see
> You walking down a lane among the poplars

and concludes with a memory of the mother's living, smiling face. Between those vivid images, the middle stanzas develop the mature artist's daydream that 'we can walk/ Together' in the familiar surroundings of the childhood countryside.[18] Kavanagh's poem and McGahern's memoir alike frame the authors' memories of their respective childhoods between images, placed at the beginning and end of each work, of a departed mother whose memory remains inextricably linked with the authors' subsequent perception of walking in the landscape of their youth.

Other plot and story elements in McGahern's fiction, too, harbour faint but definite Wordsworthian echoes. One recurring story element which may owe an unexpected debt to his reading of a poem by Wordsworth is that which deals with the rifts and failed reconciliations between fathers and sons. The same struggle seen from different points of view is a prominent feature of many of McGahern's novels and stories, from 'Wheels' to *Amongst Women*. The importance of a specific pastoral or anti-pastoral location at the end of both those works may owe something to one of Wordsworth's tragic tales. As David Malcolm has observed, 'echoes of Wordsworth's rural anti-epic "Michael" are persistent' in *Amongst Women*, both in McGahern's use of the names Michael and Luke and in events like 'Luke's estrangement in the city, [and] Moran's working with Michael [in the fields]'.[19] Indeed, when Rose and the girls are faced toward the end of Michael Moran's life with the question of why their husband and father repeatedly escapes the house in order to visit the same part of the fields (*AW*, p. 178), they may need to look no further for an answer than to the conclusion of Wordsworth's 'Michael'. In that poem the eponymous old man spends many days in melancholy solitude at the place where he had earlier taken leave of Luke, the son who has left the native countryside as an economic exile to the 'dissolute city'. *Amongst Women*'s Michael Moran has become, at the end of his life, a solitary melancholy like his Wordsworthian namesake. The reason for his repeated escapes to the sight of familiar places, McGahern may be suggesting through this subtle nod to Wordsworth, may be connected with memories of working in that place with a lost son called Luke who has now 'in the dissolute city [given] himself/ To evil courses', shrouded in 'ignominy and shame'.[20]

Once Wordsworth's 'Michael' is understood to be a vital presence in McGahern's imagination, it also becomes possible to see how a recollection of the conclusion of the same poem may have been already present twenty years earlier in the crucial, heartbreaking father–son exchange towards the end of 'Wheels'. That the conversation which confirms the rift between the narrator and his father in that story should take place on a pier by the river filled with broken glass and 'dangerous with jagged bits' (*N*, p. 18) may not just be symbolic of their barbed attitudes to one another. The setting also ironically adapts the altogether more conventionally pastoral scene of the final leavetaking between Michael and Luke in Wordsworth's poem, in which the old shepherd takes his only son to a spot near a tumultuous brook in the valley where he has planned to build a sheepfold, and where he has 'gathered up/ A heap of stones, which by the streamlet's edge/ Lay thrown together' in anticipation of this building project which will never be realised in the son's absence.[21] It is to that location of filial significance that the eponymous hero of 'Michael' continually returns, and it may be to a place of comparable connotations that the heartbroken father in *Amongst Women*, too, is drawn in his mysterious escapes from the house.

'My heart leaps up when I behold . . .'

In *Natural Supernaturalism*, his influential 1971 study of the Romantic imagination, M.H. Abrams identifies the Romantic period's 'extraordinary emphasis' on '[the poet's] mind as it engages with the world in the act of perceiving', and its 'preoccupation . . . with a radical opposition in ways of seeing the world': that between the '"outward eye," which results in a slavery of the mind to merely material objects', and the 'liberated, creative, and resurrective mode of sight . . . often called "Vision"' which characterises the work of many Romantic poets and thinkers. Abrams posits that 'of all Romantic innovations, none has so preempted the attention of poets, novelists, and painters [in later periods] . . . as the concern with the eye and the object and the need for a revolution in seeing which will make the object new'.[22] McGahern was certainly drawn to these ideas. The rest of this chapter will be concerned with his use of this specific aspect of the Romantic imagination which he encountered not only in Wordsworth and his contemporaries, but also in its later incarnations in some of the twentieth-century authors to whom he was drawn: latter-day Romantics such as Proust, Yeats, Forrest Reid and Patrick Kavanagh.

Throughout his career McGahern was constantly preoccupied with what he described as 'vision'. By this he meant that deeply personal, subjective quality, often described as a form of redemptive, religious experience, which is conferred on sights observed and scenes recollected by the artist. In 'The Image' he defines 'vision' as 'that still and private universe which each of us possess but which others cannot see' (*LW*, p. 5). The discovery — and loss — of vision are a recurring subject in McGahern's fiction. The conclusions of no fewer than four of his novels, *The Barracks*, *The Dark*, *The Pornographer* and *Amongst Women*, are concerned with the central characters' discoveries of a way of seeing — or to put it in Wordsworthian terms, with their triumphant dispersal of the 'shades of the prison house' that cloud adult vision.[23] McGahern finally borrowed that striking phrase from stanza five of Wordsworth's 'Ode: Intimations of Immortality from Recollections of Early Childhood' in a review of a collection of stories by Alice Munro in 2001, in which he wrote that 'In the early stories, Munro details with loving slowness how the shades of the prison house begin to close upon the growing girl, burdening her with the darkness of the life of adults' (*LW*, p. 419), but the idea it introduced was certainly not new to his literary preoccupations at that late date in his career. More than thirty years earlier the same process had already been the subject of the concluding paragraph of the story 'Wheels'. Its narrator's symbolically charged description of a river whose waters get muddier the farther they get from the source (*N*, p. 22) is almost certainly intended to echo the Wordsworthian process described in the 'Ode': the gradual 'sleep and . . . forgetting' which takes place as we move further from the clairvoyant source from which our lives began as we age.[24]

The most important Romantic aspect of McGahern's imagination is the constant emphasis on acts of looking, seeing and personal vision which recur at crucial moments in many of his works. Like Wordsworth, McGahern is often connected in the minds of his readers with the landscape of a particular remote rural region where he lived for most of his life and where most of his novels and stories are set. But while it is true to say, as one of his foremost critics has, that 'Only someone who has lived for many years in close proximity to nature, as McGahern has, could capture the countryside in the way that he does',[25] the purpose of his art is ultimately not, as it was not that of Wordsworth's, to simply record what he sees around him. Some of McGahern's most luminous descriptions of the natural and the urban world alike serve a very definite purpose connected less with the recording of mundane geographical fact than with the creation of a Romantic visionary consciousness.

In his essay on *The Islandman*, McGahern praised Ó Criomhthain for the total absence from his book of 'idle stretches to be filled with contemplation of the daffodil'. Such an elimination of passages of gratuitous, or 'idle', descriptiveness from his narrative may be one of the central aesthetic ideals he aimed for in the construction of his own fiction, but that does not mean daffodils are completely absent from McGahern's work. In fact, daffodils shoot from his prose in a couple of crucial places. Almost as if to show that he harboured no grudge against that particular flower, or perhaps simply in an act of homage to Wordsworth, the mother in *The Leavetaking* is greeted by just these flowers when she leaves the school after a discussion about poetry with one of the nuns and finds that 'Pale daffodils and narcissi leaned for her from the white iron railing as her crêpesoles went on the gravel of the avenue' (*L*, p. 39). It is more likely, however, that daffodils are not a reminder of Wordsworth at all here — not surprisingly, as daffodils are native to McGahern's Leitrim as much as they are to Wordsworth's Lake District; their very commonness, in fact, is one of the things that would endear them to a poet or a novelist of the everyday. McGahern's fondness for daffodils may be just that: merely a fondness, coupled with an extraordinary capacity for observation of the world as it is, not a self-conscious artistic attitude intended to align himself with Wordsworth at all. In his private correspondence, where there was no need for adopting artistic masks or striking intellectual poses, McGahern often remarked on the splendours of the landscape in bloom, and more than once these included expressions of praise for members of the genus *Narcissus*. To Patrick Swift he wrote about the 'wild mint or rose and thousands of narcissi in the pastures in Spring',[26] and Frances Byrnes, who commissioned the story 'Love of the World' for BBC Radio 4, commented later that 'All the letters that John wrote to me ended with a description of the seasons by his lake: the rowanberries were come; the daffodils were "almost unbearably beautiful"'.[27] Moran in *Amongst Women* shares the author's fondness for this style of sign-off. The short, carefully crafted letter to Luke from which all non-essential material has been purged in the many rewritings ends with a description of the springtime resurgence of the natural world which other correspondents may have considered superfluous: 'The daffodils are nearly in bloom, also shrubs, flowers, fruit, etc. It'll soon be time for planting' (*AW*, p. 176). The inclusion of that detail at the conclusion of Moran's masterpiece of scrupulous meanness suggests that for McGahern it was not a mere ornament but an essential observation.

It is, of course, not the daffodil that McGahern dislikes but the 'idle' contemplation of daffodils, or of any other natural object. McGahern's distrust of 'idle' contemplation is a deliberate aesthetic stance which is a recurring subject in his fiction. When the son in 'Wheels' suggests such an intellectually idle way of looking at the natural beauties of the landscape that surrounds them, his father momentarily proves himself to be an astute literary critic au fait with the aims of the Romantic movement. What the son, using the language of the polite school of picturesque writing, hollowly describes as 'quiet and beautiful' is to the father 'Quiet as a graveyard … stare at beauty every day and it'll turn sicker than stray vomit' (*N*, pp. 19–20). (A variation on that thought is repeated toward the end of McGahern's oeuvre by Johnny in *That They May Face the Rising Sun*, who is dismissive of the idea that the Ruttledges could ever have been attracted by the promise held out by the quiet of their new life on the lakeside. The thought of listening to 'the fucken quiet' for just a minute would not bring him peace or serenity, he says, but drive him mad instead (*TRS*, p. 77).) What the father in 'Wheels' is saying is that it is not ultimately important *what* you look at. The only thing that matters is the subjective and potentially transformative gaze of the individual observer, which can make the commonplace or the downright ugly appear beautiful just as easily as it can make the beautiful appear stale and ugly. To substitute, as the son in 'Wheels' has done, the responsiveness of real, keenly felt observation for mouthing the empty and clichéd formulae of nature poetry is to exchange the freshness of 'close and excitingly accurate' observation for the 'dead hand of English composition'. McGahern knew that these two extremes are sometimes perilously close to one another; he hinted as much in his essay on Ernie O'Malley, in whose memoirs he found examples of both types of writing side by side (*LW*, pp. 253–4).

The father in 'Wheels' is not the only character in McGahern's fiction to draw attention to this. At the other end of his career in 'Creatures of the Earth', for example, Mrs Waldron remembers a second sentence from Jane Austen's *Emma* which extends the lessons that may be learned from that novel written on the cusp between the Augustan and the Romantic era beyond the realm of manners into that of vision. '"A mind lively and at ease with itself is content to look at nothing," she recalled a favourite passage from Jane Austen, "and that nothing will always answer back"' (*CE*, p. 326).[28] Of course, the subject of Austen's sentence is the confidence of the parochial mind, in the sense in which it was defined by Patrick Kavanagh as the opposite of the insecure provincial who feels the need to ape the manners of the metropolis.[29] However, if it is taken out of context, as Mrs Waldron does when she remembers it in splendid isolation, that same sentence also describes the Romantic ideology of seeing.

McGahern's comment in 'An tOileánach/The Islandman' is not so much directed, then, against Wordsworth but rather against the grossly simplified idea of Wordsworth's poetry as it exists in the popular imagination, which believes that his verse is no more than a highly polished 'nature poetry' — that is to say, the kind of 'factual or sentimental' verse devoid of the 'essential mystery and magic in all real poetry' which is so savagely satirised by McGahern through the mother's comments in *The Leavetaking*. Of course, McGahern did not group William Wordsworth with William Allingham in the sentimental 'four ducks on a pond and a grassbank beyond' school of poetry (*L*, p. 38).[30] For McGahern, as for a Romantic poet like Wordsworth, picturesque views or sublime landscapes were of no intrinsic interest or value. The only thing that matters is the artist's individual vision, his uniquely personal way of seeing, which, as Wordsworth wrote in the preface to *Lyrical Ballads*, 'throw[s] over [incidents and situations from common life] a certain colouring of imagination, whereby ordinary things should be presented to the mind in an unusual aspect'.[31] That famous sentence may have been on McGahern's mind when he described Elizabeth Reegan's habit of seeing the world 'in the light of her own consciousness' in *The Barracks* (*B*, p. 209).

McGahern was fond of recalling Patrick Kavanagh's remark, made in one of the lectures on poetry which the young McGahern attended at University

College, Dublin, in 1956, that 'Parnassus is not a place, it is a point of view.'[32] McGahern alludes to the importance of the writer's unique, subjective point of view on many occasions in his fiction. A description in *That They May Face the Rising Sun* of the lake and the house where Mary had grown up but which has long been abandoned concludes with an interesting narratorial comment: 'Hundreds of daffodils and white narcissi still greeted each spring by the lake with beauty, though there was no one near at hand to notice' (*TRS*, p. 88). While the novel does not exactly propose, with Bishop Berkeley, that the beauty of the lakeside may not exist if there is nobody there to witness it, the implications of that observation are certainly important to understanding McGahern's attitudes towards the importance of the act of seeing. If nobody is at hand to '*behold* a rainbow in the sky'[33] or to notice a field full of daffodils, then it is of no interest to the Romantic poet. The choice of flowers in that description of the lakeside in *That They May Face the Rising Sun* is unlikely to be a coincidence in a passage so explicitly concerned with matters of perception and observation. Even if McGahern's choice of daffodils and narcissi can be explained as a realist description of the sight of Leitrim lakesides in spring, then he must still be at least conscious of the Wordsworthian connotations of invoking daffodils in a sentence primarily concerned with the act of seeing.

The same point is made more explicitly in the concluding paragraph of his essay 'My Education' (written shortly after his return from a trip to North Africa), in which he writes:

> I am back in the rushy hills now, back in my own place. Life is the same everywhere. I think that the quality of feeling that's brought to the landscape is actually much more important than the landscape itself. It is the light or passion *or love, if you like*, in which the landscape is witnessed that is more important than whether it contains rushes or lemon trees. (*LW*, p. 114, emphasis added)

Life is the same everywhere, and no landscape has intrinsically more value than any other. McGahern was certainly aware of Proust's observation that 'The only real journey . . . would be to travel not towards new landscapes, but with new eyes', an idea that is revived here.[34] However, the immediate echo in the final paragraph of 'My Education' is probably again of that same later Irish author who is also invoked on other crucial occasions.

The essay's emphasis on 'love' in the perception of the minutiae of the world is repeated in many places in McGahern's fiction. Elizabeth Reegan in *The Barracks*, for example, intuits that to 'grow into meaning' must surely be achieved as naturally 'as she grew into love' (*B*, p. 211). She feels that 'she'd no business to be in the church except she loved it and it was quiet' (*B*, p. 165), giving her an opportunity for personal reflection on the mystery of life that is often hard to come by in the hurly-burly of the barracks. The emphasis on the 'love' which colours the perception of a sight also occurs in a striking phrase in 'Mavis and the Colonel Take a Trip on the Shannon', the smutty story-within-a-novel in *The Pornographer*, which shows that even a dirty joke can become a statement of Romantic intent. Most of the profound reflections on art and life in that novel occur in the narrator's first-person descriptions of his lovemaking, not in his pornographic output. And yet it is not quite accurate to say, as a number of critics have done, that his pornography *only* 'mechanically catalogues the sexual adventures of his fictional creations'.[35] 'Mavis and the Colonel' does contain at least two important observations about the nature of art — even if, as is often McGahern's habit when it comes to incorporating borrowed expressions of core aesthetic principles in his novels and stories, these are thinly veiled in the idiom of the lowbrow, the banal or the obscene. One such occasion is the colonel's observation, while Mavis performs a sexual act which makes him very happy indeed behind the wheel of a moving car, that 'Being so feathered with those wonderful plucking fingers . . . I start to find the grey arse of that milk tanker I've been trying to pass for the last ten minutes growing beautiful. It's never a change we need. What we need is to hold the familiar eternally in love's light' (*P*, p. 154).

That last sentence echoes comments made in an essay and in a late sonnet by Patrick Kavanagh. While Kavanagh is commonly associated by many Irish readers with the bleak social realism of poems like *The Great Hunger* and 'Stony Grey Soil', McGahern was more interested in his later poems, which are lighter, more joyful and more obviously Romantic, with their emphasis on looking as a quasi-religious act. Both the colonel's observation in *The Pornographer* and the conclusion to 'My Education' recall a comment Kavanagh had made in his 1959 essay 'From Monaghan to the Grand Canal': 'The material itself has no special value; it is what our imagination *and our love* do to it.'[36] They also, perhaps more directly, echo his sonnet 'The Chest Hospital', one of the poems that had made a lasting impression on McGahern when he first read them in a typescript prepared by his friend Jimmy Swift,[37] and shortly after that when they appeared in the literary magazine *Nimbus* in 1956 (*LW*, p. 92):

> But nothing whatever is by love debarred,
> The common and banal her heat can know . . .
> This is what love does to things . . .[38]

The language of 'The Chest Hospital' was clearly much on McGahern's mind over the years, and specifically during the period in the second half of the 1970s when he wrote *The Pornographer*. So much so, in fact, that the pornographer's descriptions of his lovemaking to Josephine much earlier in the novel had already incorporated Kavanagh's statement of his visionary-Romantic intent in the closing lines of the same sonnet:

> Naming these things is the love-act and its pledge;
> For we must record love's mystery without claptrap,
> Snatch out of time the passionate transitory.[39]

When the pornographer remarks that 'We were man and we were woman. We were both the tree and the summer. There was no yearning toward nor falling away. We were one. It was as if we were, then, those four other people, now gone out of time, who had *snatched the two of us into time*' (*P*, p. 42, emphasis added), and later when he describes the preciousness of the moment of orgasm as that which allows him 'To lie still in the moment ... *to snatch it out of time*' (*P*, p. 57, emphasis added), the repeated echo of Kavanagh's visionary-Romantic declaration of his love of the world in that sonnet is unmistakable. In *The Pornographer*, then, McGahern self-consciously makes Kavanagh's metaphorical 'love-act' flesh by using it in a sex scene. The intention is not to parody or ridicule Kavanagh's idiomatic use of the word 'love-act' to describe the poet's relationship to the mundane realities of the world around him. Instead, McGahern's use of those lines in this context suggests the sacred, even mystical light with which he regards the physical love act. In a novel conceived as a study of the contrast between the mere sexual athleticism of pornography and genuine physical intimacy between individuals, this is one of the moments in which the latter is, if ever so fleetingly, achieved by the central character. Or as Eamon Grennan put it, 'sex itself is tested as a site of the mystery, as a replacement for religious loss', but the sense of wholeness with the universe and connectedness to another human being experienced by the central character during the love act are as temporary as the fleeting moments of visionary calm described in poems by Wordsworth or Kavanagh.[40]

'[W]e can only love what we know,' McGahern wrote in a set of lecture notes on Herman Melville's 'Bartleby, the Scrivener'. Writing, in those notes, about the act of reading, he suggested that the works of literature which speak to us are those that allow us to share in the experience of the narrative, 'so that its movement and images animate our memories, draws [*sic*] our lives into it, so that there exists a harmony between it and us, so that our dead or halfforgotten life assumes in the work a harmony or vision it does not have outside the animated imagination'.[41] What is true for books is also true for any other location, object or experience. To the 'animated imagination' of the artist, even conventionally undesirable or downright ugly places are as valid an object for personal vision as the picturesque sceneries of springtime lakesides in bloom — whether they are in Wordsworth's Lake District or McGahern's Leitrim. This is one of the things which, to McGahern, sets the serious artist apart from mere purveyors of 'local colour', a term of derision which recurs in his literary criticism.[42] Even bustling urban spaces can, as Wordsworth stresses in his sonnet 'Composed upon Westminster Bridge, September 3, 1802', be transformed into a personal Parnassus by the act of seeing. This is what happens in McGahern's fiction at the conclusion of *The Pornographer*, where the protagonist first finds that he is 'extraordinarily happy, the whole night and its lights and sounds passing in an amazing clarity that was yet completely calm' in inauspicious circumstances on the empty streets of London in the early morning (*P*, p. 229) before seeking to replicate that sensation in his native countryside subsequently. A similar attitude to the city is also taken in the story 'Parachutes', where small pieces of the countryside invade the metropolis and create a miniature pastoral, frozen in time amid the bustle of Dublin's fashionable Grafton Street.[43] Both those works have elements reminiscent of Wordsworth's vision of London in that sonnet, in which public buildings are described in the language and imagery of pastoral poetry, and the narrator feels a perfect 'calm' at the sight of the city steeped in the splendour of the early-morning sunlight.[44]

In *Amongst Women*, the Moran sisters are wary during an outing to the forest that they might 'trample on the colour blue' (*AW*, p. 75). The third-person description of the forest in its summer glories (which in that passage is focalised through the girls' collective consciousness) foreshadows the revelation of the uplifting beauty of his meadows eventually experienced by their father near the end of the novel. *Amongst Women* further emphasises how revelations of beauty or truth are always private, and how because of the private nature of Romantic vision the scenes or objects which may be invested with significance to any one individual observer are not usually available to any other. This is dramatised toward the end of the novel when Rose and the girls, mystified by Moran's newfound habit of slipping out of the house and looking out of the same window seemingly at nothing, remark on how 'He's always looking out at the same place. He must see something there' (*AW*, p. 179). What exactly he sees in a particular spot in the meadow, or how it may be significant to him, is unclear to them, because whatever remarkable quality the view possesses is connected with the unique point of view of the individual observer.

That the individual and subjective light of love in which things are held is much more important than any objective properties of beauty or desirability those same things may possess is starkly emphasised a final time in *That They May Face the Rising Sun.* The lake around which most of the action of McGahern's last novel takes place may be cast throughout as a vision of 'paradise' (a word that becomes ironically charged as it is used by the Shah to describe the way some estate agents would describe the ramshackle farm which the Ruttledges eventually buy (*TRS*, p. 18)), a pastoral Eden in plain view of the undesirable, barren landscape of Gloria Bog, which is brown and empty and filled with 'stunted birch trees'. But while Gloria Bog is not conventionally beautiful, the novel makes it clear that through other eyes, *that* landscape, too (even as its properties contrasts so starkly with that of the lush lakeside), can be transformed into a paradise when it is shown from the point of view of the Shah, whose loving gaze transforms it. 'On dry Sundays', the novel's narrator reveals the old man's private joys through the medium of free indirect speech, 'he loved to walk the fields, and to look ... across the lake to the acres of pale sedge of Gloria Bog, which ran like an inland sea until it met the blue of the lower slopes of the mountains where his life began, the stunted birch trees like small green flowers in the wilderness of bog' (*TRS*, pp. 35–6). His nephew Ruttledge is conscious, too, of the way 'long acquaintance and association' often breed 'affection' for a place (*TRS*, p. 227). In the same way a familiar bit of soil on a disused railway line where she has started a little garden has become an earthly paradise for the narrator's aunt in *The Pornographer*. The narrator realises as much when he visits her in hospital shortly before her death: 'I saw that it was little more than pure spirit she was living on, and from several random words I gathered that the place in eternity she most hungered for was a half-mile down the abandoned railway among the growing things in the garden' (*P*, p. 121). Like that of the pornographer's aunt in the earlier novel, the Shah's casting of his transformative gaze on his native landscape is a Kavanaghesque love act that is its own pledge, or an act of poetic transformation achieved by 'hold[ing] the familiar ... in love's light' (*P*, p. 154).

It is also true that, despite his constant fidelity to the Romantic ideology of seeing, McGahern recognises that not all men are poets, and that not all views of the landscape will lift it from drabness or anonymity. And so the expectations of the Romantic visionary can sometimes be comically deflated in his fiction. This happens in *That They May Face the Rising Sun* when the news-mad Jamesie, very much impressed with a show put on by two lorry drivers who are superbly skilled physical actors, does not at all agree with Ruttledge's teasing comment that staying at home and seeing 'the birds and the sky and the tracks of the animals' is all the diversion one can ever wish for, and dispels the Romantic myth in an eloquent complaint about the boredom of country living: 'Nothing. You see nothing. People are far more interesting. You see more in one day out than at home in a month' (*TRS*, p. 140). In a similar vein, when the sensitive Mrs Waldron in 'Creatures of the Earth' observes a stranger looking out to sea she wonders (with an echo of Rose and the girls' wonderment at Moran's eccentricity in *Amongst Women*) 'What did *he* see there?' (*CE*, p. 323), only to have her expectations of finding a Romantic visionary shattered by finding that Tommy McHugh's motives are much more mundane than she had imagined. Tommy McHugh, it turns out, is not a man whose days are bound by a Wordsworthian 'natural piety'.[45] He makes this clear when he crassly tells Mrs Waldron that he is 'not stupid enough' to be watching anything as impractical as 'the colours ... or the sea birds or just the ocean itself'. Instead, he is simply a pragmatic farmer watching his sheep, keeping his livelihood safe from the danger of falling off the edge of a cliff because, as he confides in her in what may well be the ultimate deflation of the pastoral concerns inherent in so much Romantic poetry, 'Sheep are very stupid animals' (*CE*, pp. 324–5).

The image

The artist's task is to find a way of looking at the world. McGahern's subjective personal vision, those distorted versions of memories from his past or of the familiar landscape of Leitrim and Roscommon, is often focused through striking individual images: Wordsworthian objects which, as Wordsworth writes in the preface to *Lyrical Ballads*, 'strongly excite ... feelings'.[46] The transformation of the ordinary or familiar into a vivid image of truth is an important recurring subject in McGahern's work. His own preoccupation with the importance of images was more than once projected onto his reading of other authors. One way in which he often proposed the work of a poet like W.B. Yeats might be read was exactly like this. Much of McGahern's thinking about Yeats was influenced by Donald Gordon, from whose *W.B. Yeats: images of a poet* he on more than one occasion borrowed phrases which summed up his own artistic aims. One of these is that 'For Yeats, nature and experience were a book of images ... of a truth beyond the limits of the accident that is Ben Bulben, Coole Park or Lissadell'. The text of a manuscript draft by McGahern entitled 'In Memory of Donald Gordon' consists of that sentence alone.[47] Gordon's emphasis on the centrality of images to the poetic imagination may not be the most common approach to Yeats' poetry, but it was one to which McGahern often returned because it chimed with some of the beliefs about writing which he had himself held since the beginning of his career. As is true for so many writers' readings of the works of other artists, that statement, when it was borrowed by McGahern, said as much about his own artistic aims as it did about his subject's.

McGahern could at times assume a self-consciously fatuous or dismissive stance when confronted with the importance ascribed to the imagery of his work by journalists and commentators. For instance, when he wrote to Michael McLaverty in 1965 that he was to advise a BBC documentary crew who were planning to make a film 'about the world of my work, its imagery', he added to that piece of information in facetiousness or self-deprecation that 'they give me some money for pointing out a few trees I love etc.'[48] Such protestations, however, clearly belie his very deliberate cultivation of an artistic doctrine founded around the importance of 'the image'. Time and again, the same handful of images from ordinary life — taken from nature, people, household objects and domestic interiors — return in his fiction: a bed with broken brass bells, fine white dust of the road dulling the shine of polished leather boots, the sight of pale beech chips scattered on the ground, the sound of a lone chainsaw over a quiet lake, an old brown felt hat (sometimes with a decaying headband) belonging to an old man, pink Jaffa orange wrappers on a nail by the toilet, pinpoints of sunlight piercing the dense canopy of foliage on a country lane. Striking images like these and others in his fiction are all of unremarkable things, because like James Joyce, who knew that the sacred is most likely to be manifested in a simple 'shout in the street',[49] McGahern passionately believed, as he phrased it in an interview with Myles Dungan near the end of his life, that 'the ordinary is the most precious in life'.[50] Only in the most ordinary of sights, he believed, could something enduring be discovered.

Such constantly recurring images give McGahern's work a sense of unity and coherence — though some may call it repetitiveness. They are not mere realist adornments of a fictional world, placed there to lend it an air of authenticity; nor are they autobiographical anchors inserted with the intention of tying the novels and stories to the author's own life. Instead, McGahern regarded images as the *essential* element of his writing from the very beginning of his career. He had no doubt read with interest Proust's argument in the first volume of *In Search of Lost Time* that everything in the novel, including character and plot, is dispensable except for the image, which is the only part that 'our soul can assimilate'.[51] Following the example of such grand arguments, and borrowing simultaneously from Proust and St Thomas Aquinas, McGahern had very early on come to the conclusion that, as he said later, 'The image is the basis of all writing. The writer's business is to pull the image that moves us out of the darkness.'[52] That statement recalls both an idea from *In Search of Lost Time* ('The only things that come from ourselves are those we draw out of the obscurity within us, which can never be known by other people'),[53] and the philosophical enquiries about human consciousness of Thomas Aquinas, who had written that 'The image is a principle of our knowledge. It is that from which our intellectual activity begins, not as a passing stimulus, but as an enduring foundation.'[54] McGahern made it clear that an intimate familiarity with Aquinas existed in his mind at the very start of his career. In the essay 'The Bird Swift', written in the 1990s, he recalled quoting that sentence and others in his conversations with Patrick Swift during the summer of 1960 (*LW*, p. 74). Still, a full forty-five years after the first youthful exuberance that had seen two young artists quoting medieval scholastic philosophy outside a pub on a lazy Sunday afternoon, McGahern demonstrated that his engagement with Aquinas had been more than just a drunken flirtation. In the short preface to *Creatures of the Earth* which marked the conclusion of his career he once more suggested an identical Thomist foregrounding of the importance of the image as both the point of origin and the 'enduring foundation' of his own art. In that preface, which was the last piece of writing he completed before his death in 2006, McGahern commented that many of the short stories in that volume 'began from as little as ...', before enumerating some of the most memorable and striking images spanning the length of his oeuvre of fiction (*CE*, p. vii).

If the image was celebrated a final time just before his death in the preface to *Creatures of the Earth*, then McGahern had first described the importance of images in his conception of the artistic process in an essay entitled 'The Image' which was first published near the beginning of his career in 1968 and subsequently in a revised version in 1991, and which was the closest he ever came to writing a literary manifesto. That crucial essay has obvious Romantic overtones. In it McGahern writes that the purpose of art is the 'struggle[ ] towards the single image, the image on which our whole life took its most complete expression once', but which 'may be no more than a yard of lead piping we saw in terror once'. This 'straining towards the one image that will never come, the lost image that gave our lives expression, the image that would completely express it again in this bewilderment between our beginning and end' (*LW*, pp. 5–6), is described in 'The Image' as an act of memory. More specifically, it is conceived of as a form of Proustian 'involuntary memory', as images are described as flowing 'involuntarily' (*LW*, p. 5), repeating Proust's signature term from *In Search of Lost Time*.[55] But the designation of 'The Image' in the subtitle of the original 1968 version as a 'Prologue to a Reading' strongly hints that one of its models was probably an earlier work by Proust:

the 'Prologue' to *By Way of Sainte-Beuve*, a sketch which contains the seeds of his great novel and which describes the process whereby

> as soon as each hour of one's life has died, it embodies itself in some material object, as do the souls of the dead in certain folk-stories, and hides there. There it remains captive, captive forever, unless we should happen on the object, recognise what lies within, call it by its name, and so set it free. Very likely we may never happen on the object (or the sensation, since we apprehend every object as sensation) that it hides in; and thus there are hours of our life that will never be resuscitated: for this object is so tiny, so lost in the world, and there is so little likelihood that we shall come across it.[56]

To think of the images that animate McGahern's imagination simply as memories would not be quite accurate, however. Not all images are memories, and anyhow, what matters, really, is not to *remember* things, but to learn to see clearly — what Elizabeth Reegan in *The Barracks* finally identifies as 'real seeing' (*B*, p. 211). It is here that McGahern's conception of the nature of the image can be confusing to readers coming to 'The Image' in the hope of finding there a key to unlocking the aesthetic principles of his fiction. In 'The Image' McGahern suggests — perhaps under the influence of Proust's prologue to *By Way of Sainte-Beuve* — that the image 'that moves us out of the darkness' must be a memory, something we had once seen or experienced. From his fiction, however, it is clear that such moving images can be *any* 'material impression', as the narrator in the final volume of Proust's *In Search of Lost Time* concludes, which 'enters us through our senses . . . from which it is . . . possible to extract something spiritual'. These 'material impressions' do not need to be memories but sensations which because of their familiarity often *feel* like memories. Proust draws attention to this in the final volume of *In Search of Lost Time* when his narrator says that

> obscure impressions had sometimes, even already at Combray on the Guermantes way, attracted the attention of my thoughts, in the way these reminiscences did, but not then hiding a past impression but a new truth, a precious image that I sought to discover by efforts of the same kind as those which one makes to remember something, as if our most beautiful ideas were like tunes in music which come back, so to speak, to us without our ever having heard them . . .[57]

Rather than the initial rough sketch from the prologue to *By Way of Sainte-Beuve* on which McGahern had seemingly drawn for the text of 'The Image', it is this later, more subtly developed conception of the image from *In Search of Lost Time* which properly describes just how images are significant in McGahern's fiction. The images at the heart of McGahern's vision are all profound or meaningful — like the great books Mrs Waldron happens upon in 'Creatures of the Earth' they must 'lighten[ ] and deepen[ ] life, [give] recognition and pleasure' (*CE*, p. 323) — but they do not necessarily have to be remembered. Indeed, most of the images which change the way McGahern's main characters look at the world at the conclusions of his novels are not memories at all (as 'The Image' would suggest they should be) but precisely such Proustian 'impressions' of a deeper truth. In *The Barracks*, for example, Elizabeth Reegan, despite all the time spent re-examining the past during her months of illness, does not achieve a moment of vision that moves her life 'out of the darkness' until she looks out of the window at the familiar Roscommon landscape in a frost which is at once familiar and utterly strange (*B*, p. 170). What she finds there is not a memory but simply an impression — an image — of natural beauty so profound that it communicates directly to her soul.

It seems, then, that McGahern somehow thought of the reception of certain images which cannot strictly speaking be remembered because the individual has never before witnessed them as a kind of remembering. Perhaps there is ultimately a hint, in his apparent confusion in 'The Image' surrounding the importance ascribed to memory in the reception of the images which speak to us, that McGahern was sympathetic to the transcendental ideas proposed in a poem like Wordsworth's 'Ode'. That poem proposed that the souls of some great artists can remember things that had happened to them before birth — because our birth, after all, is 'but a sleep and a forgetting'.[58]

The Barracks contains many passages concerned with Elizabeth Reegan's discovery of a way of seeing. McGahern famously told an interviewer that Elizabeth 'was as much a way of looking as a character in her own right',[59] and it is her discovery of a meaningful 'way of looking' that is at the thematic heart of the novel. That looking and seeing are the dominant themes seems appropriate in a book which begins and ends with a ritual closing of the 'blinds' in Elizabeth's barracks kitchen (*B*, pp. 7–8, 232), and which contains so many references to *King Lear*, Shakespeare's play about different types of blindness and vision. Blinds are again symbolically present much later in the novel when Elizabeth experiences her first moment of revelation brought on by a vision of the ordinary made extraordinarily beautiful:

> The heavy white frost seemed over everything at this time, the drum of boots on the ground hard as concrete in the early mornings, voices and every sound haunting and carrying far over fields of stiff grass in the evenings. The ice had to be broken on the barrels each morning. It was so beautiful when she let up the blinds first thing that, 'Jesus Christ', softly was all she was able to articulate as she looked out and up the river to the woods across the lake, black with the leaves fallen except the red rust of the beech trees, the withered reeds standing pale and sharp as bamboo rods at the edges of the water, the fields of the hill always white and the radio aerial that went across from the window to the high branches of the sycamore a pure white line through the air. (*B*, p. 170)

(The first phrase about the white frost that covered 'everything', moreover, may be intended as an echo of Gabriel Conroy's epiphany amid the 'snow [that] was general all over Ireland' in Joyce's 'The Dead'.[60]) Such sensations in the bright light of day — and light is an important aspect of McGahern's writing about moments of revelation or epiphany in many works[61] — are the opposite of the conscious searching for meaning in her life that takes place in 'her own feverish mind' at night, when in the 'flickering night light' she tries to follow patterns on the ceiling: 'but soon they were lost, the ceiling in as much confusion and emptiness over her eyes as she didn't know what' (*B*, pp. 200–1).

In a 1992 obituary essay about his late friend the short-story writer Michael McLaverty, McGahern intimated his agreement with the famous last lines of Keats' 'Ode on a Grecian Urn', those that proclaimed that:

> 'Beauty is truth, truth beauty,' — that is all
> Ye know on earth, and all ye need to know.[62]

Keats' idea that revelations of meaning or truth are available primarily through experiences of aesthetic beauty appealed to McGahern's Romantic sensibility. When he wrote about McLaverty that 'Scattered throughout all [his] books are moments of vividness, of beauty and truth' (*LW*, p. 78), that remark was not just the highest praise that could be bestowed on McLaverty's art. It also pointed to McGahern's own enduring fascination with moments of visionary clarity.

Even daffodils can, if they are observed in the right way or surprise the conscious mind and catch it off guard, again be the subject of Romantic vision and be redeemed from the stifling connotations forced upon them through the enforced study of Wordsworth for the purposes of school-leaving exams. In *The Barracks*, when the boy Willie asks his stepmother 'Is b-e-a-u-t-i-f-u-l the way to spell beautiful, Elizabeth?', she 'felt she was part of their whole lives as they worked [on their homework]. She watched them for a few minutes in a perfect wonder of peace. Then she went to the window to touch the heads of the daffodils with her fingers' (*B*, p. 62). When she returns to the kitchen the 'level glare' of the evening light in which she has observed the river and the meadows 'came so violently to the window that she'd soon to turn away, spelling the word Willie had asked her *in inarticulate wonder*' (*B*, p. 63, emphasis added). It is left deliberately ambiguous in that sentence whether that final adverbial clause refers to the schoolboy's wonder, in *asking*, at the spelling of a difficult word, or to the mature woman's wonder, while *spelling*, at the transcendent beauty of the world that renders her, not for the first or the last time in the novel, inarticulate. If the 'inarticulate wonder' is that of Willie asking about the difficult spelling of the word 'beautiful', then the exchange may perhaps have been intended to recall his namesake Willie Yeats' 'fascination of what's difficult' which can so easily '[dry] the sap out of my veins, and rent/ Spontaneous joy and natural content/ Out of my heart': a warning against the dangers of a poetry of pure intellect and little spontaneous feeling.[63] Either way, this passage in McGahern's first novel is an affirmation of the Romantic aesthetic ideology of Wordsworth and Keats.

Seeing and thinking

The act of contemplation is central to the Romantic endeavour. But Wordsworth, Coleridge and Keats are also poets of ideas, not just of feeling.[64] In many important Romantic poems — Wordsworth's 'Ode' or 'Tintern Abbey', Coleridge's 'Eolian Harp' or Keats' 'Grecian Urn' — contemplation leads to reflection and to thought. As Wordsworth remarks in the preface to *Lyrical Ballads*, 'Poems to which any value can be attached were never produced on any variety of subjects but by a man who, being possessed of more than usual organic sensibility, had also thought long and deeply.'[65] The metaphysical enquiries of the Romantic poets often gravitate towards the great questions which are so central to our experience of humanity, and about none more than about memory, imagination and the mortal and immortal existence of the soul. As Wordsworth, again, puts it in 'Tintern Abbey':

> For I have learned
> To look on nature, not as in the hour
> Of thoughtless youth; but hearing oftentimes
> The still, sad music of humanity ...[66]

This is the realisation that Elizabeth Reegan in *The Barracks* also stumbles upon during a visit to the local parish church which takes place only a few pages before her early-morning revelation of a frozen world. Sitting in the church she finds her eyes and mind drifting to the manufacturer's trade plate and the graffiti impiously cut into one of the pews:

> Her mind was giving the same attention to this old bench as it had given to the mystery of the world and Christ. There were no answers. All the mind could do was wander and wonder from object to object and find no resting-place, in the end all things were lost in contemplation. (*B*, p. 165)

Elizabeth harnesses her increasingly clairvoyant observations of the countryside around the barracks in the intense search for 'meaning' she conducts in the months and weeks of illness leading up to her death. She shares the impulse for religious speculation about her position in the world with some of Shakespeare's tragic heroes — Hamlet's fears in his most famous soliloquy that the sleep of death may not be a final resting, and Macbeth's knowledge (in a soliloquy that is echoed by a character in one of McGahern's later stories) that this life is not 'the be-all and the end-all! — here,/ But here, upon this bank and shoal of time,/ We'd jump the life to come.'[67] Unlike Shakespeare's metaphysically uncertain heroes, however, Elizabeth is not ultimately tempted to succumb to the paralysis that results from such relentless religious or philosophical questioning. She has often contemplated her position in this world in which she is 'just passing through . . . a creature of swift passage' (*B*, p. 211), and found that answers to the questions about her own mortality are not easily come by. After all, 'searching for meaning' is not the same thing as to 'grow into meaning', and it is only when she stops doing the former that she becomes capable of the latter (*B*, p. 211). 'That was how her life happened,' she concludes simply: 'nothing more could be said for certain' (*B*, p. 210). Only by accepting this simple truth can she come into the 'joy' which only the Romantic act of 'real seeing' offers (*B*, p. 211). Unlike Hamlet, Elizabeth sees clearly that the only meaningful thing she can do in the face of the mystery and uncertainty of all that surrounds life is simply 'to be',[68] and vocalises that realisation in what is one of the most intense philosophical passages in the novel, indeed in McGahern's entire oeuvre. By stoically accepting whatever something or nothing may befall her after death, Elizabeth is capable of replacing intellectual questioning with an act of Romantic seeing capable of providing more certain meaning to the inexplicable mystery of ordinary life. Meaning can now come from simple 'joy' or 'love' or 'passion':

> All real seeing grew into smiling and if it moved to speech it must be praise, all else was death, a refusal, a turning back... All the apparent futility of her life in this barracks came at last to rest on this sense of mystery. It gave hours idled away in boredom or remorse as much validity as a blaze of passion, all was under its eternal sway. She felt for a moment pure, without guilt. She'd no desire to clutch for the facts and figures of explanation, only it was there or wasn't there and if there was any relationship they would meet in the moment of her death. (*B*, p. 211)

(The joining together of the verbs 'seeing' and 'smiling' which is central to Elizabeth Reegan's final transcendent vision of reality in that crucial passage in the novel is reminiscent, again, of Proust's narrator, whose 'seeing on the water and on the face of the wall a pale smile answering the smile of the sky' is one of his earliest moments of vision.[69]) The narrative's last insight into Elizabeth Reegan's consciousness before her death confirms this one final time. As she considers the 'eternal mysteries' of the rosary she concludes that 'what it meant didn't matter, whether it meant anything at all or not it gave the last need of her heart release, the need to praise and celebrate, in which everything rejoiced' (*B*, p. 220). Like the priest in the story 'Oldfashioned' who must adapt to the new reality that the people in his congregation whom he must now face during Mass 'are the mystery' (*HG*, p. 56), Elizabeth Reegan finally acknowledges that the real mystery can only be sought for in the everyday passage of ordinary life, not in the sacraments or ceremonies of the Church. Thus, McGahern's description of the implications of the liturgical change in the Catholic Mass following the Second Vatican Council in that key story from the early 1980s is as much a restatement of the artistic beliefs which can be traced back to his earliest fictions as it is an observation of a change in religious practice that had taken place during the 1960s.

The Romantic act of 'real seeing' entered into by Elizabeth Reegan in *The Barracks* shortly before her death (*B*, p. 211) is not merely an artistic stance. Here and elsewhere in McGahern's fiction, the kind of seeing which grows naturally 'into smiling' is both a religious and a moral act, as the visionary calm it brings allows characters to relate to their 'total environment' as well as to their 'fellow-men'. This despite the fact that, normally, religion and morality were considered completely separate from one another by one of McGahern's favourite literary critics, E.R. Dodds, whose distinction between religion (which 'grows out of man's relationship to his total environment') and morality (which '[grows] out of his relation to his fellow-men') he often quoted.[70] The connection between vision, religion and morality was first made explicit in McGahern's first published novel, as it would be again in one of his final works. Elizabeth Reegan's resolution at the end of *The Barracks* that 'All real seeing grew into smiling and if it moved to speech it must be praise' is distinctly echoed near the end of McGahern's oeuvre in the short story 'Creatures of the Earth', another third-person narrative focalised through the consciousness of a solitary middle-aged woman. When Mrs Waldron in that story has finished rereading Jane Austen's *Emma*,

> She found herself repeating the sentence long after she had closed the book, seeing elements of her own life and people she knew reflected in it, elements of that life *seen* and given a *moral sweetness* that was close to *smiling*. (*CE*, p. 322, emphasis added)

In that paragraph from a late short story, Elizabeth Reegan's Wordsworthian joining together of the words 'seeing' and 'smiling' is fused with a sense of 'moral sweetness'. The latter phrase echoes Forrest Reid's 'moral fragrance', a visionary gleam that pervades all it touches to which McGahern refers in a number of his non-fictional writings (*LW*, pp. 78, 199). This 'moral sweetness' or 'moral fragrance' not only colours Elizabeth Reegan's perception of the landscape or even of her own mortality but of her whole reality, including her dealings with other people. Reid explains the term 'moral fragrance' thus in his *W.B. Yeats: a critical study*:

> The difficulty is that when one speaks of morality in art, people at once think of something didactic and aggressive. Yet a moral sense is as necessary to the artist as a sense of colour. To put it in another way, all poetry should, I think, be inspired by a spirit of love: and when I say love, I mean not only human love, but a love for all living creatures.[71]

To have attained the calm and the confidence of a visionary who knows her place in the world gives both Elizabeth Reegan and Mrs Waldron a sense of moral purpose which may in turn spill over to their attitudes to other people. Indeed, McGahern pays homage to Reid's invocation of the 'love for all living creatures' which is the result of a general moral colouring both in the *plot* — which contrasts three different types of human–animal interaction of varying degrees of cruelty or natural harmony (those with the cat, the sheepdog and the whale) — and in the *title* of 'Creatures of the Earth'.

In this mingling of the moral (social) and religious (private) impulses which E.R. Dodds had so strictly separated, McGahern was not only emulating the example of Forrest Reid but also that of some of his favourite visionary poets. In a seminar at University College, Dublin, in 1999, McGahern referred to Patrick Kavanagh's *The Great Hunger* as 'almost a great poem ... it deteriorates into sociological rant at the end, but three quarters of the poem is marvellous'. The section of *The Great Hunger* he singled out for especial praise on that occasion was section eleven.[72] It is there that the embittered protagonist experiences a momentary moral transformation brought about by a Wordsworthian act of contemplating the beauty of a daisy which makes him

> wish[ ] them happiness and whatever they most desired from life.
> He saw the sunlight and begrudged no man
> His share of what the miserly soil and soul
> Gives in a season to a ploughman.[73]

The presence of those lines, which make up one of only a handful of visionary-Romantic moments in *The Great Hunger*, may be detected behind Mrs Waldron's smiling benevolence to others. It is an even clearer presence behind the capacity to grow, through the observation of external things, 'into the one desire to love and to cause no living thing pain' which Elizabeth Reegan perceives in herself in chapter six of *The Barracks* (*B*, p. 192). Thus, the individualism to which Romantic ways of thinking could all too easily lead is alleviated in such passages in which the attainment of private moments of visionary clarity are ultimately at the root not of selfish individualism but of fellow feeling. Of course this is not a new insight but a traditional wisdom available to all readers of classic poetry. The conflation of private vision and moral feeling is deeply Wordsworthian, and may be traced back to 'Tintern Abbey's connection between a man's ability to recall 'beauteous [natural] forms' and his capacity for 'little, nameless, unremembered, acts/ Of kindness and of love'.[74]

Elizabeth Reegan's search for meaning through acts of seeing is also repeated by a very different character in a later McGahern novel. Like Elizabeth Reegan, the old revolutionary Moran in *Amongst Women* becomes capable shortly before his death of an extraordinary way of looking at the fields which surround his house — that fortress-like structure whose entrance gate is guarded by a symbolic poisonous yew tree whose psychological implications are grounded as deeply in the text as the cold, bare heath is in *King Lear*. Moran, too, uses his new powers of vision as a springboard for a series of profound thoughts about his own mortality.

That the loss and recovery of vision will be an important theme in *Amongst Women* is ironically signalled early on. Moran's performance as a comical blind man, a pantomime Lear groping about the room for the entertainment of his grown-up daughters (*AW*, p. 3) on the opening pages, is only a rehearsal for the tragic sensation of an encroaching 'deepening blindness' of which he becomes aware later in the novel (*AW*, p. 72). Moran's sense of blindness, it seems, grows more absolute as he ages, much as Wordsworth had suggested in the 'Ode' (and as McGahern had confirmed through his allusion to that famous example in 'Wheels').[75] It culminates shortly before his death in a newfound habit of 'walking the fields like a man trying to see' (*AW*, p. 130), a futile act of wishing meaning or revelation into being like Proustian voluntary memories (an idea that will be further discussed in chapter five).[76] In a turn of phrase reminiscent of the symbolic 'blinds' from the opening and closing pages of *The Barracks*, the ageing Moran develops a habit for walking his land 'field by blind field' (*AW*, p. 129). His ability to see clearly only finally develops as his physical powers diminish just before his death, when he regularly 'slipped out to the fields . . . and always in the same direction' (*AW*, p. 178). The narrative detailing these escapes is focalised through the old man's eyes. It dwells partially on scenes of obvious natural beauty such as 'the old pear tree in brilliant white blossom' which would not be out of place amid the staid idioms of mere nature poetry. Moran's consciousness is just as strongly drawn, however, to noticing a number of other, less conventionally beautiful objects like 'last year's nettles withered and tangled in the abandoned mowing machine beneath the tree, the corrugated roof of the lean-to he had built as a workshop for wet days' (*AW*, pp. 178–9). His capacity for taking in the latter kind of sights, and putting them on a level with the natural beauties that might strike a sentimental lover of the picturesque, elevates his vision onto a plane with that of the great Romantic poets of the tradition of Wordsworth. It is only after the observation of both types of sights — the derelict and the beautiful — that Moran finally comes on a revelation of truth through the act of pure seeing when he finds that the meadow 'was no longer empty but filling with a fresh growth, a faint blue tinge in the rich green of the young grass. To die was never to look on all this again. It would live in others' eyes but not in his. He had never realised when he was in the midst of confident life what an amazing glory he was part of' (*AW*, p. 179).

Repeating his daughters' earlier sensitivity to 'trampl[ing] on the colour blue' (*AW*, p. 75), colour again plays a vital role in McGahern's construction of Moran's final moment of insight at the conclusion of *Amongst Women*. The use of colour in both those passages has a number of potentially important literary antecedents both within and beyond McGahern's own oeuvre. The play of light and colour in that crucial description which marks the end of Moran's visionary quest in *Amongst Women* is reminiscent of Elizabeth Reegan watching the river and the meadows which appear to her as 'a low tangle of green and white light' in an early chapter of *The Barracks* (*B*, p. 63). Both may be reminiscent of a specific antecedent in the visionary Romanticism of the turn of the nineteenth century. The sudden attention to the 'faint blue tinge in the rich green' which plays such a crucial role in Moran's discovery of a sense of religious quietude and Elizabeth's attention to the 'low tangle of green and white light' both stir a faint but true memory of the sensuous language of the passage describing the moral effect of the play of many-coloured lights on the hero of *The Rime of the Ancient Mariner*. Coleridge's mariner is momentarily redeemed by his recognition of real beauty in a place where he had least expected it when he notices the 'tracks of shining white' in the water and the lustre of the water snakes as they appear to him in a

> rich attire:
> Blue, glossy green, and velvet black,
> They coiled and swam; and every track
> Was a flash of golden fire.

That joyful recognition of beauty leads in turn to his initial moment of spiritual salvation, as the sensation of aesthetic pleasure allows him 'love' and to 'bless[ ] them unaware'.[77] Moran's final blessing of the world in which he has so grudgingly lived finally comes courtesy of a similar moment of visionary clarity.

Seeing, smiling; loving, blessing: they are all connected in the great Romantic scheme. Like the awakening of Elizabeth Reegan in *The Barracks*, this passage near the end of *Amongst Women* is at the thematic heart of the narrative. It describes the initiation of a responsiveness to the beauties of the natural and the man-made world alike, as Moran finally realises the importance of *looking*, of things *living in his eyes*, and learns to see the 'amazing glory' of ordinary things properly perceived (*AW*, p. 179). As Denis Sampson first pointed out, at the end of the novel Moran exchanges the national pieties of Patrick Pearse for Wordsworth's 'natural piety', which is simply a responsiveness to the beauty of natural things, and the military 'glory' (*AW*, p. 14) of his younger days for the 'amazing glory' of Romantic seeing.[78] Repeated references to visionary 'glory' also abound, after all, in Wordsworth's 'Ode', a poem to which McGahern may well be paying homage in his descriptions of Moran's sense of the 'amazing glory' of the natural world.

The possibility for an old soldier like Moran to become a Romantic seer may be one aspect of that character's personality which is indebted to McGahern's reading of the memoirs and letters of Ernie O'Malley, the IRA general who read English poetry while he was on the run during the War of Independence, and whose memoir of that period, *On Another Man's Wound*, as McGahern points out in his essay about O'Malley, contains many 'descriptions of the countryside in its different seasons and weathers . . . The observation is usually close and excitingly accurate' (*LW*, pp. 253–4).[79] For McGahern, one of the most interesting things about O'Malley's life was not merely how he had transformed himself from a naive young medical student into a prominent military and political figure, but also the subsequent transformation from guerrilla fighter into a sensitive and observant reader, author and modern-art critic who had learned to see the landscape in which he moved with the eyes of a painter or a poet as well as those of a military strategist.

Similar discoveries of the importance of 'real' Romantic seeing also mark the conclusions of both *The Dark* and *The Pornographer*. In a number of essays from the late 1970s onwards McGahern returned to a letter Proust wrote to Georges de Lauris in 1903 in which, in McGahern's eloquent summary of Proust's argument, 'he protests at the exclusion of the village *curé* from the school committee, saying that he should be there with the tobacconist and newsagent and tax collector if for nothing else but the spire of his church, which lifts men's eyes from the avaricious earth' (*LW*, p. 198).[80] In his essay on Forrest Reid's *Brian Westby*, McGahern suggests that such a spire can exist in a metaphorical sense in works of literature, as 'a symbol of what Reid himself has beautifully called a moral fragrance' (*LW*, p. 199). What Proust is describing in his letter is the same sensation of seeing as a transcendent act that had been documented by Wordsworth when he wrote that 'My heart leaps up when I behold/ A rainbow in the sky'.[81] It is just this kind of spiritual, moral and imaginative lifting of the gaze, a form of redemption through looking alone, that the adolescent boy in *The Dark* envisages when he dreams of going to university. In an idea which recalls the emphasis on the uplifting potential of Gothic church spires from Proust's letter, the initiation into the 'mystery' which young Mahoney hopes to find at the university is connected in his mind with the Tudor-Gothic architecture of the university buildings in Galway which he characterises in his private fantasies as 'all stones with turrets' (*D*, p. 124). When he arrives for his first term there, however, he is disappointed to find that his fellow students choose their course of study based on nothing but the prospect of 'as much security and money as they could get' in future careers — even if it means the tedium of studying dentistry and allowing teeth to 'absorb your life' (*D*, p. 172). Far from an escape from the Famine mentality of the small tenant famer which the boy had so loathed in his father, he finds among his peers at the university a hankering after 'security' which is a curious hangover of the 'fear of the poorhouse' of the elder Mahoney's generation. Despite Proust's advice to Georges de Lauris, even the presence of the university's Gothic turrets is helpless against such earthly pessimism, no matter how high they may soar up to the sky. With 'the dream ... torn piecemeal' (*D*, p. 172), it is no wonder that young Mahoney decides to leave the university shortly after arriving. Yet even in the moment of his departure he finds an alternative architectural image which may yet lift his eyes from the avaricious earth in the manner Proust had suggested:

> It was hard to walk quiet out of the University at Mahoney's side and see the goalposts luminous in the grey light of the rain and not give savage expression to one murderous feeling of defeat ... You were walking through the rain of Galway with your father and you could laugh purely, without bitterness, for the first time, and it was a kind of happiness, at its heart the terror of an unclear recognition of the reality that set you free, touching you with as much foreboding as the sodden leaves falling in this day, or any cliche. (*D*, p. 188)

This pivotal passage in the novel's penultimate chapter marks a moment of profound change in his consciousness — what Joyce calls an epiphany — as the young man comes to a deeper understanding of life through nothing more than the recognition of the transcendent beauty of an everyday scene in the right light. He finally realises that the worldly authority of the university with its arcane academic paraphernalia was the wrong dream for him to follow all along, because real happiness is available only through finding 'an authority that was simply a state of mind, a calmness even in the face of the turmoil of your own passing' (*D*, p. 188). This realisation is triggered by the very ordinary sight of the 'goalposts luminous in the grey light' which he sees on his way out of the campus for the last time. Those goals may be symbolic of purpose, but they are also a secular reimagining of the luminous church spires of which Proust had written in his letter to Georges de Lauris. They fulfil the spiritually uplifting function, the embodiment of a sense of 'mystery', for which young Mahoney had initially fruitlessly sought in the Gothic turrets of the university buildings.

Similar ordinary structures possessed, for the right onlooker, of a mystic capacity occur elsewhere in McGahern's fiction, too. One of the characters in *That They May Face the Rising Sun* may mockingly refer to Ruttledge and Patrick Ryan's unfinished shed as a 'cathedral' (*TRS*, p. 85), but that diminutive structure, made out of concrete and iron and rough, creosoted wood, does fulfil some of the vital functions of such an important ecclesiastical building.

Like Proust's spires or the 'luminous goalposts' at the end of *The Dark* (or even the radio aerial suspended from the branches of a tree which manifests itself to Elizabeth as a 'pure white line through the air' in *The Barracks* (*B*, p. 170)), the squares of sky framed overhead by the bare rafters and beams invite an act of looking upward. Like a collection of picture windows, they draw the gaze from the earth and earthly toils toward the sky. As the same thing happens again a number of times in the novel on the lanes around the lake, where pinpoints of light pierce through the canopy and views of the lake and the sky are granted at unexpected moments through gaps in the foliage, all of nature repeatedly becomes precisely such a cathedral dedicated to ordinary spectacles made extraordinary.

The ordinary extraordinary

Elizabeth Reegan's exclamation of 'Jesus Christ' when she opens her bedroom blinds onto the beauty of the familiar Roscommon landscape is at once a curse and a prayer. She is herself aware, after all, that those two kinds of expression cannot always easily be told apart (*B*, p. 204). There may even be another literary analogy at work here. Elizabeth's curse when faced with an image of truth, a spectacle of vivid and unexpected beauty which manifests itself to her but possibly to no one else observing the same thing, replicates the profanity which is the only response of which Proust's narrator is capable when he unexpectedly encounters a beautiful sight on the way by Swann's in the first volume of *In Search of Lost Time*.[82]

Both *The Barracks* and *Amongst Women* suggest that the discovery or revelation of such a new and exciting way of seeing — in the form of the discovery of the 'amazing glory' of the world (*AW*, p. 179), or simply of the existence of a 'beauty' that can move one to smiling (*B*, p. 211) — amounts to a form of religious experience. One of the purposes of religion, after all, is to provide a way of coming to acceptance or understanding of the mysteries (a word often used in *The Barracks* and elsewhere in McGahern's fiction) of the world that surrounds us — the 'mystery of the world and Christ' to which there are no answers which Elizabeth had contemplated in the silence of her parish church (*B*, p. 165). The act of looking at the world in the light of love, as Moran in *Amongst Women* and Elizabeth Reegan in *The Barracks*, and even the conflicted protagonists of *The Dark* and *The Pornographer*, eventually learn to do, was for McGahern the closest available thing to religious celebration after he had lost his Catholic faith at an early age. One of the subplots that may be read into all four of these novels is the gradual erosion of orthodox Catholic faith in favour of a new form of religious experience rooted in a wholehearted celebration of the daily realities of the world made possible by the discovery of the simple act of seeing[83] — what Elizabeth Reegan finally sums up as 'the need to praise and celebrate, in which everything rejoiced' (*B*, p. 220). McGahern commented on what he perceived as the religious nature of the act of writing in a letter to Michael McLaverty written while he was working on *The Barracks*, in which he wrote that 'I often think the realest reason I write is, having lost my formal faith, I am self compelled to pray or praise. If I did not need to do it I would stop tomorrow, but there seems little else.'[84] *The Dark*, too, was characterised in a letter to the same correspondent as 'a religious work if it's anything at all'.[85] It, too, is essentially concerned with the protagonist's search for meaning in a world that seems to offer very little beside arbitrary cruelty and suffering, a search that is eventually achieved through a moment of visionary revelation on the university football pitch.

McGahern turned himself into a praiser of the everyday and the ordinary, one who celebrated the extraordinary beauties that can be found in even the most mundane aspects in life. In an interview with Mike Murphy recorded for RTÉ radio in 2000, McGahern attributed a sentence from *The Leavetaking* (*L*, p. 180) to a poet he had known in London in the 1960s: 'There's a line of W.S. Graham's that often comes to my mind, that "My ordinary extraordinary day is almost ended."'[86] Curiously, that line does not appear anywhere in Graham's comprehensive *New Collected Poems*.[87] Perhaps, speaking a full quarter of a century after he had originally written that line in *The Leavetaking*, McGahern simply misremembered its origins; or perhaps he deliberately attributed one of his own key sentences to another writer in order to be able to comment on its significance (because he hated discussing the significance of any aspects of his own work). Whatever its exact provenance, that line sums up the aims of McGahern's visionary imagination, which seeks to make ordinary things extraordinary by making them the subject of an extraordinary personal vision — by holding them in the light of love that may reveal, as it had for Wordsworth and for late Romantics like Proust and Kavanagh, a secret hidden truth behind the mundane realities of everyday living.

For all the other purposes which he knew great art should also serve (many of them are discussed in the other chapters of this book), McGahern was consciously committed to preserving or capturing moments when ordinary things momentarily give up their hidden extraordinariness to a careful observer. A book like *Memoir* may be read as a celebration of all the ordinary things that surround life (to adapt a sentence from one of his short stories (*CS*, p. 370)), written by a man who knew that the world would soon be taken from him by a terminal illness. Indeed, in one of the most candid and moving paragraphs in that book McGahern himself explained the need for the careful observation of everyday things in precisely such terms. Writing, as Ian Jack has observed, as much about his own situation in the early 2000s as about that of his mother in the 1940s,[88] McGahern proposed that:

> The world of the dying is different. When well they may have sometimes wondered in momentary fear or idle apprehension what this Time would bring, the shape it would take, whether by age or accident, stroke or cancer... the list is long. Then, that blinding fear could be dismissed as idle introspection, an impairment to the constant alertness needed to answer all the demands of the day. Inevitably, the dreaded and discarded time arrives and has its own shape: suddenly, the waitress pouring coffee at tables, the builder laying blocks, a girl opening a window, the men collecting refuse, belong to a world that went mostly unregarded when it was ours but now becomes a place of unobtainable happiness, in even the meanest of forms. (*M*, p. 116)

The lesson of this passage is clear: the 'demands of the day', even in the midst of confident, healthy life, should always include an element of alertness to the things most people begin to notice only shortly before death. The references to 'idle apprehension' and 'idle introspection' hark back to his comments, twenty years earlier in 'An tOileánach/The Islandman', about the habit of 'idle' contemplation of sentimental nature poets. McGahern may have admired the sparse epic vision of Ó Criomhthain that was the opposite of such a tendency, and even on occasion emulated it, but he was also at all times responsive, like a poet like Wordsworth, to the beauty and truth of ordinary things carefully, not idly, observed.

One of the perennial obsessions of McGahern's writing was with meticulously recording the small things which many people only begin to notice when they are close to death. He may only finally have come to articulate this truth clearly and concisely in that paragraph of *Memoir* (although the seeds of that paragraph can be found in the oblique, abstract credos of 'The Image'), but he had dramatised it many times throughout his career in novels such as *The Barracks* and *Amongst Women*.

CHAPTER 4

The Limits of Realism

> The mahogany bookcase stood solid. Scott, Dickens, Canon Sheehan under glass... One lone paperback, Tolstoy's *Resurrection* in a red and white Penguin, and you turned the small key to get it out, though you'd never heard of it or Tolstoy. It didn't look such a tomb as the others, there were more green leaves and living light of the day about it than the dust and memory of the others, it was too new for many dead hands to have turned the pages.
>
> *The Dark* (p. 81)

Novels were not studied at the Presentation Brothers Secondary School in Carrick-on-Shannon, or even as part of the degree course in English at University College, Dublin, in the 1950s. The curriculum still reflected traditional tastes and values that did not regard the popular form of the novel as a medium of high artistic value.[1] It is no wonder, therefore, that the adolescent protagonist in *The Dark*, who has enjoyed a solid education at the Presentation Brothers but who has never really read for pleasure beyond the set texts of the school curriculum, has never heard of Tolstoy. As it turns out, this is ironic, since the situation of his sister Joan, who is 'interfered with' by the shopkeeper Ryan for whom she is a live-in maid, is dangerously close to replicating the fate of the servant Maslova whose suffering following her seduction by a caddish aristocratic employer is at the heart of the plot of *Resurrection*, the novel of which he finds a Penguin paperback copy in Father Gerald's bookcase. Even the undefined but possibly untoward relationship which the priest maintains with his young male housekeeper may be a re-enactment of a version of the plot of the same novel. The nature of the relationship between John and Father Gerald is no more than hinted at in *The Dark*, but if a parallel is intended the invocation of *Resurrection* in the same segment of the novel may confirm some readers' darkest suspicions.[2]

Resurrection was among the first of Tolstoy's works that McGahern had read, sometime during the 1950s. Its presence in *The Dark* is not the only occasion on which McGahern's early fiction flirted with the plots of Tolstoy's novels, which he began reading in earnest in 1959 (when Michael McLaverty introduced him to *The Death of Ivan Ilych*), and which soon became 'part of my mind', as he recalled in 1991 (*PD*, p. vii).[3] One short story in particular reads like a conscious revisiting of one of the Russian novelist's most famous works. The narrator of 'Lavin' remembers his youthful infatuation with the family of his school friend Charley Casey, who 'had two dark-haired sisters of seventeen and nineteen, who were both beautiful, and a young widowed mother, and there hung about him that glamour of a house of ripe women' (*N*, p. 94). The emphasis of that memory parallels a passage from chapter six of *Anna Karenina*, in which Tolstoy explains Levin's growing fascination with the female presence in the family of his friend Shcherbatsky during his student days:

> In those days Levin had frequented the Shcherbatskys' house and had fallen in love with the family ... Konstantin Levin was in love precisely with the house, the family, especially the female side of it ... All the members of this family, especially the female side, seemed to him covered by some mysterious poetic veil, and he not only saw no defects in them, but surmised, behind the cover of this poetic veil, the loftiest feelings and every possible perfection ... [Much] that went on in their mysterious world he did not understand; but he knew that everything that went on there was beautiful, and he was in love precisely with the mysteriousness of it all.[4]

A further parallel with the same novel is gestured at in the story's title. 'Lavin's eponymous bachelor may be named with an ironic wink to *Anna Karenina*. His name is a Hibernicised version of Tolstoy's Levin, the 'earnest "seeker", addicted to intense pertinacities of meditation on death, the meaning of life, and the behest ... of the living clear-sighted conscience' who is also, in F.R. Leavis' succinct summary of his character, 'a paternal but businesslike landlord, a modernising farmer, a writer on agricultural economy, and a sportsman with the proper pride of a first-class shot'.[5] Levin embodies all the virtues and qualities which are emphatically absent from his near namesake in McGahern's story. As the story suggests, Lavin's beginnings as the son of a rich farmer had been auspicious enough, and contained the promise of an affluent and virtuous future to rival that of Tolstoy's hero; but the promise, like so many things in the stagnant post-independence world of *Nightlines*, has withered before coming to fruition. Lavin's voyeurism and his paedophilic and sadistic tendencies may also be conceived as a deliberate antithesis to Levin's exemplary capacity for maintaining meaningful adult relationships, one that provides a deliberate foil with the other central relationship in Tolstoy's novel, that between Anna and Vronsky. Even his perverted fantasies about what may be under the skirts of the two boys' older sisters is perhaps a sordid, ironic echo of the 'mysterious poetic veil' which colours Levin's idealised perception of the Shcherbatsky sisters in that same early passage of *Anna Karenina*.

McGahern's introduction to the novel did not take place in the schoolrooms where he had been introduced to Horace and Virgil, Shakespeare, Milton and Wordsworth. Instead, novels were from the beginning a purely private pleasure which did not, as he said in a different context about another set of as-yet-non-canonical texts, 'belong … to the Church and university and the worn establishment' (*LW*, p. 331). For the teenage boy, Penguin Classics and nineteenth-century editions alike of Tolstoy, Balzac and Stendhal, Dickens and George Eliot, were not 'tomb[s]' of language (that description of Father Gerald's books in *The Dark* recalls Joyce's description of the piano as a 'coffin of music'[6]) like the many books of Latin or English verse and works of devotional literature which had been officially sanctioned by professors and priests. It is important to the boy in *The Dark* that '[not] many dead hands … have turned the pages' of the 'lone' paperback copy of *Resurrection* which he finds in his cousin's bookcase, where it is surrounded by volumes of poetry and 'staunch religious books' all bound in expensive brown leather (*D*, p. 81).

The sense of novelty and excitement which gave the novel as a genre its name is repeatedly present in McGahern's descriptions, in fiction and non-fiction alike, of the total absorption that may be experienced in the act of youthful novel reading. The portrait of the engrossed young novel reader in 'The Solitary Reader' merely reprises, a quarter of a century on, the attachment to favourite novelists expressed by the boy protagonists of early stories like 'Summer at Strandhill', who longs to return from a disappointing holiday to the home where he would 'at least' have access to 'Jeffery Farnol and Zane Grey out of the library',[7] and 'Lavin', in which the hero lives for the duration of his summer holidays more fully in the exciting fictional 'world' of *David Copperfield* than in the boring real world (*N*, p. 95). Neither of those stories are simply autobiographical portraits of the artist as a young man. The youthful protagonists also replicate the professions of love for comics and cowboy novels of the first-person narrator of Joyce's 'An Encounter', who remembers his youthful attraction to the promise of 'escape' which these 'chronicles of disorder alone seemed to offer'.[8]

There were very few examples of non-religious narrative art to be found in the world of 1930s and 1940s rural Leitrim and Roscommon. There were so few, in fact, that in one unpublished autobiographical sketch McGahern remarks that 'the only book I remember in circulation [during my childhood] was an extraordinarily battered and sought after copy of *Handy Andy*', Samuel Lover's hugely popular comic novel of 1842.[9] It was in this unlikely environment that the young McGahern was turned into a narrative junkie who, as he recalls in 'The Solitary Reader', read books indiscriminately 'the way a boy nowadays might watch endless television dramas' (*LW*, p. 89). His introduction to the pleasures of novel reading was aided by two of the most fortuitous meetings of his early life. The first of these was with the Moroneys and their library. His reading there included not only early-twentieth-century cowboy novels by Zane Grey that were written in the plainest of realist idioms and the staples of popular nineteenth-century fiction by the likes of Lover and Lever, but also the work of some of the great masters of the English realist tradition, such as Austen, Scott, Dickens and George Eliot. Shortly after establishing his reading routine at the Moroneys, the young McGahern's introduction to the nineteenth-century novel was also advanced through the influence of Frank Mannion, his English teacher at the Presentation Brothers Secondary School in Carrick-on-Shannon. McGahern later recalled how Mannion would lend some of his pupils books not included among the set texts of the school curriculum. He was particularly keen to lend novels by Dickens, who was his favourite.[10] The mark of that early influence on McGahern's novel-reading life can be seen in his fiction. When he came to publish his first collection of short stories, *Nightlines*, the reference in 'Lavin' to *David Copperfield* was surely a private acknowledgement of gratitude to that one fellow reader who had made the 'worlds' (*N*, p. 95) of *Great Expectations* and *David Copperfield* available to him in Carrick-on-Shannon in the late 1940s. Also in *Nightlines*, the caricature of the Jewish shopkeeper Greenbaum in 'Hearts of Oak and Bellies of Brass' may be a tribute, reworked to suit the concerns of the post-war age, to *Oliver Twist*'s Fagin. That Greenbaum's reappearance at the very end of the story feels so out of place in a work of late-twentieth-century prose fiction is due in no small part to the heavy-handed style of the depiction (complete with unflattering animal imagery and a stage-foreigner's halting English grammar), which is characterised by what is for McGahern an uncharacteristic whiff of the Dickensian (*N*, pp. 60–1).

There are further tributes to favourite realist novelists elsewhere in McGahern's fiction. One of the books he 're-read forever', for example, was *Robinson Crusoe*. He mentioned his love for that book in a 1991 interview, but careful readers would already have noticed the little homage to Daniel Defoe's most famous novel in *The Barracks*. One of the minor characters from the 'poorer class' whose members do so much of the hard, unglamorous work around the town is known as 'Friday Gateby' (*B*, p. 78), after Crusoe's manservant. *Robinson Crusoe* is also referenced in *The Dark*. When the sight of his father's odd boots stirs the boy's fascination with the mortal coil of its absent owner (*D*, p. 131), that realist detail continues, as Richard Robinson has argued, a fictional lineage of odd shoes going back to Crusoe's discovery of 'two shoes that were not fellows' which act as *memento mori* for his perished shipmates.[11] This chapter is not primarily concerned, however, with unearthing isolated references to specific eighteenth- and nineteenth-century realist novels. Instead it will focus on how McGahern employed some of the ideas surrounding the nineteenth-century novel in his fiction. His thinking about the art of fiction was often guided by three of the late nineteenth century's most influential aesthetic thinkers: Flaubert, Chekhov and Wilde. The latter sections of this chapter will argue how McGahern's thinking was coloured by late-nineteenth-century aesthetic principles about the nature of the novel and the responsibilities of the novelist. The chapter's final section will discuss McGahern's career-long obsession with the contrast between art and life, a topic that revisits a subject that had fascinated any number of late-nineteenth-century poets and novelists. Neither McGahern's youthful excitement and continuing love of the nineteenth-century novel, nor his adoption of a selection of that century's ideas and preoccupations regarding the nature of fiction should suggest, however, that he sought to turn himself into a realist novelist in the mould of Dickens, Tolstoy or George Eliot. For all his awareness of the continuing usefulness of certain nineteenth-century ideas, he was also very clear about the very different demands placed on a prose writer in the latter half of the twentieth century. Certain well-known textbook definitions of realism's aims and objectives — definitions in common use by students and teachers of the genre which do not always stand up to scrutiny in practice — seemed outdated and ripe for parody. The first section of this chapter will argue, therefore, how McGahern's fiction repeatedly explores the limits of realism's generic conventions.

Mirrors up to nature

The great masters of the eighteenth- and nineteenth-century novel continued to give McGahern pleasure his whole adult life; he did, after all, nominate *Middlemarch*, that most expansive work of Victorian realism, as one of his desert-island books as late as 2001.[12] He did not, however, seek to emulate their style or technique in his own novels and stories. McGahern was not, as Gerd Kampen writes, the 'exclusively mimetic, truth oriented writer he is often portrayed to be', and who is so slyly parodied through the portrait of the grown-up son at the end of the story 'Oldfashioned' (as will be discussed later in this section).[13] In the description of Father Gerald's bookcase in *The Dark*, only Tolstoy exists in a contemporary paperback edition, while tomes (or 'tombs') of Scott, Dickens and Canon Sheehan are kept 'under glass', like the museum pieces — quaint reminders of writing styles now antiquated — which they had to a conscientious late-twentieth-century novelist like McGahern become. Rather than an imitator of those nineteenth-century masters, McGahern had, like some of his most distinguished contemporaries, by an early age become a brilliant student of the formal rules and conventions of the realist novel, one who adopted those generic conventions as a recurring theme in his work. So while his fiction certainly contains many recognisable realist elements, his novels and stories are not simply works of realism; they also frequently turn into books *about* realism.

McGahern was not necessarily interested in pursuing a total 'reality effect'[14] of the kind produced by the nineteenth-century novelists, whose long descriptive passages painted the worlds of their novels in exhaustive detail. Page-long descriptions of places and people by Dickens and Balzac are a staple of nineteenth-century fiction, but they were not necessarily appropriate in the age of Beckett, Auster, Coetzee and McGahern, all writers intent on making a deliberate break with aspects of the realist tradition. McGahern shared the suspicion articulated by Alain Robbe-Grillet in *For a New Novel*, a collection of essays on modern fiction first published in English translation in the same year as *The Dark*. There, Robbe-Grillet lambasted the lack of development which characterised the work of many of the most popular novelists of the twentieth century, who could 'insert long passages from *The Princess of Clèves* or *Père Goriot* into their own books without awakening the suspicions of the enormous public which devours whatever they turn out'.[15] The anti-realist bias which characterised McGahern's perception of modern fiction was concisely summarised in a joke he made to the critic Stephen Wall. He would be unwilling to sit next to Aidan Higgins on a bus, he said, 'for fear he should describe all he saw'.[16] More than once he emphasised this same aversion to unnecessary, exhaustive descriptiveness in works that do not originate in the eighteenth or nineteenth centuries. In a 1991 interview he remarked, as he often did, that 'the essence of all good writing' has as much to do with what is overlooked as with what is left in. He also suggested on that occasion that many writers and teachers do not recognise this important truth about the ruthless discipline of writing. More often than not, the English composition lessons he remembered from his schooldays tended to reinforce the perpetuation of nineteenth-century realist literary values. His frustration is clear from his remark that 'Teachers used to tell us to be "observant", noting everything you see. But that's a useless exercise because in soaking up everything you become nothing more than a camera.'[17]

His remark about photography in that 1991 interview chimes with two passages in his published oeuvre of fiction and non-fiction which are concerned with that same medium. First, it cannot but invoke the description of the documentary-film-maker's rolling camera in the final paragraph of 'Oldfashioned', which more than one critic has likened to what they perceive as McGahern's own scrupulously detailed eye for descriptive detail. However, the unproblematic equation between the film-maker's art and the desire for all-seeingness which such critics identify in McGahern's fiction misses the crucial reference in the same paragraph to the 'cunning hand of the cameraman' (*HG*, p. 58). The choice of adjective is vital here. The cameraman's 'cunning' hand achieves an act of manipulation and selection of the material even in that most objective of art forms. The fictional film-maker in that short story records only those details which correspond to his private vision, or which reinforce the narrative argument of his film, in much the same way as that described by McGahern in a later piece of critical non-fiction about the art of the photographer. In his 1995 preface to Liam Kelly's *The Face of Time*, a collection of nineteenth-century photographs taken by Leland Lewis Duncan, McGahern draws attention to how really talented photographers can bring to their craft a telling 'eye' for composition and a 'sure grasp of the ... built-in objectivity [of photography]' (*LW*, p. 17). What McGahern is suggesting in both those pieces is that the inclusion of scenery and objects, however objectively they may be depicted or described, does not always point to a desire for producing all-inclusive mimetic realism in the vein of the nineteenth-century novel.

For McGahern, a modern novelist is distinguished not just by his or her capacity for observation but also by their 'cunning' (*HG*, p. 58) selection of detail. As Joyce, another great student of literary form and genre, had pointed out in *Stephen Hero*, the artist should be possessed in equal measure of 'a selective faculty and a reproductive faculty'.[18] McGahern's fiction occasionally bears out how he found that of those 'twin faculties' it was the former that was all too often overlooked. The over-descriptive habits of bad contemporary novelists are slyly satirised in the story 'Sierra Leone'. The politician Jerry McCredy — who is ridiculed throughout by the narrator for his inability to notice important things that go on under his nose — answers the narrator's question about the outcome of a foreign job interview from which he has just returned not with a succinct account of only the salient facts but rather with a full and lengthy narrative account of his trip which makes '[no] attempt to select between details, other than to put the whole lot in' (*GT*, p. 147).

McGahern found much to admire in the exact opposite attitude to such indiscriminate descriptiveness. In his literary criticism he identified a perfect example of such an approach not in any work of modernist or postmodernist fiction but rather in the style of a work of twentieth-century prose which bypassed modern literary concerns altogether and drew instead on an epic consciousness which McGahern compared to that of Homer. When he admiringly commented on the epic style of Tomás Ó Criomhthain's *The Islandman* that 'People ... are presented only in their essential outline, and that is only in so far as their striking identities are visible to the eyes of those around them' (*LW*, p. 271), the implied contrast with the laborious descriptiveness of nineteenth-century novelists like Dickens, Tolstoy and Balzac was clear. This concern with unnecessary descriptiveness — what he characterised in his essay on *The Islandman* as the 'idle ... contemplation' of the physical dimensions and ornaments of the world (*LW*, p. 263)[19] — was a constant in McGahern's thinking about twentieth-century fiction. Inevitably, that concern is also sometimes subtly referenced in his fiction. When the narrator of 'Oldfashioned' comments on the 'endless flow of conjecture and criticism' which is invariably provoked among the guards in the barracks by as little as 'the movement of a fly across the windowpane' or the sight of somebody pushing his bicycle across the bridge (*HG*, p. 43), McGahern is not merely making a point about the importance of reticence and manners, as a previous chapter argued. The boy's condemnation of needless descriptive loquaciousness in that passage equally contains a comment on the manner of the nineteenth-century novel as it continued to exist anachronistically not only in the world of the isolated rural police barracks in the 1940s which the story depicts but also among certain contemporaries of the author of *The Barracks* in the latter half of the twentieth century. What is more, it is surely no accident that one of the narrator's examples of the guards' endless descriptions of unimportant things duplicates one of the most famous descriptive details in all of nineteenth-century fiction. The old policemen's commentary on 'the movement of a fly across the windowpane' may be read as an ironic reprise of a celebrated passage at the end of part three of *Crime and Punishment*, where the feverish mind of Raskolnikov is twice compelled to register the miniature spectacle of 'the buzzing and struggling of some large fly as it swooped ... against the windowpane'.[20]

McGahern's fiction certainly has many realist elements, not least the many authentic details which ground his fiction in the reality of an identifiable place, time and culture — what structuralist critics of the novel refer to as 'realist operators'.[21] In his early fiction he specialised in domestic interiors[22] which drew on the symbolic realism of a novel like *Madame Bovary*, and perhaps above all on that of Joyce's *Dubliners*. Compare for example the merciless attention to detail in McGahern's description of the class-conscious farmer's preparation of the front room for an important visitor in the second paragraph of chapter four of *The Dark* (*D*, p. 24), or that of the various objects and ornaments that are the markers of lower-middle-class Catholic respectability in the opening paragraph of *The Barracks* (*B*, p. 7), with Joyce's symbolically claustrophobic sitting-rooms in stories like 'The Sisters' and 'Eveline'. However, while the descriptions of the interiors and the landscapes in which McGahern's characters move are invariably 'dramatically real', his narratives do not, as Paolo Vivante put it, 'indulge in fastidious realism' — that is to say in complacent exercises in realism for realism's sake.[23] Aaron Kelly pinpoints McGahern's attitude towards the realist tradition in which his work is usually placed very accurately when he remarks that 'for all its obsessive detailing of a mundane reality, there is something overdetermined or implosive in its precision'. Or as Richard Robinson suggests about the *Crusoe*-esque attention to odd shoes in *The Dark*: 'theatrically foregrounded, they suggest how realist fiction exploits the conventions of verisimilitude'.[24] The *awareness* of the techniques employed in the pursuit of the reality effect is just as important to McGahern as the believability of the effect in its own right; on many occasions in his fiction it is clearly even more important. He could sometimes be dismissive of contemporary works of fiction that were conventionally fictitious, and which lacked the modern novelist's awareness of the nature of their art. More than once such work was described with the derogatory adjective 'novelettish'. From the very beginning of his career as a writer of fiction, McGahern saw himself as a serious and self-aware artist, not a mere teller of well-made tales. In a letter to Patrick Swift in response to the proofs of his first published work of fiction, a series of extracts from *The End or the Beginning of Love* which would appear in the April 1961 issue of *X* magazine, he registered his dissatisfaction with the title he had given the work in terms that point to this concern:

> My dislike is that it has novelettish overtones — something soft or vague.
> *THE GRINDSTONE*
> *Episodes from a novel*
> would to my mind be truer … Would *The Grindstone* seem hard and repellant, too much so? My fear was that the clumsiness and vagueness of *The End* — would offend real taste and not be true?[25]

A few years later he revealed the persistence of this same concern with the 'novelettish', the soft and vague, in a letter to Brian Friel about his dealings with the *New Yorker*, the prestigious American magazine notorious for the over-polished urbanity of its house style, its sentimental approach to Irish material, and its generally anti-avant-gardist attitude. A *New Yorker* editor had 'buggered about . . . no end', McGahern complained to Friel, with a story he had submitted because 'I think they think my work is too rough or something.'[26]

McGahern's fiction is neither soft nor vague. While on the surface it often appears to be straightforward and conventional, his uneasy relationship with the transparency of the realist style is apparent throughout his oeuvre. Particularly in his early fiction, McGahern was sometimes given to lampooning well-known descriptive tropes from nineteenth-century prose genres. This happens, for instance, when the teenage narrative consciousness of *The Dark* offers this rather clunky mock-Gothic description of the approach of morning in chapter three: 'The bats screeched continually round the eaves outside' (*D*, p. 21).

More interesting is the way McGahern's unease with the realist conventions of diction and style becomes evident from his periodic breaking of the 'looking-glass smoothness' of the language of the realist novel which Proust had so admired in a nineteenth-century novelist like Flaubert.[27] Many textbooks and critical studies devoted to the genre continue to emphasise that the language of realism aims to be 'transparent': that is to say, that it does not draw attention to itself but is calculated, rather, to allow the reader to forget that they are reading a novel. This idea may be a generalisation fraught with inaccuracy when it is scrutinised in relation to actual nineteenth-century texts, as specialised scholars have repeatedly pointed out, but it persists all the same as a commonplace in the critical discourse surrounding the realist novel;[28] and it is to the *idea* of smooth, 'transparent' language that twentieth-century novelists such as McGahern are reacting. The very roughness of the language to which McGahern thought the *New Yorker* editor had objected in one of his stories is in fact central to conveying the author's aesthetic aims, especially in the early fiction. McGahern's narrators are on more than one occasion unwilling or unable to continue in the tradition of 'transparent' realist language. The smooth surface of the prose is violently shattered at the climax of the plot of *The Dark*, for example, when the linguistic euphoria of the young man leaving the university for the last time is cut short by his unwillingness to provide any further cogent similes:

> You were walking through the rain of Galway with your father and you could laugh purely, without bitterness, for the first time, and it was a kind of happiness, at its heart the terror of an unclear recognition of the reality

> that set you free, touching you with as much foreboding as the sodden leaves falling in this day, *or any cliche*. (*D*, p. 188, emphasis added)

This is not an isolated occurrence. The same thing happens earlier in the same novel. At the end of chapter four, the narrator ends his description of the room that has been prepared for the priest's impending visit on an equally self-conscious note: 'Though even in the lamplight and the friendly hissing of logs on the fire, the cloth bleached in the frost white as snow on the table, the room remained lifeless *as any other good example*' (*D*, p. 24, emphasis added). Nor is it confined to the overtly experimental narrative that is McGahern's second novel. Already in *The Barracks*, a novel which on a casual reading appears very much like a straightforward realist study of personal suffering in the mould of *Madame Bovary* or *Anna Karenina*, Elizabeth Reegan's nocturnal musings had been cut short by an identical type of linguistic fizzling out when she reflected how 'soon they were lost, the ceiling in as much confusion and emptiness over her eyes *as she didn't know what*' (*B*, p. 201, emphasis added). The narrators of both these novels are resigned to having to express themselves in the idiom of a realist novel, but only up to the point when they are finally overcome with a weariness with an overly formalised and lyrical form of expression that ultimately fails to express the complexity of their reality.

Such ironic deflations draw attention to the generic use of language in the realist novel — to the familiar linguistic effects and devices used by novelists. Other disruptions of the structural conventions of realism in McGahern's early fiction include the obvious break with the stable point of view from which the action is viewed in *The Dark*, where the grammatical perspective shifts perpetually from first- to second- to third-person narrative — a property it shares with modernist novels by Proust and Beckett.[29] This particular experiment with narrative perspective is also not confined to *The Dark*. McGahern commenced his experiment with the use of a shifting grammatical perspective in a less obtrusive fashion in *The Barracks*, in which Elizabeth Reegan's soliloquies occasionally shift from the immediacy of the first person or the internally focalised third person, to the detachment of second-person narrative which may help her distance herself from her own suffering. This happens, for instance, in the paragraph in chapter one which begins 'It should all make you want to cry. You were lonely' (*B*, p. 32), and on a number of other occasions throughout.

McGahern admired, when he found it in the canonical realist novelists of the nineteenth century, the deployment of the 'nicely polished looking-glass' which the early Joyce of *Dubliners* (following the cue of Wilde's preface to *The Picture of Dorian Gray*) sought to hold up to his compatriots.[30] In his essay on *Dubliners*, McGahern quotes the letter to Grant Richards in which Joyce articulated that aim (*LW*, p. 201). Of course, he was also aware that in the course of his career Joyce coined not just one but two metaphorical descriptions of art that use the idea of a mirror. Just as often as emulating the aims stated by the author of *Dubliners*, McGahern's fiction followed in the tradition of the later Joyce of *Ulysses*, who proposed that the 'cracked looking-glass of a servant' would be a perfect 'symbol of Irish art'.[31] The latter pointed to a way of representing the world which deliberately breaks with the traditional nineteenth-century imperative for mirror-smoothness and transparency, and which may instead draw attention to the fact that the work is indeed but a reflection, not reality itself. It also emphasised that the modernist perception of reality — like the nineteenth-century Irish experience of colonial living — is often fractured and contradictory. It is this latter 'symbol of Irish art' from *Ulysses*, which is also a description of realism at a slant, which is so clearly recalled in the boy's description of the view from the presbytery window in *The Dark*, where 'The moon came across the graveyard, its image cut in two by a diagonal crack in the dressing-table mirror the other end of the room' (*D*, p. 68). Such a nod to the broken, multifaceted modernist rendering of reality of the later Joyce seems only appropriate in a novel whose very point of view lacks the stability of that of the nineteenth-century novel. Even the description in 'Wheels' of the 'useless pier' built by the narrator's father 'to absorb the glass about the house, dangerous with jagged bits' (*N*, p. 18) may be an emblem of the twentieth-century author's transformation of the smoothly polished surfaces of Dickens, Balzac and Flaubert into the jagged, multifaceted modernist art of Woolf, Eliot and Joyce. Its 'jagged bits' of glass may be read as provincial reincarnations of the 'shattered glass and toppling masonry' of modernity whose chaos, fragmentation and abrasiveness are reflected by the language and the structure of works like *Ulysses* and *The Waste Land*.[32]

It is perhaps not surprising, then, that the property of realism which is most frequently invoked in McGahern's fiction is the classic description of its aim — in the words of Plato, via *Hamlet* — 'to hold … the mirror up to nature'.[33] Historically, the idea of the mirror has often been used in discussions of literary realism. McGahern is not so much interested in the illusion of reality which such a process of mirroring may provide. Instead, the real subject of his work is often the very *process* of reflection itself. One of the most regularly recurring metafictional motifs in McGahern's fiction are the references to precisely that realist ideal of a mimetic art which exactly reproduces reality by holding a 'mirror up to nature'. There are many reflective surfaces in McGahern's fiction, including even (as the end of this section shall discuss) the descriptions in *That They May Face the Rising Sun* of the lake around which most of the action revolves. One of the passages in his fiction which most clearly invokes the idea of realism's 'nicely polished looking-glass' or 'mirror up to nature' is the striking description of a reflecting night-time window near the end of the first chapter of *The Barracks*. As the two Reegan children make their way up to bed, each carrying a candle and a hot brick in a heavy woollen sock, they encounter a tableau which arrests both their attention and that of the reader:

> They climbed [the stairs] without speaking a word. When they got near the top they could see their images with candles and bricks mounting into the night on the black shine of the window. It was directly at the head of the stairs, facing out on the huge sycamore between the house and the river. There was no sign of moon or star, only two children with candles reflected out of its black depth, raindrops slipping down the glass without, where the masses of wind struggled and reeled in the night. (*B*, p. 38)

With its deliberately heightened language drawing attention to itself, this passage reads like a superb pastiche of a Henry James ghost story about the children's unease at seeing their own image so chillingly accurately reflected onto the blackness of the night. More than that, the whole scene is also a knowing metafictional reflection on the idea of the 'nicely polished looking-glass' of mimetic realism. It is a paragraph *about* the reflection of reality which is the objective of realist novelists, in which the children's unease at seeing their own image so clearly reflected 'on the black shine of the window' is a version of Wilde's famous description in the preface to *The Picture of Dorian Gray* of the nineteenth century's dislike of realism as 'the rage of Caliban seeing his own face in a glass'.[34]

That passage is not the only metafictional commentary on the generic conventions of nineteenth-century realism in *The Barracks*. The novel's opening paragraph is just as self-consciously novelistic. For one, the 'glitter[ing]' of the glass that covers the faded religious pictures 'in the sudden flashes of firelight' (*B*, p. 7) is the first description in McGahern's fiction of the world seen *by reflection*. What is more, its choice of detail also references a famous scene in a specific nineteenth-century novel. The reader first discovers Elizabeth Reegan just as Charles encounters Emma in chapter three of *Madame Bovary*, amid the play of light and darkness in a farmhouse kitchen. That the comparison is intentional is clear from the way in which Elizabeth's 'darn[ing] an old woollen sock... her head bent' because of the failing light in the first sentence of McGahern's novel (*B*, p. 7) so precisely echoes Flaubert's description of Emma Bovary silently '[darning] a white cotton stocking... she worked with her head bent'.[35] Not only the situation but the style, too, pays homage to *Madame Bovary*. Domestic detail is rendered with minute precision:

> The bright golds and scarlets of the religious pictures on the walls had faded, their glass glittered now in the sudden flashes of firelight, and as it deepened the dusk turned reddish from the Sacred Heart lamp that burned before the small wickerwork crib of Bethlehem on the mantelpiece. Only the cups and saucers laid ready on the table for their father's tea were white and brilliant. (*B*, p. 7)

The attention to detail is *so* precise — almost obsessive, in fact — that it is in danger of momentarily occluding the reader's attention to the characters who inhabit this space. The novel's opening paragraph shares both its detailed awareness of kitchen clutter and its remarkable attention to lighting effects with the same passage in *Madame Bovary*, in which Charles Bovary

> at first didn't notice Emma; the shutters were closed. Through the cracks in the wood, the sun cast long narrow stripes of brightness that broke across the angles of the furniture and trembled on the ceiling. Flies, on the table, were crawling up the glasses left there, and buzzing about in the bottom, drowning in the cider dregs... Between the window and the hearth, Emma was sewing; she wore no fichu, on her bare shoulders you could see little drops of sweat.[36]

The total effect of the opening paragraph of *The Barracks*, like that of the children climbing the stairs thirty-odd pages later, is that of a heightened version of something from a realist novel which contrasts with McGahern's usual, more restrained narrative voice as it is employed in the rest of the novel. Nowhere else in *The Barracks* is there such sustained attention to gratuitous external detail. McGahern stressed how the novel is concerned with developing Elizabeth's 'way of looking', and many of the luminous details in the rest of the novel are included because they act as stimuli to Elizabeth's awakening visionary consciousness.[37] Only at the conclusion of the penultimate chapter does the narrative return to the same realist obsession with noticing insignificant external details (the inscription on the gravestone, the 'powdery white dust of the road [that] dulled the shine on their boots as they walked'

(*B*, pp. 223–5)) — and even then it is only in the light of the guards' heightened awareness of the physical dimensions of the world after the shock of losing Elizabeth. The contrast between the minute descriptive detail of the opening paragraph and the style of what follows in the rest of the novel draws attention to itself to such an extent that, together with the reference to the reflection in the glass and the fact that the situation is such an obvious homage to one of the most celebrated nineteenth-century novels, it reads more like a commentary on the properties of realism than a 'straight' realist description of a country kitchen.

Mirroring or reflective surfaces in McGahern's fiction often recall either of two particular nineteenth-century originals. The first is that famous and influential symbol of nineteenth-century realism, Stendhal's description of the novel in the epigraph to chapter thirteen of *Scarlet and Black* as 'a mirror passing down a road'.[38] Stendhal's metaphor had been freshly brought back into the Irish literary consciousness in a slightly reworked form not long before McGahern finally became a published novelist, when Frank O'Connor used it in 1957 as both the epigraph ('A novel is a mirror carried along a roadway') and the title of his book *The Mirror in the Roadway: a study of the modern novel.* However appropriate the image of a 'mirror in the roadway' may have been to the artistic aims of the nineteenth century, by the second half of the twentieth century it felt somewhat outdated. It was therefore probably as much a riposte to the aesthetic preoccupations of a self-confessed latter-day nineteenth-century realist like O'Connor[39] as it was a revisiting of Stendhal's original, when McGahern worked the idea of a mirror which is literally *in* the surface of the road into chapter eight of *The Dark*. There, the protagonist notices, as he walks back from confession with his father, how 'the pot-holes filled with water, where again and again a star shivered' (*D*, p. 44).

The second reflective surface to which McGahern often returns is a description of good writing suggested by Chekhov in 1886. In a letter to his brother Alexander, Chekhov proposed that to describe a moonlit night a writer should not try to write about the moon itself, but that instead 'you will evoke a moonlit night by writing that on the mill dam the glass fragments of a broken bottle flashed like a bright little star'.[40] The same aesthetic principle is celebrated in one of Konstantin's speeches in *The Seagull*, in which the young writer is aware of the weakness in his own prose style and contrasts it with the restrained bare style of the older novelist Trigorin in terms which echo Chekhov's own letter of a decade earlier:

> The description of the moonlit evening is too long and rather precious. Trigorin has worked out his own methods… He would just mention the neck of a broken bottle glistening on the dam and the black shadow of a mill-wheel — and there you'd have a moonlit night. But I have to put in the tremulous night, the soft twinkling of the stars, and the distant sounds of a piano, dying away in the still, fragrant air… It's excruciating![41]

McGahern had probably come across both of those passages early on in his career. Since they are concentrated on the reflection, selection and transformation of the material, rather than the efforts of Stendhal and other nineteenth-century realists to hold a passive mirror up to the totality of whatever worldly reality may pass before it, the aims expressed by Chekhov are more compatible with those of more modern, twentieth-century authors, and so his ideas have been influential on the thinking of many subsequent late-nineteenth- and twentieth-century prose writers. Chekhov, like McGahern after him, is conscious of the fact that what may appear real in realist writing can only be achieved by mastering a variety of methods or tricks. Far from suggesting that fiction is simply a 'mirror up to nature' which reflects all that comes before it in minute, exhaustive detail, Chekhov proposes in these passages how really exciting art is not achieved by pursuing an immediate or direct representation of reality in its totality but by offering a *suggestion* of reality, which is achieved by taking away unnecessary detail rather than piling it up in the manner of Tolstoy, Dickens and Balzac and the 'long and rather precious' tradition of nineteenth-century realism. It was McGahern's mastery of this stylistic habit that made Michael McLaverty remark in admiration on reading the published extracts from *The End or the Beginning of Love* in 1961 that 'all these [striking images] suggest far more than what is on the page. They give the piece substance for they are the right details in the right places… They are… poetic and not enumerative', a skill that reminded him, he added, 'of Chehov's [*sic*] famous advice to a young writer as he urged him to cut out and simplify'.[42]

The Chekhovian imperatives to reflect and to 'cut out and simplify' were central to McGahern's thinking about narrative prose. The need to *reflect* reality also had a much more ancient antecedent than Chekhov's letter. Perhaps taking his cue from W.H. Auden, who had titled one of the sections in *The Dyer's Hand* 'The Shield of Perseus', McGahern hinted in the 1968 essay 'The Image' how the artist might look to the example of Perseus as the original artist–hero. In Greek mythology, Perseus had triumphed over Medusa, whose sight turned all who looked upon her to stone, by looking at her only by reflection in the highly polished surface of his bronze shield. Like the 'Medusa's mirror' that is offered in McGahern's essay as such a potent metaphor for the artist's task to 'purely reflect on our situation through this created world' (*LW*, p. 5), a work of literature should reflect only a selection of reality, because to look directly on all of reality can only result in a form of intellectual or imaginative paralysis like that experienced by the victims of Medusa and her Gorgon sister in the Perseus myth. That the metaphorical potential of the myth about the two Gorgons who share the use of a single eye and whose sight would turn anyone who directly looks on them to stone remained important to McGahern is clear from the fact that it is not only alluded to in that early essay but also elsewhere, in the fiction of his later decades. The oblique reference in 'Gold Watch' to the narrator's one-time ambition to 'outstare the one eye of nature' (*HG*, p. 106) may be understood as a reference to the same myth. By staring *directly* into that single eye instead of regarding it only by reflection as Perseus had done, the narrator of 'Gold Watch', like so many of the emotionally stunted young men in all of McGahern's collections, turns his heart to stone as the myth had predicted. Or to translate that mythical threat into its ordinary modern equivalent, he ends up defeated and drained of the energy required for sustaining an even moderately happy or functional everyday existence.

Knowing references to the idea of reflection, always imperfectly achieved through a Joycean 'cracked looking-glass' and always calculated to pare back a spectacle to its essential elements, are a recurring element in McGahern's fiction. McGahern alluded to Chekhov's description of good writing on various occasions in his fiction and in his private correspondence alike. He uses Chekhov's example of good writing as the description of the play of moonlight on a broken bottle (but without acknowledging its Chekhovian provenance) in a letter written in 1970 or 1971 to his French translator Pierre Leyris.[43] Recognisable versions of Chekhov's example of good writing also occur in some of his works of fiction. The description of 'the pot-holes filled with water, where again and again a star shivered' (*D*, p. 44) in chapter eight of *The Dark* is not only a parody of the realist aims of Stendhal and Frank O'Connor to place a mirror in a roadway. It also puts into practice Chekhov's advice about the most effective way of suggesting a moonlit night, as the starlight reflected in the water of the potholes in that sentence in *The Dark* precisely replicates Chekhov's 'bright little star' flashing on a fragment of glass on a mill dam. The extended description of the 'perfect moonlit night ... so still that the shadows of the beeches did not waver on the moonlit grass' (*HG*, p. 118) at the end of 'Gold Watch' (the story that had warned against attempts to outstare nature's eye) also reads like a knowing reworking of Chekhov's example of good writing which took for its subject a moonlit night, as the narrator reflects how 'The night seemed so full of serenity that it brought the very ache of longing for all of life to reflect its moonlit calm' (*HG*, p. 118). Even the repeated descriptions of the great mirroring lake in *That They May Face the Rising Sun* are, in this respect, reminders that *its* surface, too, is no more than a very large Medusa's mirror which allows the artist to write about the limitless expanse of the sky only by contemplating the reflection of just a small portion of the heavens. The whole of the lake thus becomes a version of the modest pot-holes in *The Dark*, or of those Chekhovian fragments of glass by the mill dam reflecting the moonlight and the sky above. The ripples on its surface, alluded to almost every time the lake is described, make sure, like the cracks in the symbolic looking-glass of *Ulysses*, that the image of reality which it reflects can never be confused with reality itself.

Ultimately, McGahern's idea of reflection transcends the nineteenth-century obsession with mimetic realism. 'The lake was an enormous mirror turned to the depth of the sky, holding its light and its colours' (*TRS*, p. 177), the narrator observes in *That They May Face the Rising Sun*. More than a hundred pages later, again, he draws attention to how 'the lake reflected the sky and looked as deep' (*TRS*, p. 295). That property is clearly metaphorical of the aims of the conventional realist writer, but it also invokes, perhaps, Yeats' paradoxical description in his essay 'At Stratford-on-Avon' of 'nature' itself as 'but [the] looking-glass' which allows the artist to reflect on more fundamental 'ideas'.[44] It is also in this sense of the word that the idea of *reflection* is used in 'The Image', where art does not simply passively reflect the world like a huge nineteenth-century realist mirror but rather helps the artist to 'reflect *on*' his situation in the world (*LW*, p. 5, emphasis added). Similarly, in 'The Solitary Reader' the change in reading habits which marks the beginning of a reader's intellectual maturity is described with recourse to a comparison to a mirror. That process, too, is conceived as a shift away from the childish demand for mimetic realism which simply presents a recognisable world realised in great external detail, to a subtler appreciation of how the fabric of certain novels can become mirrors which may explain the complexities of one's own life (*LW*, p. 90), looking-glasses onto the soul which may help to crystallise complex thoughts and ideas that come from deep within the self.

The morality of art

A number of McGahern's ideas about the nature of fiction and the proper attitude of the artist have their origin in late-nineteenth-century thought. Many aesthetic ideas that appealed to him were articulated in the late nineteenth century by writers like Flaubert, Wilde, Henry James and Chekhov, but also by the early Joyce of *Dubliners*. Throughout his career, the moral and aesthetic guidelines set out by these authors were a constant presence in McGahern's fiction in two ways: his novels and stories often follow both their practical examples and the theoretical guidelines they set down; they also frequently self-consciously comment on many of the same principles.

A writer like Flaubert was a major influence on McGahern's thinking about the importance of creating a solid prose style. It is well known that McGahern was a scrupulous rewriter and refiner who saw himself in the tradition of the 'proper expression' which began with Flaubert and continued through the early Joyce of *Dubliners*. He made this preoccupation explicit in his essay on *Dubliners*, but self-conscious metafictional references to the importance of the same ideal are also occasionally worked into his fiction. In *The Pornographer*, for instance, the narrator notices Maloney's satisfaction at making small corrections to his pornographic prose, and remarks how 'He got curious pleasure from the changes, almost standing back to admire the line of the sentences, like someone admiring the true line of a wall he has just straightened' (*P*, p. 28). The simile does not just point in general terms to a Flaubertian concern with stylistic precision; the comparison between the shape of a sentence and that of a work of masonry is borrowed from one of Flaubert's letters about his work on the corrections to the manuscript of *Madame Bovary*:

> I have had to remove a lot of cement that was oozing out from between the stones, and the stones had to be reset so that the joints wouldn't show. Prose must stand upright, from one end to the other, like a wall whose ornamentation continues down to its very base: seen in perspective, it must make a long continuous line.[45]

Similar allusions to Flaubert's letters about writing can be found in other works. The famous letter exchange between Flaubert and George Sand about the importance of 'the well-turned sentence' is repeated in the dialogue of a pair of public-house intellectuals on a Sunday evening on Harcourt Street in the story 'Parachutes'. Flaubert had insisted that for the novelist, the task of 'rounding out a sentence' is not a frivolous act of dressing up but a labour crucial to achieving 'accurate thinking, and effective expression', and that

> The concern for external Beauty you [George Sand] reproach in me is for me a *method*. When I come upon a bad assonance or a repetition in one of my sentences, I'm sure I'm floundering in the False. By dint of searching,

> I find the proper expression, which was always the *only* one, and which is, at the same time, harmonious. The word is never lacking when one possesses the idea.[46]

This letter is clearly on the mind of one of the characters in 'Parachutes' as he bemoans the Irish habit for sloppy expression. When Mulvey, who has learned the correct names for shades of colours from a painter whom he used to know, points out to the narrator that the correct word for the colour of the sky is agate, the latter replies 'It's a beautiful word', only to be corrected that 'It's the *right* word' (*HG*, p. 20). To settle for a word that is merely beautiful would be an indulgence a serious writer can ill afford. Flaubert, McGahern and the fictional Mulvey, however little else they may have in common, are all united by their concern with finding the *right* word which alone will produce the best sentence. In his essay on *Dubliners*, McGahern twice quotes Flaubert's sentence about the importance of beauty which was for him a method (*LW*, pp. 204–5), because for him, too, it was a point that could not be overemphasised.

Flaubert constantly emphasised that much thought and effort was required for finding the correct word. McGahern also often quoted Flaubert's comment in the same letter that in order to write well one needs to, he paraphrased, 'feel deeply and think clearly'.[47] That imperative is recalled in the title story of *High Ground* when the narrator relates how 'when evening came ... I wanted to be alone, to go over the night, *to try to see clearly*' (*HG*, p. 94, emphasis added). The importance of finding the correct expression for things is a constant of McGahern's language, even if some of his characters on occasion fail to hit upon the precise word for what they are thinking or feeling.

Also among the central concerns of that late-nineteenth-century tradition which was so much on McGahern's mind was that of the morality or immorality of literary production. At the conclusion of 'The Beginning of an Idea', the opening story of *Getting Through*, what might have been a conventional moral tale about a woman cruelly taken advantage of by seedy foreign officials is deflated by Eva Lindberg's 'rage against her own foolishness' rather than against her attackers. She remembers how her poet–friend Severi in Paris is fond of repeating a maxim borrowed from Wilde's essay 'The Critic as Artist': 'There is only one real sin — stupidity' (*GT*, p. 27),[48] because it is not the sinful but the stupid which brings real shame to a person of intellectual integrity. A similar concern with the proper way of writing about keenly felt social injustices is, as this section will show, also a theme in 'Swallows', published in the same collection.

A decadent Wildean streak more generally underlies McGahern's self-definition as a serious artist dedicated to his craft, one for whom intellectual rigour and honesty, not the promotion of received notions of moral rectitude, were the highest good. His insistence after the banning of *The Dark* in 1965 that there were no moral or immoral books because 'if something is well written, it can't but be moral by definition'[49] — an attitude typical of the lofty stance assumed by many writers and intellectuals in the face of Irish censorship in the middle decades of the twentieth century (*LW*, p. 91) — repeated the confident, provocative public stance that was the default position of some of the late nineteenth century's most scandalous writers. Flaubert and Henry James had made similar comments, as had Oscar Wilde, who wrote almost exactly the same thing in the preface to *The Picture of Dorian Gray*: 'There is no such thing as a moral or an immoral book. Books are well written, or badly written. That is all.'[50] McGahern made such comments routinely in the 1990s, in his interview with Julia Carlson, in 'The Solitary Reader' and elsewhere, and his studied detachment on all those occasions may well have owed something to the passing of the years since the banning had taken place. It was much more remarkable, however, that even in the years immediately following the 'McGahern Affair', as it soon became known, he had already hit upon that same tone. His comment in an interview conducted to mark the lifting of the Irish ban on *The Dark* in 1970 that 'I'd want my work judged on the quality of my language, not on its ability to raise a rumpus'[51] replicated Byron's witty defence of *Don Juan* ('it may be bawdy — but is it not good English?') which McGahern, who was drawn to nineteenth-century ideas about the distinction between morality and art, would almost certainly have noted and stored away for future use when he read Byron's letters sometime during the 1950s.[52]

The most influential aspect of late-nineteenth-century aesthetic thought surrounding the art of the novel that was borrowed by McGahern is probably his emphasis on the ideal of the supremely objective novelist. The emphasis on objectivity and impartiality is one of the staples of nineteenth-century thought about the novel. It was championed by the same group of writers which McGahern described in his essay on *Dubliners* as the 'clearly defined tradition ... [of] Flaubert and the group of writers close to him who wrote in France at the height of the nineteenth century' who had thought clearly about the separation of art and morality (*LW*, pp. 201–2), as well as by other important late-nineteenth-century prose writers like Chekhov and Tolstoy. The latter, for example, wrote in 1876 that 'I have noticed that any story makes an impression only when one cannot make out with whom the author sympathises.'[53] James Joyce, too, in a 1928 letter which McGahern quoted with approval in his short essay on 'Mr Joyce and Mr Yeats', referred to Thomas Hardy as a 'clerk' who has the integrity not to concern himself with 'the great questions which, for all that, adjust themselves very well without his aid' (*LW*, p. 186).[54] Over the course of many decades, McGahern consistently aligned himself with that tradition. He described the relationship between the author and his characters in moral terms in a 1990 interview in which he said that 'the tradition I grew up in is that of Joyce and Flaubert, which holds that a writer's opinions as such are about as valuable as those of a footballer or anybody else who happens to be in the public eye ... Essentially, all you can do is honour your characters.'[55] His essay on *Dubliners* contains a prolonged reflection on the importance of 'objective' style which culminates in a simple observation that constitutes the highest form of praise possible of any author: that 'Joyce does not judge' (*LW*, p. 207). McGahern always measured his own fiction by those same standards, saying that 'You'd be a bad writer if you judge your people. Judgement is always bad writing.'[56] From early on in his career some readers of his work recognised McGahern's mastery of non-judgemental prose. In 1965, for example, Michael McLaverty, who remains one of McGahern's finest critics, congratulated him on how 'The final chapters [of *The Dark*], which I found compassionately moving, do justice to Mahoney as a father and as a man and demonstrate that you have the maturity and fair-mindedness of a true novelist';[57] and Gus Martin remarked, in a comment whose proximity to his own assessment of Joyce must surely have pleased McGahern, that 'there is no writer ... more free from didacticism than John McGahern'.[58]

Not only is the ideal of scrupulous authorial objectivity a constant guideline in the construction of his fiction; it is also an occasional subject in some works. For instance, when Luke in *Amongst Women* responds to Maggie's comment that 'It's not natural' that he refuses to visit his ageing father by declaring that 'It may not be natural but it's true' (*AW*, pp. 144–5), that statement becomes a metafictional marker of McGahern's own aims as a novelist — because as Maria DiBattista has brilliantly argued, Luke's acute sense of the gulf between what is 'natural', polite, conventional or expected on the one hand, and what is 'true' on the other, replicates the early Joyce's opposition between idealism and realism in literature.[59] Joyce's occasional prose was only one of the conduits through which such convictions reached McGahern. He shares his conviction of the value of 'true' material, which may be morally objectionable but which must nevertheless be rendered with complete objectivity, with the great prose writers of the late nineteenth century in whose mould much of Joyce's thought about his material was cast. More often than not, McGahern bypassed familiar Joycean phrasings of ideas to go back instead to their nineteenth-century French or Russian originals. Denis Sampson comments on how the letter to Grant Richards in which Joyce 'speaks of "dunghills as artistic materials" [*sic*] is clearly in McGahern's mind in "Parachutes".[60] That observation is true, but it does not reach far enough. When McGahern writes in that story about the backyard 'dumps' from which beautiful things may spring (*HG*, pp. 22–3), he *is* in all likelihood thinking of Joyce. Probably just as consciously, however, he is rewriting a well-known passage from Chekhov — an author whose presence is intermittently invoked throughout *Getting Through*, particularly in the opening story, 'The Beginning of an Idea', in which the main character is writing a biography of Chekhov. In a letter defending his 'immoral' art from the attacks of a prudish critic which predates that of Joyce by twenty years, the Russian master of the nineteenth-century short story invokes the 'dunghill' of everyday reality which is the artist's proper subject. For Chekhov, the artist's domain should be the entire dunghill of human nature, and to pluck only the 'pearl' of moral virtuousness from the 'heap of villains' would be to 'deny literature itself. Literature... depicts life as it actually is. Its purpose is truth, honest and indisputable. To limit its functions to special tasks, such as the finding of "pearls," does it moral injury'.[61]

Similar concerns with presenting reality without moral censure are repeated in many of McGahern's novels and stories. Following the examples of writers such as Chekhov and Joyce, Jamesie in *That They May Face the Rising Sun* emphasises the crucial wisdom that 'There's nothing right or wrong in this world. Only what happens' (*TRS*, p. 56). In *The Barracks*, too, Elizabeth Reegan — whom McGahern famously described in an interview as 'as much a way of looking as a character in her own right'[62] — is repeatedly cast as one possessed of the detachment and the eye for detail of a novelist. The detached tone of the novel as a whole is mirrored by Elizabeth's outlook, descriptions of which are as much metafictional commentaries on the author's own artistic aims as they are indications of Elizabeth's stoic calm. Thus, Elizabeth is able to confront the series of memories of her past which come to her on her sickbed 'as dispassionately as it confronted her' (*B*, p. 135), and even when the priest comes to administer extreme unction she notices the physical features which define his posture and his face because 'She was detached, she could watch' (*B*, p. 218).

The need for dispassionate, unbiased observation is of course not only an aesthetic attitude but also a basic rule of scientific procedure, an area of experience which came to maturity in the age of the nineteenth-century novelists. Readers of recent Irish fiction may associate John Banville, rather than John McGahern, with novels about scientists whose struggles and obsessions are really disguised versions of those of the artist. On more than one occasion, though, McGahern too borrows from the idiom of scientific experiment in order to emphasise the importance of objectivity or impartiality as a principle which is as crucial to the work of a novelist as it is to that of a mathematician or a physicist. Thus, the protagonist of 'Bank Holiday' — perhaps paraphrasing the epitaph Yeats wrote for himself in 'Under Ben Bulben': 'Cast a cold eye / On life, on death'[63] — looks on his own life 'with some of the cold apprehension of an experiment' (*HG*, p. 141). And when Elizabeth Reegan in *The Barracks* mulls over her life shortly before her death, she comes to the startling conclusion that 'Plainly nothing could be resolved, she had to come to this again and again ... That was how her life happened, nothing more could be said for certain' (*B*, p. 210). Elizabeth's acceptance of the limits of human knowledge is presented in the language of the scientist not in possession of sufficient evidence to reach a conclusion, which is also a description of the art of the dispassionate novelist, who can only dispassionately observe and who must be on guard against the temptation of unwarranted, irresponsible interpretation.

Probably the most striking example of McGahern's use of metafictional comments about objectivity in his fiction is the prolonged reflection on the place of judgement in 'Swallows'. In the opening section of that story a middle-aged Garda sergeant and a young state surveyor are measuring the site of a road accident where a poor young man on a bicycle has been killed by a young woman from a rich family. When the surveyor asks 'Will you be able to get manslaughter? From the measurements she wouldn't appear to have a leg to stand on', the sergeant more than hints how the law is in practice not impartial but favours the side of the affluent and the well-connected. In response, the surveyor reminds him that they, at least, can carry out their task dispassionately: 'Fortunately, Sergeant, you and I don't have to concern ourselves with the justice or injustice. Only with the accurate presentation of the evidence' (*GT*, pp. 121–2). What the surveyor in 'Swallows' is describing is not merely the role of the police force in the modern judiciary; his observation also allegorises the responsibility of the artist to present the case of each of his characters fully, accurately and dispassionately, without passing moral judgement. When he wrote this exchange, McGahern may have been thinking specifically of a letter written by Chekhov, whose correspondence repeatedly draws on the same legal analogy to explain the responsibility of the artist and the function of art. In one letter, he explains to a critic of his work how:

> In demanding from an artist a conscious attitude toward his work you are right, but you are confusing two concepts: *the solution of a problem* and *the correct posing of a question*. Only the second is obligatory for an artist. Not a single problem is solved in *Anna Karenina* and in *Eugene Onegin*,

> but you find these works quite satisfactory only because all the questions in them are correctly posed. The court is obliged to pose the questions correctly, but it's up to the jurors to answer them, each juror according to his own taste.[64]

A novel or a play should not become a forum for imposing the writer's own opinions. McGahern strongly believed in this principle. He was only half joking, therefore, when he told an audience at the Galway Arts Festival in 1991 that 'you'll be delighted . . . Like most writers, I have absolutely nothing to say.'[65]

According to an aphorism which McGahern liked to repeat, 'art is the opposite of self-expression'.[66] Fiction should be the site of discipline and clear thinking in the tradition of Flaubert, not the outlet of private passions which George Sand believed it should be. Flaubert had criticised George Sand for '[making] Art an outlet for passions, a kind of chamber-pot to catch the overflow of I don't know what'.[67] The opening of 'Swallows' — like the conclusion of 'The Beginning of an Idea' — avoids the stink of George Sand's chamber pot. Its real subject is not the revelation of McGahern's private opinions about social injustice, which it avoids, but the proper way for the artist to deal with subjects on which he may himself have strong opinions. To write about one's opinions in a work of fiction would be a form of sentimentality or self-indulgence which the artist can ill afford. The only crime that is its equal is for a reader or a critic to reduce a great work to self-expression or sentimentality, or, as the mother in *The Leavetaking* remarks about reductive readings of works of poetic genius, preferably both (*L*, p. 38). In this sense, the reticent Bill Evans in *That They May Face the Rising Sun*, who has endured great personal suffering but who, like Herman Melville's eponymous Bartleby, prefers not to discuss the details of his past, has more potential to become a great novelist than, say, Patrick Ryan in the same novel or the youthful Maloney in *The Pornographer*. The latter had once made every disappointment or setback in his personal life the subject of a highly autobiographical and self-expressive art, a tendency which, as was discussed in a previous chapter, makes him the butt of jokes and open mockery when he recites a poem about a failed love affair to the lodgers who share his boarding house.[68]

Chekhov's analogy between the legal system and the task of the novelist is one of the most celebrated statements of the importance of authorial objectivity and detachment. Perhaps even more widely known is Flaubert's comment that 'An author in his book must be like God in the universe, present everywhere and visible nowhere.'[69] That phrase occurs several times in Flaubert's letters, and it is quoted by McGahern in his essay on *Dubliners* and elsewhere (*LW*, pp. 201, 344). In *A Portrait of the Artist as a Young Man*, Joyce's Stephen Dedalus famously borrowed Flaubert's description of the ideal artist-become-deity, and added to *his* incarnation of the god–creator a wonderful touch of nonchalance, imagining him not just impartial but utterly indifferent in a pose of studied boredom as he stands 'paring his fingernails'.[70] Like Joyce, McGahern in turn gave his own comic spin to Flaubert's image of the artist standing over his creation like a god in nature. The memory of Flaubert's godlike author is clearly recalled on two occasions in *The Pornographer*. When the pornographer explains to the naive Josephine that the world is governed by *people* and their selfish motives and not in the name of an abstract moral good by some impartial deity or other by telling her that 'Since God gave the Ten Commandments he's stayed out of it' (*P*, p. 182), this echoes Flaubert's flippant rhetorical question in an argument about the importance of authorial impartiality in good writing: 'Has God ever expressed his opinion?'[71]

An earlier passage in the same novel, in which the narrator feels devoid of agency like a character in a 'farce' or a 'doomed charade' as Josephine reads one of his pornographic stories, contains another parody of Flaubert's figure of the artist standing over his creation like 'God in the universe':

> I felt time suspended as she read. If God there was, he must enjoy himself hugely, feeling all his creatures absorbed in his creation; but this was even better. It was as if another god had visited your creation and had got totally involved in it, had fallen for it. Some gods somewhere must be shaking huge sides with laughter. (*P*, p. 66)

The pornographer lacks the confident nonchalance of Stephen Dedalus' 'God of the creation … paring his fingernails'. Even though he realises, as a good Flaubertian, that his role as the author of the story Josephine is reading makes him the god of that particular universe, he cannot help but feel that he is being judged by another god 'visit[ing]' his creation. The undefined sense of mockery in the final line of the paragraph is reprised later on the same page, when the narrator's thoughts wander back to the motif of the godlike creator. 'It must have been the drink,' he reflects, 'for I felt the flat shake with an uncontrollable silent laughter, that I was both taking part in some farce and at the same time watching it from miles far off' (*P*, p. 66). He feels as if he is being mocked by a god–creator standing over his reality, only here Flaubert's impartial god of creation is transformed into a mocking Olympian. The contrast with Flaubert and Joyce could not be more marked. Far from being the ideal impartial narrator who has 'refined [himself] out of existence' as he stands over the world of the story he has created, the pornographer, like the Reegan children at bedtime in *The Barracks*, feels unreal and disempowered, like a character in someone else's fiction or an actor in a casual comedy written by a higher power.[72] In this, the pornographer is ultimately reminiscent not so much of Flaubert or Joyce's fictional worlds overlooked by benign godlike creators, but more of the self-conscious, paranoid eponymous hero of Beckett's *Molloy*, who, when he is 'play[ing], gesticulating, waving my hat, moving my bicycle to and fro before me, blowing the horn, watching the wall' and observing his 'confused shadow' cast on the wall, is convinced that he, too, can hear that 'Somewhere someone laughed.'[73]

This is not the only time the pornographer feels like a fictional character devoid of agency. Later in the novel, he again feels as if his world is not real but part of a larger fiction in which he must act when he becomes aware on the streets of London of an unsettling sensation: 'as if a beautiful incision had been made that separated me from the world and still left me at pure ease in its still centre' (*P*, p. 229). The 'beautiful incision' in the sky may be a reference to childbirth, an important plot element at this late stage of the novel, but it also contains yet another literary echo of a text concerned with the contrast between life and imitations of life. The pornographer's 'beautiful incision' recalls a much-commented-upon passage in Pirandello's novel *The Late Mattia Pascal* in which Orestes, noticing 'a little hole torn in the paper sky', realises that his situation is at once tragic and farcical, because while his problems are still real and serious to him, he is not a real human being but rather a puppet playing in front of a painted backcloth.[74]

'Art is art because it is not nature'

From his very first steps as a writer of prose fiction, McGahern displayed an acute awareness of the generic conventions which determine the shape of realist narratives. One of the central themes of McGahern's fiction is his constant highlighting of the difference between reality and the representation of reality. His obsession with the idea of mirrors and mirroring is part of this, but he also frequently returned to another set of oppositions central to the understanding of literary texts. There are many references in his writing to the contrasts between art and life, between the rules that govern fiction and those that apply in everyday reality, which are the subject of some of the most seminal literary thought of the closing decades of the nineteenth century.

When the narrator of 'Wheels' refers to the 'repetition of a life in the shape of a story' (*N*, p. 22), that phrase is not the statement of autobiographical intent for which it could easily be mistaken. Rather than in the recovery of past experience in a thinly veiled autobiographical record, McGahern is more interested in the *process* through which (as he writes in 'The Solitary Reader') 'the pattern or story is shaped' out of the raw materials one might find in real life (*LW*, p. 90). The phrase in 'Wheels', therefore, is meant to highlight the essential *differences* between art and life, not their sameness. The notion that 'shape' is the thing that distinguishes real life from a successful retelling of life is one to which McGahern returned on many occasions. That his belief in the importance of 'shape' as the defining property of successful fiction was clearly formed from a time that predated the publication of his first fictions is clear from a comment he made in a 1958 letter to Tony Whelan, in which he confidently expressed the idea that art should be an attempt to 'shape experience'.[75] All of McGahern's works are in their different ways interested in creating a sense of order, shape or pattern.

His thinking about plot is part of this. Most of McGahern's plots are, to a greater or lesser extent, characterised by their lack of elaborateness or complication. They certainly do not include unexpected twists, nor spectacular, unlikely or what McGahern himself on one occasion called 'lunatic' actions or situations. It does not necessarily follow that all of his books are plotless (he only claimed that distinction for his final novel).[76] If some of his novels can seem uneventful or undramatic, this is because of the way McGahern conceptualised what 'plot' meant. In a letter to Patrick Swift written shortly after the publication of the extracts from *The End or the Beginning of Love* in *X* in 1961, McGahern explained what he intended to do — and not do — in his fiction:

> The insistence that to string a few lunatic situations into a plot is more valuable and difficult than to give passion and pattern to the lives of people being eroded out of their existence in the banality and repetitiveness of themselves and their society is the real maddening thing.[77]

This avoidance of stringing together a series of 'lunatic situations' in favour of the simple desire to 'give ... pattern' to a life is not a refusal of plot but a return to its core meaning. The *Oxford English Dictionary* defines 'plot' as 'The plan or scheme of a literary or dramatic work ... considered or presented as an interrelated sequence'. The aim which McGahern describes in his letter to Patrick Swift duplicates this original sense's emphasis on the interrelation of things. To 'give ... pattern' to a life is for McGahern one of the most important functions of art, one that is at the heart of all his fiction. It is alluded to by his first major character, Elizabeth Reegan, who longs to attain an 'ordered vision on her life' (*B*, p. 50). Elizabeth's effort to 'keep [their days] *in order*' (*B*, p. 20, emphasis added) is a constant concern in *The Barracks*, one that is repeatedly linked with the many religious and domestic rituals which make up the daily life in the barracks. In the *Nightlines* stories, both the fascination of the narrator of 'Wheels' with the 'repetition of a life in the shape of a story' and Sinclair's explanation in 'Why We're Here' that the meaning of existence consists of the effort to '*Try to see some make or shape on the nothing we know*' (*N*, p. 25) repeat McGahern's discussion in a 1963 letter of his labours on a short story based on his experience of attending his mother's deathbed when he was a boy. It was, he wrote to C.M. Newman at the *New Yorker*, 'a story that I have been working on and giving up for a very long time, trying to find shape for the personal experience out of which it began'.[78]

The relationship between art and life is a theme that recurs constantly throughout McGahern's work. It is discussed in the greatest detail in *The Pornographer*. As Denis Sampson points out, the first sentence of one of Maloney's maxims — that 'Art was art because it was not nature. Life was a series of accidents. Art was a vision of the law' (*P*, p. 27) — repeats a credo of the young W.B. Yeats ('Art is art because it is not nature') which McGahern had found both in *Autobiographies* and in the 1901 essay 'At Stratford-on-Avon'.[79] In addition, the last two sentences of Maloney's same maxim paraphrase a passage from chapter ten of Forrest Reid's *Brian Westby* in which Brian and Linton discuss the art of the novel:

> Art isn't just life in the raw: it is a selection from life: it *is* a vision: — life seen through a temperament, as Zola said. And its quality depends on the quality of that temperament far more than on the material out of which the actual pattern is woven.[80]

It is evident that Reid's novel about a novelist was much on McGahern's mind in the years leading up to the publication of *The Pornographer*, when he was engaged in a private campaign to have *Brian Westby* republished, first by Faber & Faber and later by his American publisher, Alfred A. Knopf. In his 1977 essay on *Brian Westby*, McGahern introduces this quotation from the novel with the speculative remark that 'There is much talk of writing. Reid, through Linton's words, states his own true vision of the activity' (*LW*, p. 194). This may be true. It is equally tempting to assume that *Brian Westby*'s 'talk of writing' also expressed, in a way that appealed to him, a number of ideas in which *McGahern* believed deeply. His fascination with Reid's novel may stem to an important degree not from its merits as a work of prose fiction but from the quality of its characters' discussions of what are essentially nineteenth-century ideas about the novel. Even the phrasing of Elizabeth Reegan's desire in *The Barracks* to achieve an 'ordered vision on her life' probably harks back to McGahern's reading of the same passage in *Brian Westby*.

One of the subplots of *The Pornographer* concerns the narrator's naive lover Josephine's inability to distinguish between the way things tend to happen in real life and the lines along which fictional plots are constructed. Although she shares this fault with the heroines of classic novels like *Madame Bovary* and *Northanger Abbey*, McGahern decided to illustrate her condition through a reference to a very different work of fiction. In a letter she sends to the narrator, Josephine misremembers the last line of dialogue from *Some Like It Hot*, a film McGahern may have seen when he was a young teacher in Dublin: 'We can't all be perfect, she quoted from her favourite movie' (*P*, p. 224). The reference is to the eccentric millionaire Osgood's response to the objection raised by 'Daphne' (played by Jack Lemon) that she/he cannot accept his proposal of marriage because he/she is really a man in disguise. That is no reason, Osgood retorts, because 'Well, nobody's perfect!'[81] Josephine's invocation of that line is charged with multiple ironies. *Some Like It Hot* may be her favourite film, she may glibly quote the joke in its final line, she may even be named after 'Josephine', the cross-dressing ladies' man played by Tony Curtis; yet despite all that she finds it impossible to accept the limitations and imperfections of real life in the way Osgood does at its conclusion. For most of *The Pornographer*, Josephine suffers from a condition sometimes called 'Bovaryism', which is to say an inability to accept that her own life is not subject to the conditions which render the lives of the virtuous heroines of the novels she is apparently accustomed to reading so perfect.[82] Even in her scheme for acquiring a husband by getting pregnant and trapping him into a marriage which she believes will still somehow be happy, she follows her instincts as a reader of sentimental fiction. When she does get pregnant and still finds herself rebuffed by her lover, she repeatedly assures herself, with all the confidence of somebody who habitually mistakes poetic justice for the laws that actually preside over real life, that everything will work out fine: '"Because," she said, "because both of us are good people"' (*P*, p. 106), a phrase that soon becomes something of a refrain running through her dialogue.

Only after she extracts herself from the sheltering influence of her protector Jonathan does Josephine find out that the world is really run by people all pursuing their own selfish motives, and that her life may not automatically follow the typical narrative arc of a certain type of novel. Talking about her discovery of the ways of the world, she confides in the narrator that

> I thought things were run on lines of good and bad, according to some vague law or other. *Virtue was rewarded*, vice was punished. My eyes were certainly opened. I sure had some catching up to do (*P*, p. 182, emphasis added)

It can be no accident that her speech on that occasion invokes the subtitle of one of the early canonical English novels, Samuel Richardson's *Pamela: or, virtue rewarded* (1740). That is how she has so far been reading the events of her own life: as a series of events which may, like those described in *Pamela*, seem unfair at first but which are in the end revealed to be part of an intricate plot which sees the just and the pure rewarded. The reader is of course expected to recognise the authorial irony that is at work in Josephine's belief in the existence of 'some vague law or other' which rewards the pure and punishes the wicked. Maloney's casual reference to *Moll Flanders* (1722) a few pages earlier (*P*, p. 165), by contrast, alludes to a truth which remains largely hidden from Josephine, who for much of the novel struggles to come to terms with the disjunction between what she thinks ought to happen and what actually does happen. Defoe's early-eighteenth-century novel about a thriving prostitute, bigamist and petty thief is not a moral fable in which the virtuous are rewarded. In *Moll Flanders*, the morally corrupt, not the pure and virtuous, profit most from the twists and turns of fate, as they often do in real life but not usually in the plots of nineteenth-century novels.

A similar belief that their lives are subject to the restorative justice that belongs in the realm of fiction also influences the thinking of one of McGahern's earliest central characters. While Elizabeth in *The Barracks* slowly comes to terms with the randomness of the universe in the face of her own death, Reegan is disturbed by the memory of the death of his first wife during childbirth, which he regards as a tragedy or a severe injustice. At the same time, however, he also takes a strange kind of solace from that same misfortune when he persuades himself, perversely recycling one of Wilde's jokes in *The Importance of Being Earnest*, that 'Elizabeth could not die . . . ; it was impossible that two could die; it would be ludicrous' (*B*, p. 47).[83] Clearly neither Josephine in *The Pornographer* nor Reegan in *The Barracks* are readers of Wilde, because the inherent unfairness which distinguishes life from fiction is one of *his* constant themes, too. In *The Importance of Being Earnest*, Miss Prism, who had in her younger days herself written one of those three-volume novels of which Cecily in the play speaks so slightingly (and of which Josephine in *The Pornographer* is evidently such an aficionado), comically draws attention to exactly this distinction between fiction and reality when she says that 'The good ended happily, and the bad unhappily. That is what Fiction means.'[84] In 'The Critic as Artist', Gilbert wittily suggests that 'Anybody can write a three-volume novel. It merely requires a complete ignorance of both life and literature.'[85] The arbitrary nature of real life, on the other hand, is summed up in the cynical Wildean simile coined by the priest in McGahern's story 'The Wine Breath', who can refer to something being 'as unfair as life' (*GT*, p. 105).[86]

Real life is characterised by its unfairness, fiction by the triumph of the moral order. One of the defining properties of the realist novel is that it is, in this sense at least, wholly *un*realistic. One paradoxical contrast between life and art in which McGahern marvelled was first expressed by him in an interview with Denis Sampson in 1979:

> I actually think that art and life are very different for very simple reasons, and a reason which has always amused me is that fiction always has to be believable, I mean that you have to convince the reader that it happened; but actually life shows its superiority in that it doesn't have to be believable, and that has always amused me.[87]

The same observation was repeated with undiminished gusto at the very end of his career in the 2006 preface to *Creatures of the Earth*, which stated that 'Among its many other obligations, fiction always has to be believable. Life does not have to suffer such constraints, and much of what takes place is believable only because it happens. The god of life is accident. Fiction has to be true to a central idea or vision of life' (*CE*, pp. vii–viii).[88] It is this idea of an 'idea' that is alluded to in the title of the story 'The Beginning of an Idea', in which the protagonist Eva Lindberg goes in search of a sense of 'calm and order' which she feels is missing from her life (*GT*, p. 24). In his development of this idea, McGahern may have taken his cue from a nineteenth-century example such as Dickens' ironic defence, in the author's preface to *Nicholas Nickleby*, of some of the more 'curious' and improbable aspects of his depictions:

> It is remarkable that what we call the world, which is so very credulous in what professes to be true, is most incredulous in what professes to be imaginary; and that while every day in real life it will allow in one man no blemishes, and in another no virtues, it will seldom admit a very strongly-marked character, either good or bad, in a fictitious narrative, to be within the limits of probability.[89]

Alternatively, his model may have been Pirandello's *Six Characters in Search of an Author* (a play that had made a lasting impression on him when he saw it in a small theatre in Dublin in the 1950s), in which the Father remarks to the Director that 'you must be well aware that life is full of endless absurdities which, bold-faced as they may be, do not even have to appear plausible, since they are true.'[90] The phrasing in the Sampson interview suggests that the latter was perhaps the more immediate source.

Even the narrator's uncle in *The Pornographer* adheres to this same principle. When the pornographer wonders whether the mourners at his aunt's funeral will believe the fiction he has concocted to explain the bruises to his face, his uncle cynically explains: 'What do you care whether they believe it or not? As long as they have no way of finding out!' (*P*, p. 232). What the pornographer's uncle is expressing is one of the generic aims of the eighteenth- and nineteenth-century novel as it was conceived by Defoe and his contemporaries, those great professional liars whose only ambition was to make the reader believe, by the sheer conviction of the narrative voice, that what they had made up had really happened.

A preference for coherent fictions — even if they are outright lies — over the mediocrity that often characterises real life is a trait shared by a number of the artists and intellectuals who appear in McGahern's fiction. That flamboyant mouthpiece of nineteenth-century thought Mulvey in 'Parachutes', for example, responds to the narrator's reminder that he had told him that Halloran was 'all right... You said he was a sensitive person' by offering a competing, opposite truth in the style of one of Oscar Wilde's plays: 'Oh, I was just making him up... You don't have to take what I say about people so solemnly. I am always making people up. People need a great deal of making up. I don't see how they'd be tolerable otherwise' (*HG*, pp. 20–1). Thus, far from being but a pale imitation of life as it is reflected in the 'looking-glass' of a painter or a writer, art is actually superior to life. McGahern, like a number of his protagonists, shares this paradoxical thought with nineteenth-century aesthetes like Wilde. The presence of an essay like 'The Decay of Lying' is clear in one of Maloney's assertions in *The Pornographer*: that a story is 'like a life, but with none of life's unseemly infirmities' (*P*, p. 21).[91] A few pages later he can in the same spirit adapt a joke of Mark Twain's (who had said that 'Everything human is pathetic. The secret source of Humor itself is not joy but sorrow. There is no humor in heaven'[92]) and volunteer the opinion that 'One of the reasons of art's supremacy is just because of the very limitations of life. There will be no art in heaven' (*P*, p. 25), a thought that was repeated by McGahern in his own voice when he wrote in a written response to an interviewer that 'The only fact about heaven that I can be certain about — if it does exist — is that there will be no writers there.'[93]

A Wildean belief in the superiority of art over life affects the way in which the narrator of *The Pornographer* looks at nature. During a romantic boat trip on the Shannon with his lover, he cannot bring himself to accept the beauty of the surrounding landscape at the fall of evening:

> the evening seemed so beautiful that it was hard to believe it was real. There had been so many interpretations of beauty as such an evening and scene that it had grown abstract and unreal. (*P*, p. 89)

It seems that fiction, not real experience, has become the protagonist's primary frame of reference. Every genuine sensation is translated into literary or painterly terms, so that a sunset is unfavourably compared to more awe-inspiring renditions of the same event in art. In this, the pornographer follows the example of Vivian, Wilde's mouthpiece in 'The Decay of Lying', who had argued that 'Nature, no less than Life, is an imitation of Art', and for whom the 'mysterious loveliness' of a sunset or a morning fog as it appears outside his drawing-room window appears as no more than a second-rate imitation of the work of any number of first-rate painters.[94] The pornographer is not alone among McGahern's narrators and protagonists in his preference for representations of reality over reality itself. The narrator of 'Faith, Hope and Charity', a story from the same period, at one point apparently suffers from the same affliction which makes him confuse things that are real with things that merely *mimic* reality and foreground the latter over the former. One of the apparently conventional realist description of things found in the countryside on a hot summer's day is concluded with the curious observation that 'Across the lake, just out from a green jet of reeds, a man sat still in a rowboat *as if* fishing for perch' (*GT*, p. 53, emphasis added). The two italicised words introduce a welcome sense of unreality into the narrator's world, which may temporarily distract him from the terrible news he has been sent to deliver at the Cunninghams. The addition of 'as if' transforms the paragraph from a straightforward realist description into one which questions the very reality of the tangible world which realism so confidently takes as its subject.

Even in his non-fictional prose does McGahern on one occasion allow himself a similar thought. This happens in his essay on 'County Leitrim', where he remarks that a stretch of the river Shannon near Knockvicar 'could have been painted by Constable' (*LW*, p. 23). Perhaps such a way of thinking about the unreality of the physical world was unavoidable for a writer like McGahern who had been introduced from a very early age through the teachings of the Catholic Church to the idea that the world itself was but a kind of fiction which merely reflected a deeper truth. This is a connection McGahern himself proposed in a fascinating aside in a 1991 *Irish Times* article about Ireland in the 1950s, 'From a Glorious Dream to Wink and Nod', in which he playfully reflected on the existence of a way of thinking which encouraged a sense of unreality in this Irish-Catholic environment. According to the rhetoric of the all-powerful Church in the mid-twentieth century, as he cynically remarked in that article, 'the doctrines and truths of the Church were realities besides which all worldly things were shadows, though the Church politic was increasingly intent on controlling and ordering the same shadow' (*LW*, p. 127). McGahern was not the first writer to describe the theocratic, inward-looking state during that period as a latter-day incarnation of Plato's cave, in which shadowy figures play out unreal lives. In fact, that idea in 'From a Glorious Dream' is a development of the historian F.S.L. Lyons' use of the same metaphor to describe Ireland's isolation during the Second World War in his *Ireland since the Famine*.[95] In 'From a Glorious Dream', however, the shadows contrive to be less constrained than those in *Ireland since the Famine*, as the Church can do no more than be *intent on* controlling what McGahern elsewhere describes as the 'sensible pagan lives' of the people (*LW*, p. 87).

McGahern's fiction constitutes a striking development of this idea that the external life is only an unreal reflection — and that art, no less than the heavenly ideal promised by the Church, may be the perfect original which life so haltingly imitates. The contrast between art and life in its various forms is an important subject throughout McGahern's career. His work is aware of their essential differences as acutely as that of some of his great nineteenth-century predecessors. Like those predecessors also, he knew that writing about the world involves not merely an act of *mirroring* the realities that can be found there, but of improving them by introducing a sense of coherence generally lacking in the original.

CHAPTER 5

A Modernist Mind I: Proustian Thought and Forms

> Lightfoot, not my friend since he found friendship disgusting, quoting Proust that it is the halfway house between physical exhaustion and mental boredom ... and I respect Lightfoot too much to claim him for a friend against his will.
>
> *The Leavetaking* (pp. 30–1)

The narrator's friend Lightfoot in *The Leavetaking* is quoting from *The Guermantes Way*, the third volume of Proust's *In Search of Lost Time*, one of the central achievements of European literary modernism.[1] A number of Proustian themes and ideas return in McGahern's fiction at different stages of his career. Many of the technical innovations and new ways of thinking about form and representation that were brought to bear on the novel by Proust and his modernist contemporaries were absorbed and adapted, and occasionally alluded to, in McGahern's fiction.

McGahern's introduction to modernism took place during his student days at St Patrick's College, Drumcondra, between 1953 and 1956, when through a number of fortuitous encounters he was introduced to the work of T.S. Eliot, Joyce, Proust and Beckett within the space of just a couple of years. The years spent reading the cornerstones of European modernism between classes as a live-in student at St Patrick's College, and later in his bedsit on the Howth Road while he was a young teacher at St John the Baptist's National School in Clontarf, mark a turning point in the development of his literary sensibilities. The turn from George to T.S. Eliot was for the young McGahern a crucial milestone on the road to becoming an artist equipped for expressing the fears and longings of the twentieth century. McGahern's teenage reading in Leitrim and Roscommon had been that of a previous age, shaped as it was by the Presentation Brothers' curriculum and by the contents of the Moroneys' library and his English teacher Mr Mannion's private shelves. As he remarked in retrospect, 'Mannion would not have known of Lawrence's or Joyce's existence; or Proust or even T.S. Eliot.'[2] The story 'Crossing the Line' alludes to the outmoded literary tastes McGahern had observed in many teachers in small provincial schools, perhaps first during his time as a pupil in Carrick-on-Shannon but especially later when he worked briefly as a teacher in Athboy and Drogheda. The newly qualified teacher who is the protagonist of that story is asked by the branch secretary of the teachers' union for the part of the country where he has just taken up a post 'what poets my generation was reading. He seemed unimpressed by the names I mentioned. His own favourite was Horace' (*HG*, p. 89).[3] Later in Clontarf, at least, McGahern joined a staff which also included the modern Irish-language short-story writer Donncha Ó Céileachair, whose conversation at break times allowed him to feel connected again to a vibrant modern tradition in a way he had probably not experienced in an educational institution since his fraternity with certain fellow-students in Drumcondra a couple of years earlier. When Ó Céileachair died young in July 1960, McGahern was just as keenly affected by the break in the continuity of what was best and most modern in the Irish tradition, and by the severing of his own link with that modern tradition, as he mourned the personal loss of a friend.[4]

In later decades McGahern would describe not only the creation of the modernist aesthetic but also its readership as a predominantly urban phenomenon. In a 1987 interview he contrasted his own sheltered literary upbringing in the country with that of a precocious, urban, Jesuit-educated author like Joyce, or by extension with that of those of his classmates in St Patrick's College who had been reared and educated in the capital.[5] Yet the course of his own life, and the trajectory he imparted to his work, are among the most powerful pieces of evidence against such a simplistic distinction between urban and rural forms. For McGahern succeeded in creating some of the most subtle works of late-twentieth-century modernism not from a fashionable self-imposed Parisian exile but from the artistic hinterland that is County Leitrim.

That Lightfoot in *The Leavetaking* should quote, of all the ideas coined by the narrator of *In Search of Lost Time*, Proust's disavowal of friendship is ironic because some of the friends McGahern made when he first moved to Dublin were crucial to his development as a reader of literary modernism. It is especially ironic since, as Denis Sampson points out, embedded in the same paragraph is McGahern's acknowledgement of one special literary friendship in particular. Lightfoot, who appears as the respective narrators' faithful bookish drinking companion in both 'Wheels' and *The Leavetaking*, is based on McGahern's friend Jimmy Swift, whom he met regularly in Dublin pubs and dance halls from late 1955 onwards to discuss books. In a letter written only a matter of weeks before his death, he described Jimmy Swift as 'Other than books, the main influence' of his literary life during that period.[6] Particularly important here is that it was through Swift that McGahern was first introduced to Proust, an author whose influence on his thinking about the themes and techniques of modern literature in the twentieth century, and on his expression of those newly formed aesthetic ideas and beliefs, was more obviously pervasive than that of almost any other author.[7]

During that same brief period in the mid-1950s he also discovered the work of Samuel Beckett. McGahern's initial introduction to Beckett was Alan Simpson's first Irish production of *Waiting for Godot*, which he saw either at the Pike Theatre in November 1955 or after it transferred to the Gate Theatre in 1956.[8] The memory of seeing that production — wherever precisely it took place during the course of that Dublin winter — remained vivid all his life. The revelation he experienced at that performance led him in the first place to read Beckett's prose in small magazines like *Irish Writing* (which published extracts short enough to be read in a single standing in the Eblana Bookshop), and then to seeking out the novels. McGahern would certainly have read *Watt* and *Murphy*, but when pressed on the matter in an interview he said that his favourite of Beckett's novels were *Molloy* and *Malone Dies*, while of the plays he returned most often to *All That Fall* and *Happy Days*, but also to *Krapp's Last Tape* and 'sometimes, but not so much [to *Waiting for Godot*]'.[9] (The latter phrase is a downplaying belied by the many incarnations of that play throughout his fiction.) All these novels and plays would become palpable presences in McGahern's own novels, stories and occasional dramatic writings over the next five decades, as he repeatedly turned to Beckett for ways of achieving narrative authenticity in the latter half of the twentieth century.

Other influences led him simultaneously to discover many of the other seminal authors of European modernism. Some were no doubt picked up at random from second-hand bookshops and from 'the extraordinary Mr Kelly', who sold books of uncertain provenance '[that] would now be described as modern classics' from a barrow on the corner of Henry Street (*LW*, p. 91). Just as importantly during those halcyon days of Irish literary censorship, he also sold banned books.[10] In a 2003 interview McGahern recalled that Kelly's stock included items such as first editions of Beckett, but his early enthusiasm for a writer like Thomas Mann may also have originated at the same fishy barrow.[11] Curiously, at least two of the other pivotal influences on his reading of modernist literature at this time were connected in some way or other with

St Patrick's College, that bastion of clerical anti-intellectualism in Upper Drumcondra. One of his teachers there fostered McGahern's appreciation of Yeats — whose early work, he recalled in an interview half a century later, 'was well known and in the school books, but not the great later poems'.[12] At the same time he was introduced to the work of both Joyce and T.S. Eliot by Éanna Ó hEithir, a 'brilliant classmate' who was a nephew of Liam O'Flaherty, the novelist and short-story writer whose life was spent between the Aran Islands, Dublin and Paris (*LW*, pp. 112, 115). Like many Irish writers of his generation, McGahern would later live for a brief spell in the Bohemian circles of Paris. Unlike many, he soon reassessed the sagacity of that choice after realising that much of what went on in those circles had very little to do with writing, and he eventually lampooned that Bohemian life in the 1974 story 'The Beginning of an Idea'. His friendship with the nephew of O'Flaherty a decade before that brief Parisian sojourn of the mid-1960s, however, was arguably his first tangential link to the culture of European modernism.

McGahern was more interested in the works and the ideas of that turbulent period in literary history than in anecdotes about the colourful private lives of that earlier generation of Parisian exiles. The parochial world of a novel like *That They May Face the Rising Sun* could not be further from the Bohemian metropolis, yet it appears as if the afterlife of literary modernism momentarily becomes an explicit topic on a late page of that novel. With its two separate references to Proustian 'involuntary' memories as well as an overt evocation of the title of T.S. Eliot's most famous poem, that single page towards the end of McGahern's final novel reads like a conscious act of homage to the classics of literary modernism, a page very much about the continuing importance of some of the key ideas of early-twentieth-century modernism in the literature of our time. When he looks at the site of the Shah's business empire, Ruttledge is struck by how:

> For a moment, the old living railway station stood there so vividly in his mind, like an oil painting of great depth, that the substantial square looked deranged. Nobody could ever have imagined that the little station, then the hub of the town, would become this half-wasteland… (*TRS*, p. 227)

This passage encodes the romantic yearning, undoubtedly experienced on many occasions by any number of contemporary novelists, for the unproblematic clarity of expression and representation which had been possible before the age of Proust, Joyce, Woolf and Eliot. It also acknowledges that giving in to such a longing would be foolish for a serious artist writing in the wake of high modernism. The 'deranged', broken-up vision of reality that belongs to modernist art — to T.S. Eliot and *The Waste Land*, say, or a painting by Picasso or Francis Bacon — is juxtaposed in this passage with the 'vivid' representational solidity of 'an oil painting of great depth'. While Ruttledge may prefer to see the world through the nostalgic eyes of a realist painter, he cannot escape from modernism's legacy of fragmentation and disjunction — what Virginia Woolf describes as the '[tearing] asunder' of the unity of perception of the Victorian world.[13] The Shah's 'deranged' half-wasteland of a square is no less than a version of Joyce's 'ruin of all space, shattered glass and toppling masonry' or Eliot's 'heap of broken images'.[14] The half-wasteland, though, is the contemporary reality which the characters must accept and inhabit. The vividness of realist art which appeals to Ruttledge so much, on the other hand, is no more than a dream or a reverie or an illusion which may momentarily displace the infinitely more complex and disorienting realities of modern experience. This is not a regrettable fact. After all, for all its visual unattractiveness or undesirability compared to the picturesque sight of a nineteenth-century railway hub in its full working glory, a wasteland is not imaginatively barren. Even the 'stony rubbish' of a wasteland, as Eliot demonstrates in the opening stanzas of his poem of that title, is capable of nourishing the branches on which memory and desire may flourish.[15]

These two chapters on McGahern's engagement with the legacies of European and Irish literary modernism, respectively, are concerned with McGahern's indebtedness to what are for him some of the key writers of the modernist period. Chapter six will focus on his interaction with Yeats and Joyce and with the Irish modernist tradition which developed in their wake. This chapter is concerned with McGahern's absorption of some of the ideas he had first encountered in his reading of Proust in Drumcondra and on the Howth Road in the second half of the 1950s. Inevitably, Beckett is an important presence in both these chapters on McGahern's modernist influences, as well as the foremost exponent of the post-war writers whose significance to McGahern's sensibility is the subject of the final chapter.

McGahern's Proust

McGahern would have read *In Search of Lost Time* in C.K. Scott Moncrieff's translation, in which it was controversially called *Remembrance of Things Past*, a title by which it remains known to many English speakers. It is clear that both English titles were presences in McGahern's mind, since he alludes in deliberate ways to both at different points in his fiction. The presence of Proust haunts McGahern's work in many ways. Not least of these are the obvious Proustian echoes in 'The Image', the essay which is at once a serious literary manifesto and a cheeky literary joke, a rewriting on a single page of typewriter paper of Proust's great multi-volume novel. The style as well as the contents of that early manifesto are deliberately reminiscent of that of Proust. Unlike that of any of McGahern's other prose — which is rich in Proustian ideas but generally shirks the rhetorical flourishes of *In Search of Lost Time* — the self-consciously literary, overtly allusion-laden voice of 'The Image' is a loving pastiche of flamboyant Proustian style. Many of the ideas in 'The Image' are as deliberately Proustian as its showy, intrinsically un-McGahernesque style. As chapter three discussed, its foregrounding of memory (especially of the involuntary variety) and image are obviously Proustian concerns, but other ideas and sentences in the same short essay equally bear the stamp of the recluse of the Boulevard Haussmann. Both the suggestion from volume two of *In Search of Lost Time* that 'great writers are gods, each of them reigning over a kingdom which is his alone' and the assertion in *By Way of Sainte-Beuve* that 'Style is . . . largely a record of the transformation imposed on reality by the writer's mind', for example, can be clearly heard in the prose of 'The Image'.[16]

McGahern's feeling of kinship with Proust is so deep that even when he came to write about the formative experiences of his own childhood in 'The Solitary Reader' in the 1990s, what seems like a straightforward autobiographical confession is really a deeply Proustian moment expressed in appropriate Proustian language. When he remarks in that essay that 'There are no days more full in childhood than those days that were not lived at all, the days lost in a favourite book' (*LW*, pp. 89–90), that thought is lifted word for word from the opening sentence of Proust's essay *On Reading*.[17] The rest of this chapter will concentrate not on such superficial echoes but on two key Proustian ideas central to McGahern's thinking. The first is his treatment of the complex nature of the individual subject and the self's relationship to the external world. The second is that of time, including, but not exclusively, Proust's celebrated treatment of memory.

'two things that have obsessed me all my life, . . . the Self and the Other'[18]

When Ruttledge and Kate in *That They May Face the Rising Sun* observe Robert Booth as he waits on a railway platform for the train that will take him back to the professional day-to-day reality of his London life, the narrator remarks on how the latter lives his life in a series of 'closed compartments' (*TRS*, p. 158). That remark not only makes for an immediately satisfying pun on the traditional layout of railway carriages; it also contains a self-conscious, even ironic commentary on one of the central concerns of McGahern's earlier fiction. Especially in the overtly experimental middle period of his career which spanned the period from *The Dark* to *The Pornographer*, McGahern regularly shows a Proustian awareness of the mutability of the individual subject, which inevitably affects his protagonists' relationships with all the other constantly changing individual subjects around them.

The effects of such compartmentalisation may be most obvious in a character like Robert Booth, the Irishman who has made a career for himself in England through the help of acting lessons which have helped him to perfect an English accent which makes him, like many Anglo-Irish writers throughout the nineteenth and twentieth centuries, appear like a foreign interloper to Irish ears when he is at home (Jamesie, for example, at one point describes him simply and without malice as 'The big Englishman' (*TRS*, p. 157)). However, a more subtle and imperceptible form of the compartmentalisation of the individual subject over time is at work in everybody. McGahern stresses this in many of his works. Thus, the protagonist of *The Pornographer* is wary of re-establishing contact with an old university friend because he knows that 'Calling him up out of the past was like calling up a ghost. There are more awkwardnesses than with a total stranger because of the dead barrier of memory' (*P*, p. 104). Similarly, the narrator of *The Leavetaking* realises, when he looks at a photograph of himself and a former lover, that he can no longer summon any feelings for that person. The significance of the outline of a woman's body in the photograph is to him no more than 'simple celluloid ... nothing, as the corpse we search for the person that has fled becomes any skin and bones ... We know leaving the house of the dead that the person we came to look on a last time has totally fled us and lives only among the shadows of memory' (*L*, p. 92). McGahern sharpened the observation of that passage from *The Leavetaking* by taking away the unnecessary whiff of poeticism when he rewrote it in the revised edition a decade after its first publication: 'the more I looked the further she went away. I was looking at celluloid that merely looked back. There was not even the sense of persons missing from empty spaces that will never be filled that way again' (*Lrev*, p. 91). In the revised version the idea can be applied not only to lovers or to friends but more universally to *all* things given to change or decay over time. That more universally applicable thought from the revised edition of *The Leavetaking* is reprised towards the end of McGahern's career when Fonsie in 'The Country Funeral' remarks that 'There's nothing more empty than a space you knew once when it was full' (*CS*, p. 386). The observation in the later story is ultimately just as much at home in the elegiac descriptions of the death of another ancient realm of Irish experience in the work of a novelist like Elizabeth Bowen (who implicitly makes a similar point in the description of the empty space where a house once stood on the final page of *The Last September*) as it is in Proust's elegy for lost youth and lost love.

The respective narrators' comments in *The Leavetaking* and *The Pornographer* both acknowledge, in a way that had been overtly argued by a modernist writer like Proust, how the self is far from constant. The 'impossible obstacle facing love', says Proust's hero Marcel in a famous passage from *The Prisoner*, the fifth volume of *In Search of Lost Time*, is that 'We imagine that love has for its object a being which can lie down before us, enclosed in a body. Alas! It is the extension of that body to every point in space and time which that being has occupied or will occupy.'[19] The changeable nature of selfhood is poignantly demonstrated in *The Pornographer* in the inevitable failure of that meeting between old friends who find that they have nothing left in common not because one party has had the audacity of wilfully changing his personality but because by the very nature of selfhood *both* have in the interval become different people. Proust dissects that process at length in the section in volume one of *In Search of Lost Time* which deals with the affair of Swann and Odette, and again in the Marcel–Albertine love story in volume five. That McGahern had early on identified the centrality of that theme in *In Search of Lost Time* is clear from a 1959 letter to Michael McLaverty in which he refers to 'Proust's great novel: the quarrel about the changing of love in time'.[20] In those volumes, which were later summarised by Beckett in some of the most famous and often-quoted passages of his early critical study of *In Search of Lost Time*, Proust elaborates his conviction that the individual is really 'a succession of individuals' because the individual subject and his aspirations die many deaths every day.[21] Proust's famous characterisation of the changeable nature of selfhood which is at the heart of all doomed love affairs as a kind of death is obliquely but unmistakably referenced, of course, when the narrator of *The Leavetaking* compares the sensation of encountering the likeness of a former lover with that of seeing a corpse.

The way in which McGahern's early characters conceive of the fractured multiplicity of their individuality is essentially Proustian. The most sustained exploration of that idea in his fiction is his use of the fluctuating point of view in *The Dark*, which has been likened by critics both to Proust and to Beckett.[22] Through the use of different pronouns, the reader is made to feel in each successive chapter of that novel how the narrator has become a different person from the one he had been before. Beside that audacious early experiment with form, more than one of McGahern's subsequent narrators also make explicit reference to the same Proustian instability of the individual subject. The narrator of *The Pornographer*, for example, refers to 'this painful becoming of ourselves' (*P*, p. 20), an idea which implies that an individual is never finished or completed but always a work in progress, subject to constant changes and revisions. The narrator of the story 'Doorways', too, experiences a sensation similar to that of the pornographer visiting his old university friend when he meets his old friend Jimmy at the Sligo train station at the start of his holidays. Encountering Jimmy is like seeing a ghost from a long-gone past, and so he reflects on how 'walking with him and remembering the part of our lives that had been passed together ... was like walking in a continuance of days rather than in the broken worlds of ourselves' (*GT*, p. 78). McGahern's constant recourse all the way through his career (including in that same story) to the force of 'habit', which works to resist change by offering to make every day of our lives into the same day, is one way of countering the painful effects of such fragmentation. The use of habit will be discussed in the final chapter of this book.

McGahern's analysis of selfhood is Proustian in another way, too. Not only does the individual's perception of his or her own identity and that of others exist in a state of constant change; the self's capacity for connecting with things external to it — including the individuals closest and most beloved to it — is also fraught with difficulties. Lightfoot in *The Leavetaking* is not the only one of McGahern's characters to share Proust's disgust with friendship. The central character in *Amongst Women* is as separate and inward-turned as the 'enclosed world' of Great Meadow which he has so deliberately created for himself and his family. The narrator comments on how, after the row with McQuaid on Monaghan Day, Moran 'had lost his oldest and best friend', but how, like Proust and like Lightfoot in *The Leavetaking*, 'in a way he had always despised friendship' (*AW*, p. 22). (That last sentence *also* contains an echo of the conclusion of Joyce's 'An Encounter': 'And I was penitent; for in my heart I had always despised him a little', a sentence McGahern had previously echoed at the conclusion of 'Lavin' (*N*, p. 100).[23]) In *The Guermantes Way*, Proust had written that 'friendship ... is totally bent on making us sacrifice the only part of ourselves that is real and incommunicable (except through art) to a superficial self', where it is 'hospitalized in the individuality of another person'. Friendship, Proust famously concludes, 'seemed to fall half-way between fatigue and boredom'.[24] And so, instead of the superficial attachment which friendship offers, Moran prefers 'that larger version of himself — *his* family' (*AW*, p. 22) or other versions of selfhood. References to Moran's self-sufficiency abound in *Amongst Women*. Rose is first attracted to his 'distinct sense of separateness' (*AW*, p. 23) — a description that is repeated in *That They May Face the Rising*

Sun when the narrative voice, probably focalised at that moment through the consciousness of Ruttledge, observes how Frank Dolan's 'very separateness was as impressive as the Shah's' (*TRS*, p. 211). When Moran realises that his annual Monaghan Day ritual with McQuaid is 'about to be broken up', he 'withdrew back into himself' (*AW*, p. 21); when his brother is late turning up to drive the family to the church on Moran's wedding day, he remarks that 'I should have learned by now never to rely on anybody' (*AW*, p. 40); and near the beginning of the novel, after reminding himself of his estranged son Luke, 'He went silent and dark *and withdrew into himself*, the two thumbs rotating about one another as he sat in the car chair by the fire' (*AW*, p. 4, emphasis added). Even the remark he makes while he is composing a letter to Luke — 'I suppose I might be as well off writing to myself for all the answer I'm likely to get' (*AW*, p. 4) — may be read as an ironic expression of his inwardness and self-sufficiency.Unlike Patrick Moran in *The Leavetaking*, Michael Moran in *Amongst Women* does not at any point seek to know the people around him. The closed-off, fortress-like structure of Great Meadow symbolically mirrors its owner's closely guarded individuality. Proust, after all, had already suggested how the self is like a self-contained building. Beckett's summary of the crucial passage from *In Search of Lost Time* is better known than the original:

> 'Man,' writes Proust, 'is not a building that can receive additions to its superficies, but a tree whose stem and leafage are an expression of inward sap.' We are alone. We cannot know and we cannot be known. 'Man is the creature that cannot come forth from himself, who knows others only in himself, and who, if he asserts the contrary, lies.'[25]

(McGahern had echoed precisely that passage in his interview with Denis Sampson in 1979 when he said that 'I happen to think that the person cannot emerge from the Self'. He echoed it again in another interview conducted in the year following the publication of *Amongst Women*.[26]) That Moran 'knows others only in himself', that he imagines them as creatures in his own image whose needs and interests and desires mirror his own, is confirmed by his attitude to his family, who are, to him, not individuals but simply an extension, a 'larger version' of himself. The narrative suggests that this is why he is 'ill at ease by the very suggestion of a shape other than his own' when it comes to his children taking on their own lives (*AW*, p. 74).[27]

Proust's narrator's awareness of the unknowable, secret nature of selfhood obviously affects his ability to make friends, even as he yearns to connect with another human being. The Saint-Loup section in *The Guermantes Way* from which the quote about friendship in *The Leavetaking* is taken makes this very clear. But the essential separateness of the self in the face of the unknowable other, the tragedy of a species who 'cannot know and ... cannot be known', had already been dramatised by Proust at much greater length in the love story of Swann and Odette in the first volume of *In Search of Lost Time*. The dynamics of McGahern's love stories from the 1970s are heavily indebted to Proust's analyses of selfhood, love and sexual jealousy. McGahern's love stories are often philosophical enquiries more than they are exercises in romantic escapism. The tales of jealousy and desire from his middle period invariably serve as ways of observing the nature of selfhood and human interaction, and often they follow a Proustian trajectory. Patrick and Isobel's light-hearted dance-hall banter in *The Leavetaking* about whether it is better to be in love or to be loved, and whether it would not be 'tiresome to have someone love you that you don't want' (*L*, p. 94), rehearses the difficult dynamic of unreciprocated desire that would be explored in greater detail in *The Pornographer*. The protagonist's description in that second novel from the 1970s of the 'usual enough pattern' of a previous failed relationship is more than a little reminiscent of the reasons for the failure of Marcel's pursuit of Albertine in *The Prisoner* and *The Fugitive*:

> We went out casually for a year. At first she did most of the running, and when she tired I took up the pursuit. It's a usual enough pattern. The more I pushed myself on her the more tiresome I became to her, and that speeded up her withdrawal, which made her ten times as attractive. I felt I couldn't live without her. Which made me ten times as tiresome. I was ill, lovesick, mad. If she'd finished it then it might have been easier, but who knows. She kept the thing going, interested in my madness ... (*P*, p. 80)

Clearly, Josephine's alienation of the protagonist could have been prevented if she had paid closer attention to this story instead of repeating the same classic Proustian dating offence of which the narrator's younger self had been guilty all those years earlier. The same pattern is repeated a number of times throughout the novel. Josephine will later chase the pornographer, which increasingly repels him; Jonathan's pursuit of Josephine makes her reject him; and the pornographer's obsession with the black-haired nurse does not exactly spur on her desire for him. What is more, the protagonist finds further sanction for his behaviour between the covers of a book — just as the young McGahern may have found his own youthful lover's pangs mirrored (in the manner that was discussed in the introduction of this book) in his reading, at an age when many find themselves most troubled by such things, of novelists like Proust and D.H.

Lawrence. When he searches for wisdom by picking random volumes from his shelves, he is struck by a sentence in Thomas De Quincy's *Recollections of the Lakes and the Lake Poets*, a book McGahern probably owned because it had recently been published in a Penguin Classics edition edited by David Wright, the London acquaintance who had co-edited *X* magazine with Patrick Swift in the early 1960s. The quote from De Quincy appositely sums up the same Proustian nature of human interrelations: 'Everybody must feel that a man who hates any person hates that person the more for troubling him with expressions of love; or, at least, it adds to hatred the sting of disgust' (*P*, p. 137).[28]

Proust suggests that the beloved, like any other stranger, has no unique individuality when we first meet them. As Beckett summarises Marcel's first glimpse of Albertine in Balbec: 'She has no individuality. She is merely one blossom in this fragile hedge of Pennsylvanian roses'.[29] This same idea is hinted at in McGahern's fiction. The notion of falling in love with the *idea* of love, rather than with an individual person, is one McGahern had already encountered when he read St Augustine's remark in the *Confessions* that 'I had not yet fallen in love, but I was in love with the idea of it ... I began to look around for some object for my love'.[30] He would find it expressed again in a sentence from John Williams' *Stoner* which he would later borrow in a short piece of non-fictional prose called 'Five Drafts' (*LW*, pp. 3–4).[31] It is important, though, that that idea is introduced in his earliest work by way of a Proustian allusion. The poetic title of McGahern's first, unpublished novel, *The End or the Beginning of Love* (a title about which he expressed his misgivings in a letter to Patrick Swift),[32] is taken from a passage in the second volume of *In Search of Lost Time* which describes the process of falling in love in a particularly unromantic way:

> *At the very beginning of love, as at its end*, we are not exclusively attached to a single beloved: it is the yearning to love, of which that person will be the loved outcome, and later the echo left in the memory, which wanders voluptuously in a place full of charms — sometimes deriving only from contingencies of nature, bodily pleasures or habitation — interchangeable and interrelated enough for it to feel in harmony with any of them.[33]

The repercussions of that Proustian observation survive in the characterisation of *The Dark*, the novel into which sections of that earlier unpublished novel were later incorporated. Neither the woman in the ad for a hair-removal product in the *Irish Independent* over which young Mahoney masturbates, nor Mary Moran, a local girl with whom he falls in love, have a strongly defined personality in the narrative. Both are little more than random ciphers in the narrator's 'yearning to love', no less so than the sexual 'athletes' (*P*, p. 21) who are the main characters of the titular pornographer's smutty stories in that later novel are only faceless (and initially nameless) placeholders onto which his readers can project the particularities of their own sexual desires. Such an understanding of the nature of love undermines the romantic notion of fate and destiny inherent in the traditional discourse of the romance novel.

The individuals who are to become our lovers begin their existence in our imaginations faceless; one of the great Proustian tragedies of the world of McGahern's fiction is that they are doomed to remain so ever after. Proust had remarked in numerous passages of his great novel that the essence of another person is condemned to remain an enigma even to the closest and most sympathetic of observers. McGahern repeatedly returns to that Proustian theme. His most sustained treatment of it is that in *The Leavetaking*. Patrick Moran, the narrator of that novel who is clearly a reader of either E.M. Forster or Aldous Huxley, is conscious of the difficulty he encounters in his attempt to relate to his beloved, and (in the original edition of the novel at least) he 'remember[s] in some dismay that we can only love what we know' (*L*, p. 121).[34] The essentially Proustian concern with the separation of self and other is visible in the text of both editions of that novel — perhaps most explicitly during a meeting between Patrick Moran and Isobel in a café near Liverpool Street Station which was cut from the 1984 revised edition, its central idea displaced into the argument of the author's preface (*L*, pp. 120–1; *Lrev*, p. 5). Its significance in the novel has been well documented by critics of McGahern's fiction, as well as by the author himself in repeated efforts to explain the rationale behind a novel which had often been mercilessly criticised by critics for its stylistic imbalance. Both in his 1979 interview with Denis Sampson and in his remarks on the novel's duality in the 1984 preface to the revised edition, McGahern discussed why he deliberately wrote the second half of the novel in a style of 'poor reportage' (*Lrev*, p. 5).[35] In the preface he explained how he conceived of *The Leavetaking* as an experiment to see whether the 'disparate' realities of the self (written in McGahern's habitual mellifluous prose) and the other (which is translated by the first-person narrator into the language of 'poor reportage') could be 'made true to one another' (*Lrev*, p. 5). That phrase from the preface to the revised edition echoes the exhortation from Matthew Arnold's 'Dover Beach' which had also come to the narrator's mind on the final pages of the original edition (*L*, p. 194): 'Ah, love, let us be true/ To one another!'[36] McGahern had a lifelong obsession with 'Dover Beach', and this, it seemed, was one of a number of subjects on which that poem had begun to answer back to him. It did so on more than one occasion throughout his career. Its tidal imagery can, after all, again be detected as a presence behind one of those reflective passages in which *Memoir* is so rich. Arnold's sea-tide metaphor is enlisted there to explain the distance between close friends or lovers: 'it may be… difficult to understand those close to us, whether that closeness be of enmity or love *or their fluctuating tides*' (*M*, p. 226, emphasis added).

The treatment of the self and the other in *The Leavetaking* has over the decades become a recurrent theme in the criticism of McGahern's work. Much less frequently remarked upon is the fact that the same 'obsession' is a theme also addressed in some of his other works dating from both before and after either edition of *The Leavetaking*. Many of McGahern's characters recognise the epistemological difficulty inherent in truly knowing or understanding another human being. That process is described as an almost mystical act in 'Along the Edges', a story that may be best read as a companion piece to *The Leavetaking* which in its two parts chronicles a doomed love affair from the perspective of the man and the woman, respectively. In the penultimate paragraph the narrator of that story points out that to imaginatively enter into the life of another is like an act of supplication, or even pilgrimage, when he says that 'They would have to know that they could know nothing to go through the low door of love, the door that was the same doorway between the self and the other everywhere' (*GT*, p. 120). The central metaphor of that sentence is borrowed from Evelyn Waugh's *Brideshead Revisited* (the 'worst book' of a writer whose sensibility and whose prose he admired),[37] in which Charles Ryder, looking back on his youthful search for love, also refers to the literal and metaphorical 'low door' which must be negotiated in order to gain access to the secret enclosed world of Sebastian.[38]

If the other cannot be reliably known, then it is equally clear to many of McGahern's protagonists how their own inner lives are just as inscrutable to those around them. The protagonist of *The Dark* is startled to discover how his sister Joan perceives him. The picture of himself in the eyes of another is strangely unfamiliar: 'You didn't know very much about yourself so. The mirror was before you now, temptation to probe to see other pictures of you in her mind, but it was no use, she had her life as well as you, every life had too much importance and unimportance to be only a walking mirror for another' (*D*, p. 94). That mirror-metaphor is revived in the late story 'The White Boat', in which the protagonist explains to himself why pretty young girls enjoy going to dances: 'She'd have seen, here, her beauty reflected more excitingly in men's eyes filled with desire and fear than in any mirror.'[39] Even amidst the apparently mirror-smooth third-person narrative of *Amongst Women*, the same preoccupation is once more raised in the narrator's summing-up of the aftermath of an argument between Moran and Rose, when 'Instead of recognition, all that the quarrel had incurred was a deepening blindness. He now knew less about her than the day they had first met in the post office, standing beside one another on the scrubbed hollow boards, waiting for the evening mail van to come' (*AW*, pp. 71–2). As if to mirror the impenetrable front presented by the appearance of another person, the only *certain* things, in that last description, are the external dimensions and textures of the physical world.

Tracing the lines of literary influence is rarely pure and never simple.[40] It must be added, therefore, that while the idea underlying the broken structure of *The Leavetaking* is essentially Proustian, and while McGahern seems to have found that it could be further poeticised with recourse to the language and imagery of Matthew Arnold, he had most likely also taken notice of extended treatments of it elsewhere in his wide reading. McGahern's interest in writing a novel about man's essential 'aloneness' and the futile attempts to connect to an unknowable other may be traced to his interest in D.H. Lawrence. In a passage in *Lady Chatterley's Lover* by which he may have been struck when he read Lawrence as a student at St Patrick's College in the 1950s or as a young teacher in the early 1960s (possibly in a copy illicitly obtained via 'the extraordinary Mr Kelly'), the heroine reflects how 'It's no good trying to get rid of your own aloneness. You've got to stick to it — all your life. Only at times, at times, the gap will be filled in. At times! But you have to wait for the times. Accept your own aloneness and stick to it, all your life.'[41]

In addition, it seems that his interest in the same idea was also renewed through the example of two of his favourite twentieth-century American novelists, F. Scott Fitzgerald and John Williams. In *Augustus*, first published two years before *The Leavetaking*, Williams had written a sentence which neatly sums up the same intentions that McGahern would ascribe to *The Leavetaking* in his 1984 preface to the revised edition: 'if one loves a friend, he does not become that other; he remains himself, and contemplates the mystery of one that he can never be, of selves that he has never been'.[42] It has been noted that McGahern in later years cited relevant passages from Williams' novels *Stoner* and *Augustus*, as well as from his preface to an anthology of English Renaissance verse, both in one of his interviews with Eamon Maher and in his introductions to new editions of those two novels.[43] The other American example that may be discerned behind *The Leavetaking* is F. Scott Fitzgerald's *Tender Is the Night*. In that, Fitzgerald's last completed novel, Dick Diver, a young psychiatrist, attempts to 'plunge over the Alpine crevasse between the sexes' in order to comprehend his wife Nicole who is also his patient. Dick, Rosemary and others in *Tender Is the Night* are painfully aware throughout, like Patrick Moran in *The Leavetaking*, of the impenetrable external surfaces that will not reveal the true thoughts and feelings of those to whom they are closest, as they regard their lovers' physical forms 'without the slightest idea as to what was in [their] head'.[44] That *Tender Is the Night* is employed as a conscious intertext in *The Leavetaking* is particularly suggested by the way certain story elements recall Fitzgerald's plot. Patrick Moran's wife Isobel reveals that she, like Nicole Diver, had started reading Freud and developed an interest in psychoanalysis as a tool for overcoming the traumas of the past (*L*, p. 131). There is also a passing resemblance between the incestuous relationship between Nicole and her father in *Tender Is the Night*, and that between Isobel and her father in the long section in part two of *The Leavetaking* which describes the traumatic past that has led Isobel to reading Freud in her maturity.

'Remembrance of things past . . .'

'Who cares about time? We know the time well enough' (*TRS*, p. 99), says Jamesie in *That They May Face the Rising Sun*, in a question reminiscent of Winnie's concern in Beckett's *Happy Days* with whether one 'may . . . still speak of time' in the current age.[45] Twenty years earlier in the story 'Gold Watch', the father had already rhetorically asked his son the same question — 'What use have I for time here anymore?' — before setting out methodically to destroy the flashy modern reminder of *tempus fugit* from the Montreal duty-free (*HG*, p. 116). If McGahern's characters often have no use for time, then many of them are also given, like St Augustine, to the melancholy knowledge that the course of time cannot be retarded. Thus, Maloney in *The Pornographer* parodically invokes the image of Cuchulainn facing down the sea in Yeats' *On Baile's Strand* when he suggests that turning back time and reversing the ageing process would be as futile as 'thrash[ing] the tide back with mere sticks, [or] even with the pure spirit' (*P*, p. 205).[46] Mary in *That They May Face the Rising Sun* more gently makes much the same point when she poignantly wonders 'how can time be gathered in and kissed? There is only flesh' (*TRS*, p. 125).

An acute awareness of the nature and perception of time permeates much of McGahern's fiction. As the next chapter will discuss, the narratives of his novels are rarely arranged chronologically. One reason for this is that McGahern knew how the strict chronology of the traditional realist novel, which relies on linear clock time, corresponds very poorly to the way time is perceived by actual human subjects. McGahern shares this interest in the subjective perception of time with modernist novelists like Virginia Woolf and Proust, as well as with early-twentieth-century thinkers like Henri Bergson and Walter Benjamin. The importance of clock time is repeatedly disparaged in *That They May Face the Rising Sun*. It is with deliberate irony that the novel begins with the sound of church bells ringing out over the lake, because nobody pays any heed to the time of day announced by the bells any more than they do to the teachings of the Church who put them there in the first place to remind the people of the urgency of their religious duties. At a public reading shortly after the publication of *That They May Face the Rising Sun*, McGahern remarked that when he began writing that novel, 'I decided to fill the house with at least fourteen clocks,' before pausing and adding with a mischievous smile, 'and none of them telling the right time.'[47] The image of a house filled with clocks all telling a different time to the exasperation of an owner — in this case, ironically, Jamesie, who so forcefully denies time's mandate — who has inherited them from a previous inhabitant is on the most basic level of course simply a marvellous comic touch, one that was first introduced into McGahern's work in the 'broken medley' of clocks chiming their different hours in Father Gerald's house in *The Dark* (*D*, pp. 65, 75).[48] In both novels, however, the same clocks are not just comic props but also a constant *memento mori*. This is especially obvious when the clocks in the later novel are all stopped as part of Johnny's funeral ritual, or when in *The Dark* they become a reminder of the oppression that can often be experienced at the hands of the 'whirligig of time'.[49] That phrase from the conclusion of *Twelfth Night* seems to be on the mind of the narrator of *The Dark* when he endeavours to fall asleep despite the ceaseless chiming of the many clocks, only to find that 'it was impossible to sleep, the mind a preying whirl' (*D*, p. 75).

It is clear from comments he made about certain other authors during the 1980s and 1990s that as he entered middle age, McGahern began increasingly to conceive of his perfect work of fiction as timeless, in the sense that 'people, as well as the setting and action, exist[ ] outside of time' (*LW*, p. 346). In his essays and reviews McGahern identified this quality of 'timelessness' in the epic art of Homer and that of Tomás Ó Criomhthain's *The Islandman*, as well as in the short stories of more recent writers like George Mackay Brown and Alistair MacLeod. He also found it in Primo Levi's account of life in Auschwitz in *If This Is a Man*, a book he overtly compared with *The Islandman* in a 1999 seminar for its identical sense of a life lived in a succession of individual days.[50] As he remarked, none of those narratives have a sense of time beyond that of 'the day, a single day breaking continually over the scene and the action' (*LW*, p. 265), so that anecdotes and incidents separated by hundreds of years and thousands of miles can easily become, in the imagination of such artists, 'all part of the same eternal day' (*LW*, p. 405). Those thoughts were repeated, in more or less identical sentences, in an essay and in two reviews whose publication spanned fifteen years.

Variations on these ideas can be found in many places in McGahern's occasional critical prose. In what may be intended as a deliberate play on the English novelist L.P. Hartley's famous remark that 'The past is a foreign country: they do things differently there', he wrote about Mavis Gallant's stories that 'Her prose can move seamlessly from the present to the past and back again, as if they were *one time and the same country*' (*LW*, p. 374, emphasis added).[51] Similar concerns are also referenced in his fiction. A version of McGahern's thoughts about Ó Criomhthain, Mackay Brown and MacLeod is projected onto the shape of the Shah's life in *That They May Face the Rising Sun*, whose habits are so perfectly regular that he manages to 'turn[ ] each day into the same day, making every Sunday into all the other Sundays' (*TRS*, p. 41). The whole of that novel is to some extent an embodiment of the timeless epic narrative ideal that McGahern had long observed and praised in other writers. In a novel such as *That They May Face the Rising Sun*, written after more than a decade of thinking about 'timeless' narratives during the 1980s and 1990s, there is no sense of linear progression, no time-dependent plot. Instead, each episode follows the last more like a succession of paintings in an art gallery than a series of carefully plotted events in a novel.

McGahern shares his sense of timelessness not only with the epic imaginations of ancient Greece and modern-day Orkney and Nova Scotia but also with the sensibilities of early-twentieth-century modernists like Proust, Woolf and Eliot. The theme of timelessness is explicitly addressed in *That They May Face the Rising Sun*. Early in that novel, Patrick Ryan tells a story about a farming accident that had happened long ago when he was just a young boy, and which he had not witnessed first-hand. The narrator remarks how even though Patrick Ryan had never actually seen any of the things of which he speaks, 'he could see the man sitting on the single-bar mowing machine and the young horse and the big trees of an enclosed meadow as real, as real as if he had been there'. When Kate remarks in response to this that she believes that 'The past and present are all the same in the mind . . . They are just pictures' (*TRS*, p. 73),[52] she is echoing the Irish-language poet Seán Ó Ríordáin, who had said, as McGahern recalled in a 1999 seminar, that 'There are no differences between the living and the dead in our mind'[53] — or indeed the opening lines of T.S. Eliot's *Four Quartets*:

> Time present and time past
> Are both perhaps present in time future,
> And time future contained in time past.
> ... all time is eternally present ... [54]

Kate's remark also replicates McGahern's own convictions about the function of art. It is reminiscent of a comment he made in an interview not long before the publication of *That They May Face the Rising Sun*, when he said that 'We can say that writing memorializes, stops time, allows us to see more clearly, enables us to find out certain things'.[55] It also recalls a sentence which McGahern often identified as one of his favourite descriptions of art: the reference of Donald Gordon (McGahern's old mentor at the University of Reading) to Yeats' poems as an 'art that abolishes time and establishes memory'.[56] In such an art the significant 'permanent or impermanent images'[57] at the heart of the literary imagination are not *placed in time*, as they are in a realist novel, but rather 'Snatch[ed] out of time' as they might be in an important poem.[58]

There is, of course, a great paradox at the heart of this. Memories exist *within* time and are dependent on time, because the remembering subject must grow older and time must pass in order for things to be forgotten and then again remembered; yet they are simultaneously also *outside* and independent of time, impervious to its passing. So while their plots often rely on the passing of time, the majority of McGahern's novels and stories, like those of Proust and Woolf and many other modernist writers, are anti-chronological or 'timeless' — in nature. Following the example of novels like *Mrs Dalloway* and *In Search of Lost Time*, which had, in the words of one commentator, 'brought into a simultaneous relationship the past and the present of [the] narrator', McGahern's fiction often seeks to abolish the linearity of the realist novel.[59] His novels and stories often follow a more fluid narrative pattern which moves effortlessly between memories of things past, experiences of things present, and even dreams of things still to come.

Many of McGahern's narrators are aware of the Proustian conundrum that it is easier to live in the anticipation and memory of things than in the immediacy of the present moment. The narrator of *In Search of Lost Time* talks about the way our pasts 'project in front of [us] that shadow of itself which we call our future', which makes us think that the purpose of our lives is to make 'past dreams com[e] true' rather than revelling 'in the simple bliss of the passing moment'.[60] Such Proustian knowledge sits heavily on the minds of various narrators from the fiction of the 1970s. During his recollection of a hospital visit to his dying aunt, for example, the narrator of *The Pornographer* remarks that:

> Now that it was taking place it amounted to the nothing that was the rest of our life when it too was taking place. It would become part of our life again in the memory. In both the apprehension and the memory it was doomed to live far more vividly than in the taking place. Nature had ordered things well in that we hardly lived our lives at all. (*P*, p. 13)

The opening paragraph of 'Doorways', from *Getting Through*, revisits the same idea when the narrator observes how 'There are times when we see the small events we look forward to — a visit, a wedding, a new day — as having no existence but in the expectation. They are to be, they will happen, and before they do they almost are not: minute replicas of the expectation that we call the rest of our life' (*GT*, p. 69). The reliving of key events from the past in the memory, in particular, is of course a generally acknowledged constant of McGahern's fiction, as a majority of his narrators are engaged in a reconstruction in the past tense of episodes from their early lives.

Memory is one of the major themes of McGahern's fiction. The narrative strategy of much of McGahern's fiction relies on his narrators' ability to bring memories from the past into the present day. Proust is undoubtedly a crucial presence behind the technical challenge of imaginatively recovering the past, although memory is not a theme he found *exclusively* in Proust when he first read *In Search of Lost Time* during the 1950s. McGahern had encountered, or would encounter around the same time, reflections on the nature of memory in other texts as various as Wordsworth's poems, Tolstoy's *The Death of Ivan Ilych* and Thomas Hardy's 'Under the Waterfall', with its invocation of 'The sweet sharp sense of a fugitive day/ Fetched back from its thickening shroud of gray'.[61] In addition to such modern literary texts, he had also become fascinated with 'the great passage on memory in St Augustine's *Confessions*' (*LW*, p. 74), which remained a staple in the reading of young Irish Catholic intellectuals during the middle decades of the twentieth century, and which often prefigured later Proustian insights. Over the decades he singled out the treatment of memory in all those texts and authors in essays, letters and interviews.[62]

Despite all those other influences on his thinking about time and memory in the novel, however, McGahern on more than one occasion unambiguously signalled the centrality of his debt to the example of Proust's novel. Perhaps the most obvious instance of this is that in 'The Wine Breath', a story described by Denis Sampson as a 'perfect Proustian exercise'.[63] The main character of that story is transported, through the vision of white beech chips scattered on the ground like snow which suddenly take on 'an incredible sweetness of light', from the 'solid world ... everywhere around him' into 'another day, the lost day of Michael Bruen's funeral nearly thirty years before' (*GT*, p. 95). Critics have convincingly established the story's passing similarities with *The Death of Ivan Ilych* and Joyce's 'The Dead'. It seems certain, however, that the analogy with *In Search of Lost Time* is uppermost in McGahern's intentions for the treatment of memory in 'The Wine Breath'. The presence of Proust is palpable throughout in the story. His description of the protagonist's sensation of 'suddenly falling through time' (*GT*, p. 97) contains an unmistakable nod to Marcel's description of a man falling asleep in the opening pages of *The Way by Swann's*: 'then the confusion among the disordered worlds will be complete, the magic armchair will send him travelling at top speed through time and space'.[64] What is more, the repeated references to 'the lost day' and 'these dead days' (*GT*, pp. 95–7) pay even more unambiguous homage to the lost time of the title of Proust's novel. The example of Proust is present on the level of the narrative's formal structure, too. Proust is famous for his introduction of sense-memories, as Marcel is transported back to his childhood initially through the smell of the madeleine dipped in tea and later through other tastes, sights and sounds. In 'The Wine Breath', as Bertrand Cardin has noticed in his scrupulous close reading of the story, McGahern dutifully replicates Proust's use of all the senses by ensuring in a meticulous act of narrative patterning that 'Each transition period which causes the character ... to slip into a past memory is associated with a particular sense. Indeed, the five transition periods which are driving forces triggering recollections, correspond to the five senses.'[65]

McGahern is at all times aware of the distinction between what Proust calls 'voluntary' and 'involuntary memory' — a term that is borrowed in 'The Image', where he writes about the artist's business of recording images from the past as they flow 'involuntarily' through his mind (*LW*, p. 5). 'It is a waste of effort for us to try to summon [the past], all the exertions of our intelligence are useless. The past is hidden outside the realm of our intelligence and beyond its reach,' Proust writes in a well-known early passage of *In Search of Lost Time*, and so to summon a 'voluntary memory' can only yield images that are 'really quite dead'.[66] Despite these warnings, the past can on some rare occasions be deliberately invoked by McGahern's protagonists. Elizabeth Reegan in *The Barracks* knows that opening the trunk she always keeps locked upstairs (like something from a Gothic novel) and handling the contents associated with an earlier period of her life can sometimes mean being allowed again to 'experience blindingly' what she then felt (*B*, p. 39). In other works such as *The Leavetaking* and the story 'A Slip-up', the respective main characters patrol in their minds the stretch of river or the rundown farm they have left to come to the city. Each voluntarily conjures at a time of great mental crisis what the narrator of the latter story refers to (in a Proustian phrase identical to that used by the narrator of 'The Wine Breath') as the 'dead days' of an earlier period when they had been happier (*L*, p. 102; *GT*, pp. 31–3). As Denis Sampson was the first to point out, in those works McGahern borrows a visualisation technique used by republican prisoners during the War of Independence which he had found described in Ernie O'Malley's *On Another Man's Wound*, and which offered, Sampson suggests, 'an implication ... that a conscious mental training may lead to a kind of escape from consciousness which McGahern associates with the creative state'.[67]

Generally, however, conscious or 'voluntary' attempts to regain lost time are as doomed as the wilful attempts to achieve visionary clarity of a character like Moran in *Amongst Women* 'walking the fields like a man trying to see' (*AW*, p. 130).[68] To an imaginatively void character like Maloney in *The Pornographer*, who regretfully concedes that to fight the passing of time would be like trying to 'thrash the tide back with mere sticks' (*P*, p. 205), the idea that the past might be reclaimed by any other means than with brute force is unimaginable. The very different sensibility of an artist like Eva Lindberg in 'The Beginning of an Idea', by contrast, is constantly aware of the power of things spontaneously or involuntarily entered upon. Thus, Eva is enabled to find a rare period of happiness during an unplanned stopover in Barcelona, where she spends her days wandering around purposelessly. The very lack of purpose or intention makes her enjoyment possible, as the Proustian narrator of the story explains: 'As an army in peacetime she was doing what she had to do by being idle and felt neither guilt nor need to strive to make the holiday, always the death of any chance of actually enjoying it' (*GT*, p. 22). Ruttledge in *That They May Face the Rising Sun*, too, is worried on more than one occasion that to will or wish a moment of complete happiness into being, or even to be consciously aware of it as it occurs, would dispel the magic of the moment:

> he felt that this must be happiness. As soon as the thought came to him, he fought it back, blaming the whiskey. The very idea was as dangerous as presumptive speech: happiness could not be sought or worried into being, or even fully grasped; it should be allowed its own slow pace so that it passes unnoticed, if it ever comes at all. (*TRS*, p. 183)

That thought was anticipated by the priest in 'The Wine Breath', who had also considered with hindsight that 'He must have been what is called happy' when he lived with his mother in the presbytery before her death (*GT*, p. 102). Both those works' descriptions of the elusive nature of happiness, which it is acknowledged can only exist with recourse to memory, probably owe something to a passage on the nature of happiness in St Augustine's *Confessions*.[69]

Ruttledge even explains the shape of the local town using the same Proustian psychology which dictates how involuntary processes are generally more likely to succeed than premeditated acts:

> No two houses were alike in the long, wide, winding main street. People had come in from the country and mountain and put down a new house next to the last built house without any thought other than to shelter together and survive and trade. To prosper was such a distant dream that it was both dangerous and unlucky to even contemplate. (*TRS*, p. 227)

The danger of such deliberate anticipations of happiness is most starkly demonstrated in the same novel in the tragedy of Bill Evans. Earlier, his neighbours have realised that his weekly outings to the town on 'the bus' as part of a charitable scheme must be 'pure heaven' for the elderly recluse (*TRS*, p. 112). It is only inevitable that as soon as he begins 'living these bus rides on Thursday in the mind', he sows the 'seeds of calamity' (*TRS*, p. 212). The pleasures of anticipation which Bill Evans allows himself on that occasion only serve to make him vulnerable to the disappointment of 'being stopped' from going on the bus one Thursday, a shock which temporarily destroys the stability of his world. Equal disappointment awaits Miss McCabe, the spinster who pursues the narrator's father in the story 'The Stoat'. Miss McCabe's 'dream of her future life, of what she hoped to become', was 'still in the womb of time' (*GT*, p. 60), and its gestation is cut short despite, or perhaps because of, the fervidness of her wish for the dream to become reality.

Proustian involuntary memories can be found at crucial moments in McGahern's fiction at all stages of his career. In the opening chapter of *The Barracks*, when Elizabeth can suddenly see herself as others see her and is shocked by what she realises she has become, she is troubled by a sudden memory of her youth which contrasts with the reality of the present day in the barracks kitchen: 'to plague her, a vision of herself in London before the war flashed on her mind, a spring Sunday in London, when the light is grey and gentle as anything on earth' (*B*, p. 21), a sentence which faintly but surely echoes Wordsworth's sonnet about the awakening of visionary powers in central London:

> Earth has not anything to show more fair . . .
> This City now doth, like a garment, wear
> The beauty of the morning; silent, bare . . .[70]

In *The Pornographer*, the novel which most closely imitates the circular narrative structure of *In Search of Lost Time*, the narrator is repeatedly conscious of how 'fragment[s] of another day' may 'linger' in the present (*P*, p. 252). This happens during his visits to his dying aunt in the hospital, as well as during a taxi ride in the hospital grounds with nurse Brady, when a familiar 'old sweet scent' of freshly cut grass reminds him of the smells which 'surrounded the summers of my life' in the country (*P*, pp. 172–3). A lingering 'fragment of another day' also presents itself to him during the drive in the rain with Maloney with which the novel ends, when a lingering memory of the raincoated figure of his uncle brings him to complete the Proustian narrative circuit of the novel.[71] At the other end of McGahern's career, near the conclusion of his writing life in 'Creatures of the Earth', Mrs Waldron also finds, in a moment very similar to that experienced by Elizabeth in her barracks kitchen, how 'without warning, a buried memory of her father scattered the day' and 'displaced this actual day of her life' (*CE*, pp. 325–6). Even McGahern's retrospect on his own life in his final book contains at its core a description of the involuntary Proustian sensations, so similar to those experienced by Marcel on the Guermantes Way in the first volume of *In Search of Lost Time*,[72] which connect the mature novelist to the world of his childhood. On rare occasions when he walks in his maturity along the same lanes he once walked with his mother, he writes in *Memoir*, 'the actual lane and the lost lane becom[e] one for a moment in an intensity of feeling, but without the usual attendants of pain and loss. These moments disappear as suddenly and as inexplicably as they come, and long before they can be recognized and placed' (*M*, p. 4).[73] So the novelist's life can momentarily seem as timeless as the narratives of some of his favourite books.

'. . . and dreams of things to come'

Not only memory but anticipation, too, is a potent force in McGahern's fiction. Often anticipation takes the form of 'waiting' (a word whose Beckettian connotations will be discussed in the final chapter of this book), but it also extends beyond the often crippling effect of that idea into the realm of the joyous. Reegan in *The Barracks* lives not only for the theatrical re-enactments of his confrontations with Superintendent Quirke but also for the anticipation of the witty repartee that might ensue from future meetings. Old Mahoney in *The Dark* derives great pleasure from the prospect of taking his son to the Royal Hotel for a celebratory meal, even if the subsequent experience of actually being there turns out to be, for a variety of reasons, a prolonged act of torture for both father and son.

In his later years McGahern increasingly refined his technical mastery of working in a novelistic tense between past and future. Much of the drama of his final novel is played out in the spaces between the past and the future tense. It has been remarked by one of McGahern's most careful readers that the ideal tense of a novel like *That They May Face the Rising Sun* is the future-perfect, 'the tense in which one can say that this will have been a happy day'. That line from Beckett's *Happy Days* is a palpable presence underlying the Ruttledges' deep unspoken sense 'that there would come a time when these days would be looked back on as happiness' (*TRS*, p. 206).[74] Perhaps the best example of McGahern's use of the future tense in that novel is the introduction of Jamesie's brother Johnny. Long before he actually makes his appearance in the here and now of the lakeside world, Johnny's life is outlined in a series of utterances in the future and the past tense, respectively. The story about Johnny's youthful misfortunes, like many of the characters' anecdotes about the past in that novel, uses the third-person preterite which is the preferred mode of many a nineteenth-century novel. Before the commencement of that history, however, Johnny is first introduced not in the past but in the future tense. His impending annual visit home is initially reported in a dazzlingly brilliant piece of writing which moves between Jamesie's wildly enthusiastic dreams of things to come in the simple future tense ('I'll meet the train with Johnny Rowley. We'll have several stops on the way from the station. When we get to the house, Mary will put the sirloin down') and the narrator's more dispassionate subjunctive, both of which are based on the predictable pattern of previous instalments of Johnny's annual visit to his native lakeside:

> The house and the outhouses would be freshly whitewashed for the homecoming, the street swept, the green gates painted, old stakes replaced in the netting wire that held Mary's brown hens in the space around the hayshed. Mary would have scrubbed and freshened all the rooms. Together they would have taken the mattress from the bed in the lower room . . . and left it outside to air in the sun. (*TRS*, p. 4)

This kind of vivid, quickening anticipation is a kind of remembering, too — remembering of things which have not yet happened but which are no less vivid for it, due to the power of the imagination coupled, in this case and in many others, with a deeply ingrained sense of habit. Eamon Grennan insightfully comments on McGahern's use of this unusual grammatical tense when he writes: '*would* generates a tense poised between past, present, and future — a sense of continuous and repeated action, the consequence of which is to give to ordinary acts the quality of ritual — which is action repeated and repeated ... [a] sense of the ceremonial, of ritual'.[75] The final paragraphs of *Memoir*, a book written in the past tense about a world that no longer exists, are narrated in the same wishful, wistful subjunctive:

> If we could walk together through those summer lanes ... we probably would not be able to speak, though I would want to tell her all the local news.
>
> We would leave the lanes ... I would want no shadow to fall on her joy and deep trust in God. She would face no false reproaches. As we retraced our steps, I would pick for her the wild orchid and the windflower. (*M*, p. 272)

Like all anticipations, the repeated *woulds* of these future scenarios which the young boy had once imagined, and which the mature novelist, by now in his seventies, imagines still, will never come to pass. Yet despite this they can still bring immense solace.

It is also true, however, that McGahern is aware of the delusions which are often contained in living so purely through dreams of a rosy future. The same events so joyfully anticipated by Jamesie on the opening pages of *That They May Face the Rising Sun* are again invoked much later in the novel when Mary, in a piece of future-tense writing of her own which draws on her experiences of things past, offers a cynical corrective to Jamesie's initial childlike excitement: '"This fella gets all excited every summer when Johnny is coming. The place is done up. The best sirloin is ordered. Then what does he do when Johnny *does* come home? He disappears ...," Mary accused' (*TRS*, p. 190). *That They May Face the Rising Sun* contains various cautious reminders of the drawbacks of living exclusively in the past and in the future tense. The Ruttledges may sometimes share the temptation for looking back or forward in time with characters in McGahern's earlier novels and stories. At the same time, however, they are more consciously aware of the way the present can easily be squandered by anticipating the future or dwelling on the past. In a conversation about the way the dominant religious culture in Ireland has long influenced the way people think about their time in the here and now, Ruttledge remarks (with what may be intended as an echo of Hamlet's description of death as an 'undiscovered country'[76]) on how

> 'The greatest country in Ireland was always the world to come.'
>
> 'And all we have is the day.'
>
> 'We better make the most of it,' Ruttledge kissed her lightly as they rose. (*TRS*, p. 200)

The married couple at the centre of *That They May Face the Rising Sun* are acutely aware of how the future tense of the anticipation of things to come has been officially sanctioned by the Catholic Church to repress their flock's enjoyment of the present. The many references in the same novel to the obsession felt by some with the historical past suggest that *it*, too, has a habit of being more real for people such as Jimmy Joe McKiernan or Big Mick Madden, the book's two militant nationalists, than the present they actually inhabit. Harbouring feelings of preference for a rosy historical past in which things were (or were reported to be) more pleasant than in the present, or for a wishful future that may yet be achieved by military, political or cultural means, is in many ways a stereotypically Irish trait, one fit for a country whose history remains partially unresolved. As the novel shows, though, such ways of thinking are ultimately unsatisfactory, because to live so fully in the past or in the imagined future will soon become an obstacle to experiencing the simple joys of the present. Big Mick Madden may mock Jamesie's obsession with hearing the year's first cuckoo when he says that 'Elsewhere they are putting men on the moon and flying to the stars and here we have clients with their ears to the ground trying to be first to hear the cuckoo!' (*TRS*, p. 246), but his own obsession with commemorative parades equally blinds him to contemporary concerns, and leaves him out of step with the historical era in which he is condemned to live just as much as his neighbour.

McGahern found an expression of the malaise that may result from living exclusively in religious or political anticipation in Kate O'Brien's *The Ante-room*. In his notes on that novel he copied the sentence from the conversation in book two, chapter four from which it takes its title. That sentence draws attention to how many of the characters live in 'expectancy' — of renewed political energy following the fall of Parnell, of the start of a love affair, or simply of gaining access to heaven — so that 'Today is an ante-room', merely a vestibule in which they listlessly await the better political, romantic or spiritual fortunes of tomorrow.[77]

One of the philosophical challenges of everyday living, it appears then, is to live fully in the present, in what Proust described as 'the simple bliss of the passing moment'. While for Proust's narrator it is neither possible nor desirable to fully live in the present moment — Marcel does after all feel light-hearted, anxious and disoriented on that occasion when he feels the present minutes 'segregated' from the rest of his life[78] — it is a skill considered increasingly desirable in McGahern's later fiction. In the central passage about mortality in *Memoir* which was quoted in an earlier chapter, for example, McGahern warns that the 'blinding fear' of death, like the 'idle apprehension [of] what ... Time would bring', can easily become 'an impairment to the constant alertness needed to answer all the demands of the day' (*M*, p. 116).[79] Or as the narrator of *Amongst Women*, who is it seems as effortlessly versed in Horace as the classically schooled protagonist of *The Dark*, observes: 'There is nothing more difficult to seize than the day' (*AW*, p. 106).

The idea of 'the day' is a central one in McGahern's thinking. He articulated the idea that 'the basic unit of time is the day' (*LW*, p. 265) in the essay about *The Islandman* which was originally written under the critical sway of Paolo Vivante and E.R. Dodds in the mid-1980s, when he had already started working on the novel that would become *Amongst Women*.[80] Critics have naturally taken to identifying the aesthetic aims of that novel published in 1990 with the example McGahern had found in *The Islandman*,[81] but the same emphasis on seizing the day is also present, arguably in more concentrated form, in a short story from the same period. The titular anti-hero of 'The Creamery Manager', first published in *Krino* in 1987, stresses the same wisdom when he reminds Guard Casey and the sergeant of the importance of unconditionally enjoying their day out, without questioning either the expense or the possible future repercussions of things that give pleasure in the here and now. To do so would make us, as the narrator of *The Pornographer* had feared, 'hardly live[ ] our lives at all'. The creamery manager's repeated insistence on the importance of enjoying 'a day out, a day out of all our lives' which becomes the story's refrain (*CS*, pp. 368, 373) echoes a sentence from Robin Flower's translation of *The Islandman* which McGahern singled out for attention in his essay on that book. 'There is a haunting phrase that echoes like a refrain throughout,' McGahern wrote in the essay:

> *lá dár saol.* Flower translates it simply as 'a day of our lives', but it is probably untranslatable. The phrase conveys the whole life of a person as being formed by a succession of single days. When he apologizes for the waste of a day in Dingle ... there is the physical sense of the day being taken out of the succession of days and squandered like money. (*LW*, pp. 264–5)

By echoing that same phrase, 'The Creamery Manager' explicitly takes up the challenge of the 'untranslatable' wisdom of Ó Criomhthain's archaic, insular epic, and suggests how its relevance continues, perhaps with increased urgency, among the many distractions of late-twentieth-century middle-class modernity.

For all the joys and consolations that living in the present brings, it can also be hazardous, if it is the only way one *can* live. To seize the day must be a conscious choice, and not a life sentence one is condemned to serve. In McGahern's world, access, where necessary or appropriate, to memory and anticipation are as crucial a prerequisite to happiness as an ability to enjoy the passing moment. While the realisation that much of their life is lived in anticipation and retrospect is coloured for the narrators of earlier works like 'Doorways' and *The Pornographer* with more than a tinge of regret, *That They May Face the Rising Sun* shows the necessity for possessing an ability for entertaining those alternative temporal perspectives. This is demonstrated above all in the descriptions of a recurring minor character called Bill Evans, a survivor of institutional violence who is conceived as a kind of antithesis to Moran in *Amongst Women*. While Moran had found it impossible to let the past be the past and spends his whole life reminiscing about lost glories even as he ironically demands that his life should be seen as a 'continuing present' (*AW*, p. 3), Bill Evans can *only* live 'from moment to moment, from blow to blow, pleasure to pleasure, refusing to look forward or back' (*TRS*, p. 212). McGahern had found a philosophical exposition of the circumstances which lead to living exclusively and obsessively in the present moment in one of the most harrowing works of twentieth-century prose, and transposed it to the idyllic lakeside setting of *That They May Face the Rising Sun*. In a seminar on Primo Levi's *If This Is a Man* at University College, Dublin, in 1999, when the work on *That They May Face the Rising Sun* was slowly beginning to come to a conclusion, he had remarked how he saw 'sorrow as a kind of blindness'.[82] What he meant by this is illustrated when the narrator of *That They May Face the Rising Sun* remarks how Bill Evans has been so badly scarred by the experiences of his past that he has disavowed the use of memory altogether and lives his life confined in 'a small closed circle of the present' (*TRS*, p. 167). That observation closely echoes a sentence from Levi's analysis of the psychological trauma suffered by the inmates of the Nazi death camps in their attempt to cope with their loss of humanity in *The Drowned and the Saved*: 'We had not only forgotten our country and our culture, but also our family, our past, the future we had imagined for ourselves, because, like animals, we were confined to the present moment.'[83] The same important lesson from Primo Levi can be felt behind a comment McGahern made shortly after the publication of *Amongst Women*, that novel about a man who unreasonably demands that his life be seen as a 'continuing present' (*AW*, p. 3), when he explained to an interviewer that 'Anyone who wants to ignore the past becomes uncivilised: without a past things become brutish.'[84]

Bill Evans has learned to live completely in the present moment, and questions about his past are invariably greeted with the same hostile response as reminders of things to come. McGahern uses a wide range of appropriate literary allusions in his depiction of this trait. Early in the novel, when Ruttledge questions Bill Evans about the painful past life which he knows only in outline from local gossip and first-hand knowledge of seeing similar cases during his time as a student in Drumcondra, 'A look of rage and pain crossed his face. "Stop torturing me," he cried out' (*TRS*, p. 12). His tortured cry echoes through the novel. Most notably, it is repeated during a car journey to John Quinn's third wedding lunch, when Patrick Ryan teases Bill Evans with the prospect of the big meal which awaits them there (a detail which itself revives Primo Levi's description in *If This Is a Man* of a fellow-inmate who 'talks endlessly about some marriage luncheon and remembers with genuine regret that he failed to finish his third plate of bean soup', a detail described in comical language which fails to veil the tragic realities of such an existence[85]):

> 'Stop it, Patrick,' Bill Evans called out as if in pain … 'Stop torturing me, Patrick.' The cry was terrible … The cry cut through the years to the evening he was questioning Bill Evans after he came starving to the house: 'Stop torturing me.' It was the same unmistakable cry that had to be bowed to then as the silence in the car respected it now. Bill Evans could no more look forward than he could look back. He existed in a small closed circle of the present. Remembrance of things past and dreams of things to come were instruments of torture. (*TRS*, p. 167)

The hungry savage dependent Bill Evans may strike readers initially as a latter-day Caliban. Unlike the wild creature from *The Tempest*, however, Bill Evans cannot look forward in joyful anticipation to meals to come. In the end his repeated plea to 'Stop torturing me' whenever he is reminded of the passing of time is probably intended not so much as a reminder of Caliban's repeated plea toward his social superiors in *The Tempest* ('Do not torment me!') but rather of Pozzo's violent outburst in Act 2 of Beckett's *Waiting for Godot*: 'Have you not done tormenting me with your accursed time! It's abominable! … one day we were born, one day we shall die … is that not enough for you?'[86] In addition, of course, the most obvious allusion in that same paragraph from *That They May Face the Rising Sun* is that to C.K. Scott Moncrieff's English translation of the title of Proust's novel as *Remembrance of Things Past*. Curiously, that echo of a twentieth-century classic also has a Shakespearean element. It is well known that Moncrieff had taken his title from Shakespeare's Sonnet 30 ('When to the sessions of sweet silent thought/ I summon up *remembrance of things past*'), and it seems that McGahern returned to that the same original source not just once but twice when he composed that sentence about Bill Evans, as the original of the invocation of 'dreams of things to come' as a counterpart to 'remembrance of things past' may be traced back to the opening lines of Shakespeare's Sonnet 107:

> Not mine own fears nor the prophetic soul
> Of the wide world *dreaming on things to come*
> Can yet the lease of my true love control,
> Supposed as forfeit to a confined doom.[87]

The allusions to Proust and to Shakespeare's sonnets in that key passage of McGahern's final novel confirm one last time the importance of memory and anticipation as ways of cancelling time. To cancel time, however, is not the same as wishing it did not exist, but merely to find a way to suspend its relentless forward momentum. In a variation on the familiar conceit of many of Shakespeare's sonnets, the final couplet of Sonnet 30 promises how memory is a force that may 'losses ... restore[ ] and sorrows end', and which may even cheat death. It is this promise for longevity and communion with the past and its inhabitants that McGahern explores in many of his fictions about memory. Those who, like Bill Evans, are unable to achieve this connection are the most pitiable of all.

CHAPTER 6

A Modernist Mind II: After Yeats and Joyce

> There are two lovely old apple trees just below Merrill House, earlier the President's House, and now the Faculty Club of Colgate University. They had been pruned and shaped once and though they grow close together are very different. I fell into the habit of thinking about them as Mr Joyce and Mr Yeats . . .
>
> 'Mr Joyce and Mr Yeats' (*LW*, p. 185)

When McGahern described the two foremost Irish modernists of the early twentieth century as two great trees in his 1979 foreword to an exhibition catalogue, he was unashamedly borrowing Austin Clarke's famous description of Yeats as a mighty oak tree casting his formidable shadow over the Irish imaginative landscape.[1] Like that of Clarke, McGahern's relationship with his immediate Irish predecessors — whether it is with Yeats and Joyce or with early-twentieth-century Revivalists and post-Revivalists like J.M. Synge, Patrick Kavanagh and Daniel Corkery — is often deeply ambivalent.[2] It is well known how McGahern's admiration for the stylistic achievements of Yeats and Joyce was unstinting, even if he did not wholeheartedly embrace the experimental turn of Joyce's later work. The challenge facing a modern Irish-born author like McGahern was to separate important works like 'Easter 1916' and *Dubliners* from the biographies and the reputations of their authors, and in the process to wrest himself free from the expectations that cling to an Irish author writing in the wake of Yeats, Joyce and Beckett.

Those expectations extended so far as to suggest how and where, as a serious aspiring Irish artist, one should live. In his interview with Julia Carlson,

McGahern talked candidly about how, when he was young, he 'resented' the idea that an Irish writer needed to live in exile.[3] The Joycean trope of exile — including internal exile — is revived with some regularity in McGahern's novels and stories from the late 1960s onward, particularly in those works composed immediately following his enforced departure from Ireland after the banning of *The Dark*. Roberta Gefter Wondrich has drawn attention, for example, to McGahern's self-conscious invocation of the Irish writer's choice between exile or inner exile in *The Pornographer*: 'But why, why have you to go into exile since your whole life and work is an embodiment of the idea of exile?' (*P*, p. 125)[4] Ultimately, however, first in transitional works like *The Pornographer* and 'Oldfashioned' and finally in the late phase of 'The Country Funeral' and *That They May Face the Rising Sun*, the counter-trope of the prodigal return to the native soil was of more interest to McGahern than that of the departure into silence, exile and cunning. It more naturally expressed his own attitudes towards the locality to which he had himself returned in 1970, after a five-year European exile, and from the rooted security of which he was from that point onward to write many of his greatest fictions.

Ever since he was a young man finding his way in Dublin in the 1950s, it seems, McGahern had studied the pitfalls of what he described in a different context as that 'not unusual Irish strategy' of defining itself 'more by what it was against... than by what it was' which he had perceived in other authors, and in the culture of mid-century Ireland at large (*LW*, p. 331). For that reason he was determined from the very beginning of his career to become neither a detractor of past indigenous genius (in the manner of some of his more bitter or insecure precursors and contemporaries), nor a mere modish imitator of Joycean or Yeatsean poetics. While, in the aftermath of the Irish Literary Revival, he forged an independent artistic path that followed English and European models, he simultaneously also insisted that Irish modernist masters like Yeats and Joyce continued to offer valuable insights to a new generation of writers. He emphasised that conviction through the inclusion of many overt references and oblique allusions to the work of both authors in all of his books. This chapter traces McGahern's engagement with his most illustrious Irish predecessors. It will deal both with how the weight of their reputations pressed on emerging Irish writers, and with some of the key ideas, themes and techniques in their novels, stories and poems which McGahern continued to revisit throughout his career. The final part of the chapter will consider McGahern's wider relationship with some of the central tropes of modernist fiction as it developed specifically in an Irish context.

Paralysis and epiphany

Comparisons with Joyce, in particular, were commonly projected onto McGahern when he first emerged in the 1960s as a stylistically restrained teller of truths about Ireland's rural paralysis. (It has been remarked before now that McGahern appeared to have set out, in the first half of his career, to write the volume about provincial life which Joyce at one time conceived as a sequel to *Dubliners*.[5]) In an otherwise positive review, for instance, Derek Mahon's only criticism of *Nightlines* was that it was perhaps rather *too* close to familiar Joycean territory.[6] When McGahern was asked about this influence by interviewers, though, he usually sought to disarm any suggestion that he might harbour feelings of anxiety toward the legacy of Joyce. 'I've been compared to everyone', he responded when he was reminded in a 1984 interview for *Books Ireland* of how reviewers of his early work had routinely drawn comparisons with Joyce's style of 'scrupulous meanness', 'and I find it tiresome. One is doomed, I believe, to one's own unfortunate self.'[7] As happens so often in McGahern's interviews, he is quick to adopt a commonsensical tone, a tactic calculated, in this case, to hide any possible 'anxiety of influence' behind the mask of a farmer who can insist with impunity that he has never even *heard* of either Harold Bloom or the central argument of his most famous book![8]

The truth is, of course, that the presence of the early Joyce can certainly be keenly felt in McGahern's fiction, extending long beyond the early novels and stories from the 1960s. For one thing, despite his downplaying in that interview of the importance of Joycean 'scrupulous meanness', McGahern was certainly aware that his compositional aims replicated those of Flaubert and Joyce. His essay on *Dubliners* more or less makes this explicit. More strikingly, the idea of scrupulous meanness is also occasionally invoked — sometimes in parodic ways — in his fiction. In 'The Stoat', a story written in the mid-1970s, the protagonist is grateful that the dismay he experiences due to the contents of his father's lonely-hearts ad cancels the laughter provoked by the extreme brevity of its style (*GT*, p. 62). In *That They May Face the Rising Sun*, Luke Henry tends bar with the same practised effortlessness with which Joyce or Flaubert might write a sentence: 'His movements were slow but precise; they had been refined by practice to their essentials' (*TRS*, p. 229).[9] The same obsession with brevity and with the process of refining things to their essentials also momentarily becomes a subject in *Amongst Women*, the novel published in the same year as McGahern's essay on *Dubliners*. Moran's habit of drafting and redrafting his letters to Luke in 'a clean, bare style' allows him 'to slip the burden of his personality' (an ability which contrasts, in the same paragraph, with the 'slips and repetitions' that mar his imperfect delivery of the rosary) (*AW*, p. 66). That ability is clearly a version of the Joycean–Flaubertian need for the artist to 'refine [himself] out of existence' behind perfectly polished sentences to which McGahern subscribed in the composition of his own prose.[10] So many critics have noticed this that to point it out has almost become a commonplace in McGahern criticism.[11] What is normally overlooked, though, is that the preceding paragraph already harbours another arch parody of 'scrupulous meanness' (or perhaps equally of the idea of a Beckettian minimalism which strives for silence, an idea that fascinated McGahern but which, in the end, he found impracticable).[12] There, the narrative implicitly suggests that it is but a short step from the 'clean, bare style' which characterises Moran's letter writing to the logical but pointless extreme of scrupulously pared-down writing which Moran perceives in Maggie's response to his letters. When Moran becomes convinced he can see the influence of Luke on his sister's missives to the homestead, he complains to Rose that 'Your man warned her not to say anything about what he is doing. That's why she wrote nothing' (*AW*, p. 66).

It is clear from a casual allusion to Joyce in a 1960 letter to Michael McLaverty that the shadow of Joyce loomed large in the mind of the young aspiring novelist. McGahern congratulated the older novelist on having started to write again beside the demands of his teaching job. He also commiserated with McLaverty about the difficulty of finding time to write during the teaching term because, he wrote, echoing a well-known line from *Ulysses*, 'I understand only too well what it is, the impossibility, of serving two masters.'[13] That statement should not be read, however, as an arrogant attempt to establish a connection between his own situation and that of either Joyce or Stephen Dedalus. Instead, Joyce was even at that early stage held at an ironic distance which bespoke great intellectual independence and maturity in the young unpublished writer. Unlike many of the reviewers of *The Dark* who five years later would insist on unfavourably comparing the path chosen by young Mahoney with that of Stephen Dedalus, McGahern already recognised in that letter written six months before he became a published author that the stance taken by an individual, even one possessed of artistic ambitions, in relation to the social norms and conventions of his day is never given a priori, as McGahern told Patrick Swift during one of their conversations about art and artists, but remained 'more a matter of temperament and background' (*LW*, p. 74). McGahern knew better than anyone that his temperament was not that of Joyce, just as young Mahoney's in *The Dark* is not like that of Stephen Dedalus. Like McLaverty before him and the protagonist of *The Dark* after him, McGahern had chosen the security of steady paid employment above the impractical 'dream' of the purely intellectual life.[14] That choice was not for the young McGahern a defeat of artistic or intellectual ambition but rather a way of achieving the same goal by another path, and so he knew that any comparison with Joyce's or Stephen Dedalus' example could only be cast in *ironically* Joycean terms. And if McGahern had begun his career with a letter to one would-be sympathetic reader of his work which contained an ironic echo of Joyce's artistic aims, then he was to bookend his career with another one when shortly after the publication of *That They May Face the Rising Sun* he humorously wrote to Declan Kiberd that he was worried about venturing out of the house in Leitrim lest his neighbours should be wondering 'Am I in it?' That comment was no doubt intended to recall, to a long-standing reader of his own work who is also one of Joyce's foremost contemporary critics, the supposed response of the citizens of Dublin to the publication of *Ulysses* in 1922.[15] By parodying one of Joyce's most famous statements about his relationship to his native country, McGahern was self-consciously casting himself in an ironic post-Joycean role as a writer, and specifically as an *Irish* writer.

Despite these ironic acts of distancing from the example of Joyce, McGahern's aesthetic and thematic concerns often echo those of the author of *Dubliners* and *Ulysses*. If his exposition of the importance of getting lost in a book as a young 'solitary reader' (*LW*, pp. 89–90) had been pilfered from that other giant of the early-twentieth-century modernist novel, Marcel Proust (as the previous chapter showed), then McGahern's awareness of the 'shape', 'weight' and 'colour' of words as physical presences of which he often talked to interviewers (*LW*, p. 9) is just as shamelessly taken from Stephen's Dollymount reverie in chapter four of *A Portrait of the Artist as a Young Man*.[16] Joyce's early fiction no doubt helped the young McGahern to see more clearly some of the preoccupations with class, gender, religion and society that were to become his own themes. McGahern had lost his religious belief early in life, yet he was aware that his mind, and consequently the language and imagery of his art, remained, as Cranly says in *A Portrait of the Artist as a Young Man*, curiously 'supersaturated with the religion in which you say you disbelieve'.[17] McGahern's lifelong search for a suitable literary form imposed on the materials of a claustrophobic Irish Catholic childhood — an experience which includes the confusion and guilt surrounding the discovery of male physical sexuality, the guilt at failing to fulfil the wishes of a devout dead mother, and the eventual rejection of a religious vocation in favour of a ministry of art — certainly revives Joycean themes in the second half of the twentieth century, while many of the protagonists of stories set in Dublin and the countryside alike 'remain as fixed in their destinies as the various victims of Joycean paralysis in *Dubliners*'.[18] The narrator's memory of a less-than-heroic confrontation with a school inspector in *The Leavetaking* — 'I blush still as I hear the slavish caution of *my whole forever overmastered race* in my voice' (*L*, p. 174, emphasis added) — is certainly ironically reminiscent of Stephen Dedalus' famous statement of intent in the closing pages of *A Portrait of the Artist as a Young Man*.[19]

Like Joyce, McGahern could often be devastatingly satirical of the institutions which govern morality and religious belief in Ireland. What is more, several of his more overtly critical or satirical utterances in fiction and non-fiction alike invoke deliberate memories of the language of Joyce. Thus, the assertion in *Memoir* that 'Church and State worked hand in hand' in mid-twentieth-century Ireland (*M*, p. 210) clearly echoes Joyce's famous satirical invocation, in 'Gas from a Burner', of 'Christ and Caesar ... hand in glove' (a line that had previously been parodied in *The Barracks*, where Reegan gains immense satisfaction from 'fulfilling two obligations at the one time' by attending Mass in uniform while he is officially on duty (*B*, p. 182)).[20] The assessment of the sinister motives of the Church in determining the state's Irish-language policy in 'Oldfashioned' — 'At home a vaguely worried church joined a dying language to declare that learning Irish would help to keep much foreign corrupting influence out' (*HG*, p. 36) — owes a debt to Joyce's cynical identification in *Stephen Hero* of priests who 'encourage the study of Irish that their flocks may be more safely protected from the wolves of disbelief; they consider it is an opportunity to withdraw the people into a past of literal, implicit faith'.[21] McGahern's borrowing of Joyce's social critiques extends even to Maloney's crude aphorism about Church-sponsored sexual repression in *The Pornographer*: 'Ireland wanking is Ireland free. Not only wanking but free. Not only free but wanking as well' (*P*, p. 25). The structure of the latter recalls both the slogan of the nineteenth-century temperance movement ('Ireland sober is Ireland free') and Joyce's satirical rewriting of that same po-faced original in *Finnegans Wake* as 'Ireland sober is Ireland stiff.'[22]

McGahern made it clear that his favourite of Joyce's books was *Dubliners*. Versions of the language, imagery and even the plots of those stories are everywhere in his fiction. In the *High Ground* story 'Parachutes', for example, McGahern's treatment of sexual jealousy, one of his recurring themes, is not written as a Proustian drama as it had been in certain works from the 1970s (as the previous chapter showed), but rather as a homage to the plot of 'The Dead'. Like that of Gabriel Conroy in Joyce's story, the protagonist's love for a young woman in 'Parachutes' must exist in the shadow of the woman's memories of another, recently ended, relationship. But while Gabriel Conroy is paralysed by compulsively comparing himself with the idealised example of Michael Furey, in McGahern's deflated version of one of Joyce's most famous plots that jealousy is replaced with a harsh, unattractive cynicism as the narrator prosaically concludes that 'I used to be jealous of Willie Moran but by now even that had been burned away. I just thought him a fool for not marrying her, wished that I'd been he' (*HG*, p. 19).

McGahern's adaptations of the Joycean epiphanies of *Dubliners*, especially in stories about childhood from *Nightlines* like 'Christmas', 'Lavin', 'Bomb Box', 'Coming into His Kingdom' and 'Strandhill, the Sea', all of which deal with Joycean themes of Catholic guilt and shame, have been well documented.[23] The symbolical-realist texture of *Dubliners* is also recalled in other ways, however. Its example is particularly prevalent in McGahern's early fiction (although the continuing importance of *Dubliners* to the imagination that conceived the later fiction is suggested by his revisiting, in Moran's pointed question in *Amongst Women* about why a priest should be afraid of death if he believes in what he preaches (*AW*, p. 179), of the laughing priest's unspoken epiphany at the centre of Joyce's 'The Sisters', a story to which McGahern felt close enough to have adapted it for BBC television in 1973[24]). When, on the opening page of McGahern's first published novel, the reader encounters Elizabeth Reegan sitting in the fading light of evening (*B*, p. 7), that situation may not only be intended as a reminder of *Madame Bovary*, or even of the image of a drudging peasant on the stage of the Abbey Theatre.[25] It also suggests a parallel with the eponymous heroine of Joyce's 'Eveline' as she 'sat at the window watching the evening invade the avenue'.[26] Eveline's struggle with the choice between staying at home or escaping Irish dreariness for romantic foreign places has its parallel in McGahern's fiction not only in the deadly dilemma that remains unresolved at the end of 'Korea', but also in Elizabeth's memories of her homecoming from London in *The Barracks*. On one level, McGahern's first novel can be read as a kind of sequel to Joyce's story which offers a version of an Eveline figure who has initially escaped from but then again returned in middle age to the localities she found it so hard to leave in the first place.

Allusions to *Dubliners* and the early episodes of *Ulysses* can be found throughout *The Barracks* — particularly in matters connected with death and the rituals and superstitions which surround it. When Elizabeth Reegan finds that 'She couldn't pray' in the face of her own impending certain death (*B*, p. 123), she is repeating the predicaments of famous literary exemplars including not just Macbeth but also the Stephen Dedalus of the Telemachus episode of *Ulysses*. The ritual pulling down of the blinds and the lighting of the lamps which forestall Elizabeth's death on the first page replicate the opening paragraphs of 'The Sisters' and 'Araby', both of which begin with references to blinded windows symbolic of death.[27] And when Elizabeth Reegan absent-mindedly says an extra Hail Mary in her decade of the rosary — a lapse that remains unnoticed by her family, though not by herself (*B*, p. 33) — this duplicates the fate of Maria in 'Clay' as she sings the first verse of a song twice.[28] As readers of Joyce we know, just as Elizabeth herself knows and as McGahern intends for us to know, that such a slip is symbolic of the failing strength of her disintegrating body, her waning powers of mental concentration and, like other symbolic details in Joyce's story and in McGahern's novel, of her impending death. The symbolism of impending death from the same story in *Dubliners* is again recalled by McGahern in 'Korea', in which the young man condemned to kill or be killed is attracted to the vision of worms intended as fishing bait wriggling in the 'clay' of the outside lavatory, and in which both the clay and the worms become emblems of his own inevitable fate. In that last example, though, the imagery is perhaps equally tied up with McGahern's memory of Kavanagh's clay-encrusted living dead in *The Great Hunger*, a poem to which he returned frequently.

Poets of place, poets of ideas

When the narrator of *Amongst Women* comments how '*like a shoal of fish moving within a net*, Rose and the girls started to clear the table, to brush away crumbs, to wash, to dry, to return each thing to its own place, all done with a muted energy' (*AW*, p. 79, emphasis added), he is reiterating a variation on Rose's ability to move within the limits of the social frameworks designed to confine her (*AW*, p. 24). The image of confinement in a net of social convention is forever tied up, in Irish writing, with Stephen Dedalus' desire in the final chapter of *A Portrait of the Artist as a Young Man* to fly the nets of various forms of patriarchal control.[29] However, the resonance in this particular sentence is as much Yeatsean as it is Joycean, recalling as it does the middle line of Yeats' enigmatic three-line poem 'Three Movements':

> Shakespearean fish swam the sea, far away from land;
> Romantic fish swam in nets coming to the hand;
> What are all those fish that lie gasping on the strand?[30]

Like Yeats' 'Romantic fish', the Moran women are not wild, expansive or impulsive. They do not aggressively assert their individuality like heroic social outcasts adrift on the open sea, nor do they exhaust their life force in open conflict with the status quo (in the form of a Joycean '*non serviam*'), a tactic that might leave them gasping for air on the hostile strands of a traditional, male-dominated society. Instead they prefer to work *within* systems rather than against them, ordering rather than rejecting the particulars of a hostile world in order to gain imaginative mastery over their environment. Rose and the girls go with the flow, so to speak: an idea which McGahern found elsewhere in Yeats and which was, as this chapter will argue, influential on his thinking about literary form in its own right.

Yeats is probably quoted or alluded to even more often than Joyce in McGahern's work. His presence haunts all of McGahern's writing like the ghost of Plato who materialises out of Yeats' late poem 'What Then?' into McGahern's last essay, 'God and Me', which revisits that poem's theme of spiritual uncertainty even in the face of 'material ease and scientific advancement' (*LW*, p. 151).[31] McGahern's relationship with Yeats is based, probably more than that with any other author except Shakespeare, on a detailed mnemonic catalogue of lines and rhythms that had become internalised over many decades of careful and loving rereading, and whose compulsive involuntary recitation was triggered by the lightest touch. McGahern's first serious introduction to the work of the most important Irish poet of the early twentieth century was facilitated through the influence of one of his English lecturers at St Patrick's College, Drumcondra. James Rigney represented another instance of the 'great good fortune' (*LW*, p. 87) McGahern experienced in his encounters with teachers who were willing to share their enthusiasm about literature. McGahern felt this debt sufficiently strongly to credit Rigney, in a letter written on the eve of his debut as a published novelist, with having introduced him — even amid the otherwise 'stultifying' anti-intellectual atmosphere of St Patrick's College — 'to many things that were to enrich my life, Yeats above all, and the joy of rhythmic speech'.[32] It is no coincidence, therefore, that the two examples of the 'essential mystery and magic in all real poetry' chosen by the narrator's mother during her defence of poetry to the nun in *The Leavetaking* are both taken from Yeats' early lyrics (*L*, pp. 37–8).[33] When Maloney in *The Pornographer* refers to Yeats as 'Our national poet' (*P*, p. 165), he probably intends the epithet with more than a shade of bitter irony; for McGahern himself, on the other hand, the description was fully warranted, and versions of the same praise for Yeats in interviews from the same period are not veiled in even the slightest hint of irony. As he emphasised to Denis Sampson, Yeats continued to give him, in the decades following his departure from St Patrick's College, 'more pleasure than any other writer, and more constant pleasure'.[34] Or as he would later emphasise about his intellectual maturation during the 1950s and 1960s in 'The Solitary Reader': 'The more we read ... the more clearly it emerged that not only was Yeats a very great poet but that almost singlehandedly he had, amazingly, laid down a whole framework in which an indigenous literature could establish traditions and grow' (*LW*, p. 92). McGahern was acutely aware of Yeats' immense influence on successive generations of readers and writers. That influence is also subtly acknowledged in some of his books. When the narrator in *The Leavetaking* notices, for example, 'the clay of the young flesh reflecting their master's character' (*L*, p. 21) as one of the other teachers at the school marches his class back inside, McGahern is paying homage to Yeats' noble ambition of intellectually moulding the fledgling nation 'like soft wax'.[35]

McGahern was undeniably critical of the more mythical aspects of Yeats' involvement in the revival of national consciousness. Like many of his contemporaries who emerged in the early 1960s, he was keen to distance himself from the romantic conventions of the Irish Literary Revival. His deflation of the ease with which the Cuchulainn myth is put to work in the pursuit of self-aggrandisement on the final page of *The Barracks* (where Reegan admonishes Mullins that 'It's always easy to make a Cuchulainn outa the other fella' (*B*, p. 232)) is telling of McGahern's suspicion of Revivalist pieties.

Yet he was at the same time certainly interested in other ways in which Yeats fostered the creation of a localised Irish consciousness. Yeats offered the young McGahern ways of imagining Irishness, and of seeing familiar or alien localities mediated through beloved poems, often taking on shades of meaning in the process. In a 1979 interview with Denis Sampson he recounted how his first encounters with Yeats had taught him, as a young man on the brink of becoming a writer, that the places he knew intimately were valid material for great art. He was delighted to find the names of places he had visited during family holidays to the Sligo seaside in memorable lines of verse.[36] On that occasion he singled out Yeats' use of place names as an important aspect of his work:

> To actually see the names like Knocknarea and Queen Maeve's Grave, and you know, 'I stood among a crowd at Drumahair, His heart hung all upon a silken dress,' to actually know that those placenames were places that I knew, like Boyle or Carrick on Shannon ... I've always ... admired place names in fiction. I mean actual names; in the Yeats poem, I'm always delighted that he used the word Drumahair because I think both conferred distinction on one another.[37]

McGahern's own use of place names in his fiction may be traced back to that early pleasure of recognition first experienced in his reading of Yeats' poetry and prose. These even occasionally include places in Sligo with strong

Yeatsean connections. First published in *Getting Through* not long before he made that remark about the importance of Yeatsean place names, the decision to set the original version of 'The Stoat' in a Sligo golf resort overlooking Ballisodare and Knocknarea is probably as much an act of tribute to Yeats as it is an autobiographical element. That a connection with Yeats' early lyrics is intentional is immediately suggested by the way the first three paragraphs of that story, those that poetically describe the titular stoat (a close relative of the weasel) stalking his prey, revisit a detail from the opening stanza of Yeats' 1893 poem 'Fergus and the Druid': 'This whole day have I followed in the rocks,/ ... A weasel moving on from stone to stone'.[38] Immediately following that three-paragraph overture, the protagonist finds his father 'reading *The Independent* on the front lawn of the cottage ... facing Knocknarea, his back to the wind that blew from the ocean' (*GT*, p. 59). Looking inland at Knocknarea is associated in 'The Stoat', as it is in another early Yeats poem, 'Red Hanrahan's Song about Ireland', with the wind blowing from the ocean:

> The wind has bundled up the clouds high over Knocknarea,
> And thrown the thunder on the stones for all that Maeve can say.
> Angers that are like noisy clouds have set our hearts abeat;
> But we have all bent low and low and kissed the quiet feet
> Of Cathleen, the daughter of Houlihan.[39]

The invocation of the place name coupled with the blustery weather conditions make for a distinctly Yeatsean mix. McGahern is issuing both the protagonist and the reader with a challenge to read the situation through their knowledge of Yeats. The result of such an exercise is at best ambivalent. First of all, the stoat's hunt is symbolic of the human actions that unfold in the rest of the story. Thus both the young student's pursuit of knowledge and Miss McCabe's romantic quest may gain an air of nobility through an association with a mythical Yeatsean model. That model, however, simultaneously suggests the futility of any search for wisdom or knowledge, as the eponymous Fergus must eventually accept that he has 'grown nothing, knowing all'.[40] More obviously ironic is the association with 'Red Hanrahan's Song', Yeats' poem about idealised romantic (and nationalist) passions that are as thunderous as the clouds above Knocknarea. Much less 'thunderous' or romantic passions are at work in this story about an ageing, widowed schoolteacher's comically pragmatic search for companionship among the 'wrecks and battleaxes' who can be expected to answer an ad in the lonely-hearts column (*GT*, p. 62), and about the less-than-chivalrous abandonment of his courtship of one of those women.

In *Amongst Women*, too, the place names associated in the narrative with the characters' various outings away from Great Meadow include not only the towns and villages of Leitrim and Roscommon but also landmarks on the Sligo coast. Places like Strandhill, Ballisodare and Rosses Point (where first Moran and Rose, and later Michael and Nell Morahan travel in their cars in search of sexual fulfilment, like 'motorised version[s]', as Eamon Maher joked, of the legendary interlopers Diarmuid and Gráinne who were a favourite subject of Yeats, Lady Gregory and Synge[41]) are all associated both with McGahern's memories of childhood holidays and with his reading of the early sections of Yeats' *Autobiographies*. It is only fitting, therefore, that McGahern should obliquely acknowledge the part Yeats had once played in the first youthful instilling of regional pride by employing a version of a clearly identifiable Yeatsean thought on the opening pages of that same novel. The Moran girls' realisation that 'On the tides of Dublin or London they were hardly more than specks of froth' (*AW*, p. 2) repeats a lesson the young Yeats had learned from one of his aunts before leaving Sligo for London in *Reveries over Childhood and Youth*: 'Here you are somebody. There you will be nobody at all.'[42]

Perhaps more unexpectedly for a writer from the rural north-west of Ireland who is known primarily as a chronicler of the ordinary lives of that region, Joyce, too, was of interest to McGahern among other things as a writer of place. McGahern's perspective on Dublin life sometimes owes something to the Dublin of Kavanagh and Flann O'Brien. Those two writers appear as minor characters in the stories 'Bank Holiday' and 'My Love, My Umbrella' respectively; what is more, in an essay from the 1990s McGahern even viewed his youthful self with comic detachment by casting it as a stock figure in the literature of the mid-century, 'one of those National Teachers Flann O'Brien observed as they came into Earlsfort Terrace after work on their bicycles' (*LW*, p. 75). Once, Dublin even has Yeatsean connotations. When the protagonist of 'Bank Holiday' points out Howth during a romantic seaside outing with his new American lover and adds that this was the place 'where Maud Gonne waited at the station as Pallas Athena', the woman immediately recognises the allusion to one of Yeats' 'Beautiful Lofty Things', and is even able to quote from that poem (*HG*, pp. 145–6). Thus these two outsiders to the city bond over the intimate knowledge of Dublin's literary landscape which they share but which remains a mystery to many a native. Above all, though, the descriptions of the capital in McGahern's novels and stories are indebted to Joyce's various mythic-symbolic renderings of the city and its environs. In 1956, when he settled into what was intended to be a long-term teaching post after short stints teaching in provincial postings in Drogheda and Athboy, he found himself working and living in the environs of Clontarf and Howth. Those north-Dublin suburbs were foreign territory to a young man who had grown up in Leitrim and Roscommon. As a close reader of Joyce it was almost inevitable that McGahern came to see the places where his own life now played out through pivotal scenes of *A Portrait of the Artist as a Young Man*, *Ulysses* and *Finnegans Wake* which had been set in those same locations. The descriptions of Clontarf and Howth in *The Leavetaking*, in particular, contain extended acts of homage to scenes in Joyce's fictions set on the north-Dublin coastline. The pavement outside the railings of St Anthony's on the seafront in Clontarf on which Patrick Moran waits while the headmaster asks for the local priest's permission to give him a job in the school (*L*, p. 16) is that on which Stephen Dedalus had paced 'From the door of Byron's publichouse to the gate of Clontarf Chapel' as he waited for his father to enquire about a place for him in the university in chapter four of *A Portrait of the Artist as a Young Man*.[43] Following the controversial ending of *The Dark*, with its hero's anti-Joycean retreat into the security of the social order, in *The Leavetaking* McGahern yet again invites comparisons with Stephen Dedalus' soaring consciousness in *A Portrait of the Artist as a Young Man* only to deflate the expectations which such a comparison inevitably raises with readers and critics. Dedalus had set off from the suburban seafront to the Bull and Dollymount strand, where he encounters the 'bird girl', that sensuous 'wild angel … of mortal youth and beauty' who makes him experience feelings of ecstasy and 'profane joy';[44] for the young teacher in *The Leavetaking*, by contrast, there is no such escape from the forces of Joycean paralysis. In McGahern's ironic reimagining of the bird-girl episode, only the gulls (to whose possible further significance in the intricate Joycean tapestry of the novel this chapter will return later) make the journey 'over the trees in the direction of Dollymount strand and the Bull', while the main character stays behind and remains sexually and professionally frustrated and unfulfilled (*L*, pp. 24–5).

In Joyce's fiction, the various beaches and promontories around Dublin Bay are often associated with sexual instincts, desires and acts. Beside Dollymount, Howth is particularly prominent in Joyce's imagination in that respect, since it is the setting for the conclusion of *Ulysses* and the beginning of *Finnegans Wake* — if indeed 'beginning it ever had', as one of McGahern's narrators remarks about his own circular narrative (*P*, p. 252). As one critic observes, Joyce had '[used] the image of the sea-tides to explain the ebb and flow of [Leopold and Molly Bloom's] sexual desire' in the final episode of *Ulysses*, in which the middle-aged couple remember their youthful courtship on Howth head.[45] Patrick Moran and Isobel in *The Leavetaking* (like his parents before them) also court on Howth; and McGahern, too — via a line remembered from Matthew Arnold's 'Dover Beach' (*L*, p. 193)[46] — uses the surging of the tides against the harbour wall in Howth as a potent metaphor for the retreating and resurgence of the natural rhythms of life, death and sexual feeling. Allusions to this aspect of Joyce's imagination are not confined to *The Leavetaking*. McGahern's first reworking of a detail from the conclusion of *Ulysses* can probably be found in 'Korea'. In that early story, the father's memory of seeing bursting seed pods during his honeymoon on Howth Head — which had in turn reminded him of an execution he had witnessed during the War of Independence (*N*, pp. 85–6) — contains an oblique tribute to Leopold and Molly Bloom sharing the seed cake (a reference to sex as well as food) on Howth Head in the Penelope episode of *Ulysses*. The mature attitude to sex adopted by the Blooms in *Ulysses* was something McGahern was only gradually able to use in his work during the latter half of his career. A number of the major characters in later works like 'Love of the World' and *Amongst Women* are capable of making love in private without experiencing feelings of shame or guilt. This is in stark contrast with the furtive and predatory attitudes that had characterised the sexual exploits and fantasies of the protagonists of works like *The Dark* and *The Leavetaking*, 'Two Gallants' and *A Portrait of the Artist as a Young Man*. That McGahern identified a parallel for that capacity for emotional and sexual maturity which characterises the outlook of his own later fiction in that of the older Joyce is signalled by the insertion of an echo of Leopold Bloom's appetites into *Amongst Women*. Moran, like the libidinous and sensual Bloom, repeatedly eats 'with relish' (an echo of the famous first sentence of the Calypso episode of *Ulysses*) — including once during a romantic seaside picnic in Sligo with Rose (*AW*, pp. 12, 59) during which their hunger for food is suggestive of the couple's appetites for one another.[47]

'my own conviction about this world and the next'[48]

Ultimately, the examples of Yeats and Joyce alike were of Irish authors of international stature whose themes and subjects are relevant to particularly Irish thoughts, ideas and experiences as well as to more universal ones. Yeats may in the first instance have offered the young McGahern a securely grounded regional model after which an Irish writer might fashion himself, but as a mature novelist he also habitually approached him as a poet of ideas — many of them adapted from modern and ancient philosophy. When McGahern writes in 'The Solitary Reader' about the sense of social and metaphorical truth which, for a group of writers who came of age around the turn of the 1960s, clung to '[Yeats'] proud words, "The knowledge of reality is a secret knowledge; it is a kind of death"' (*LW*, p. 92), he is referring to Yeats' discussion, in one of the later volumes of *Autobiographies*, of the separation of soul (intelligence) and body (power) in the Eastern and Western philosophical traditions.[49] Given his interest in this aspect of Yeats' thought, it is clear that McGahern is not collusive in the act of casting Yeats as a dirty old man which takes place in *The Pornographer* when Maloney wilfully or obtusely misinterprets Yeats' remark that 'The tragedy of sexual intercourse is the perpetual virginity of the soul',[50] and turns it into a misogynistic joke about sex (*P*, p. 165). When Yeats wrote that line he was alluding to an idea from the Epicurean poet Lucretius, which he knew in Dryden's eighteenth-century translation, about the separation of body and soul, and the consequent incompleteness of any sensation of pleasure that is purely physical. Sex may intertwine two individuals' body parts but it cannot 'force their way to t'others heart... For bodies cannot pierce, nor be in bodies lost'.[51] On occasions such as this, McGahern maintains a clearly defined ironic distance from the misconceptions of his characters. The rest of the novel suggests that McGahern, unlike Maloney, had understood Yeats very well. Despite Maloney's best efforts at masking truth with vulgarity, a kernel of the original idea which Yeats had found in Dryden's translation of Lucretius survives in one of the key themes of *The Pornographer*. That novel, like *The Leavetaking*, is concerned with the 'tragedy' of imperfect human relationships — with the 'irredeemable imprisonment' of individual selves to which McGahern refers in the preface to the revised edition of *The Leavetaking* (*Lrev*, p. 5). The pornographer, like Mavis and the colonel in the pornographic stories he writes, has plenty of sex, but most of the time the physical act of love fails to connect the souls of the participants, thus leaving it 'tragically' virginal, as Lucretius, Dryden and Yeats predicted. Throughout, the novel juxtaposes the purely physical sexual pleasures of both the narrator and his pornographic creations with the more profound spiritual fulfilment that may be found in other realms.

This is not the only occasion on which McGahern uses ideas from classical philosophy surrounding sex and procreation as they are handed down to him through literary history mediated through the eyes of Yeats and Joyce. An obvious case in point is the way in which the grown-up sons in *The Dark* and *The Leavetaking* retrospectively define their late mothers by the way they had imagined the futures of their young and their unborn children respectively. On the most basic level, McGahern may have based that trait on his relationship with his own mother (as he intimates in *Memoir* when he observes that after a while 'it was impossible to tell to whom [that is, to mother or son] the dream [about the son's future] belonged' (*M*, p. 62)). But by the time he came to write those novels he had also found such animated 'mother's reveries' to be a universal passion through his familiarity with Yeats' mythic treatment of it in 'Among School Children', in which the dreams of a youthful mother are compared with a nun worshipping religious images or Plato looking at the shadows of reality playing out against the walls of his cave.[52]

In the early schoolroom episode in *The Leavetaking*, the narrator reflects — *Tristram Shandy*-style — on the uncertainty of the circumstances of his own conception (*L*, p. 35) and that of the boys in his class. 'They have all certificates of birth and will all one day have death certificates but their certificates of conception would be more interesting', he reflects, before indulging in a 'cruel' game of imagining some of the more salacious possible scenarios for the latter (*L*, p. 45). Patrick Moran is in that passage continuing the favourite Joycean question with the 'legal fiction' of paternity.[53] He is not *only* alluding to that single Joycean idea introduced by Stephen Dedalus in the Scylla and Charybdis episode, however; he also shares his fascination with the endless historical possibilities that have not come to pass with Stephen's thinking elsewhere in *Ulysses*. McGahern is mischievously reviving Stephen Dedalus' application of Aristotle's definition of 'a movement', which is 'an actuality of the possible as possible', to the troubled history of Ireland in that other famous schoolroom in the Nestor episode.[54] Andrew Gibson's explanation of the significance of that passage is useful here: 'A historical actuality', he writes, 'was one possibility among others ... These other possibilities cannot be granted the same status as an actuality. But that does not mean that they were without value, nor does it render them null and void. They are still available *to thought* (and therefore to art).'[55] Gibson's reading of that passage is as true for the fictitious certificates of conception of the schoolboys in *The Leavetaking* as it is of the alternative histories imagined by Stephen Dedalus. In appropriating Stephen's awareness of the importance of possibilities, McGahern is extending Joyce's resistance to the sense of inevitability at the heart of colonial historiography (a theme that is treated elsewhere in *The Leavetaking*)[56] to encompass the equally mysterious question about the unknowable pasts of our mothers and fathers, the reconstruction of which makes up such a large part of Patrick Moran's narrative in part one of *The Leavetaking*.

McGahern regularly returns to Yeats as a poet of ideas. As the end of this chapter will discuss, McGahern's use of various kinds of circularity as a leitmotif throughout his career drew on many literary exemplars both ancient and modern, but one of his earliest and most explicit explanations of the significance of the circle as a symbol clearly draws on a specific Yeatsean model. The 'ritual wheel' of human existence which is described by the narrator in the opening story of *Nightlines* (*N*, p. 19) is not only reminiscent of such allegories of the ageing process as Jaques' 'seven ages of man' speech in *As You Like It*, as has been suggested;[57] the title and central image of 'Wheels', as well as the reference to the 'sections' of the wheel of life both at the conclusion of that story and later in *The Pornographer* (*N*, p. 22; *P*, p. 172), more immediately reference Yeats' description in *A Vision* of the 'Great Wheel' and its phases which is universally metaphorical of every cyclical process — what he describes in that book as 'every completed movement of thought or life'.[58]

The titles of two stories from *Getting Through* also contain allusions to Yeats' poems. As Eamon Grennan first suggested, the title of 'The Wine Breath' is more than likely intended as a reminder of Yeatsean themes in 'All Souls' Night', a poem first published as an epilogue to *A Vision*.[59] That story is about the 'intensity' of the poetic vision of the past as compared with the dullness of the priest's experience of the present moment (*GT*, p. 96), a concern which shadows Yeats' contrast in 'All Souls' Night' between the 'sharpened' palate of the ghosts who 'drink from the wine-breath/ While our gross palates drink from the whole wine'. As the previous chapter showed, 'The Wine Breath' has routinely been connected by critics with Proust and with Joyce's 'The Dead' because of its emphasis on the priest's involuntary memories of old friends; but 'All Souls' Night', too, is a poem profoundly engaged with the importance of 'thoughts [that] rise up unbid'. In addition, the fates of both the priest and his elderly mother in McGahern's story slyly mirror those of two of the narrator's old friends in 'All Souls' Night'. The lonely priest's doubts about his vocation, which had meant giving up the opportunity for human, physical love (a regret which is dramatised in particular in the last paragraph, in which the red altar wine of his vocation is replaced in the priest's thoughts with the image of a young man offering a bottle of white wine to the woman whose body he hopes to conquer in the kind of life he knows he has renounced in order to become a priest), repeats Yeats' description in 'All Souls' Night' of Horton's pangs of 'platonic love' which causes

> Two thoughts . . . [to be] so mixed up I could not tell
> Whether of her or God he thought the most . . .

Meanwhile, the metaphorical

> ravell[ing] out
> From a discourse in figurative speech
> By some learned Indian
> On the soul's journey

which characterises the lonely end of Florence Emery's life in Yeats' poem is humorously rewritten in McGahern's story in the form of the subplot about the priest's elderly seamstress–mother, who in the dementia of her final days feels compelled to *literally* tear up (or un*ravel*) every garment she has ever made (*GT*, pp. 101–2).[60]

Similarly, Denis Sampson suggests that the cryptic title of *Getting Through*'s 'Swallows' — a story in which these birds do not appear — may contain a reference to Yeats' poem 'Coole Park, 1929'. In a story about the contrast between the sergeant who has lost his artistic vocation and the surveyor who remains dedicated to his art, the allusion to swallows in the title seems to recall, Sampson suggests, Yeats' description of 'the security artists and intellectuals found in [Lady Gregory's] presence: "They came like swallows and like swallows went,/ And yet a woman's powerful character/ Could keep a swallow to its first intent."'[61] The burning intensity of the powers of artistic vision had already been cast in Yeatsean terms in the earlier story 'Christmas', from *Nightlines*, a story rich in literary allusions to many authors. In that story McGahern not *only* borrows the death of Lady Gregory's airman–son in a dogfight over Italy (an event cast in tragic terms by Yeats in a number of poems) as a plot element; the youthful protagonist's burning of his painted toy — an object which itself contains a hidden allusion to an earlier Yeatsean lyric[62] — in a handful of straw in the barn at the conclusion of the story *also* repeats, in anti-mythic terms, Yeats' symbolic description of the fires of the imagination in 'In Memory of Major Robert Gregory':

> Some burn damp faggots, others may consume
> The entire combustible world in one small room
> As though dried straw . . . [63]

This insistence on the intensity of the poetic vision which must be brought to bear on all his material by the artist is a central principle in McGahern's thinking about his art. Like Yeats, he knew that even the most 'trivial event' can 'change[ ] some childish day to tragedy' (a line from 'Among School Children' which is echoed in the recollection of a formative incident from the mother's childhood in *The Leavetaking* (*L*, p. 68)),[64] and so the fates of his central characters are always rendered with the intensity of tragic poetry. Thus, while McGahern's novels and stories — particularly those from the 1960s and 1970s — often focus on lives lived in a turmoil of doubt and uncertainty, the quality of his prose is invariably capable of 'mak[ing] that very uncertainty sing' (*LW*, p. 361), as he wrote in a review of a collection of stories by Richard Ford, with an unmistakable echo of one of Yeats' most frequently quoted ideas about poetry: that paragraph from *Per Amica Silentia Lunae* which argues that the poet, unlike the rhetorician, must live in solitude and metaphysical doubt and yet 'sing amid our uncertainty'.[65]

While that artistic imperative from *Per Amica Silentia Lunae* sums up the quality of the narrative voice of the narrator of an early novel like *The Dark*, there is a distinct moving away from the embodiment of Yeatsean turmoil in McGahern's later fiction. Intriguingly, the direction of that move itself owes a debt to Yeats. At the end of his life, two ideas with a distinctly Yeatsean flavour emerged chief among McGahern's convictions about this world and the next. An early paragraph in *Memoir* reflects on how

> We grow into an understanding of the world gradually. Much of what we come to know is far from comforting, that each day brings us closer to the inevitable hour when all will be darkness again, but even that knowledge is power and all understanding is joy, even in the face of dread, and cannot be taken from us until everything is. *We grow into a love of the world*, a love that is all the more precious and poignant because the great glory of which we are but a particle is lost almost as soon as it is gathered. (*M*, p. 36, emphasis added)

That paragraph invokes, on the one hand, the Yeatsean 'tragic joy' of the man approaching death who experiences a final ecstatic 'enlargement of... vision'.[66] McGahern had already made that concept his own, both in his essay on Alistair MacLeod's stories about the 'oblivion' of traditional communities in Nova Scotia which 'take on the truth of the Gaelic songs their people sing. In the mystery of their art they take joy from that very oblivion of which they so movingly sing' (*LW*, p. 212), and in his descriptions in essays like 'Rural Ireland's Passing' and 'Terrible Tales from the Mart' of the death of similar ancient ways of life in the Irish countryside.[67]

The same paragraph from *Memoir* also emphasises the more uncomplicated joy that springs from loving the world. McGahern's use of the phrase 'love of the world' is of particular interest. He used the same phrase as the title for one of his last short stories, which begins and ends with lyrical descriptions of the natural world that contrast with the 'violent and shocking' acts of domestic abuse and murder that make up the story's central plot (*CE*, p. 336).[68] 'Love of the World' embodies his final preference for writing about the 'quiet' life, lived in places where 'Nothing much ever happens' (as the narrator of 'Love of the World' stresses in the opening paragraph, in what reads like a tribute to the joys of *Waiting for Godot* (*CE*, p. 336)), over the conflict that drives most conventional plots, or even the inner turmoil of a certain type of Yeatsean poetics. McGahern's widow Madeline maintains that his use of the phrase 'love of the world' originated from his reading of Hannah Arendt.[69] It is just as likely, however, that McGahern's references to the importance of living and writing from a 'love of the world', both in *Memoir* and in the title of this late story, were intended as a response to a question raised in Yeats' 'Ego Dominus Tuus', a poem first published as a verse prologue to *Per Amica Silentia Lunae*.

'Love of the World' may be read as, among other things, a response to the conflict between different classes of writing on which Yeats ruminates in 'Ego Dominus Tuus'. That poem, a notoriously difficult one, is written in the form of a dialogue between Hic and Ille, each of whom represents conflicting aspects of Yeats' personality (leading Ezra Pound to refer to it as the dialogue of 'Hic and Willie').[70] The romantic Hic believes that art can be created by

> Impulsive men that look for happiness
> And sing when they have found it.
> . . .
> No one denies to Keats *love of the world*;
> Remember his deliberate happiness.

The worldly Ille, on the other hand, is convinced that all art arises from the 'dissipation and despair' of their creators, and that to simply sing out of happiness is a form of naivety or sentimentality. Ille argues that while Keats' art is happy, the 'deliberate happiness' that is a feature of his art was probably contrived out of the private dissatisfactions of the heart.[71] With the echo of the concluding flourish of Hic's argument in its title, 'Love of the World' may appear to simply endorse the former set of convictions. Indeed, like many of McGahern's central consciousnesses, the narrator of 'Love of the World' apparently shares the 'deliberate happiness' that comes from loving the world and singing out of that love which Hic in 'Ego Dominus Tuus' identifies in Keats. However, other parts of the narrative may bear out that 'Love of the World' is not quite the uncomplicated endorsement of the sentimentalist's art of self-deception which it may at first appear. McGahern shares Yeats' awareness that nourishing a 'love of the world' may be useful in the everyday pursuit of happiness, but that it does not automatically follow that it is also a prerequisite in the creation of great art. To wit, Ille's counter-argument to Hic's proposition that loving the world is the only artistic imperative is also a presence in 'Love of the World', though one that is perhaps less clearly defined. The action of

'Love of the World' is framed by two lyrical paragraphs describing the lakeside setting:

> It is very quiet here. Nothing much ever happens. We have learned to tell the cries of the birds and the animals, the wingbeats of the swans crossing the house
>
> ......
>
> The moon was bright on the lake, turning into a clear, still sky. The fields above the lake and the dark shapes of the hedges stood out ... Wildfowl scattered from the reeds along the shore out towards the centre of the lake ... They squawked and shrieked for a while before turning into a dark silent huddle. (*CE*, pp. 336, 368)

The emphasis on the sounds made by the birds on the lake at night in the opening and closing paragraphs of 'Love of the World' may be traced to the final stanza of the dialogue poem by Yeats from which it takes its title. Significantly, the final word in 'Ego Dominus Tuus' is given not to the romantic Hic but to the worldly Ille, who reveals that he is not opposed to writing about the subjects proposed by Hic; he is concerned, however, that art should not be a form of self-expression but a mastery of passions or ideas which come from beyond the self. In the final stanza, Ille finally reveals how he intends to create his art through summoning a 'double' or an 'anti-self', one who 'yet/ Shall walk the wet sands by the edge of the stream',

> And standing by these characters disclose
> All that I seek; and whisper it as though
> He were afraid the birds, who cry aloud
> Their momentary cries before it is dawn,
> Would carry it away to blasphemous men.[72]

While both Hic and Ille finally find a way to write about the world as they find it, there is a crucial difference in the way in which they arrive at their respective perceptions. Ille's love of the world is a consciously adopted artistic mask, not the idle expression of private passion advocated by Hic. As 'Love of the World' bears a title taken from 'Ego Dominus Tuus', it is only reasonable that the attention to the crying, squawking and shrieking of birds in the first and last paragraphs should be read as a nod of acknowledgement to Ille's intention to discover, through hard labour, a delicate 'image' of truth amid the cries of birds before the dawn. The two paragraphs which frame the action of 'Love of the World' are not simply unguarded expressions of McGahern's personal love of the natural world, then. They may also be read as his affirmation of Yeats' lesson that manifestations of happiness, satisfaction or calm in an artist's work do not necessarily correspond to feelings of private inner peace in the individual who created it, but that artistic expressions must instead be the result of sustained and disciplined intellectual activity — that art, as Ille/Willie in 'Ego Dominus Tuus' puts it, 'Is but a vision of reality'.[73] The paragraph from *Memoir* in which the same phrase occurs confirms, after all, that McGahern regarded his 'love of the world' as something to 'grow into', to be acquired or achieved over time (*M*, p. 36), rather than as a superficial, uncritical response to natural beauties.

McGahern also turned to Yeatsean thought when it came to formulating his own and some of his characters' beliefs not just about the importance of loving the world when we are alive but also about the *termination* of one's mortal span. In the opening story of *Getting Through*, a dim memory of some relevant lines from Yeats offers itself to the main character who, like McGahern himself, possesses the kind of mind given to storing and involuntarily recalling beloved lines of verse. It is clear that the Finnish writer Eva Lindberg in 'The Beginning of an Idea' shares some of her ideas with Samuel Beckett. Her self-effacing remark on being praised for her fluent command of English that a talent for foreign languages means only that 'you can manage to say more inaccurately in several languages what you can say better in your own' (*GT*, pp. 22–3), for example, recalls Beckett's long and painful search for accuracy and authenticity in two languages — or indeed the struggle of a writer like Seán Ó Ríordáin, who had grown up in a 'fractured linguistic background ... where his father's Irish was gradually being replaced by his mother's Hiberno-English'.[74] When she considers that 'once alive it is better to go on than die, the best not to have been born at all' (*GT*, pp. 23–4), the first half of that stoic thought appears to be an equally clear invocation of the Beckettian imperative to 'go on' which concludes *The Unnamable* (or perhaps of Camus' 'absurd revolt').[75] The final word in that same passage belongs not to Beckett or to Camus, though, but to Yeats. Eva's initial articulation of Beckettian endurance somehow brings to her mind, through an involuntary process of association, a memory of the chorus in Yeats' version of Sophocles' *Oedipus at Colonus*:

> Never to have lived is best, ancient writers say;
> Never to have drawn the breath of life, never to have looked into the eye
> of day;
> The second best's a gay goodnight and quickly turn away.[76]

That memorable tercet was ever present in McGahern's mind as much as it is in that of the unfortunate protagonist of 'The Beginning of an Idea'. Like many Irish writers, McGahern was a lapsed Catholic, whose private belief in the absence of an afterlife was summed up by young Mahoney's image of life as a 'haphazard flicker between nothingness and nothingness' in *The Dark* (*D*, p. 69), and later by Mary's belief in the fleetingness of human existence in *That They May Face the Rising Sun*: 'We're no more than a puff of wind out on the lake' (*TRS*, p. 115) (a thought that echoes St Augustine, who had written that 'Men give voice to their opinions, but they are only opinions, like so many puffs of wind that waft the soul hither and thither and make it veer and turn'[77]). In the verse rhythms of Yeats' Sophocles, he found a graceful expression of acceptance of that fact.

The tercet from Yeats' *Oedipus at Colonus* was in the end one of the main articles of McGahern's agnostic faith. So central was it that when it came, near the end, to choosing a text to sum up his convictions about the span of his life that might be recited at his funeral service, he turned again to those same lines.[78] The lack of sentimentality which they bespeak is one of the hallmarks of McGahern's Yeatsean philosophy, which exists in the knowledge that, as Yeats wrote in another poem, 'Everything that man esteems/ Endures a moment or a day.'[79] If one is confident in that knowledge, then to regret the passing of beloved things, or even of one's own life, would be a sentimental folly, because human beings have 'no choice' in the matter (as the priest in 'The Wine Breath' has had to acknowledge) and can only stoically endure or accept their fate (*GT*, p. 95). The reverberation of such Yeatsean thoughts can be felt throughout McGahern's oeuvre. Its graceful stoicism underlies passages as varied as Ruttledge's and Jamesie's matter-of-fact elegies for dying ways of life in *That They May Face the Rising Sun*, and the elderly priest's reflection on his own mortality in the opening paragraph of 'The Wine Breath'. '[H]e was doomed to die', the latter reflects, 'and being dead he'd miss nothing, being nothing' (*GT*, p. 95). The priest's thought, which he knows flies in the face of the Christian teachings about the afterlife which he is supposed to preach, repeats not the Holy Scripture but the play in which Yeats summed up his beliefs about this world and the next. Its words and rhythm echo the Old Man's remark about the apparition of his dead father in the window in *Purgatory*, the play which haunted McGahern's imagination in so many ways throughout his life: 'That beast there would know nothing, being nothing.'[80] Finally, then, through this echo of *Purgatory*, the 'nothing' that had oppressed the protagonists of *The Barracks*, *The Dark* and *King Lear* could also become a source of comfort and solace.

The shapes of modern narrative

McGahern's engagement with Joyce, too, did not begin and end with the repetition of Joycean themes of economic, social, spiritual and sexual repression or discovery, or even with his borrowing of an array of Joycean symbols of paralysis which might just as easily be applied to mid-century rural Leitrim and Roscommon as to Dublin's urban and suburban realities at the turn of the century. His response to Joyce and other early-twentieth-century modernists extends to his thoughts on what might be the appropriate narrative structure with which to most accurately reflect the experience of everyday living.

McGahern had abandoned realism's faith in the ideal of linear narrative from the earliest beginnings of his career as novelist and short-story writer. Serious and humorous allusions to the plainest of differences between what the narrator of 'Wheels' calls 'the shape of a story' (*N*, p. 22) and that of a life are repeated in a number of McGahern's works, which occasionally share the explicit questioning of the uses of beginnings and endings which may be found in the work of prominent modernist and postmodernist contemporaries like Salman Rushdie, Paul Auster and Samuel Beckett. The latter's protagonist in *Molloy* remarks that according to the man who comes to take away the pages of his life story, 'I should have begun differently ... I began at the beginning, like an old ballocks, can you imagine that?'[81] The joke, like so many in Beckett, serves to highlight a serious point, one that McGahern also makes on a number of occasions in his fiction. On the last page of *The Pornographer*, when the narrator circles back to the image with which the novel began and refers to 'the beginning of the journey — if beginning it ever had — that had brought each to where we were, in the now and the forever' (*P*, p. 252), he is, like Molloy, engaging in an act of metafictional commentary which calls attention to what it is that sets novels and stories apart from the experience of real life. While every novel and every story has a beginning, in life things are never so simple, and no single moment can ever really be assigned the privileged role of 'beginning': all are merely points 'in the now and the forever'.

The nature of beginnings is problematised on a number of occasions in McGahern's fiction. A realisation of the difficulty encountered in assigning one moment the privileged status of 'beginning' is why Patrick Moran in *The Leavetaking*, like the eponymous hero of Laurence Sterne's *Tristram Shandy*, finds it so difficult to determine just how far back he should go in his family history before reaching the point where he can properly begin the story of his own life. Like Tristram, Patrick decides that this beginning must be placed sometime before his birth, or even his conception. Even in the published episodes from *The End or the Beginning of Love*, McGahern already draws attention to the way in which religious rituals seek to make real life more like an endless series of short stories, each with their own clearly defined beginnings. As Francie and his father walk back from confession, the narrator of that early work comments on how

> The lonely and ignorant never realise that sin is as common as flesh. For them it is always the first sin and through confession they are always beginning — as if they were beginning life again with their first innocence. And in some measure Francie and his father walked in the joy of this beginning.[82]

The idea of an ending is just as much of a fiction as that of a beginning. In *The Sense of an Ending* (1966), an influential work of literary criticism that McGahern would probably have read in the late 1960s or the 1970s, Frank Kermode argued how every work of fiction 'unwinds to have an Ending', and how it is from the sense of its going towards a clearly defined ending that it derives its meaning.[83] Young Mahoney in *The Dark* is aware of a version of Kermode's argument *avant la lettre*, casting it in the religious terms of divine judgement and eternal afterlife, when he considers that 'The moment of death was the one real moment in life; everything took its proper position there, and was fixed for ever' (*D*, p. 69). Kermode's argument about 'end-determined fiction' proposes that experiences may be understood and analysed from the vantage point of a time when the action is finished, when it can be made sense of as a coherent whole, with a beginning, a middle and an end.[84] McGahern considers the artificiality of neat fictional endings in the closing sentences of a couple of his stories. In 'Gold Watch', despite the destruction of the titular timepiece, 'time, hardly surprisingly, was still running; time that did not have to run to any conclusion' (*HG*, p. 119), and in 'The Wine Breath', the young man on the doorstep feels himself 'immersed in time without end' (*GT*, p. 106). These conclusions, anathema as they are to the conventional narrative arc of the realist novel or story, reflect an appreciation of the true complexity of the world, in which — as the narrator of 'The Recruiting Officer' also considers — nothing can ever be truly finished (*N*, p. 153). How could it be otherwise, really, in the mind of an author who had from a very early age been instructed by the Catholic liturgy about the existence of a 'world without end. Amen'?[85] — a line that is so obviously echoed in the last sentence of 'The Wine Breath'.

Since the fixed beginnings and endings of realism are obviously unsatisfactory to an artist with an essentially modern sensibility like McGahern, it seems inevitable that he should consider the solutions of Joyce and Proust in his search for an alternative to the linear narrative structure of the realist novel. One seemingly inconsequential detail in a novel may well point to his debt to those examples. The seagulls who make their presence so keenly felt in *The Leavetaking* are on one intertextual level urban cousins of the gabbling crows from the opening stanza of *The Great Hunger* — a text to which McGahern pays oblique homage in the masterful *tableau vivant* of the opening pages, which depicts schoolboys on their break stooping to pick up discarded lunch wrappers supervised by the headmaster who, with 'mechanical' movements, 'hounds vigorously between the still figures in search of any papers left on the concrete' (*L*, p. 11). The narrator's view of the figures of boys and headmaster alike recalls *The Great Hunger*'s 'mechanized scare-crows' on the hillside, while the imagery of paper lunch wrappers blowing aimlessly in the wind and the seagulls falling on scraps of bread 'in a white frenzy' (*L*, p. 10) are transplanted versions of the crows that 'gabble over worms and frogs' and the gulls that 'like old newspapers are blown clear of the hedges' in that poem's opening stanza.[86] The allusions to *The Great Hunger* point to the novel's social-critical concerns. But the prominent presence of those same gulls also serves another intertextual purpose. They whish into *The Leavetaking* straight out of *Finnegans Wake*, a novel whose well-known narrative structure McGahern here evokes and celebrates. *Finnegans Wake*, too, is set in the 'environs' of the mouth of the Liffey in north Dublin, and begins and ends with a meandering description of the running water of the river and the 'Whish[ing]' of the gulls.[87] Like *Finnegans Wake*, *The Leavetaking* is a circular novel, and the circularity of both novels is first announced by the gulls, who begin to make themselves heard again in the final pages. On the final pages of *The Leavetaking*, the action returns to where it had begun in time and space, and the narrator circles back, in the long monologue on the penultimate page of the novel, to some of the most striking phrases and images from the opening paragraph — 'the first constant was water, the gull's shadow floats again on the concrete' (*L*, pp. 9, 194).

The introduction of circularity as a viable alternative narrative mode by modernists like Joyce in *Finnegans Wake* and Proust in *In Search of Lost Time* is taken up in some form by McGahern in most, if not all, of his novels. *The Leavetaking* signals its debt to *Finnegans Wake* explicitly through the whishing of Joyce's seagulls in its opening and closing paragraphs. In *The Pornographer*, the narrator draws explicit attention to the peculiar circularity of first-person retrospectives such as his own or that of Marcel in *In Search of Lost Time* when he refers to 'the beginning of the journey — if beginning it ever had — that had brought each to where we were, in the now and the forever', a comment which allows him to become the narrator of the story up to this point (*P*, p. 252). Even *The Dark*, the only one of McGahern's novels without an obvious circular narrative structure, nevertheless contains the seeds of the same kind of circularity. When, after spending the whole novel uncertainly shifting between the first-, second- and third-person pronoun, young Mahoney's narrative voice is finally allowed the detachment of a dispassionate, god-like Flaubertian narrator following his epiphany on the football pitch in Galway, the newfound stability of the point-of-view in the final chapter reads like a prologue to a future retrospect — a retrospect that may well be, in fact, following that same familiar Proustian conceit, the very novel that the reader is just about to finish. In reading *The Pornographer*, *The Leavetaking* and *The Dark* as the autobiographies of their respective protagonists, told up to the moment when they are set free to become the narrators of their own lives, it is useful to keep in mind Roger Shattuck's lucid explanation of the significance of the structure of *In Search of Lost Time*:

> Proust's ending leads us firmly out of the *Search* as *Marcel*'s story of growing up and across into a symmetrical mirror-novel, consisting of all the same words and incidents, this time recording the *Narrator*'s story of recording Marcel's story. A new circumambulation begins, this time not of living the events but of writing them. As Proust's *I* contains two persons, his novel contains two stories.

A skilled reader of Proust, Shattuck argues, will be able to read both stories simultaneously,[88] and so will readers of McGahern's three autodiegetic circular novels.

The circularity of McGahern's other three novels is of a very different order. In *The Barracks*, *Amongst Women* and *That They May Face the Rising Sun*, words, images and phrases from the opening paragraph are repeated on the final pages: the blinds being drawn by the children in Elizabeth's kitchen, Moran's daughters turning into the father who has become part of their lives even in death, the bells ringing out for Mass over the still lake and the conversation between Jamesie and the Ruttledges that follows (*TRS*, pp. 1–2, 238). In those three novels, however — and most clearly in *That They May Face the Rising Sun* — the narrative structure has evolved away from the perfectly hermetic circularity of Joyce, Proust and others, as well as from that of McGahern's own novels from the 1970s. In *Finnegans Wake* and *The Third Policeman*, *The Pornographer* and *The Leavetaking*, circularity denotes stagnancy, as the nightmare of history endlessly repeats without a possibility of reprieve. The image of the narrator's uncle carrying his raincoat on the last page of *The Pornographer* is the same as that on the first, and the details of another day which Patrick Moran remembers on the final page of *The Leavetaking* are of the day which opens that novel.

In those other three McGahern novels, by contrast, what first seems like Joycean or Proustian circularity is not precisely that. When the bells ring out for Mass a second time on page 238 of *That They May Face the Rising Sun*, or when in the final chapter of *The Barracks* the Reegan children go to draw the blinds they had first drawn on the first page, those narratives are describing a day *similar* to that of the first page a year on rather than re-circling to the *same* day. There is in the Reegans' mourning and acceptance and eventual forgetting of Elizabeth's death in *The Barracks*, and in the Morans' overcoming of the traumas of personal, domestic and national history in *Amongst Women*, more a sense of the rhythm of natural life which combines the circularity of the seasons with the birth, growth and eventual decay of all living things. As Hermione Lee writes in a review of McGahern's last novel, 'A year's cycle frames the lives on the lake', and seasonal events (many of them from the farming calendar) 'are re-created continually, different each time, with intense, eloquent simplicity'.[89] It is the deviation from the precise details of each previous cycle which makes such circling so interesting and so true to the vitality of real life as it is experienced day after day, year after year. 'Everything that had flowered had now come to fruit' (*TRS*, p. 177), the narrative voice of the novel reports at one point, with a sense that this is the universal law of existence much more real to our experience of living than the abrupt beginnings and endings of realist novels. In what are arguably his three best novels, *The Barracks*, *Amongst Women* and *That They May Face the Rising Sun*, McGahern routinely abandons the strict modernist circularity of Proust and Joyce and replaces it with what he himself described as a 'rhythm'. McGahern had always been interested in the idea of 'rhythm'. That concept extended, in his usage, beyond that of the sounds of individual words or syllables within a sentence or a paragraph to include the repetition of images, words and phrases (even sometimes of whole conversations, as in the case of *The Barracks* or *That They May Face the Rising Sun*), a process which he compared to refrains in verse.[90]

Like Virginia Woolf before him, McGahern was very interested in the idea that entire works of fiction might be patterned following such social and natural *rhythms*, rather than according to the strict linearity of realist plots or even the closed-circuit circularity of certain other modernist novels. Woolf planned for her most audacious narrative experiment to be written 'in the rhythm of the waves'.[91] As she wrote in a letter about the composition of

The Waves: 'my difficulty is that I am writing to a rhythm and not to a plot... though the rhythmical is more natural to me than the narrative, it is completely opposed to the tradition of fiction'.[92] McGahern may have remembered these comments, or indeed the strange haunting quality of *The Waves*, when he determined to pattern the narrative of *That They May Face the Rising Sun* to follow the course of the seasons and the days. Another, perhaps more immediate, cue for the use of natural rhythms as a way of patterning fiction was probably a line from Arnold's 'Dover Beach': 'Begin and cease, and then again begin.' McGahern's memory of that line had earlier in his career allowed the narrator of *The Leavetaking* to conceive of his life using the imagery of ebb and flow, as 'the long withdrawing tide of memory becoming imagination' moves like the sea surges against the harbour wall in Howth (*L*, pp. 45, 193). Patrick Moran's ease in applying that sound to a metaphysical reflection is facilitated by the way in which Arnold's poem itself unpacks the metaphor. 'Dover Beach' is a reflection not just on the sounds of the sea, but on the way those sounds foster thoughts about 'the turbid ebb and flow/ Of human misery' in observers in all places and throughout all historical ages.[93]

Ultimately, however, a recurring echo from a well-known poem in his last two novels, and a piece of literary criticism from the 1980s about an Irish classic, may well suggest how McGahern's reading of two favourite Irish authors probably informed his eventual embracing of the great tides of nature as a narrative model in his later fiction, after the flirtation with Joycean and Proustian circularity respectively in *The Leavetaking* and *The Pornographer*. Yeats, certainly, had his part to play as an exemplar of how the rhythms of natural things may be an appropriate template for modes of living. When Rose in *Amongst Women* talks about her time in Glasgow as a young woman, 'Mona and Sheila were so poised on the edge of their own lives that they listened as if hearing about *the living stream* they were about to enter' (*AW*, p. 80, emphasis added). The echo of 'Easter 1916' which is contained in the italicised phrase in that sentence[94] is revived in *That They May Face the Rising Sun*. By the time McGahern wrote his last novel, that phrase from the contemplative third section of Yeats' poem, the one describing the immovable pace of ordinary life in the midst of political turmoil (or that at least is how McGahern appears to have read it), had become something of a touchstone in McGahern's thinking about the flow and vitality of harmonious urban living as it can be idealised by those who live in rural isolation; to the Ruttledges, part of the 'attractiveness' of London is the 'living stream of its people' (*TRS*, p. 156). The place itself is ultimately immaterial, though. The sensation of entering a 'living stream' can be applied equally to the experience of the running succession of days spent in *any* place, as both the Ruttledges' failure to leave the lake and the Moran girls' eventual return to Great Meadow suggest.

Like so much of what is freshest and most radically modern in McGahern's ideas about literature, perhaps his main aesthetic cue in radically re-conceiving of the shape of the novel appears to have come from his reading of Tomás Ó Criomhthain's *The Islandman*, a book that enabled him to articulate many of his most deeply held beliefs about writing. In his essay on *The Islandman*, McGahern observes how the action is punctuated by settings out and returns, and how its narrative is patterned by the immutable changing of the seasons and the continual breaking of new days (*LW*, pp. 264–5). In that essay he first introduces into his thought the idea that the rhythm of each individual human life can be seen as analogous to that of the sea tides:

> [A] haunting phrase — *rithe mo laethse* or *rithe mo bhearthain* — runs throughout the book. 'In the running of my days' is Flower's literal translation, but it has more the sense of a great tide, filling the strand with the vigour and glory of youth coming to a fullness, and then gradually and weakly withdrawing (*LW*, p. 269)

— a reading which may itself have been influenced by Matthew Arnold's 'melancholy, long withdrawing roar' of the tides.[95] It is in *Amongst Women*, again, that the presence of McGahern's thinking about *The Islandman* can be most acutely felt. To say that *Amongst Women* recalls Ó Criomhthain's style would perhaps not be as accurate as to suggest that it recalls McGahern's *reading* of Ó Criomhthain. The references in the opening passage to the 'tides' of the great outside world (*AW*, p. 2), and later to the girls' 'regular comings and goings' to and from Great Meadow which 'flow like relief through the house' (*AW*, p. 93), certainly echo McGahern's reading of Ó Criomhthain's sense of the cyclical movements of time. More than in the example of Joyce or Proust or Woolf or even Matthew Arnold, then, it is here, in McGahern's individual, idiosyncratic readings of classic texts as much as in the actual properties of those texts themselves, that the origins of his final reimagining of the structure of the modern novel may be found.

'Talk will save us'

McGahern's fiction should also be regarded in a specifically Irish modernist tradition, in the context of a narrative trope shared by a number of prominent twentieth-century Irish writers. McGahern was temperamentally wary of writing which seemed to him to be no more than the showing off of technique. He told the critic Keith Hopper, for example, that while he admired Flann O'Brien, he found *At Swim-Two-Birds* 'too tricksy' for his own liking,[96] and on more than one occasion he made it known that he preferred the pared-down scrupulousness of Joyce's *Dubliners* and the early episodes of *Ulysses* to the formal experimental exuberance of *Finnegans Wake* (*LW*, p. 207). He voiced his despair with the aesthetic trajectory of Joyce's later fiction in the essay 'Mr Joyce and Mr Yeats':

> It was a long journey: from the scrupulous clarity of *Dubliners*, where the first shapes are, where the wonderful aural wit first stirs, crux upon crux — out into *Finnegans Wake*, the words now losing their definite line to merge and chime and swim, calling up other words, always changing, always taling, summoned by the incredible energy of that comic genius, always expanding, expounding, playing. Words alone seem certain good. Talk will save us. (*LW*, p. 185)

The quotations in the final two sentences from Yeats' 'The Song of the Happy Shepherd' and from *Finnegans Wake*, respectively, are obvious.[97] Both are expressions of Irish writing's belief in the power of spoken language.Many works of fiction by Irish authors display a reliance on talk which is highly self-referential, and which often takes the place of any other action. Characters either fill the void of inactivity forced upon them through other causes with incessant storytelling (as Beckett's bedridden narrators in the Trilogy do) or they are immobilised by their compulsive chattering like Sterne's Tristram Shandy. Characters and narrators in such works do not only talk as if their continuing existence or salvation depended on it; they are also characterised by an awareness of this compulsion, as the subject of their talk is often the very need to talk. Beckett draws attention to the persistence of this trope in his own work and that of others when the tramps in *Waiting for Godot* conclude that 'To have lived is not enough for them … They have to talk about it.'[98] Examples of an Irish fondness for this trope go back over centuries: Declan Kiberd, for instance, traces the Beckettian trope of the man lying on his back in the dark summoning voices and narrating his own death as it occurs to the Gaelic bards.[99] Its use is particularly noticeable in twentieth-century writing, though. 'Ho, talk save us' is the unofficial credo of many of the central representatives of Irish literary modernism. That sentence from *Finnegans Wake* sums up a preoccupation that is at the heart of an Irish tradition which encompasses writers like Synge, Beckett, Flann O'Brien and the Joyce of *Finnegans Wake*, as well as the Irish-language novelist Máirtín Ó Cadhain, in whose most famous novel, *The Dirty Dust* (*Cré Na Cille*; 1949), even the dead who lie buried in the graveyard cannot stop talking, taling, gossiping and arguing.

More than once McGahern self-referentially places his own work in this tradition of insatiable and self-aware talkers. Far from supporting the case for the marginality of *Finnegans Wake* in the Irish literary tradition, as is ostensibly its purpose in the essay, the quotation of that line from *Finnegans Wake* in 'Mr Joyce and Mr Yeats' actually points to a recognition of a major concern in McGahern's *own* work. In an interesting spin on Joyce's 'talk save us', Patrick Ryan in *That They May Face the Rising Sun* believes in the *literal* healing power of conversation and anecdote. When he is stung by the Ruttledges' angry bees, he turns not just to whiskey — which he wittily dubs 'Yer Irishman's morphine' — but more significantly to *storytelling* as an anaesthetic, so that soon 'He talked as if talk itself could ease the pain' (*TRS*, pp. 72–3). McGahern also deliberately aligns himself with Synge as a exponent of the same tradition, as the same novel references the emphasis on talk in Synge's most famous play. Old Mahon concludes *The Playboy of the Western World* by stating his intention of becoming a wandering purveyor of comic tales much like Patrick Ryan in *That They May Face the Rising Sun* when he says that 'we'll have great times from this out telling stories of the villainy of Mayo and the fools is here'.[100] Patrick Ryan had once acted in that play but is now condemned to relive the afterlife of one of its central characters, having turned into a theatrical itinerant purveyor of the stories of the villainies of his native county and the fools who live there. The connection with *The Playboy* is cemented on the final page by a clear allusion to Old Mahon's farewell to the village, as Patrick marks his departure from the novel with the buoyant announcement that 'I'll go and entertain them all in their own houses' (*TRS*, p. 298).

Talk is central to the experience of many of McGahern's characters as they rehearse their lives in retrospective tales with no hope of reaching the catharsis of classical narrative forms. The list of purgatories and confessionals in which his characters are trapped is seemingly endless. *The Dark*, *The Leavetaking* and *The Pornographer*, and stories like 'My Love, My Umbrella', 'Doorways' and 'Parachutes', are all first-person records of narrators who are struggling to put the events of their lives in order. The reliance on talk to bring salvation or enlightenment is not confined to the narrators or even the main characters of his works. A character like Tipperary in 'Hearts of Oak and Bellies of Brass' feels compelled to go over his failure in the school-leaving exams like the responses to the catechism, while Tommy McHugh in 'Creatures of the Earth' stops unwilling passers-by on the cliff path with his tale of woe like Coleridge's mariner. All of these are in stark contrast with Bill Evans in *That They May Face the Rising Sun*, who, in his refusal to talk at all about his past, appears to be as divested of one as Beckett's Vladimir and Estragon, who only rarely allude to their past and are scornful of 'all the dead voices' who feel a constant need to talk about it. Rather than talking about the past and its many traumas, Bill Evans, like the eponymous Molloy in Beckett's novel, prefers to speak only 'of the things that are left'.[101]

A fascination with talk and stories which may take the place of real action is obvious from the opening sentence of 'Wheels', the first story in *Nightlines* and in both his *Collected* and his *New and Selected Stories*, in which the narrator settles down to listen to a conversation between three railway porters because he can do 'nothing but wait and watch and listen, and I listened to the story they were telling' (*N*, p. 11). The only tool that Guards Reegan, Brennan, Casey and Mullins in *The Barracks* possess to alleviate their boredom consists of a considerable gift of the gab. Like the titular character of Beckett's *Molloy*, the guards in *The Barracks* spend their days 'speak[ing] of the things that are left' as they live out their final years in a rural backwater. There is very little else for them to do now that the heroic roles that once defined their position in society have been made redundant by the Anglo-Irish Treaty of 1922. For as the narrator points out in a sentence which captures the essence of twentieth-century tragedy, 'Now they sat and remembered, thirty years later, waiting to go to their homes in the rain' (*B*, p. 29). It is a theme to which McGahern returns with some regularity. That other pair of old revolutionaries in his fiction, Moran and McQuaid in *Amongst Women*, are closer to death but still they continue to talk once every year of what the narrator, not without irony, refers to as 'the days of their glory' (*AW*, p. 14). Most of the stories McGahern's characters tell themselves and others are about their own past. Even on the occasions when they are not, they still serve a not dissimilar purpose. When the first-person narrator of 'My Love, My Umbrella' remarks on how he and his lover had met regularly during the course of a summer and that 'Sometimes we told each other stories' (*N*, p. 106), McGahern is clearly invoking the resolve of the eponymous hero of Beckett's *Malone Dies*: 'While waiting [for death] I shall tell myself stories.'[102] The lovers' stories in 'My Love, My Umbrella' can be 'cruel' or pointless, and often they are only tangentially related to the tellers' own lives. What these stories have in common is that they all serve the Beckettian function of 'passing the time' — a phrase that reverberates through the consciousness of so many of McGahern's central characters and narrators — before they are allowed to end the evening's date by having sexual intercourse under his umbrella.

Despite this, McGahern can simultaneously also be deeply sceptical of the implications of the Irish-modernist literary trope of ceaseless talk within which his novels and stories so consistently operate. The well-mannered silence of the Protestant characters in *High Ground* whose reticent temperaments are so sympathetic to McGahern as man and author (as chapter two discussed), for one thing, is a powerful antidote to the 'blather' of the heroes of Ó Cadhain, Beckett and Flann O'Brien. Even Moran in *Amongst Women*, as that same passage of indirect speech about his annual meetings with McQuaid suggests, refuses to endorse his old comrade's idea of the 'glory' of the past they endlessly narrate (*AW*, p. 14). Perhaps he knows, like Joyce and Stephen Dedalus before him, how ridiculous a professional qualification it is to be 'a praiser of his own past'.[103]

McGahern is practical enough to know that talk can in fact not always save us. The healing it offers is at best only temporary. In a sentence reminiscent of the reasons given by the eponymous hero of Beckett's *The Unnamable* for *his* endless stream of talk, the narrator of *The Dark* refers to his father's maniacal 'midnight heart-easings' as 'All this talk and struggle to get to terms or understanding'. He is painfully aware that the 'understanding' conjured by his father's endless talk is doomed to 'last for no longer than the sleep of this night. It was always changed by the morning' (*D*, p. 19). The father probably knows this too, yet he indefatigably persists with his efforts to 'get to terms or understanding'. In *The Dark*, as in *Malone Dies* or *The Unnamable*, the cycle of talk must be endlessly repeated, each time in the hope that speech will make sense of events or situations, and each time also in the knowledge that it never will. This is even true of the passage in *That They May Face the Rising Sun* which introduces Patrick Ryan's belief in the power of talk as medicine. When he 'talked *as if* talk itself could ease the pain' (*TRS*, p. 73, emphasis added), the two italicised words are crucial, because while Patrick may be convinced of the anaesthetic properties of chit-chat, those two words make it clear that the narrator, at least, is more sceptical about that possibility.

On other occasions, McGahern's fiction also operates from an awareness that not only can talk not bring real or lasting salvation but that it often works instead to perpetuate, or even instigate, trouble and pain. *Amongst Women*, with its pair of Beckettian talkers, also contains at least two ironic reminders of the shortcomings of this typical Irish-modernist response to the past. In the first of these, Moran's family notice how their attempt 'to start him back to himself' (*AW*, p. 1) through the kind of rehearsal of his wartime past which he had always enjoyed in the company of McQuaid is a failure because, on this last occasion, 'Monaghan Day had revived nothing but a weak fanciful ghost of what had been' (*AW*, p. 7). W.B. Yeats' late poems are full of the regretful ghosts of the past, and perhaps McGahern intended an analogy between Moran and McQuaid reminiscing for the last time and one of Yeats' final reassessments of the heroism of 1916 in 'The Statues', with its invocation of an undefined pale ghost from the past that 'stalked through the Post Office', doing untold damage in the present.[104] The havoc which this kind of talk can cause to the ordinary business of living is also a theme in the Big Mick Madden episode of *That They May Face the Rising Sun*. The second instance in *Amongst Women* comes later, when Rose tries to assuage Moran's disapproval of what seems to him to be Luke's shady business plans as she 'ventured edgily' that 'It may be just talk'. After his experience of the unspeakable things that may result from nationalist rhetoric, not to mention the subsequent glorification of those same deeds in the form of old-soldiers' war stories, Rose's use of that word does not produce the desired calmative effect. Moran's response is a wry rhetorical question which is reminiscent of some of the statements of Beckett's disillusioned protagonists from *Malone Dies* or *The Unnamable*, and which ironically counters the confident thrust of the talk-centred Irish-modernist tradition: 'How does anything start but in talk?' (*AW*, p. 67)

After *Amongst Women*'s self-conscious interrogation of the usefulness of talk, McGahern nevertheless returned to write about a community made up almost exclusively of brilliant conversationalists in *That They May Face the Rising Sun*. The difference with much of his earlier fiction is that in that final novel most of the characters are no longer seeking to 'escape', like Beckett's protagonists, from '"blather", an endless verbality... to reach the silence that lies beyond it'.[105] Nor is their talk the self-important going over of one's own past of Moran and McQuaid in *Amongst Women* or the guards in *The Barracks*. 'Talk' in *That They May Face the Rising Sun* is not very Beckettian at all.

McGahern's last novel celebrates the arts of bantering neighbourly conversation, small talk, and even gossip. As an earlier chapter showed, such varieties of talk were generally condemned with the ferocity of an eighteenth-century satirist in his earlier work.[106] James Sharkey and the parish priest in 'All Sorts of Impossible Things', for example, matter-of-factly discuss the way 'Everything gets round these parts', and drily mock how hardly any of what is reported in that small-town gossip is even remotely accurate (*GT*, p. 42), while the father in 'Wheels' feels the need to condemn both the sharp edge of the late Mrs McGreevy's tongue and the savage gossip which ensued from that same Mrs McGreevy's ignominious last journey out of the village, her coffin roped to the top of the bread van (*N*, p. 20). *That They May Face the Rising Sun* marks an important shift in attitude. The main characters are still censorious of the more aggressive kinds of gossiping that go on around the lake — such as the case of the boy being mugged by neighbours on the road 'until they had extracted every word of flesh' like newsy vultures (*TRS*, p. 45) which demonstrates how curiosity can be as aggressive as any other intervention into one's private life. At the same time, the narrative also finds much to admire in the lively exchange of gossip and local news. Talk and gossip are central to the structure of *That They May Face the Rising Sun*. Many of the central characters can talk without an attendant sense that keeping up an endless stream of talk is necessary to achieving a moment of catharsis which deep down they know is unattainable, or even that it is required to numb the pain of living. The likes of Jamesie simply revel in banter and gossip. In his last major work of fiction, McGahern increasingly embraces the insight that gossip, as long as it is not malicious, can be a great art form in its own right. That form is particularly virulent in Ireland. Gossip is the structural backbone of such loosely patterned Irish prose narratives as *Tristram Shandy* and *The Dirty Dust*, as well as of *Finnegans Wake*, with its nosy washerwomen exchanging all the local news by the river of life. The characters' constantly repeated enquiries for local news and gossip — 'What's the news?' 'No news. Came looking for news' (*TRS*, p. 3) — bind the action of *That They May Face the Rising Sun* together. The novel begins with a spirited exchange between the eavesdropper and his prey, in which the former playfully complains that, even after listening in on a private conversation for several minutes, he has not heard a bad word spoken about anybody yet (*TRS*, p. 1). Even the arrival of the first cuckoo is awaited each year by Jamesie with the anticipation of a great gossip who takes pleasure from being the first to report the news of its arrival (*TRS*, p. 239). Thus, the novel revives Joyce's brilliant discovery of the rhythmic and structural potential of such newsy entreaties in *Finnegans Wake*, where the washerwomen's constant refrain of 'Tell me all. Tell me now... Tell me moher. Tell me moatst' manages to drive the narrative of the Anna Livia Plurabelle chapter forward at a steady pace despite the absence of anything resembling a formal plot.[107]

What makes *That They May Face the Rising Sun* such a compelling book is the centrality of *small talk*, not big talk. The latter invariably gets short shrift throughout from all the novel's central characters, who, like Joyce and Stephen Dedalus before them, 'fear those big words... which make us so unhappy' (McGahern cited that line from *Ulysses* on more than one occasion).[108] In a 1995 piece of travel writing about the west of Ireland for an American newspaper, McGahern humorously pointed to this Irish habit that can be so exasperating to outside observers and foreign visitors when he quoted a 1934 letter by Virginia

Woolf about the countryside near Galway: 'It is a lovely country, but very melancholy, except that the people never stop talking' (*LW*, p. 28).[109] Woolf's comment not only serves to highlight the contrast between English and Irish sensibilities; her observation of Irish character is also a perfect description of the local character that was to be so lovingly reconstructed in McGahern's next novel, on which he began working around the time that essay was published, and which would, when it was finally published, inevitably provoke uncomprehending responses from some English reviewers which in turn echoed Woolf's letter's exasperation with unrelenting Irish loquaciousness.[110] *That They May Face the Rising Sun* celebrates the lively exchange of talk and gossip and the propagation of stories and narratives. In doing so, it enables a transcending of the traumas of the past which other kinds of 'talk' only work to refresh and renew through the obsessive repetition of failures and injuries. *This* kind of talk, on the other hand, may indeed go a long way to save us.

CHAPTER 7

Post-war Philosophies

> 'What the hell is all this living and dying about anyway?' would come as a scream of frustration and hate at some time or other of those grisly evenings. Then came the car crash on the Leytonstone Road to solve nothing and everything...
>
> *The Barracks* (p. 94)

The euphemistic description of the circumstances of Michael Halliday's death in *The Barracks* may be read as a cloaked reference to a loss recently sustained by the world of letters: that which occurred when the Algerian-born Nobel Prize winner Albert Camus died in a car crash, the circumstances of which have never been satisfactorily established, in early January 1960. McGahern was an admirer of Camus' prose, and the shock of his sudden loss must still have been fresh when he wrote *The Barracks* in 1961–62. The silent homage to Camus, if one is intended, would be appropriate in the context of McGahern's first published novel. Halliday's predilection for what he himself describes as 'pessimistic' thoughts is not just the result of his training as a surgeon, his pursuit of that profession during the horrors of the London Blitz, or even his juvenile devotion to A.E. Housman's verses of doomed youth (*B*, p. 92). The self-proclaimed 'Master of Suffering' who has travelled in Europe before the War and who takes Elizabeth to a restaurant where the menus are in French (*B*, pp. 92, 88) is also influenced by trends in contemporary Continental philosophy.

This chapter will be concerned with McGahern's post-war sensibility, as it developed through his reading of some of the defining voices of the period. It will consider McGahern's work in the light of some of the literary ideas that emerged in the post-war period. The subject is not the presence in his writing of the *historical* realities of the Second World War. It is concerned instead with McGahern's digestion of some of the key literary and philosophical debates and trends which developed in response to those realities in continental Europe, either during or in the years immediately following the War. The first section will take in McGahern's occasional engagements with Sartre's and Camus' contrasting strategies for coping with what the latter described as a godless 'universe suddenly divested of illusions and lights' in which 'man feels an alien, a stranger'.[1] It will also consider his interest in Claude Simon and the *Nouveau Roman*, and in Primo Levi's literary response to the revelation of forms of inhumanity in the concentration camps. All these ideas can be found in isolated places in McGahern's work. These probably remained isolated because McGahern did not have time to digest those recent authors and their ideas as fully as he did those of writers from earlier centuries, or even of early-twentieth-century presences like Yeats, Joyce and Proust, who had by the 1950s already assumed the status of 'traditional' writers in the sense used by T.S. Eliot. Samuel Beckett, it seems, was more easily digestible for the young McGahern. This was perhaps partly because of his more profound affinity with a 'Beckettian' sensibility, and partly because of his more constant and sustained reading of and thinking about Beckett's writing as it appeared. The second half of the chapter is dedicated to McGahern's lifelong engagement with Beckett, and with the various versions of Beckettian strategies for coping with modern life that can be found throughout McGahern's oeuvre.

Post-war thought

Intermittent references to the global events of the 1940s in novels and stories such as *The Barracks*, 'Hearts of Oak and Bellies of Brass' and 'Oldfashioned' testify that Irish writers of the post-war generation such as McGahern were not, as has all too readily been assumed in the past, isolated from the realities of the Second World War.[2] Nor were they out of touch with the intellectual culture which emerged during the conflict and in its aftermath. *The Barracks* shows evidence of McGahern's sensitivity to contemporary literary and philosophical thought. It does so by introducing a version of a Parisian literary-philosophical debate of the 1940s into a narrative about living and dying in rural Roscommon.

Elizabeth Reegan's memories of her conversations with the morbid surgeon Halliday in wartime London are essentially a rewriting of the philosophical disagreement between Camus and Jean-Paul Sartre which split what is popularly, but erroneously, thought of as the existentialist movement. Camus' position was fundamentally different from that of Sartre and the existentialists, yet they are often linked together. Camus explained why he found it odd that these two thinkers should be yoked together under a single adjective when he said in an interview that 'Sartre is an existentialist, and the only book of ideas that I have published, *The Myth of Sisyphus*, was directed against the so-called existentialist philosophers.'[3] Halliday's fate in *The Barracks* may echo Camus' tragic end, but the tenor of his living thoughts are not those of the Algerian-born novelist. Elizabeth's recollections of her conversations with Halliday record a clash of sensibilities. In these, the 'pessimistic bastard' Halliday (as he describes himself (*B*, p. 92)) is squarely aligned with the hopeless philosophical stance of Sartre's existentialism — or at least with a popularised version of it. Halliday fantasises about making available an institutionalised course of study of 'The Human Drama of Suffering' which would lead to the awarding of an 'M.Sf.... the degree of degrees... Master of Suffering!' (*B*, p. 92) Further, the question he repeats constantly to Elizabeth, and which she repeats to herself in later years, 'What is all this living and dying about anyway?', revives that concerning the purpose of existence which had led Sartre to conclude, as he wrote in *Being and Nothingness*, that 'being' is 'without reason, without cause, without necessity'.[4] It is easy to be defeated, as Halliday is, by the meaninglessness contained in that conclusion. Its pessimism did not appeal to McGahern, though. He had no religious faith to convince him that life *wasn't* strictly speaking without purpose, but he did not believe that this should automatically extinguish the will to go on living.

McGahern did not like being labelled an existentialist any more than Camus did. He was occasionally reminded of having been described as one by some French reviewers earlier in his career. On one such occasion he deftly sidestepped an interviewer's question whether he was 'influenced by any French existentialists' with the response, 'I'm not sure what the word means.'[5] The fact is that McGahern's outlook was ultimately much closer to Camus' philosophy of 'the absurd' than to that of Sartre's existentialism. This rival strain of 1940s French thought is dramatised in the character of Elizabeth Reegan in *The Barracks*. Elizabeth is initially fascinated by what seems to her the intellectual independence of the dashing young surgeon, but she cannot accept Halliday's philosophy of pointlessness. In response, she begins to write her own version of a philosophy to cope with the futility of a life which seems both short and arbitrary, and to which there may very well not be a celestial sequel. Sitting in a riverside café in the small Irish town where she has made her home after the war, she daydreams of her wartime days with Halliday:

> She was in London, with Halliday, the enriched and indestructible days about her, 'What the hell is all this living and dying about anyway,

> Elizabeth? That's what I'd like to know,' removed to the fixity of death and memory and coming now [i.e. when she remembers it years later in Ireland] *like a quality of laughter*. (*B*, p. 86, emphasis added)

It is important that remembering his question about the pointlessness of existence should make Elizabeth laugh. As Denis Sampson writes, despite the hopeless situation faced by the central character, *The Barracks* 'is actually a study of the personal qualities that counter despair with endurance and serenity'.[6] In the resounding final sentence of *The Myth of Sisyphus*, the book in which he argues against suicide, Camus famously concluded that 'One must imagine Sisyphus happy.'[7] Elizabeth's 'laughter' is that of the Sisyphus we encounter in Camus' essay. Camus' Sisyphus must laugh in the face of the arbitrary cruelty of an uncaring world and choose, in what Camus stresses repeatedly is the only possibility for 'absurd revolt', to not commit suicide but to continue living and even somehow, despite all the odds, to achieve a state of happiness.

Elizabeth, in contrast to Halliday, learns like Camus' Sisyphus to look upon the world that has proven so cruel and yet to 'smile' on her deathbed (*B*, p. 211), even to laugh in the face of her own suffering and the certain knowledge of her imminent death. Thought similar to that which enables Elizabeth Reegan to laugh and smile at her 'absurd' predicament can be found to underpin the original 1968 version of 'The Image'. In that essay, written under the apparent sway of *The Myth of Sisyphus* and its lessons in the art of absurd revolt, McGahern proposed that we can 'create a world in which we can live' by 'absurdly' 'celebrat[ing] even the totally intolerable' (*LW*, p. 5). Not only is the choice of the adverb 'absurdly' (which is used twice in the very short essay) as telling of Camus' influence on McGahern's thinking as the choice of 'involuntarily' is of that of Proust; the underlying philosophical stance of those paragraphs from 'The Image' certainly shares a close affinity with a remark in Camus' 1955 preface to the English-language edition of his book, in which he described *The Myth of Sisyphus* as 'a lucid invitation to live and to create, in the very midst of the desert'.[8] The urge to smile or laugh in the face of futility first introduced into McGahern's work in *The Barracks* and subsequently encoded in his literary philosophy in 'The Image' is also repeated in other works of fiction from the later 1960s and 1970s. It can be seen, for example, in the pornographer's awareness of feeling 'extraordinarily happy' on the streets of London after a beating at the hands of Josephine's protector (*P*, p. 229). Even the title of 'The Beginning of an Idea', a story first published in 1974 in which the protagonist undergoes intense acts of arbitrary cruelty, may have been intended as a nod of acknowledgement to the first sentence of Camus' preface, which states: 'For me

The Myth of Sisyphus marks the beginning of an idea which I was to pursue in *The Rebel*.'[9]

The presence of Camus' conclusions about the importance of imagining Sisyphus happy can perhaps above all be seen at the end of *The Dark*. There, young Mahoney conjures the ability to transcend suffering by 'laugh[ing] purely, without bitterness, for the first time, and it was a kind of happiness, at its heart the terror of an unclear recognition of the reality that set you free' (*D*, p. 188). The protagonist's attitude at the end of the penultimate chapter of that novel has an antecedent in Camus' fiction as well as his non-fiction. Young Mahoney's peculiar discovery of the openness of human destiny reprises the climactic moment at the conclusion of what is probably Camus' best-known novel, *The Outsider*, in which the aimless drifter Meursalt finally opens his heart 'to the benign indifference of the universe'.[10] Meursalt and Mahoney are both liberated from the crippling pressures brought to bear on their existence by the expectations of social convention through their knowledge that in an absurd world, as the narrator of *The Pornographer* was eventually to sum up the aimless freedom of an existence devoid of real purpose, 'any one thing was as worth doing as any other' (*P*, p. 251). McGahern wholeheartedly embraced that kind of thinking when he wrote *The Dark* as a young man defining himself against inherited social values in the early 1960s. By the time he wrote that sentence in *The Pornographer*, however, the potential dangers of such apathetic attitudes to the continuing stability of the world of manners had come to dampen the initial excitement of the philosophy of individual liberty which he had first found in Camus. As an earlier chapter showed, McGahern was ultimately acutely aware of how the absurd sense that 'any one thing was as worth doing as any other' could all too easily become a sanction for imaginatively apathetic acts of antisocial behaviour towards one's fellow man.[11] It is this hazard presented by casually existential attitudes to the delicate world of manners which is the real subject of that much-quoted existential sentence from *The Pornographer*. It is probably for this reason that McGahern's flirtations with the literature of the absurd remain confined to the work of the early decades of his career.

McGahern's fiction also shows evidence of his immersion in some of the other major themes of post-war European, and particularly French, literary culture. In *The Leavetaking*, a novel written during the brewing storm of violence in Northern Ireland in the early 1970s, the schoolteacher–protagonist Patrick Moran confronts the headmaster at his school about the way Irish history is portrayed in 'the official *Notes For Teachers* on history' as a simplified mythical struggle between powerless virgin (Ireland) and overpowering black beast

(Britain). He concludes his point by saying that 'most of us know it's a lot more complicated than that. And yet we teach it', an accusation against which the headmaster can only respond with a complicit silence and an immediate change of subject (*L*, p. 186). By drawing critical attention to the propagation of such highly emotive versions of the nation's history in Irish schools, McGahern showed that he was in step with the new generation of revisionist Irish historians who, spurred on by the same escalation of events north of the border, began to campaign for an overhaul of the piously nationalist school curriculum which could only lead — and indeed *had* led — to violence.[12]

The Leavetaking's vocal suspicion of the shape of historical narratives is not, however, *exclusively* a manifestation of a politically attuned Irish writer's awareness of the dangers which may result from substituting propaganda for real knowledge at a specific moment in history. Its discussion of the Irish history curriculum is part of a larger epistemological argument about the nature of historical narratives as much as it is a plea for *Irish* historical revisionism. Other remarks about the nature of history elsewhere in the novel have a more obviously universal scope. Following his discussion with the headmaster about the way history is taught, Patrick Moran goes to meet his friend Lightfoot in a pub. He finds him at the counter engrossed in a history book. The narrator may have gone to the pub to escape his conversation with the headmaster, yet it becomes immediately clear that this passage is thematically linked to the preceding conversation in the school when Lightfoot expresses a preference for reading works of history because, he proclaims grandly, 'it stays still. *It* at least is settled' (*L*, p. 187). The foolishness of that statement is not made explicit by the narrator, but it must nonetheless be abundantly clear to any reader of the novel. Patrick Moran's, and indeed McGahern's, suspicion of the intrinsic mutability of the narratives presented as 'still' or 'settled' truths in history textbooks points to a more general concern with the nature of written histories. The same concern is illustrated by McGahern's recollection in the opening paragraph of a lecture script of meeting the historian J.C. Beckett, author of *The Making of Modern Ireland* (1966), one of the classics of modern Irish historiography. That short paragraph is revealing of one of McGahern's key beliefs about the nature of narratives, historical and otherwise, and it can usefully be read as a companion piece to that late passage in *The Leavetaking*. McGahern recalls how Beckett had told him with a 'sly twinkle' how 'Of course, [my books] are prejudiced', and remarks by way of explication that 'What this has always seemed to me to imply is that there is no such thing as a "true" history. Each is a version of what has taken place, and everybody who writes is coming from somewhere' (*LW*, p. 12). In recounting the eminent historian's caveat about his life's work, McGahern was not only reiterating a point about the formal discipline of academic historiography; he was also enlisting J.C. Beckett's comment to make a more universal statement about the uncertainty of *all* types of histories, stories, and even memories.

The awareness, both in *The Leavetaking* and in the anecdote about J.C. Beckett, of the ever-changing nature of all historical narratives was as much a response to recent trends in French literary and intellectual culture as it was a sign of McGahern's sympathy with the revisionist streak in Irish historiography. The narrator's suspicion in *The Leavetaking* of 'still' or 'settled' versions of history is perfectly in tune with the poststructuralist approach to 'history as a discourse' (that is to say, as a narrative or story) popularised by thinkers such as Foucault in the 1970s. This argued how 'history is never objective because it cannot be independent of the historian and his ... own time or cultural context, and it is the power of language to create meaning rather than to discover the true direction that history has taken that is important ... The reasoning behind this position is Foucault's sustained attack on the ... belief in the adequate representation of reality through the narrative form.'[13]

It is doubtful, however, whether McGahern had read Foucault. Even if he did, it is unlikely that he would have taken much heed of such a purely theoretical approach. It is certain, on the other hand, that he *had* read widely in the *Nouveau Roman* which flourished as a genre of experimental fiction in France during the 1950s and 1960s, and which shared many of the concerns of historians and philosophers of the same period. McGahern particularly admired the novels of Claude Simon, whose novels began appearing in English translation in the early 1960s, and whom he described in a 1971 book review as the only 'true poet' among the group of writers 'unfairly labelled together as the post-war French experimentalists' (*LW*, p. 295).[14] The nature of stories and histories is one of Simon's master themes, and it is not unreasonable to assume that the narrator's questioning of the use of Irish-history textbooks in *The Leavetaking* in 1974 owes something to McGahern's recent reading of novels like *The Grass* and *The Flanders Road*. Both of these deal with what the narrator of the latter calls the 'excessively confiscated, disinfected and finally edible' versions of the past constructed 'for the use of official school manuals and pedigreed families ... But actually what do you know?'[15] Such awareness of the way all stories and histories, both personal and national, refuse to stay 'still' or 'settled' is one of the thematic mainstays of late-twentieth-century literature in English. McGahern's interest in it connects his work not only with Claude Simon and the post-war moment in avant-gardist French fiction but also with certain of his prominent Irish and international contemporaries, from John Banville and Brian Friel to Salman Rushdie and J.M. Coetzee.

McGahern's admiration for Claude Simon was unstinting. The presence of that novelist can be felt not only in McGahern's preoccupation with the fraught nature of the construction of historical narratives but also occasionally behind striking thoughts and sentences on other topics in his early fiction. One of these is Sinclair's obscene misogynistic mockery of his own ritual sacrifice at the high altar of seductive female sexuality in 'Why We're Here'. Sinclair's downfall because of his marriage to an unsuitable woman, and particularly his crude remark that '*All candles were made to burn before the high altar of their cunts*' (*N*, p. 26), appears to be indebted to a passage in *The Flanders Road*. One of the characters in that novel is privy to the dreadful knowledge that proposing marriage to a particular, sensual woman would amount to organising the 'Passion' of his own crucifixion, 'with this difference that the site the centre the altar wasn't a naked hill but that smooth and tender and hairy and secret crease in the flesh ... Yes: crucified, agonizing on the altar the mouth the cave of ... But after all wasn't there a whore at the other crucifixion too[?]'[16]

One post-war voice who haunted McGahern's imagination more profoundly than either Camus or Simon was Primo Levi, the Italian Jew who had survived the Nazi death camps only to be condemned, like one of Beckett's characters, to endlessly repeat the experiences of those years in works of fiction and documentary non-fiction for the rest of his life. McGahern first made reference to having read *The Truce* and *If This Is a Man*, which he described as 'possibly ... a great book', in a letter to Michael McLaverty shortly after the publication of *The Dark* in 1965.[17] That Levi continued to occupy McGahern's thoughts ever since is evident from the inclusion of *If This Is a Man* on the syllabus of the course on modern writing which he taught at University College, Galway, in 1993 and again at University College, Dublin, in 1999. On the latter occasion Catriona Clutterbuck, a lecturer at the English Department, noticed that McGahern knew a lot of the book by heart. McGahern was eventually to characterise Primo Levi as an artist made by chance, not by natural calling: one who had been hurt into speech (as Auden said of Yeats, in a line McGahern borrowed in one of his book reviews (*LW*, p. 352))[18] by events beyond his control with which he spent a lifetime trying to come to terms or understanding. The model of Levi's unusual career as a writer provided McGahern with ways of understanding the generation of Ernie O'Malley, the most talented writer of the Irish revolution, as well as that of his own father and uncles who had fought in the War of Independence and the Civil War. In his series of seminars on modern writing, McGahern included sessions on both *If This Is a Man* and O'Malley's *On Another Man's Wound*, and he made it explicit on those occasions how he saw those texts as kindred works by accidental artists. More than that, however, he was interested in the *ideas* that Levi's books developed.

What is remarkable about Primo Levi's books is that they are not accusations, calls for sympathy or even simply expressions of individual suffering. They are primarily books of ideas that provide extraordinarily lucid insights into what Levi calls the 'fundamental values' of human experience from the vantage point of a place designed to strip away every shred of humanity.[19] McGahern was highly receptive to the ideas and analyses Levi's books offered. For one thing, it appears that his reading of *If This Is a Man* brought into new relief a lesson first gleaned from one of Edgar's asides in Act 4 of *King Lear*, that which taught that 'The worst is not,/ So long as we can say "This is the worst."'[20] McGahern stressed to the students in his University College seminar on Levi that one of the profound wisdoms to be found in *If This Is a Man* is that it is impossible to pursue happiness since the objects of the aspirations which would make us happy are constantly replaced before they can be fulfilled, but that total *un*happiness is equally impossible.[21] The conversation between Ruttledge and Patrick Ryan about gradations of happiness and unhappiness in *That They May Face the Rising Sun* ('"Are you happy, lad?" he demanded . . . "I'm not unhappy," he answered, surprised' (*TRS*, p. 203)) may owe as much, then, to McGahern's thinking about Primo Levi as it does to his memory of the ludic cadences of Vladimir and Estragon's banter about the word 'happy' in *Waiting for Godot*, or indeed to the blind man's insistence in Beckett's *Rough for Theatre I* that he is not ready yet to kill himself because 'I'm not unhappy enough!'[22] Most likely, that passage in his final novel is the result of a conscious or unconscious convergence of McGahern's memories of all these texts.

In his University College seminar on *If This Is a Man*, McGahern remarked on how Levi sees Auschwitz as 'an extraordinary model for ordinary life', as the laws which apply in ordinary life are distorted and thrown into very sharp focus there.[23] For a novelist like McGahern, the insights and revelations offered by *If This Is a Man* and *The Drowned and the Saved* were as true in twentieth-century Ireland, or in any other time and place, as they were in Auschwitz in the 1940s. He made some of these parallels explicit in his seminar. His understanding of the culture of shrewd, unattractive individualism of post-Famine rural Ireland, for example — what he describes in the 1995 essay 'The Christmas Rose' as 'the "Famine mentality", a blind rancour against neighbours coupled with an equally blind grasping after even useless advantages' (*LW*, p. 155) — is thrown into relief by his reading of Levi's analysis of life in Auschwitz. McGahern remarked to his students that 'Very few of us are truly alone, but in the Lager

[camp] everyone is against everyone else', before coming to the controversial conclusion that, in this sense, 'Rural Ireland is one enormous Lager.'[24] The scale of the Great Famine is in some way comparable to that of the Holocaust, and so the comparison was subversive but tenable. It may seem in more dubious taste to suggest that Primo Levi's writing about life in Auschwitz also gave McGahern a way of understanding his own responses — not all of them cause for moral pride — to things he had experienced in the institutions of Catholic Ireland in the 1950s. However, once the scale and the intensity of the atrocities committed are left out of the equation, the psychology of the human responses to institutional violence in twentieth-century Ireland can easily be transferred from those so patiently and so painfully excavated by a Holocaust survivor like Levi. As the previous chapter discussed, the description of Bill Evans' confinement to the 'small closed circle of the present' as a result of an unknown childhood trauma in *That They May Face the Rising Sun* (*TRS*, p. 167) reprises one of Levi's most dreadful psychological insights from *The Drowned and the Saved*.[25] McGahern turned to the same book to 'lighten[ ] and deepen[ ]' (*CE*, p. 323) his understanding of the collective responses of his own generation to shocking acts of institutional violence such as the ones he had himself witnessed as a student at St Patrick's College, Drumcondra. An incident in the refectory which McGahern remembered from his time there is reworked in the early pages of *That They May Face the Rising Sun*. When Ruttledge recalls a savage beating administered to one of the kitchen skivvies by the 'sinister' dean of studies, he dwells not so much on the beating itself as on the effect it would leave on the onlookers:

> Only the students who were seated close to the accident saw what happened next, and even they weren't certain ... The beating was sudden and savage. Nobody ate a morsel at any of the tables while it was taking place. Not a word was uttered. In the sobbing aftermath the silence was deep and accusing until the scrape of knife and fork on plate and the low hum of conversation resumed. Many who had sat mutely at the tables during the beating were to feel all their lives that they had taken part in the beating through their self-protective silence. (*TRS*, p. 11)

In the final sentence, the guilt of the survivors who feel complicit in their silence, powerless to come to the aid of the victims of a crime which took place before their eyes, is reminiscent of Primo Levi's accounts of the guilt of surviving the Nazi death camps — these are the drowned and the saved of Drumcondra. Levi had remarked that survival is rarely possible 'without renunciation of any part of one's own moral world'.[26] McGahern was interested in the price of survival: in 'The Christmas Rose' he wonders at the guilt that must have been felt by those who lived through the Great Famine at the expense of others (*LW*, p. 154). More than in exposing the austerity of conditions or the brutality of officials, this passage from *That They May Face the Rising Sun* is interested in the lasting effect on the 'moral world' of survivors like Ruttledge or Primo Levi.

McGahern's Beckett

The author who most consistently articulated the conditions of living in the late twentieth century was Samuel Beckett. As the preceding chapters have shown, Beckett's work is a constant presence in McGahern's imagination. The remainder of this chapter will endeavour to place McGahern's work alongside elements of Beckett's writing which seem particularly grounded in the 'absurd' conditions of the post-war era.

One of the things that first attracted McGahern to Beckett was undoubtedly the ear for local speech and dialogue which he also admired in Joyce.[27] For instance, the exchange about a variety of rose absurdly named Climbing Mrs Sam McGredy in 'Strandhill, the Sea' (*N*, p. 65), while like the rest of that story it shares the 'vituperative' quality of Joyce's dialogue in a story like 'Grace' for which McGahern expressed his admiration in his essay on *Dubliners* (*LW*, p. 206), is certainly in the comic register of plays like *All That Fall* or *Happy Days*. Equally Beckettian, in its different way, is the peculiar anecdote about two city gents using their umbrellas as dangerous weapons with which the nervous young man in 'My Love, My Umbrella' bizarrely serenades his lover (*N*, p. 107). McGahern was aware that some colloquial Irish turns of phrase in his own fiction as much as in that of Beckett can sound to foreign ears like exercises in morbid 'Beckettian' fatalism — or as Derek Hand was later to summarise it rather pithily: 'Some critics have called McGahern's work "existential", but we in Ireland know better: we know he simply tells it like it is.'[28] Thus, when McGahern told Hermione Lee during a public interview that 'a lot of the things that are thought existential in Beckett [are] just local speech', this was a hint of which readers of his own fiction were as well advised to take heed as critics of Beckett's novels and plays.[29]

Certain distressing features of contemporary Irish reality in the post-war decades could also be more clearly seen through Beckettian eyes. Beckett had divided his life between different places, and even different languages.[30] McGahern was interested in the sense of liminality which Beckett's life and work embodied, and which seemed to him and countless others to be symptomatic of the experiences of the 'lost generation' who had been forced by economic crisis to leave Ireland in the middle decades of the twentieth century — or indeed of those who, like Moran in *Amongst Women*, had been left behind.[31] The absent figure of Luke is in some relevant ways at the heart of that novel: his name is often invoked by Moran, yet he is destined, like Godot, never to make an actual appearance on the stage of Great Meadow. A type of Beckettian liminality (a favourite word in Beckett criticism) is a feature of many passages in McGahern's work concerned with exile and emigration. When Ruttledge in *That They May Face the Rising Sun*, who has spent most of his adulthood living and working in London before returning to Ireland in middle age, comments that after years of living in England 'I never feel it's quite real or that my life there is real... It's like being present and at the same time a real part of you is happily absent', while life in Ireland would be 'Far too real' (*TRS*, p. 19), that feeling of disembodiment in exile is unmistakably Beckettian.[32] Ruttledge's analysis of exile anticipates McGahern's blatantly Beckettian analysis of the lives of Irish emigrants in Britain in his own voice in *Memoir*. There he characterised the experience of Irish exiles in urban Britain as a purgatorial, suspended state of being in which 'the small communities they had left were more real to the emigrants than the places where their lives were happening and where their children were growing up with alien accents' (*M*, p. 210). In addition, Ruttledge's feeling of in-betweenness, like that of many emigrants, recalls the unreal sense of disembodiment, of being not quite there, experienced by Moran on his wedding day in *Amongst Women*. The latter's demand 'that the continuing present he felt his life to be should not be shadowed or challenged' (*AW*, p. 3), like his 'violent, dissatisfied feeling that his whole life was taking place in front of his eyes without anything at all taking place... All seemed a kind of mockery. It was as if nothing at all had happened' (*AW*, p. 45), is of course borrowed from his namesake Jacques Moran in Beckett's *Molloy* (who in turn all but shares *his* name with the melancholy clown from *As You Like It* who feels like a fictional character in a play). Beckett's Moran, too, is aware of the dreadful unreality of his present condition as he laments: 'My life, my life, now I speak of it as of something over, now as of a joke which still goes on, and it is neither, for at the same time it is over and it goes on, and is there any tense for that?'[33]

Among McGahern's favourite works by Beckett were *Waiting for Godot* and the radio play *All That Fall*, which he may have heard when it was first broadcast on the BBC Third Programme in 1957, and which he certainly read soon after that when it was published by Faber & Faber. The influence of those two works on McGahern's earliest writing in the genres of prose and drama is clear from a number of apprentice pieces. When as a young writer in the 1960s he first came to search for an appropriate literary or dramatic model for reimagining the material connected with his early acquaintance with the Protestant Moroneys, in whose house he had found both domestic squalor and a culture of learning and scholarship, it was perhaps only natural that he should turn to his memory of Beckett's radio play about the final days of an elderly Protestant couple in reduced physical and economic circumstances. McGahern's treatment of those dishevelled old gentlemen in the early prose and drama of the 1960s is in a completely different mood from his later return to the same memories in the *High Ground* stories of the early 1980s, in which (as was discussed in chapter two) they were to be seen through the lens of Goldsmith's Augustan pastoral and that of Yeats' idealisation of enlightened eighteenth-century Anglo-Irish culture. The stamp of *All That Fall*, which was at once comic and intensely moving, may be discerned in the *Nightlines* story 'Why We're Here'. It is even more evident in the mixture of learning and colloquial obscenity that marks the monologues of Gillespie in a version of the same material called *Sinclair*, written for radio and first broadcast on BBC Radio 3 on 16 November 1971. Gillespie's monologues in *Sinclair* switch effortlessly between a vocal appreciation of the smell of his own farts and second-hand invocations of popular scholarly works like the *Encyclopaedia Britannica* and the sermons of Martin Luther. These interests and pastimes replicate those of the blind Mr Rooney in *All That Fall*, who tells his wife about a particularly satisfying fart he has had in a railway carriage which he hopes was empty, before the pair go on to recall snippets from lectures of various scientific topics which they had attended in their youth.[34] As McGahern revisited and revised his work, he often moved further away from his original sources and inspirations. It is hardly surprising, therefore, that the rawest likeness to *All That Fall* can be found not in *Sinclair* or 'Why We're Here' but in an incomplete draft of another dramatic piece for radio written sometime earlier during the 1960s, and now held in the archives at the National University of Ireland, Galway. That early fragment builds up to the perfect little comic tour de force that is Old Mr Moroney's lecture on bees. In that disquisition the old man seeks to illustrate his cynical views about the harsh and arbitrary nature of human existence by channelling the tone and vocabulary of an apicultural textbook in a way that recalls Mr and Mrs Rooney's conversational use of half-remembered fragments of books and lectures on a range of scientific disciplines in *All That Fall*:

OLD MR MORONEY The virgin queen usually emerges in a colony from which the old queen has flown. She starts her adult life by searching

> among the combs for any possible rivals, those still in the cells or having just come out like herself. Any she finds she stings to death through the walls of [the] cell. It is, my dear, if I can suggest as much, just like life itself, and almost equally inefficient.[35]

Long before this flirtation with the style and subject of *All That Fall*, McGahern had already toyed with the much more infinite dramatic possibilities offered by *Waiting for Godot* for transforming some of the defining experiences of his own early life. As an earlier chapter discussed, one of the curious paradoxes in the development of McGahern's reading was that he should have discovered modernist literature through influences connected with the bastion of anti-intellectualism that was St Patrick's College, Drumcondra, in the 1950s. Among other things, McGahern had first been introduced to Beckett when he saw *Waiting for Godot* at the Pike or the Gate Theatre during his time as a student there. Perhaps even more curiously, St Patrick's College was also the scene of his first successful act of homage to the example of Beckett. This took place when McGahern and his friend Éanna Ó hEithir collaborated on 'a short sketch about the training college, loosely based on *Godot*' which they performed in front of a full house as part of the college's Saturday-night entertainment. He later conceded that the enterprise was not without youthful pretension. Still, anyone who remembers the culture of St Patrick's College during those dark decades in the mid-century would assent how apposite the connection was between the Continental absurdism of writers like Kafka and Beckett and the reality of an educational institution which took the punctual observance of religious rituals and duties very seriously, but which did not intend to provide its inmates with any real education (*LW*, p. 115). As it turned out, the students' homage to the master proved nearly as controversial as the original, and the performance very nearly led to the expulsion of McGahern and Ó hEithir by unamused college authorities.[36] Perhaps McGahern came in time to realise the serendipitous parallel that had seen the future author of *Waiting for Godot* himself chastised by another set of college authorities for his involvement in a performance of a burlesque based on a play by Corneille a quarter of a century earlier.[37] What is certain is that this youthful skit was the first of many imaginative returns to a play that would continue to haunt his imagination for the rest of his life.

Of course, while Beckett was often 'Irished' in McGahern's rereadings and rewritings of his work, his fascination with the most distinguished living Irish writer, like that with Yeats and Joyce, went further than seeing him merely as an author of local interest who wrote about exclusively Irish phenomena. Many of the concerns of living and writing in the post-war period could be understood through reading and rereading Beckett, and when they were expressed it was often with a distinctly Beckettian inflection. Over the decades McGahern was on several occasions to channel Beckettian thoughts not only in his fiction but also — often playfully — in talks and interviews. In 1991 an interviewer asked him what he expected his next move to be after the critical failure of *The Power of Darkness*. When McGahern laughed and replied 'I'll begin again', he was slyly citing the same refrain from Matthew Arnold's 'Dover Beach' which he had employed so many times in his fiction.[38] But this laconic response to a reminder of failure also invoked, of course, the indefatigable spirit of the narrators of novels like *Molloy*, *The Unnamable* and *How It Is* — or even the famous artistic imperative of *Worstward Ho* to 'Try again. Fail again. Fail better.'[39] Similarly, when he stoically told another interviewer who had asked him about the inevitability of his own eventual demise that 'We can't know anything about it and there is nothing we can do about it. So, one leaves it as one leaves all hopeless things',[40] he was plainly echoing *Godot*'s Estragon's unsentimental resignation at the fact that there is 'Nothing to be done.'[41] Sometimes he could also echo specific Beckettian aesthetic aims. When, for example, he proclaimed at a public appearance shortly after the publication of *That They May Face the Rising Sun* that during the writing of that novel he decided he 'wanted everything in the novel to happen at least twice',[42] the echo of Vivian Mercier's famous description of *Waiting for Godot* as 'a play in which nothing happens, twice' could not have been more clear.[43] The fascination with Beckettian repetition invoked on that occasion was one with which McGahern had been fascinated for a long time. He explained it with uncharacteristic candour — uncharacteristic, that is, for a writer known for an unwillingness to discuss the details of his methods — in a 1993 interview in which he remarked that '"Sameness attracts me more than novelty. If you can deepen the work it seems far more interesting than gadding about with trickery, although," he adds with a slightly sly smile, "repetition is a trick in itself. I am a great admirer of Beckett's clever use of repetition."'[44]

From the very beginning of his career as a writer of prose fiction, McGahern consciously adopted key elements from Beckett. Years later he recalled that when he expressed his dissatisfaction with *The End or the Beginning of Love* in his correspondence with Peter du Sautoy of Faber & Faber in 1961, he offered in its place another novel which he had not yet started to write. He told du Sautoy that the new novel, which was to become *The Barracks*, would be 'about boredom. And I am going to set it in a police barracks.' When it was politely pointed out to him that novels about boredom often tend to take on some of that quality themselves, the unpublished novelist assured the seasoned editor with the cockiness of youth that that all depended on who wrote them.[45] Boredom did indeed become one of McGahern's recurring themes, both in *The Barracks* and in many of his subsequent novels and stories. In making these great themes of fashionable urban modernism or postmodernism fully his own, McGahern deliberately transplanted them to a distinctly unfashionable setting in the rural counties of the Irish midlands in the 1930s and 1940s. Like his contemporary Derek Mahon, McGahern knew that there were many places where a thought might grow.[46] His deliberate setting of a treatment of such contemporary themes in a rural backwater was not just an act of homage to Beckett (whose most famous play is, after all, set on a country road): he was also staking a fundamental claim that the 'boredom of living' which defines the experience of twentieth-century living was not an exclusively cosmopolitan complaint but one which also existed in remoter places — as, for that matter, did the 'suffering of being' with which it was famously associated by Beckett in *Proust*.[47] Even in a police barracks in deepest Leitrim, the evidence of McGahern's book suggests, could one experience the ennui of the twentieth century. That this was not completely unknown is clear from the fact that the boredom of bicycling policemen in the Irish countryside is also the subject of Flann O'Brien's postmodernist classic *The Third Policeman*, a novel of ideas set in and around a police barracks somewhere in the Irish midlands written in the 1940s but only published posthumously in 1967, four years after *The Barracks*.

Beckett had observed that life exists somewhere between 'the boredom of living' and 'the suffering of being'. In *Proust*, he discusses at length how anaesthetising the pain of the latter requires the full force of 'habit', which he famously compares to a 'drug' — because habit, as Vladimir says in *Waiting for Godot*, 'is a great deadener'.[48] Throughout his work, McGahern repeatedly alludes to Beckett's famous descriptions of habit as either a 'drug' or a 'great deadener'. Thus, the famous contrast between the boredom of living and the suffering of being is perhaps deliberately invoked in an obscure sentence in *The Dark* which describes the line waiting outside the confessional in the local church. The narrator remarks (insofar as the idiosyncratic syntax and punctuation allow us to work out precisely what he intends to say) on how there are two possible ways of approaching that sacrament: while some choose to solicit forgiveness 'in the listless performance of habit and duty', the alternative would be to engage in an altogether more painful act of 'torturing and turning over their sins and lives' (*D*, p. 39). On several occasions in his fiction, the effects of habit are compared with those of drugs. The narrator of *The Pornographer* refers to two specific popular legal drugs when he remarks on the 'scent' of 'habits and tobacco and alcohol' which envelops the nervous courting men and women in a Dublin dance hall (*P*, p. 31);[49] in 'Like All Other Men', the narrator remarks how the two confused and distressed lovers 'now leaned completely on those small acts of ceremony that help us better out of life than any drug' (*HG*, p. 67); and Guard Casey in *The Barracks* lives much of his days in 'repetitions that had become more than his nature … He was at least master of these repetitions, they had no power to disturb him, he knew them in his blood; *and they ran there like a drug*' (*B*, p. 24, emphasis added). In the autobiographical essay 'The Solitary Reader', even the contrast between different types of readers is cast in those same terms. When McGahern observes in the central paragraphs of that essay how for some people the reading habits of youth, when we read for nothing but the escapism of the story, continue into adulthood 'as an indolence or pastime or *drug*', while others discover in their teens or twenties how a 'new, *painful* excitement enters the way we read' (*LW*, p. 90, emphasis added), that contrast ultimately derives from the influence of Beckett's *Proust* and its distinction between 'the boredom of living' and 'the suffering of being'.

Many of McGahern's characters are drawn to the small ways in which life can be made into a series of habits by turning parts of it into automatic actions resembling the games and rituals which help Vladimir and Estragon and Molloy and Malone get through their days. The numbing habits in which McGahern's characters engage often display a close resemblance — not surprising to those who remember their Marx — to the rituals of religious ceremony. The labourers in 'Hearts of Oak and Bellies of Brass' make the working day pass more easily by endlessly reciting, like obscene monks, the same monotonous chants: 'shovel or shite; shite or burst … gravel, sand, gravel; gravel, sand, gravel; cement' (*N*, pp. 49ff). The repetitious quality of their chant is recalled in a later story, 'All Sorts of Impossible Things', in which the description of the two dogs moving about the frozen ground chasing a hare as it is focalised through the consciousness of Sharkey and Lennon takes on the quality of a ritual seen through to its predictable conclusion: 'The two men below in the rushes watched in silence as the old dance played itself out on the bare side of the hill: race, turn, race again' (*GT*, p. 37). In what is a more regularly recurring motif in his fiction, the adolescents and young men working their fathers' fields in so many of McGahern's novels and stories develop a liking for the work because it is repetitive and allows them not to think about the many painful realities which make up the suffering of their being. The boy in *The Dark*, for instance, takes 'savage delight' in 'the total unconsciousness of the night afterwards … the same dogtiredness after, not a shadow of thought'

(*D*, p. 149). The debt to Beckett which lies behind the need for the 'deadening' force of habit and ritual in all of these and many other novels and stories is most explicitly signalled in 'Doorways'. That story opens with a description of the unvarying daily routine of a pair of nameless tramps, whom the narrator calls Barnaby and Bartleby (after the urban oppressed in classic nineteenth-century works of prose fiction by Dickens and Melville), and who like Vladimir and Estragon are somehow simultaneously interchangeable and utterly distinct in character and appearance. The analysis he offers of their lives is both poignant and comical in its absurdity. Ultimately, though, the significance that warrants their inclusion at the top of the story is that their behaviour offers a solution to a great philosophical quandary. It strikes the narrator that Barnaby and Bartleby never once deviate from the pattern of movements and activities that he describes in meticulous detail. The absolute, unchangeable regularity of their daily observances offers a secular version of the 'habit of unchanging death-like days' which the narrator, like so many of McGahern's protagonists, had once hoped to find in a religious vocation (*GT*, p. 69). (The pun in that phrase on the religious *habit* worn by monks is particularly satisfying.)

Another central Beckettian preoccupation, that with boredom and waiting, is also omnipresent in McGahern's fiction. The sense of indebtedness he felt to the older writer on this front was also explicitly signalled from very early on. McGahern was undoubtedly aware of the Beckettian connotations he was sure to invoke in readers when, with the same brimming youthful confidence that had seen him assume a faux-Beckettian stance in his negotiations for a contract for the as-yet-unwritten *The Barracks* with Faber & Faber not long before, he gave not just one but two of the published promotional extracts from the opening chapter of that novel the simple title 'Waiting'.[50] When the narrator of *The Pornographer* refers to his acts of 'passing time, and killing time, and lessening time *that'd lessen anyhow*' (*P*, p. 30, emphasis added), the emphasis of that thought is obviously reminiscent of a conversation between the two tramps in *Waiting for Godot*:

> VLADIMIR That passed the time.
> ESTRAGON It would have passed in any case.
> VLADIMIR Yes, but not so rapidly.[51]

The entire opening page of 'Wheels', too, is an extended act of homage to the presence of such themes and preoccupations in some of Beckett's novels and plays. In the opening paragraph the narrator, stranded at a Dublin railway station in the early morning, observes 'three porters pushing an empty trolley up the platform ... the loose wheels rattling, and nothing but wait and watch and listen, and I listened to the story they were telling' (*N*, p. 11). The resolution voiced in the latter phrase is perhaps intended as an echo of the opening of *Malone Dies*, in which the immobilised hero resolves that 'While waiting I shall tell myself stories'.[52] At the same time, the sight of the porters pushing an empty trolley up the platform replicates a detail from the first chapter of *Watt*, in which a solitary porter at another Dublin railway hub is seen wheeling empty cans up and down the platform, 'perhaps', as Watt reflects, as 'a punishment for disobedience, or some neglect of duty', like a modern-day Sisyphus.[53] The story to which the protagonist decides to listen in order to pass the time is both macabre and very funny. It is not merely a darkly ribald diversion from the seriousness of the rest of McGahern's plot, however. The plot of the porters' story about a colleague who 'tried to hang himself from a branch out over the river but the branch went and broke and in he fell roaring for help' (*N*, p. 11) shows more than a passing resemblance to the sequence in Act 2 of *Waiting for Godot* in which Vladimir and Estragon try to hang themselves only to find that that final opportunity for making a decision which would restore to them a measure of control over their lives is no longer available when the rope they intend to use breaks. That early story of McGahern's revisits the contrast between willed and endured death which had been a prominent theme for early-twentieth-century thinkers like Walter Benjamin,[54] as well as for Beckett and Camus. By referencing a well-known moment in *Waiting for Godot*, McGahern introduces into *Nightlines* an awareness of twentieth-century philosophical responses to suicide — a theme which reappears with some frequency in other stories from that same early collection.

McGahern's reasons for placing 'Wheels' at the head of *Nightlines* and that of subsequent collected and selected editions of his short stories were undoubtedly many and varied, and he never discussed them in detail. It is certain, however, that that story's nod of acknowledgement to Beckett is well placed on the opening page of the *Collected Stories* to signal one of McGahern's most important lifelong debts.[55] Waiting is a constant concern in his fiction. Sometimes waiting can be a cause for boredom, while on many other occasions it is acknowledged to be the cruellest form of torture imaginable, one that is unlike any other in its protracted intensity. McGahern came good on the Beckettian promise he made in his early negotiations for *The Barracks* with Faber & Faber. Elizabeth Reegan, like the eponymous hero of *Malone Dies*, does indeed spend most of the novel simply passing the time as she waits for her own death — on one occasion, in fact, the phrase 'to pass the time' comes straight from Estragon's lips into the description of Elizabeth's stay in hospital (*B*, p. 135).[56] So, too, in a sense, does a character like Moran in *Amongst Women*.

To most readers of McGahern's fiction, however, probably more memorable than either of those acts of waiting is that which opens McGahern's second and most controversial novel. The thoughts of the young boy in *The Dark* as he waits for a beating which, as it turns out, never actually comes, turn to imagining the 'unreal… horror' of his fate. The *anticipation* of pain, he discovers, is much worse than pain actually experienced: 'He'd never imagined horror such as this, waiting naked for the leather to come down on his flesh, would it ever come, it was impossible and yet nothing could be much worse than this waiting' (*D*, p. 9). In the first sentence of chapter three of the same novel the narrator draws renewed attention to the same terrible fate of suffering the 'strain of waiting for [his father] to come to bed, no hope of sleep in the waiting… Turn and listen and turn' (*D*, p. 17), a sentence that anticipates the cadence of the long opening sentence of 'Wheels' five years later.

On the very first page of *Nightlines* McGahern first introduced the *Godot*-like resignation at the necessity of waiting on a railway platform into his work. Those places embody like no other the senseless boredom of the twentieth century, as Beckett had also suggested when he originally intended Lucky in *Waiting for Godot* to be dressed in the uniform of a railway porter.[57] He returned to that same suggestive location twenty years later in *Amongst Women*. In his old age, Moran spends much of his time reminiscing about the glory days of his youth, and ironically one of the things he most vividly remembers is how much of his most action-filled years in his twenties were spent waiting. In his recollection of the raid on a British train which had been one of his greatest moments of triumph during the War of Independence he, like the boy in *The Dark*, is at pains to emphasise the torture of waiting. In the process he echoes Estragon's less-than-enthusiastic review of the play in which he is condemned to act ('Nothing happens, nobody comes, nobody goes, it's awful!'[58]) when he 'violently' says: 'Then there was the waiting… The waiting was terrible. It's like getting old. Nothing happens and then the whole bloody thing is on top of you before you know it' (*AW*, p. 16). The oppressive weight of waiting is felt throughout that novel. The narrator's condemnation in 'Wheels' to doing 'nothing but wait and watch and listen' at the train station (*N*, p. 11) is not only echoed in that later novel in Moran's anecdote about waiting for an ambush (in which even the detail of a trolley with loose wheels makes another appearance (*AW*, p. 16), like some sort of incestuous intertextual reference to an earlier work by the same author) but also in the family's anticipation of Moran's brother before his wedding day, when 'They were all dressed. There was nothing to do but wait for their uncle' (*AW*, p. 40). If 'Waiting' was a title

McGahern gave to early extracts from his first novel, then it could easily be applied also to many of his subsequent works, which return obsessively to this same concern he shared with Beckett.

McGahern's echoes of Beckettian themes and preoccupations are not intended to flaunt his knowledge of an author who is often considered simultaneously fashionable and difficult. The concerns about living and writing in the modern age that McGahern shares with Beckett are indicative of each author's fundamental beliefs. Here more than at any point in this book, therefore, a note of caution may be in order. Often writers have things in common with their contemporaries precisely because they *are* contemporaries. This is no doubt as true of some of McGahern's apparently 'Beckettian' concerns as it is of the overlap between his interest in the idea that historical narratives are not 'still' or 'settled' with that of contemporaries like Banville, Friel and Coetzee which was discussed earlier in this chapter. McGahern was writing in the first place about his own experience of twentieth-century living; it just so happened that Beckett provided the most subtly polished mirror with which to observe many of the phenomena which defined that experience. His interest in, and the manner of, his treatment of some of the contemporary themes and concerns in a way that strikes readers and critics of his work as 'Beckettian' was sometimes undoubtedly as much a case of his responsiveness to the demands of his own time and place, of an openness to ideas which circulated in a particular cultural moment of which he was as much a part as Samuel Beckett, as it was an outcome of his immersion in an established Beckettian literary tradition.

For all his self-conscious adoption of Beckettian masks in the infancy of his career in the late 1950s and early 1960s, McGahern quickly matured into a writer who sometimes did indeed pay overt homage to or borrowed from Beckett, but who at other times just shared Beckett's concerns as a contemporary. This accounts for the way the 1968 story 'Why We're Here' could pre-empt by some fifteen years one of the most quintessential Beckettian aphorisms of all. When the Protestant Sinclair in that story defines the reason for existence as '*Scratching our arses, refining our ignorance*' (*N*, p. 25), readers after 1983 will perhaps hear superimposed on that statement Beckett's much more famous 'Try again. Fail again. Fail better.' But McGahern could not possibly, on this occasion, be echoing Beckett; nor is it likely that Beckett was thinking of McGahern's story when he wrote *Worstward Ho* in the early 1980s. The basic thought which both these statements express — that failure and ignorance cannot be prevented, only mitigated — is merely one shared by two comparable literary sensibilities writing in the same era.

In his engagement with Beckett and the Beckettian, and in that with other post-war contemporaries, therefore, we reach the limits of McGahern's uses of tradition. In time McGahern's prose became itself a touchstone against which the authentic rendering of contemporary experiences might be measured. The possibility that his work had become truly 'traditional' in this sense even during his lifetime will be the subject of the epilogue.

Epilogue

tradition . . . must be continually renewed; and tradition is civilization.

'*Ní bheidh sibh ar ais*: St Patrick's College Drumcondra' (*LW*, p. 116)

In the essay on 'Tradition and the Individual Talent' on which McGahern drew for the argument of his 2003 honorary-doctorate acceptance speech in Drumcondra, T.S. Eliot had stipulated that for a writer to be truly 'traditional' they must not only assimilate the example of all the great writers who came before; they must also, as both Eliot and Borges had emphasised, become part of the continuing tradition by reshaping it in their own image, and casting new light on all the classic works that come before and after. There is evidence to suggest that, by this standard, McGahern became a 'traditional' writer at a relatively early stage in his career.

Nobody would deny that McGahern's influence in the *Irish* literary landscape, in particular, over the past half-century has been pervasive. Echoes of his language and themes can be found in many key works of the past forty years, and numerous younger Irish prose writers have during that period paid overt tribute to the importance of his example. (He has made occasional inroads, too, into the consciousness of writers from other cultures, but these are more sporadic than his presence at home.) The Belfast novelist Glenn Patterson, for example, referred to McGahern as 'the father of the Irish novel' — with all the Oedipal baggage which that label implies.[1] More recently, Mike McCormack and Claire Keegan, two of the most celebrated short-story writers of the present moment, have spoken of their admiration for McGahern's early and his later stories and novels, respectively.[2] Perhaps the most intriguing instance of McGahern's presence in contemporary fiction, however, is embodied by the rise of Joseph O'Connor, who has on numerous occasions told the story of how the first work of fiction he wrote was in fact a story by John McGahern. O'Connor recalls how as a young man he took his first tentative steps to becoming a successful novelist in his own right by repeatedly copying McGahern's story 'Sierra Leone', changing more of the story's details with each rewriting until, a hundred versions later, the original story had almost completely disappeared.[3] The ghostly presence of that and other McGahern stories about the urban experience of the Irish male in the twentieth century can certainly be felt in some of O'Connor's own early fiction. It was Joseph O'Connor, too, who pointed out that while McGahern is most often 'praised as the most gifted chronicler of rural Ireland, he also recorded the realities of Dublin life more memorably than did many a native'.[4] That observation suggests how McGahern was not just a straight 'influence' on a single young writer, but how he became in a more intangible way a 'traditional' figure shaping the outlooks and experiences of a whole culture. That is to say, while he started out writing of his youthful bewilderment with the alien rhythms of city life, he ended up inadvertently laying the foundation not just for a new flourishing of stories about the besieged ways of the countryside, such as Claire Keegan's, but for a whole genre of fiction about the urban and suburban experiences of young rural migrants to the city in the late twentieth century by writers with roots in various regions of the country.

Beckett's McGahern

More tantalising than any of these influences among younger Irish prose writers is a suggestion that McGahern's honest and truthful but simultaneously often poetic prose may also have fed back as an example into the language of that older, most eminent of late-twentieth-century authors, Samuel Beckett. It is important to remember that for most of their careers — during the quarter-century that elapsed between the publication of *The Barracks* in February 1963 and Beckett's death in December 1989 — Beckett was not a dead writer who belonged to a previous era but rather, as McGahern emphasises in 'The Solitary Reader', a 'living, exciting presence' in the contemporary Irish literary scene (*LW*, p. 92). It is known that Beckett, at the behest of their mutual friend Peter Lennon, a left-wing Irish journalist living in Paris, had read and admired *The Dark* after it was banned in Ireland under the Censorship of Publications Act in June 1965.[5] McGahern himself recalled in later years that when Beckett was asked to lead the protest against the banning, he said he would first have to read the novel and apparently concluded after doing so that it was 'a good job'.[6] Judging from the English-language version of one of Beckett's plays from the 1970s, at least one sentence from *The Dark* had stuck in his memory and become part of his poetic imagination. The forward- and backward-looking literary resonances of that sentence suggest how through the hard graft of getting the words and the sentences of his books right McGahern had started to become, sometime during the first dozen years of his career, a truly 'traditional' writer.

In chapter three of *The Dark*, young Mahoney describes the clumsy nocturnal advances of his father during 'the nights he wanted love' (*D*, p. 17). The 'love' the widower craves does not just take the form of types of physical contact which overstep the bounds of decency. Old Mahoney is also given to 'midnight heart-easings' through which he seeks to achieve a greater emotional proximity to his terrified and disgusted son. The boy knows very well, however, that the big plans made by his father during the night will vanish by morning, when they are invariably replaced by 'shame and embarrassment and loathing, *the dirty rags of intimacy*' (*D*, p. 19 emphasis added). That last phrase is 'traditional' in the sense in which that word is defined by Eliot. When McGahern wrote it he was probably thinking of the final couplet of one of Yeats' last poems, 'The Circus Animals' Desertion':

> I must lie down where all the ladders start
> In the foul rag and bone shop of the heart.[7]

The unstoppable wave of tradition did not terminate in *The Dark*, however, but kept rolling into the future of writing as McGahern's novel, too, became in turn 'traditional'. An echo of that sentence from chapter three of *The Dark* can be found in *Rough for Theatre I*, Beckett's 1975 English translation of a dramatic piece he had originally written in English in 1956 and then reworked in French during the 1960s.[8] The cripple in the published text of *Rough for Theatre I* speaks of his intention to 'Find *a few rags of love* in my heart and die reconciled . . . '[9] That striking poetical phrase does not appear in the manuscript of 'The Gloaming', the earlier abandoned English version from the 1950s, which suggests that Beckett must have composed that phrase sometime *after* 1956.[10] Nor does the French text of *Fragment de théatre* from the 1960s include a precise equivalent for the 'rags' of the later English version: it refers to 'quelques lambeaux d'amour dans mon cœur' (literally: some shreds, or fragments, of love in my heart).[11] Of course, Beckett's choice of the word 'rags' in his English rendition of the speech of the cripple may also have drawn on a conscious or subconscious memory of the same well-known line from 'The Circus Animals' Desertion'. It is striking, however, that the word first made its way into the play only after Beckett had read *The Dark* in 1965, and that, moreover, the phrasing as well as the idea of *Rough for Theatre I*'s 'few rags of love' is much closer to McGahern's 'dirty rags of intimacy' than it is to Yeats' 'foul rag and bone shop of the heart'. Both to the young McGahern and to Beckett during this period, it is clear that there can be no simple, *unqualified* affirmation of love and intimacy. Those qualities can only exist in tattered fragments, not in the resplendent, idealised shapes belonging to romantic fiction. This is not to say, however, that they are undesired. Even if they are ragged, the metaphorical vestments of love and intimacy are nevertheless important because, as both authors had learned from Act 3, Scene 4 of *King Lear*, to have only dirty rags to protect one from the storm is better than to face it completely naked.

It appears, therefore, that when Beckett came to translate *Fragment de théâtre* into English in 1975 he drew not only on his memories of theatrical texts by Shakespeare, Synge and Yeats, as critics have suggested;[12] he also reached back to a lingering memory of a novel by a young Irish writer called John McGahern which had impressed him when he had read it exactly a decade earlier.

Notes and References

References in the notes to NUIG refer to archival materials in the John McGahern Papers, James Hardiman Library Archives, National University of Ireland, Galway.

Preface

1. Eamon Maher, 'John McGahern, a Writer in Tune with His Time', *Crosscurrents and Confluences: echoes of religion in twentieth-century fiction* (Dublin: Veritas, 2000), pp. 139–54, at p. 139.

Introduction

1. 'The Solitary Reader' appeared in print no fewer than five times in 1991. For the original publication details of McGahern's non-fictional writings, see the notes and references section at the back of *Love of the World: essays*. For those of his short stories I rely either, for stories first published up to 1991, on Denis Sampson, 'John McGahern: a preliminary checklist', *Canadian Journal of Irish Studies*, vol. 17, no. 1 (July 1991), pp. 93–101; or, for stories after that date, on Stanley van der Ziel, 'John McGahern — an annotated bibliography', *Irish University Review*, vol. 35, no. 1 (spring/summer 2005), pp. 175–202.
2. Gerd Kampen, 'An Interview with John McGahern', appendix in Kampen, *Zwischen Welt und Text: narratologische Studien zum irischen Gegenwartsroman am Beispiel von John McGahern und John Banville* (Trier: Wissenschaftlicher Verlag Trier, 2002), pp. 336–42, at p. 336.
3. John McGahern, letter to Michael McLaverty, 19 June 1961, *Dear Mr McLaverty: the literary correspondence of John McGahern and Michael McLaverty 1959–1980*, ed. John Killen (Belfast: Linen Hall Library, 2006), p. 24.
4. That phrase, from one of his last short stories, echoes the idea of 'moral idleness' which McGahern attributed to Proust in 'The Solitary Reader' (*LW*, p. 87).
5. The quote is from John Williams' 1986 interview with Bryan Woolley: it is quoted by McGahern in his 2003 introduction to Williams' novel *Stoner* [1965] (*LW*, p. 223).
6. John McGahern, untitled manuscript draft: NUIG, P71/1303.
7. W.H. Auden, *Secondary Worlds* (London: Faber & Faber, 1968), p. 141. John McGahern, typescript fragments about John Butler Yeats: NUIG, P71/933 (p. 4). In a conversation with the present author, Declan Kiberd remembered John and Madeline McGahern's conversational use of that quote from Auden.

8. [Joyce Andrews], 'John McGahern' (profile), in Daniel Murphy (dir. of research), *Education and the Arts: the educational autobiographies of contemporary Irish poets, novelists, dramatists, musicians, painters and sculptors: a research report* (Dublin: Trinity College Department of Higher Education, 1987), pp. 129–43, at p. 132.
9. See his comment on Yeats and tradition in 'The Solitary Reader', quoted on pp. 190–1 below.
10. T.S. Eliot, *Selected Essays 1917–1932*, rev. edn (London: Faber & Faber, 1934), pp. 14–15.
11. Jorge Luis Borges, *Labyrinths: selected stories and other writings*, ed. Donald A. Yates and James E. Irby (London: Penguin, 2000), p. 236.
12. John McGahern, draft of a letter to an American university (probably Colgate), *c.* 1968–69: NUIG, P71/1177.
13. Eliot, *Selected Essays*, p. 14.
14. Guard Casey quotes the lines 'God's in His heaven —/ All's right with the world!' from Robert Browning's 'Pippa Passes', *The Poetical Works of Robert Browning*, ed. Ian Jack et al., 15 vols (Oxford: Clarendon, 1983–), vol. iii, p. 40.
15. W.H. Auden, *The Dyer's Hand and Other Essays* (New York: Random House, 1962), p. 5.
16. See James Whyte, *History, Myth, and Ritual in the Fiction of John McGahern: strategies of transcendence* (Lewiston: Edwin Mellen, 2002), p. 55; and Belinda McKeon, '"Robins Feeding with the Sparrows": the Protestant "Big House" in the fiction of John McGahern', *Irish University Review*, vol. 35, no. 1 (spring/summer 2005), pp. 72–89.
17. See p. 49 below.
18. See p. 152 below.
19. John McGahern, 'The End or the Beginning of Love: episodes from a novel', *X: a quarterly review*, vol. 2, no. 1 (April 1961), pp. 36–46, at p. 46.
20. See Michael C. Prusse, 'Symmetry Matters: John McGahern's "Korea" as hypertext of Ernest Hemingway's "Indian Camp"', in Georges Letissier (ed.), *Rewritting/Reprising* (Newcastle: Cambridge Scholars, 2009), pp. 22–39; and Michael C. Prusse, 'Repetition, Difference and Chiasmus in John McGahern's Narratives', *Language and Literature*, vol. 21, no. 4 (November 2012), pp. 363–80.
21. See Horace, *Complete Odes and Epodes*, trans. W.G. Shepherd (London: Penguin, 1983), p. 125.
22. Many of McGahern's most deeply held convictions about life and death echo those he had found in other writers. As a case in point, his comment in an interview that 'I do see the human condition as mostly solitary … I see companions and conviviality as much more on the sidelines of life than at the centre' no doubt reflected a genuine belief; but it also repeated a comment of Philip Larkin's, who had said: 'I find the idea of always being in company rather oppressive; I see life more as an affair of solitude diversified by company than an affair of company diversified by solitude.' Joe Jackson, 'Tales from the Darkside' (interview), *Hot Press*, 14 November 1991, pp. 18–20, at p. 20; Philip Larkin, *Required Writing: miscellaneous pieces 1955–1982* (London: Faber & Faber, 1983), p. 54.
23. Introductory note preceding Christopher Murray's lecture at the John McGahern International Seminar, Dock Arts Centre, Carrick-on-Shannon, 25 July 2008: sent by email to the present author.
24. Borges, *Labyrinths*, p. 236.
25. A.C. Bradley, *Oxford Lectures on Poetry* [1909], 2nd edn (London: Macmillan, 1970), p. 26, quoted by McGahern in Andrews, 'John McGahern', p. 135.
26. Compare those paragraphs from 'The Solitary Reader' with this passage from *The Dyer's Hand*: 'A child's reading is guided by pleasure, but his pleasure is undifferentiated; he cannot distinguish, for example, between aesthetic pleasure and the pleasures of learning or daydreaming. In adolescence we realize that there are different kinds of pleasure, some of which cannot be enjoyed simultaneously … Between the ages of twenty and forty we are

engaged in the process of discovering who we are, which involves learning the difference between accidental limitations which it is our duty to outgrow and the necessary limitations of our nature beyond which we cannot trespass with impunity. Few of us can learn this without making mistakes, without trying to become a little more of a universal man than we are permitted to be. It is during this period that a writer can most easily be led astray by another writer or by some ideology.' Auden, 'Reading', *The Dyer's Hand*, p. 5. McGahern's adherence to that last sentence of Auden's might explain his own inclusion of the sentence about the need to 'discard all the tenets' which otherwise sits slightly uneasily in the argument of those paragraphs of 'The Solitary Reader'.

27. In an undated draft of a letter (*c.* 1968–69) to a contact at Colgate University, where he would shortly be spending the next academic term, McGahern identified the 'burden' of 'students... overloaded with compulsory reading' as one of the problems of a university degree course in English: NUIG, P71/1177. See also Declan Kiberd's recollection of McGahern's similar concerns in the 1990s, in his introduction in McGahern, *Love of the World*, p. xxii.
28. John McGahern, letter to Patrick Swift, 5 September [1961?]: The *X* Mss, Lilly Library, Indiana University.
29. Eamon Maher, 'Drawing from a Life of Fugitive Days' (interview), *Irish Book Review*, vol. 1, no. 2 (autumn 2005), pp. 12–13. On the importance of the shape given to the material, and the difference between art and life, see also chapter four.
30. Dermot McCarthy, *John McGahern and the Art of Memory* (Oxford: Peter Lang, 2010), p. 46. The quote is from James Whyte, 'An Interview with John McGahern', appendix in Whyte, *History, Myth, and Ritual in the Fiction of John McGahern: strategies of transcendence* (Lewiston: Edwin Mellen, 2002), pp. 227–35, at p. 235.
31. John McGahern, untitled manuscript of a speech introducing Seamus Heaney, *c.* 1983–84: NUIG, P71/1074 (emphasis added).
32. John McGahern, letter to Patrick Swift, 5 September [1961?]: The *X* Mss, Lilly Library, Indiana University.
33. Perhaps this is because, as Paul Ricoeur argues, 'facts' are always inextricable from their 'representation in the form of events in a history'. See Ricoeur, *Memory, History, Forgetting*, trans. Kathleen Blamey and David Pellauer (Chicago: University of Chicago Press, 2004), p. 257 and *passim*.
34. For the Proustian original, see p. 156 below.
35. Linda Hutcheon, *The Politics of Postmodernism* (London: Routledge, 1989), p. 89.
36. See D.H. Lawrence, *Sons and Lovers* [1913], ed. Keith Sagar (Harmondsworth: Penguin, 1989), p. 50. The 'remarkable parallel' with Lawrence was first pointed out by Denis Sampson, 'The "sacred weather" of County Leitrim: John McGahern's *Memoir*', *Irish Review*, no. 36/37 (winter 2007), pp. 120–8, at p. 125.
37. Paul John Eakin, *Fictions in Autobiography: studies in the art of self-invention* (Princeton: Princeton University Press, 1985), p. 129.
38. Declan Kiberd, 'Fallen Nobility: the world of John McGahern', *Irish University Review*, vol. 35, no. 1 (spring/summer 2005), pp. 164–74, at p. 168.
39. W.B. Yeats, *Collected Plays* (London: Macmillan, 1963), p. 687.
40. John Cronin, 'Art and the Failure of Love: the fiction of John McGahern', *Studies*, vol. 77, no. 306 (summer 1988), pp. 201–17, at pp. 209, 210.
41. On the unknowable nature of the inner lives of other people, see also the section on 'two things that have obsessed me all my life' in chapter five.
42. Lawrence, *Sons and Lovers*, pp. 101–2.
43. Ibid., p. 102.

44. See for example his remark about the lacunae in the literary knowledge of his English teacher in Carrick-on-Shannon, quoted on p. 152 below.
45. The term 'intertextuality', which has largely replaced the older notion of direct 'influence' in current scholarship, has been subject to much theorising ever since it was first coined in the 1970s. For an exposition of an approach sympathetic to my own views, see Susan Bassnett, 'Influence and Intertextuality: a reappraisal', *Forum for Modern Language Studies*, vol. 43, no. 2 (April 2007), pp. 134–46, at p. 138 and *passim*.
46. Eileen Battersby, 'John McGahern Receives PEN/A.T. Cross Literary Award', *Irish Times*, 6 March 2003, p. 9.
47. John McGahern, letter to Stanley van der Ziel, 14 February 2006. Private collection. The review of *Memoir* in question was published in *Irish University Review*, vol. 35, no. 2 (autumn/winter 2005), pp. 463–9: the quote is at p. 465.
48. John Banville, 'Butler's Window on the World', in Chris Agee (ed.), *Unfinished Ireland: essays on Hubert Butler* (Belfast: Irish Pages, in association with The Butler Society, 2003), pp. 142–3, at p. 142.
49. Colm Tóibín, 'Out of the Dark: a profile of John McGahern' [1985], *The Trials of the Generals: selected journalism 1980–1990* (Dublin: Raven Arts, 1990), pp. 94–102, at p. 101.
50. Ovid, *Metamorphoses*, trans. Mary M. Innes (Harmondsworth: Penguin, 1955), p. 231. McGahern echoes that famous line in his praise of Alistair MacLeod's short stories when he refers to 'that high art that conceals itself' (*LW*, p. 212).
51. See p. 65 below.
52. See Stanley van der Ziel, editor's preface in McGahern, *Love of the World*, pp. xxvi–xxvii.
53. Bob Minzesheimer, Letters, *Colgate Scene*, vol. 35, no. 2 (September 2006), www4.colgate.edu/scene/sept2006/letters.html (accessed 1 March 2012).
54. John McGahern, letter to Stanley van der Ziel, 14 February 2006. Private collection. On Jimmy Swift's role in McGahern's discovery of modern literature, see pp. 152–3 below.
55. Outline for McGahern's course on Modern Writing, University College, Dublin, 1999. He had previously taught the same course at University College, Galway (now the National University of Ireland, Galway) in 1993. I am indebted to Catriona Clutterbuck for providing me with the outline, and with copies of her detailed notes taken during most of McGahern's seminars between 20 January and 7 April 1999. All further references to these seminars refer to Dr Clutterbuck's notes.

Chapter 1: Shakespearean Antics

1. William Shakespeare, *Macbeth*, ed. G.K. Hunter (Harmondsworth: Penguin, 1995), II.iv.8–10.
2. See also Stanley van der Ziel, 'Learning to Read', *John McGahern Yearbook*, vol. 4 (2011), pp. 20–9.
3. Janet Clare and Stephen O'Neill (eds), *Shakespeare and the Irish Writer* (Dublin: University College Dublin Press, 2010), p. 9.
4. The role of the alcoholic labourer Paddy as the play's chorus or 'moral voice' (*PD*, p. ix) is an original element of McGahern's version of the play which does not appear in the Tolstoy original. For a discussion of more Shakespearean echoes, principally of *Macbeth*, which may be found in McGahern's only stage play, see Christopher Murray, 'The "fallen world" of *The Power of Darkness*', *John McGahern Yearbook*, vol. 2 (2009), pp. 78–90.
5. [Joyce Andrews], 'John McGahern' (profile), in Daniel Murphy (dir. of research), *Education and the Arts: the educational autobiographies of contemporary Irish poets, novelists, dramatists, musicians, painters and sculptors: a research report* (Dublin: Trinity College Department of Higher Education, 1987), pp. 129–43, at p. 134.

6. Paul Clements, 'The Book and Magazine Collector Interview: John McGahern', *Book and Magazine Collector*, no. 208 (July 2001), pp. 80–9, at p. 89. The other two desert-island books he selected on that occasion were George Eliot's *Middlemarch* and Yeats' poems. On the selection of Shakespeare plays McGahern studied in those institutions, see *M*, p. 169, and Denis Sampson, *Young John McGahern: becoming a novelist* (Oxford: Oxford University Press, 2012), pp. 7, 11.
7. Cf. William Shakespeare, *Twelfth Night*, ed. M.M. Mahood (London: Penguin, 2005), II.iii.111–12.
8. On McGahern's obsession with morals and manners, see chapter two.
9. William Shakespeare, *Hamlet*, ed. T.J.B. Spencer (Harmondsworth: Penguin, 1996), I.iii.75–6.
10. Only three of Shakespeare's plays were performed at the Abbey Theatre during the first fifty years of its existence: *King Lear* (1928), *Macbeth* (1934) and *Coriolanus* (1936).
11. The complex issue of the Irish writer's 'struggle' with Shakespeare as 'both their own cultural inheritance and yet a cultural representation of their colonial oppression' is the subject of Robin E. Bates, *Shakespeare and the Cultural Colonization of Ireland* (London: Routledge, 2008), p. 2 and *passim*.
12. Shakespeare, *Macbeth*, I.i.9.
13. Ibid., I.vii.1–28. The echo of *Macbeth* does not appear in the original version of 'Oldfashioned' (cf. *HG*, p. 47).
14. See also Stanley van der Ziel, 'John McGahern: *Nightlines*', in Cheryl Alexander Malcolm and David Malcolm (eds), *A Companion to the British and Irish Short Story* (Malden and Oxford: Wiley–Blackwell, 2008), pp. 488–97, at pp. 490–2. The 'obvious homage to *Hamlet*: "the funeral baked-meats/ Did coldly furnish forth the marriage tables"' (I.ii.180–1) in *The Pornographer*'s 'The christening party becomes the funeral' (*P*, p. 30) was pointed out in Raymond Mullen, '"The womb and the grave": living, loving and dying in John McGahern's *The Pornographer* and Albert Camus' *L'Étranger*', in Eamon Maher, Eugene O'Brien and Grace Neville (eds), *Reinventing Ireland through a French Prism* (Frankfurt: Peter Lang, 2007), pp. 229–43, at p. 237.
15. Declan Kiberd, 'Fallen Nobility: the world of John McGahern', *Irish University Review*, vol. 35, no. 1 (spring/summer 2005), pp. 164–74, at p. 170.
16. William Shakespeare, *The Merchant of Venice*, ed. W. Moelwyn Merchant (London: Penguin, 2005), I.iii.140–8, IV.i.16–309.
17. The climax of a flashback concerning Maloney's youthful humiliation in love is summed up in a mocking Shakespearean epithet. The audience of an impromptu poetry recital, 'shepherded' into the upstairs lounge of a small-town boarding house by the lovesick Maloney, endure his reading of a long poem in rhyming couplets about lost love amid 'much nudging, low giggles, scraping of chairs and feet … When he finished, everybody applauded, relieved that *love's labours at last had ended*' (*P*, p. 27, emphasis added). The mockery of the pun is directed not against Maloney's romantic suffering but against the poor quality of the verse in which his feelings are expressed.
18. Cf. Shakespeare, *Hamlet*, V.ii.213–14. The echo was first pointed out in Graham Price, 'The Fact Is a Fiction: representations of memory, place and modernity in Friel and McGahern's short stories', in Raymond Mullen, Adam Bargroff and Jennifer Mullen (eds), *John McGahern: critical essays* (Oxford: Peter Lang, 2014), pp. 155–72, at p. 167.
19. Sampson, *Young John McGahern*, p. 11.
20. William Shakespeare, *King Lear*, ed. G.K. Hunter (London: Penguin, 2005), I.ii.22.
21. Denis Sampson refers to this echo as 'an emblem of ordinary life enriched by literary analogy'. Sampson, *Outstaring Nature's Eye: the fiction of John McGahern* (Washington, DC: Catholic University of America Press, 1993), p. 45.

22. John Locke, *An Essay Concerning Human Understanding* [1689], ed. Peter H. Nidditch (Oxford: Clarendon, 1979), pp. 394–401.
23. Shakespeare, *Hamlet*, V.ii.330. This echo was first identified in Dermot McCarthy, *John McGahern and the Art of Memory* (Oxford: Peter Lang, 2010), p. 304.
24. John McGahern, 'The End or the Beginning of Love: episodes from a novel', *X: a quarterly review*, vol. 2, no. 1 (April 1961), pp. 36–46, at p. 45.
25. Shakespeare, *King Lear*, I.i.90.
26. Ibid., V.iii.304–5.
27. See chapter three, note 42.
28. Shakespeare, *Twelfth Night*, V.i.386–405.
29. Shakespeare, *King Lear*, III.ii.74–7.
30. Ibid., III.ii.42–3, III.i.12–15.
31. Cf. ibid., V.iii.8.
32. John D. Sheridan, 'Classic Tragedy in the Barracks' (rev. of *The Barracks*), *Irish Independent*, 16 March 1963, p. 10.
33. Sampson, *Outstaring Nature's Eye*, p. 45.
34. In the introduction to his *Collected Plays* (London: Cresset, 1958), Arthur Miller pointed out that the standards by which tragedies are traditionally measured belong to a pre-modern world, and argued that in twentieth-century drama no common man can be debarred from the tragic or heroic role 'so long as [he] may be said to have had alternatives of a magnitude to have materially changed the course of his life' (pp. 27–38).
35. That McGahern was from early on in his career preoccupied with the intensity and the intention of the experience which defined a 'tragic' death is also clear from a set of handwritten lecture notes on Herman Melville which probably date to the time of his appearance at the Belfast Arts Festival in November 1967: 'Gladiator is not the death of a kinglike tragic hero. The tragic fall was not his. Death was for the amusement of the spectators in the circus.' NUIG, P71/1294 (p. 2).
36. The thematic development of blindness and vision later in that and other of McGahern's novels will be discussed in chapter three.
37. Antoinette Quinn draws attention to the contrast between the 'traditional … male code of chivalry' associated with Moran, and the 'secular, commercial outlook' of McQuaid and others. See Quinn, 'A Prayer for My Daughter: patriarchy in *Amongst Women*', *Canadian Journal of Irish Studies*, vol. 17, no. 1 (July 1991), pp. 79–90, at p. 82.
38. Stephen Greenblatt, *Will in the World: how Shakespeare became Shakespeare* (London: Cape, 2004), p. 328.
39. Shakespeare, *Macbeth*, V.v.19–28. Macbeth's 'Tomorrow, and tomorrow, and tomorrow' is also loosely echoed in the final paragraph of a later short story, 'Like All Other Men', in which the young protagonist knows that his aimless walk along the pavements of the big city 'could only take him to the next day, and the next' (*HG*, p. 67).
40. Shakespeare, *Macbeth*, V.v.23.
41. W.B. Yeats, *Autobiographies* (London: Macmillan, 1955), p. 47.
42. In his review of *The Dark*, Anthony Cronin remarked that although readers may find the protagonist's anxious swotting and the 'grotesquerie of the examination emphasis' too repetitive and lacking in 'humour and such alleviations of the spirit as are common to all adolescents … they should not miss Mr McGahern's irony … We discover we are reading grim and terrible farce. The writer who is capable of such a double-take deserves esteem.' [Cronin], 'Swotting out of the Farm', *Times Literary Supplement*, 13 May 1965, p. 365.
43. Stanley van der Ziel, 'An Interview with John McGahern', appendix ii in van der Ziel, 'Medusa's Mirror: art, style, vision and tradition in the fiction of John McGahern', PhD dissertation, University College, Dublin, 2008, pp. 361–81, at p. 381.

44. Cf. Shakespeare, *King Lear*, V.iii.255.
45. See also Sampson, *Young John McGahern*, pp. 27–8.
46. Henri Bergson, *Laughter: an essay on the meaning of the comic* [1900], trans. Cloudesley Brereton and Fred Rothwell (London: Macmillan, 1911), pp. 4–5. Richard Murphy remembers McGahern quoting from Bergson on laughter in his lecture on Melville's 'Bartleby, the Scrivener' at the Belfast Arts Festival in November 1967: see Murphy, *The Kick: a memoir* (London: Granta, 2002), pp. 261–2. For a more prolonged discussion, see also van der Ziel, 'John McGahern: *Nightlines*', pp. 490–1.
47. *Horace Walpole's Correspondence*, ed. W.S. Lewis, 48 vols (London: Oxford University Press, 1967), vol. xxiii, p. 166.
48. 'Bomb Box' was rewritten in the third person and retitled 'The Key' for inclusion in the *Collected Stories*. It is not included in *Creatures of the Earth: new and selected stories*.
49. See Katharine Cooke, *A.C. Bradley and His Influence in Twentieth-century Shakespeare Criticism* (Oxford: Clarendon, 1972), especially chapter six (at pp. 119–52).
50. Shakespeare, *King Lear*, IV.vi.184.
51. Frank Kermode, *Shakespeare's Language* (London: Penguin, 2001), p. 66. NB that in an interview thirty years after the publication of the novel, McGahern erroneously attributed the quote from *Twelfth Night* to Falstaff in *Henry IV* or *Henry V*. This is not to say, however, that he misidentified the play when he wrote the novel in 1961–62. See Nicole Ollier, 'Step by Step through *The Barracks* with John McGahern' (interview), *La Licorne*, no. 32 (1995), pp. 55–86, at p. 77.
52. Shakespeare, *Macbeth*, V.v.24–6.
53. *Long Day's Journey into Night* had its Irish premiere at the Abbey Theatre in 1959. In an interview with Mike Murphy, McGahern recalls seeing it there in the late 1950s. Clíodhna Ní Anluain (ed.), *Reading the Future: Irish writers in conversation with Mike Murphy* (Dublin: Lilliput, 2000), pp. 137–55, at pp. 151–2. In a letter to Michael McLaverty, he wrote that he was planning to see it again when it returned to the Abbey in September 1962: *Dear Mr McLaverty: the literary correspondence of John McGahern and Michael McLaverty 1959–1980*, ed. John Killen (Belfast: Linen Hall Library, 2006), p. 26.
54. Eugene O'Neill, *Long Day's Journey into Night* [1956] (London: Cape, 1966), p. 111.
55. Shakespeare, *King Lear*, I.iv.285–6.
56. William Shakespeare, *As You Like It*, ed. H.J. Oliver (Harmondsworth: Penguin, 1996), II.vii.140–1.
57. C.L. Barber, *Shakespeare's Festive Comedy: a study of dramatic form and its relation to social custom* (Princeton: Princeton University Press, 1959), p. 226.
58. Shakespeare, *As You Like It*, II.vii.143; William Shakespeare, *Henry V*, ed. A.R. Humphreys (Harmondsworth: Penguin, 1996), Prologue, lines 11–14.
59. Shakespeare, *King Lear*, IV.vi.183–4; Shakespeare, *The Merchant of Venice*, I.i.77–9.
60. Samuel Beckett, *Play*, *Complete Dramatic Works* (London: Faber & Faber, 1986), p. 317.
61. W.B. Yeats, *The Poems*, ed. Richard J. Finneran (London: Macmillan, 1984), p. 386. See Stanley van der Ziel, 'Fionn and Oisin in the Land of Wink and Nod: heroes, history, and the creative imagination in John McGahern's *Amongst Women*', *Canadian Journal of Irish Studies*, vol. 31, no. 2 (autumn 2005), pp. 10–18, at pp. 14–15.
62. O'Neill, *Long Day's Journey into Night*, p. 111.
63. John Montague, 'John McGahern', in D.L. Kirkpatrick (ed.), *Contemporary Novelists*, 4th edn (Chicago: St James, 1986), pp. 592–3, at p. 592.
64. See Richard Pine, *The Diviner: the art of Brian Friel* (Dublin: University College Dublin Press, 1999), pp. 3–4.
65. Friel may well have read the relevant opening passage of *The Barracks* when it appeared as 'A Barrack Evening', in Thomas Kinsella and John Montague (eds), *The Dolmen Miscellany of Irish Writing* (Dublin: Dolmen, 1962), pp. 84–94.

66. See pp. 128–9 below.
67. T.C. Murray, *Selected Plays*, ed. Richard Allen Cave (Gerrards Cross: Colin Smythe, 1998), p. 121.
68. See p. 230 below. See also van der Ziel, 'Fionn and Oisin in the Land of Wink and Nod', pp. 12–13.
69. Edward Dowden, *Shakspere: a critical study of his mind and art* [1875], 3rd edn (London: Routledge & Kegan Paul, 1957), p. 79 (emphasis added). Dowden, Trinity College Dublin professor of English in the late nineteenth and early twentieth centuries, is an important figure in McGahern's writing about John Butler Yeats' Dublin (*LW*, p. 230). It is likely that he had read Dowden's books around the same time he read J.B. Yeats' letters as a student at St Patrick's College or University College, Dublin, sometime during the 1950s.
70. William Shakespeare, *King John*, ed. Robert Smallwood (London: Penguin, 2005), II.i.374–6.
71. Yeats, *Autobiographies*, pp. 470–1; W.H. Auden, *The Dyer's Hand and Other Essays* (New York: Random House, 1962), p. 376.
72. Shakespeare, *King Lear*, IV.i.36–7.
73. Sampson, *Young John McGahern*, p. 24.
74. Shakespeare, *Macbeth*, I.iii.108.
75. Shakespeare, *Hamlet*, I.iii.72.
76. See also James Whyte's comment that 'Throughout the novel, clothes are repeatedly related to social identity.' Whyte, *History, Myth, and Ritual in the Fiction of John McGahern: strategies of transcendence* (Lewiston: Edwin Mellen, 2002), p. 40.
77. William Shakespeare, *The Taming of the Shrew*, ed. G.R. Hibbard (London: Penguin, 2006), IV.ii.121.
78. When Patrick quotes 'And when all is said and done, who can tell the man who wore the ragged jacket?' (*TRS*, p. 51), the reference is to an anonymous ballad which teaches the simple moral that 'It's not the coat that makes the man, but the deeds through life that bears it … // And, when we're laid beneath the sod, with a hundred years to back it,/ Who can tell which were the bones that wore the ragged jacket.' www.traditionalmusic.co.uk/songster/35-the-broadway-swell-and-the-bowery-bum.htm (accessed 25 September 2014). The undertaker in *The Pornographer* 'expansively' quotes the last lines of the same ballad in his questioning of the usefulness of expensive coffins (*P*, p. 246).
79. Shakespeare, *The Taming of the Shrew*, IV.iii.165–70.
80. Frank McGahern Sr to Seán [John McGahern], 8 January 1960: NUIG, P71/1201, quoted in *Memoir*, p. 225. Shakespeare, *King Lear*, I.iv.147–8.
81. J.M. Synge, *Collected Works*, gen. ed. Robin Skelton, 4 vols (London: Oxford University Press, 1962–68), vol. iv, p. 171.
82. Cf. '[They] Should know what issue is at stake:/ It is myself that I remake.' Yeats, *The Poems*, p. 548.
83. Auden, 'The Joker in the Pack', *The Dyer's Hand*, pp. 256–8.
84. Shakespeare, *Hamlet*, I.ii.84.
85. John McGahern, *Memoir*, uncorrected proofs (London: Faber & Faber, 2005), p. 229. Cf. 'Man is least himself when he talks in his own person. Give him a mask, and he will tell you the truth.' *Complete Works of Oscar Wilde*: centenary edition (Glasgow: HarperCollins, 1999), p. 1142.
86. Cf. Marx's comment that all history is repeated twice, the first time as tragedy and the second time as farce. Karl Marx, 'The Eighteenth Brumaire of Louis Bonaparte', *Surveys from Exile*, ed. David Fernbach (Harmondsworth: Penguin, 1973), p. 146.
87. See Mikhail Bakhtin, *Rabelais and His World*, trans. Hélène Iswolsky (Bloomington: Indiana University Press, 1984).

88. Beckett, *Complete Dramatic Works*, p. 20. On McGahern's discovery of *Waiting for Godot*, see p. 153 below.

Chapter 2: An Augustan Sensibility

1. Cf. Jane Austen, *Emma* [1815], ed. Ronald Blythe (Harmondsworth: Penguin, 1985), p. 180.
2. Linda Grant, 'Private Isle' (profile), *Independent on Sunday*, 11 October 1992.
3. I am indebted for this information to Patrick Gilligan, in conversation with the present author, 21 February 2012.
4. [Joyce Andrews], 'John McGahern' (profile), in Daniel Murphy (dir. of research), *Education and the Arts: the educational autobiographies of contemporary Irish poets, novelists, dramatists, musicians, painters and sculptors: a research report* (Dublin: Trinity College Department of Higher Education, 1987), pp. 129–43, at p. 134.
5. This idea is further developed in my forthcoming essay on 'McGahern, Post-Revival Literature and Irish Cultural Criticism', in Adam Bargroff, Raymond Mullen and Tom Walker (eds), *John McGahern: ways of seeing*.
6. Samuel Beckett, *Complete Dramatic Works* (London: Faber & Faber, 1986), p. 219. McGahern listed his favourite works by Beckett in an interview with Stanley van der Ziel, quoted on p. 153 below.
7. See Marilynn J. Richtarik, *Acting between the Lines: the Field Day Company and Irish cultural politics 1980–1984* (Oxford: Clarendon, 1994), especially the postscript, on the *Field Day Anthology of Irish Writing* (at pp. 256–69).
8. Fintan O'Toole, 'The Family as Independent Republic' (profile), *Irish Times*, 13 October 1990, Weekend, p. 2.
9. Jane Austen, *Persuasion* [1817], ed. Gillian Beer (London: Penguin, 2003), p. 41; Goldsmith, *The Vicar of Wakefield* [1766], *Collected Works of Oliver Goldsmith*, ed. Arthur Friedman, 5 vols (Oxford: Clarendon, 1966), vol. iv, p. 50.
10. Denis Sampson, *Young John McGahern: becoming a novelist* (Oxford: Oxford University Press, 2012), p. 91.
11. Edmund Burke, *Reflections on the Revolution in France* [1790], ed. Conor Cruise O'Brien (London: Penguin, 1986), pp. 135, 315.
12. John McGahern, letter to Tony Whelan, 16 July 1959, *John McGahern Yearbook*, vol. 2 (2009), pp. 32–3. See also Sampson, *Young John McGahern*, pp. 58–65.
13. Quoted in Richard Ellmann, *James Joyce* [1959], rev. edn, with corrections (Oxford: Oxford University Press, 1983), p. 505. See also Stanley van der Ziel, editor's preface in McGahern, *Love of the World*, p. xxxii.
14. Alexander Pope, *An Essay on Criticism*, *The Major Works*, ed. Pat Rogers (Oxford: Oxford University Press, 2006), p. 27.
15. *Complete Works of William Hazlitt*, ed. P.P. Howe, 21 vols (London: Dent, 1930–34), vol. iv, p. 71.
16. See pp. 134–5, 137–8 and 148 below.
17. W.B. Yeats, *Explorations* (London: Macmillan, 1962), p. 345.
18. John McGahern, *The Rockingham Shoot*, BBC 2 Northern Ireland, 10 September 1987: typescript screenplay, BBC Written Archives Centre, Caversham Park, Reading: TV Drama Scripts 1987 [microfilm], film no. 545 (p. 7).
19. See also Declan Kiberd, 'Nostalgia as Protest: Goldsmith's "Deserted Village"', *Irish Classics* (London: Granta, 2000), p. 115.
20. John Montague, 'The Sentimental Prophecy: a study of *The Deserted Village*', in Thomas Kinsella and John Montague (eds), *The Dolmen Miscellany of Irish Writing* (Dublin: Dolmen, 1962), pp. 62–79, at pp. 74–5, 76.

21. Kiberd, *Irish Classics*, p. 108.
22. Oliver Goldsmith, *The Deserted Village* [1770], *Collected Works of Oliver Goldsmith*, vol. iv, p. 295.
23. McGahern, *The Rockingham Shoot*, p. 9.
24. John McGahern, notes on Yeats' *Purgatory*: NUIG, P71/1290 (p. 3). The papers are undated, but it is not unlikely that they are McGahern's speaking notes for the seminar series on Modern Writing from the 1990s (see note 55 of the introduction).
25. W.B. Yeats, *Collected Plays* (London: Macmillan, 1963), p. 684.
26. Another source for the description in 'Oldfashioned' of Rockingham House as it had been and the empty shell it became after the burning, and the feelings of sadness and loss which its remains provoked, may have been the eyewitness account of a *Roscommon Herald* reporter which appeared about a fortnight after the burning. 'Before us was the blazing shell of the once beautiful mansion that was Rockingham House', the report concludes: 'a hundred years ago it would have been an occasion for rejoicing. But to the people of the area in the late years Rockingham house was something of which they were proud, a stately home which was an architectural gem and which had somehow symbolised the changes that had taken place, without being changed itself. Now it was gone, into dust and ashes, a smouldering ruin that cast a red glow in the eastern sky as we wended our way down the avenue, along the famous beech walk, back to the sleeping town of Boyle. Somehow or other we were sorry that Rockingham was burned.' *Roscommon Herald*, 21 September 1957, p. 7. It is possible that this vivid piece of reportage, the concluding paragraphs of which move beyond the mere reporting of fact of most journalism, was the first report of the event McGahern read while he was still in Dublin. Its tone and imagery may have been stored away in his mind and made his own over the decades that followed.
27. See Patrick Kavanagh, *A Poet's Country: selected prose*, ed. Antoinette Quinn (Dublin: Lilliput, 2003), p. 237.
28. John McGahern, untitled manuscript [*c.* 1992–93]: NUIG, P71/1337 (p. 2).
29. Denis Sampson, *Outstaring Nature's Eye: the fiction of John McGahern* (Washington, DC: Catholic University of America Press, 1993), p. 149. The idea that *The Pornographer* marks a turning point in McGahern's fiction is elaborated in George O'Brien, 'Going Inland' (rev. of *Memoir*), *Dublin Review*, no. 22 (spring 2006), pp. 36–46, at p. 39; and Denis Sampson, '"The Day Set Alight in the Mind": notes on John McGahern's late style', *Irish University Review*, vol. 39, no. 1 (spring/summer 2009), pp. 122–8, at p. 125.
30. James Joyce, *Ulysses* [1922]: annotated students' edition (Harmondsworth: Penguin, 1992), p. 430.
31. Declan Kiberd, 'Fallen Nobility: the world of John McGahern', *Irish University Review*, vol. 35, no. 1 (spring/summer 2005), pp. 164–74, at p. 170.
32. Cf. David Hume, *An Enquiry Concerning Human Understanding* [1748]: a critical edition, ed. Tom L. Beauchamp (Oxford: Oxford University Press, 2000), p. 98.
33. See for example Cathy Herbert, 'Window on the World' (profile), *Magill*, vol. 10, no. 13 (October 1987), pp. 56–62, at p. 60.
34. *Letters of Anton Chekhov*, sel. and ed. Avrahm Yarmolinsky (London: Cape, 1974), p. 40. See also for example Clíodhna Ní Anluain (ed.), *Reading the Future: Irish writers in conversation with Mike Murphy* (Dublin: Lilliput, 2000), pp. 137–55, at p. 149.
35. John McGahern, 'A Note on the Stories', in the programme for the touring production of *My Love, My Umbrella: a new opera by Kevin O'Connell and James Conway, based on John McGahern's short stories* (Opera Theatre Company, Ireland, 1997), pp. 12–13, at p. 12. Copy at NUIG, P71/696.
36. John McGahern, notes on Yeats' *Purgatory*: NUIG, P71/1292 (p. 4).

37. John McGahern, notes on Yeats' *Purgatory*: NUIG, P71/1286. Yeats' defence of *Purgatory* is quoted in Donald T. Torchiana, *W.B. Yeats and Georgian Ireland* (Washington, DC: Catholic University of America Press, 1992), p. 357.
38. Burke, letter to Charles-Jean-François Depont, November 1789, quoted in Conor Cruise O'Brien, *The Great Melody: a thematic biography and commented anthology of Edmund Burke* (London: Sinclair-Stevenson, 1992), p. 390.
39. Burke, *Reflections on the Revolution in France*, p. 151.
40. See also, in particular, the shortened, sharpened version of the passage in which that statement appears in the revised version of the story: *CS*, p. 269; *CE*, p. 259.
41. Vivian Mercier, *Beckett/Beckett* (Oxford: Oxford University Press, 1977), p. 47.
42. J.M. Synge, *Collected Works*, gen. ed. Robin Skelton, 4 vols (London: Oxford University Press, 1962–68), vol. ii, p. 59.
43. Joyce, *Ulysses*, p. 98.
44. Colin Murphy, 'The Calm Journey through the Day' (profile), *Village*, 16–22 September 2005, pp. 32–3, at p. 33.
45. George Eliot, *Daniel Deronda* [1876], ed. Terence Cave (Harmondsworth: Penguin, 1995), p. 180 (emphasis added).
46. Oscar Wilde, *Lady Windermere's Fan*, *Complete Works of Oscar Wilde*: centenary edition (Glasgow: HarperCollins, 1999), p. 457.
47. Philip Larkin, *Required Writing: miscellaneous pieces 1955–1982* (London: Faber & Faber, 1983), p. 49.
48. Stanley van der Ziel, 'An Interview with John McGahern', appendix ii in van der Ziel, 'Medusa's Mirror: art, style, vision and tradition in the fiction of John McGahern', PhD dissertation, University College, Dublin, 2008, pp. 361–81, at p. 361.
49. For this aspect of Joyce, see Declan Kiberd, *Ulysses and Us: the art of everyday living* (London: Faber & Faber, 2009). On Kate O'Brien, see the conclusion of an early version of this chapter: 'McGahern, Austen and the Aesthetics of Good Manners', *Essays in Criticism*, vol. 63, no. 2 (2013), pp. 203–22, at p. 218.
50. Joyce, *Ulysses*, p. 490. Cf. Burns: 'O wad some Pow'r the giftie gie us/ To see oursels as others see us!/ It wad frae monie a blunder free us/ An' foolish notion'. Robert Burns, *Poems and Songs*, ed. James Kinsley (London: Oxford University Press, 1969), p. 157.
51. Adam Smith, *The Theory of Moral Sentiments* [1759], ed. Ryan Patrick Hanley (London: Penguin, 2010), p. 6.
52. Samuel Johnson, *The Major Works*, ed. Donald Greene (Oxford: Oxford University Press, 2000), p. 204.
53. Austen, *Emma*, p. 166. On Austen in the context of such a late-eighteenth-century intellectual tradition, see Peter Knox-Shaw, *Jane Austen and the Enlightenment* (Cambridge: Cambridge University Press, 2004).
54. McGahern called *Persuasion* 'a very great novel' in Fred Johnston, 'John McGahern at Fifty' (interview), *Irish Times*, 13 August 1985, p. 10.
55. Austen, *Persuasion*, p. 37.
56. McGahern's various fictional and non-fictional depictions of literary Dublin in the 1950s, in works like *The Pornographer* and *Memoir* (*M*, p. 243), suggest that he shared Wilde's view that 'Good artists exist simply in what they make, and consequently are perfectly uninteresting in what they are ... But inferior poets are absolutely fascinating.' *The Picture of Dorian Gray*, *Complete Works of Oscar Wilde*, pp. 52–3.
57. Oscar Wilde, 'The Soul of Man under Socialism', *Complete Works of Oscar Wilde*, pp. 1194–5.
58. Ní Anluain (ed.), *Reading the Future*, p. 148.

59. On the importance of rhythm and ritual in McGahern, see also Stanley van der Ziel, 'The Aesthetics of Redemption: John McGahern's *That They May Face the Rising Sun*', *Studies*, vol. 93, no. 372 (winter 2004), pp. 473–86.
60. Ní Anluain (ed.), *Reading the Future*, p. 148.
61. Declan Kiberd, introduction in McGahern, *Love of the World*, p. xxi.
62. Jane Austen, *Sense and Sensibility* [1811], ed. Ros Ballaster (London: Penguin, 2003), p. 18.
63. Austen, *Persuasion*, p. 134 (emphasis added).
64. John Butler Yeats, *Letters to His Son W.B. Yeats and Others 1869–1922*, ed. Joseph Hone [1944], abridged and with an introduction by John McGahern (London: Faber & Faber, 1999), pp. 59–60.
65. Jane Austen, *Mansfield Park* [1814], ed. Kathryn Sutherland (London: Penguin, 2003), p. 363. The similarity between the two texts was first pointed out in Belinda McKeon, '"Robins Feeding with the Sparrows": the Protestant "Big House" in the fiction of John McGahern', *Irish University Review*, vol. 35, no. 1 (spring/summer 2005), pp. 72–89, at p. 87 n. 17.
66. Austen, *Persuasion*, p. 134.
67. *The Letters of John Keats*, ed. Maurice Forman, 4th edn (London: Oxford University Press, 1952), p. 71.
68. Cf. the eponymous Bartleby's refrain, 'I would prefer not to', in Herman Melville, 'Bartleby, the Scrivener', *Billy Budd, Sailor and Other Stories* (Harmondsworth: Penguin, 1986), pp. 13 and *passim*. Bartleby's refrain was something of a constant in McGahern's literary imagination even before he used it as the leitmotif of his celebrated lecture on Melville's story at the Belfast Arts Festival in November 1967. As becomes clear from a sentence in an early manuscript draft excavated by Fergus Fahey, he also originally conceived of the Homeboy's fascination with the sound of the word 'prefer' in 'Christmas' (one of his earliest stories, written about four years before his Belfast lecture) as an *explicit* homage to the refrain of 'Bartleby'. See Fergus Fahey, 'Reinvented, Reimagined and Somehow Dislocated', *Journal of the Short Story in English*, no. 53 (autumn 2009), pp. 39–51, at p. 43.
69. McGahern quotes Beckett's question about the quality of silence with approval in Denis Sampson, 'A Conversation with John McGahern', *Canadian Journal of Irish Studies*, vol. 17, no. 1 (July 1991), pp. 13–18, at p. 18.
70. Austen, *Emma*, p. 62.
71. Sampson, 'A Conversation with John McGahern', p. 16. See also the section on 'two things that have obsessed me all my life' in chapter five.
72. Austen, *Sense and Sensibility*, pp. 263–6.
73. Austen, *Emma*, p. 159. See also Tony Tanner, *Jane Austen* [1986], rev. edn (Basingstoke: Palgrave Macmillan, 2007), p. 42.
74. Sampson, *Outstaring Nature's Eye*, p. 234. Sampson's book is the only study of McGahern to date to make repeated references to McGahern's affinity with Austen's novels of manners and morals.
75. Ní Anluain (ed.), *Reading the Future*, p. 148.
76. O'Toole, 'The Family as Independent Republic', p. 2. On the novelist's imperative for objectivity, see also the section on 'The morality of art' in chapter four.
77. The other mention of Austen in McGahern's essays is the reference to *Mansfield Park* as one of the 'books that act as mirrors' reflecting our own lives in 'The Solitary Reader' (*LW*, p. 90).
78. Austen, *Persuasion*, p. 115.
79. James Whyte, *History, Myth, and Ritual in the Fiction of John McGahern: strategies of transcendence* (Lewiston: Edwin Mellen, 2002), p. 206.

80. McGahern cited that sentence as one of his favourites in private conversations and public talks during the 1990s and early 2000s. He eventually used it in *Memoir*, pp. 2–3.
81. John McGahern, 'The White Boat', in A.S. Byatt and Peter Porter (eds), *New Writing 6: an anthology* (London: Vintage, 1997), pp. 342–72, at p. 350.
82. John McGahern, untitled manuscript of a speech introducing Seamus Heaney, *c.* 1983–84: NUIG, P71/1074. The quote from Heaney is actually from 'A Dream of Jealousy', *Field Work* (London: Faber & Faber, 1979), p. 47.
83. Primo Levi, *If This Is a Man and The Truce* [1958/1963], trans. Stuart Woolf (London: Abacus, 1987), p. 178. Cf. John McGahern, notepad marked 'Notes on reading Primo Levi': NUIG, P71/1490 (p. 9). The notes were probably made for his Modern Writing seminars in the 1990s (see note 55 of the introduction).

Chapter 3: A Romantic Imagination

1. John McGahern, 'An tOileánach/The Islandman', *Canadian Journal of Irish Studies*, vol. 13, no. 1 (June 1987), pp. 7–15, at p. 8. The essay was first published in an Irish translation in 1985. It was later republished in expanded, reworked form as 'What Is My Language?' (*LW*, pp. 260–74).
2. William Wordsworth, *Poetical Works*, ed. Thomas Hutchinson, rev. Ernest de Sélincourt (Oxford: Oxford University Press, 1973), p. 149.
3. See for example Eamon Maher, *John McGahern: from the local to the universal* (Dublin: Liffey, 2003), pp. 99ff; Declan Kiberd, *Irish Classics* (London: Granta, 2000), pp. 521, 535; and especially Paolo Vivante, 'McGahern and the Homeric Moment', *Canadian Journal of Irish Studies*, vol. 17, no. 1 (July 1991), pp. 53–6.
4. George Gordon, Lord Byron, is invoked in McGahern's tribute to the Presentation Brothers' secondary curriculum in 'Oldfashioned', in which 'boys... came long distances from the villages and outlying farms to grapple with calculus and George Gordon and the delta of the River Plate' (*HG*, p. 37). *Don Juan* is quoted by characters in *The Barracks* (*B*, p. 162) and *The Rockingham Shoot*: typescript screenplay, BBC Written Archives Centre, Caversham Park, Reading: TV Drama Scripts 1987 [microfilm], film no. 545 (p. 85).
5. John McGahern, in conversation with the present author, 2005.
6. John McGahern, seminar on Patrick Kavanagh, Modern Writing series, University College, Dublin, 3 March 1999 (see note 55 of the introduction).
7. Clíodhna Ní Anluain (ed.), *Reading the Future: Irish writers in conversation with Mike Murphy* (Dublin: Lilliput, 2000), 136–55, at p. 150.
8. *The Prose Works of William Wordsworth*, ed. W.J.B. Owen and Jane Worthington Smyser, 3 vols (Oxford: Clarendon, 1974), vol. i, p. 135. McGahern first publicly announced that he was 'only interested... in poetry, which occurs more often in verse than in prose' in his celebrated lecture on Herman Melville's 'Bartleby, the Scrivener' at Queen's University, Belfast in November 1967: quoted in Seamus Heaney, 'Shedding the Skin of Youth' (rev. of *The Leavetaking*), *Sunday Independent*, 26 January 1975, p. 9.
9. Cf. Wordsworth, *Poetical Works*, pp. 62, 460.
10. McGahern started a set of handwritten lecture notes with some thoughts on *Tristram Shandy*. Regrettably, he did not detail in those notes what these thoughts were. See 'The Idea of Reading and Writing': NUIG, P71/1300–1303.
11. On the literary allusion in the latter phrase, see p. 95 below.
12. Dermot McCarthy, *John McGahern and the Art of Memory* (Oxford: Peter Lang, 2010), p. 32. See also Denis Sampson, *Young John McGahern: becoming a novelist* (Oxford: Oxford University Press, 2012), p. 7.

13. Christopher Salvesen, *The Landscape of Memory: a study of Wordsworth's poetry* (London: Edward Arnold, 1965), p. 1.
14. John McGahern, on *The South Bank Show*, UTV/ITV 1, 29 January 2006.
15. John McGahern, typescript of *The Leavetaking* with amendments and typesetting instructions: NUIG, P71/107 (p. 27). Reproduced in the *John McGahern Yearbook*, vol. 4 (2011), p. 51.
16. George Eliot, *The Mill on the Floss* [1880], ed. A.S. Byatt (London: Penguin, 2003), p. 71.
17. Wordsworth, *Poetical Works*, p. 165.
18. Patrick Kavanagh, *Collected Poems*, ed. Antoinette Quinn (London: Allen Lane, 2004), p. 129.
19. David Malcolm, *Understanding John McGahern* (Columbia: University of South Carolina Press, 2007), p. 116.
20. Wordsworth, 'Michael', *Poetical Works*, p. 109.
21. Ibid., p. 108.
22. M.H. Abrams, *Natural Supernaturalism: tradition and revolution in Romantic literature* [1971] (New York: Norton, 1973), pp. 375–7, 411.
23. Wordsworth, *Poetical Works*, p. 460.
24. Ibid., p. 460.
25. Maher, *John McGahern*, p. 134.
26. John McGahern, letter to Patrick Swift, 5 September [1961?]: The *X* Mss, Lilly Library, Indiana University.
27. Frances Byrnes, 'John McGahern' (obituary), *The Guardian*, 31 March 2006.
28. Cf. Jane Austen, *Emma* [1815], ed. Ronald Blythe (Harmondsworth: Penguin, 1985), p. 241.
29. Patrick Kavanagh, *A Poet's Country: selected prose*, ed. Antoinette Quinn (Dublin: Lilliput, 2003), p. 237.
30. See also Frank Shovlin, 'Four Ducks', *John McGahern Yearbook*, vol. 4 (2011), pp. 48–53.
31. *The Prose Works of William Wordsworth*, vol. i, p. 123.
32. Quoted by McGahern in his seminar on Patrick Kavanagh, Modern Writing series, University College, Dublin, 3 March 1999 (see note 55 of the introduction). See also Antoinette Quinn, *Patrick Kavanagh: a biography* (Dublin: Gill & Macmillan, 2001), p. 372.
33. Wordsworth, 'My Heart Leaps Up', *Poetical Works*, p. 62 (emphasis added).
34. Marcel Proust, *In Search of Lost Time* [1913–27], gen. ed. Christopher Prendergast, 6 vols (London: Allen Lane, 2002), vol. v, p. 237 (*The Prisoner and The Fugitive*, trans. Carol Clark and Peter Collier).
35. Suzanne J. Fournier, 'Structure and Theme in John McGahern's *The Pornographer*', *Éire–Ireland*, vol. 22, no. 1 (spring 1987), pp. 130–50, at p. 142.
36. Kavanagh, *A Poet's Country*, p. 273 (emphasis added).
37. See Sampson, *Young John McGahern*, pp. 48–52. NB that the poem McGahern first read as 'The Chest Hospital' in 1956 is in later editions entitled simply 'The Hospital'.
38. Kavanagh, *Collected Poems*, p. 217.
39. Ibid., p. 217.
40. Eamon Grennan, 'Presence, Absence, Amputations: post-Catholic McGahern', *Facing the Music: Irish poetry in the twentieth century* (Omaha, NE: Creighton University Press, 1999), pp. 119–30, at p. 123.
41. John McGahern, notes on Herman Melville's 'Bartleby, the Scrivener' (*c.* 1967?): NUIG, P71/1293. The reference to 'the animated imagination' of the artist sounds Wordsworthian, but it can actually be found in Kant, who proposed that 'Spirit is the principle of animation, of upward movement — of talent, of the soul's powers — through ideas; and therefore it is the principle of a purposeful, animated imagination.' Quoted in James Engell, *The Creative*

Imagination: Enlightenment to Romanticism (Cambridge, MA: Harvard University Press, 1981), p. 139.

42. See McGahern's essay on *The Islandman* and his review of Frank McCourt's *Angela's Ashes* (*LW*, pp. 264, 400). In his review of a collection of stories by George Mackay Brown, he damningly refers to 'the poor gaudy beads of local colour' (*LW*, p. 347).
43. The rural invasion of the city in 'Parachutes' was first discussed in Declan Kiberd, *Inventing Ireland: the literature of the modern nation* (London: Cape, 1995), p. 485.
44. Wordsworth, *Poetical Works*, p. 214.
45. Wordsworth, 'My Heart Leaps Up', *Poetical Works*, p. 62.
46. *The Prose Works of William Wordsworth*, vol. i, p. 127.
47. D.J. Gordon, *W.B. Yeats: images of a poet: my permanent or impermanent images*, with contributions by Ian Fletcher, Frank Kermode and Robin Skelton (Manchester: Manchester University Press, 1961), p. 25; John McGahern, 'In Memory of Donald Gordon' (*c.* 1977?): NUIG, P71/1260.
48. John McGahern, letter to Michael McLaverty, 2 November 1965, *Dear Mr McLaverty: the literary correspondence of John McGahern and Michael McLaverty*, ed. John Killen (Belfast: Linen Hall Library, 2006), p. 43.
49. James Joyce, *Ulysses* [1922]: annotated students' edition (Harmondsworth: Penguin, 1992), p. 42.
50. Myles Dungan, interview with John McGahern at Vicar Street, Dublin, RTÉ Radio 1, 8 June 2002.
51. Proust, *In Search of Lost Time*, vol. i, p. 87 (*The Way by Swann's*, trans. Lydia Davis).
52. Arminta Wallace, 'Out of the Dark', *Irish Times*, 28 April 1990, Weekend, p. 5. Three years earlier, McGahern had written almost exactly the same thing about Patrick Kavanagh: 'He had an individual vision ... and he was able to bring the images that move us into the light' (*LW*, pp. 330–1).
53. Proust, *In Search of Lost Time*, vol. vi, p. 188 (*Finding Time Again*, trans. Ian Patterson).
54. St Thomas Aquinas, *Philosophical Texts*, trans. Thomas Gilby (London: Oxford University Press, 1951), p. 234.
55. On voluntary and involuntary memory, see also chapter five.
56. Marcel Proust, *By Way of Sainte-Beuve*, trans. Sylvia Townsend Warner (London: Chatto & Windus, 1958), p. 17.
57. Proust, *In Search of Lost Time*, vol. vi, pp. 186–7.
58. Wordsworth, *Poetical Works*, p. 460.
59. Eileen Kennedy, 'Q.&A. with John McGahern', *Irish Literary Supplement*, vol. 3, no. 1 (spring 1984), p. 40.
60. James Joyce, *Dubliners* [1914] (Harmondsworth: Penguin, 1992), p. 225.
61. McGahern loved the paintings of Constable, but just as much, he writes in the essay 'The Bird Swift', he loved the letters in which the great English landscape painter wrote extraordinarily well 'about trees and clouds and light and water' (*LW*, p. 66).
62. John Keats, *Poetical Works*, ed. H.W. Garrod (London: Oxford University Press, 1970), p. 210.
63. W.B. Yeats, 'The Fascination of What's Difficult', *The Poems*, ed. Richard J. Finneran (London: Macmillan, 1984), p. 93.
64. The Romantic poets' interest in ideas is the subject of Jack Stillinger's *Romantic Complexity: Keats, Coleridge and Wordsworth* (Urbana: University of Illinois Press, 2006).
65. *The Prose Works of William Wordsworth*, vol. i, p. 127.
66. Wordsworth, *Poetical Works*, p. 164.
67. William Shakespeare, *Hamlet*, ed. T.J.B. Spencer (Harmondsworth: Penguin, 1996), III.i.56–89; *Macbeth*, ed. G.K. Hunter (Harmondsworth: Penguin, 1995), I.vii.5–7. See also p. 28 above.

68. '... she'd be consumed at last in whatever meaning her life had. Here she had none, *none but to be*' (*B*, p. 211, emphasis added).
69. Proust, *In Search of Lost Time*, vol. i, p. 156.
70. E.R. Dodds, *The Greeks and the Irrational* (Berkeley: University of California Press, 1951), p. 31. See for example *LW*, p. 323. McGahern said in an interview with Paul Clements that he read *The Greeks and the Irrational* 'every two or three years'. Clements, 'The Book and Magazine Collector Interview: John McGahern', *Book and Magazine Collector*, no. 208 (July 2001), pp. 80–9, at p. 89.
71. Forrest Reid, *W.B. Yeats: a critical study* (London: Secker, 1915), p. 218.
72. John McGahern, seminar on Patrick Kavanagh, Modern Writing series, University College, Dublin, 3 March 1999 (see note 55 of the introduction).
73. Kavanagh, *Collected Poems*, pp. 80–1.
74. Wordsworth, *Poetical Works*, p. 164.
75. See the beginning of this chapter's section on 'My heart leaps up when I behold ...'.
76. See the section on 'Remembrance of things past ...' in chapter five.
77. Samuel Taylor Coleridge, *Poetical Works*, ed. Ernest Hartley Coleridge (Oxford: Oxford University Press, 1978), p. 198.
78. Denis Sampson, *Outstaring Nature's Eye: the fiction of John McGahern* (Washington, DC: Catholic University of America Press, 1993), p. 240.
79. On other aspects of the presence of O'Malley in *Amongst Women*, see Stanley van der Ziel, 'Fionn and Oisin in the Land of Wink and Nod: heroes, history, and the creative imagination in John McGahern's *Amongst Women*', *Canadian Journal of Irish Studies*, vol. 31, no. 2 (autumn 2005), pp. 10–18.
80. The passage in question is quoted in full by McGahern in 'The Church and Its Spire' (*LW*, pp. 133–4).
81. Wordsworth, *Poetical Works*, p. 62.
82. Proust, *In Search of Lost Time*, vol. i, p. 156. See also Roger Shattuck, *Proust's Way: a field guide to* In Search of Lost Time (Harmondsworth: Penguin, 2001), pp. 109–10.
83. See Grennan, 'Presence, Absence, Amputations', pp. 119–30. See also van der Ziel, 'Fionn and Oisin in the Land of Wink and Nod', pp. 14–16.
84. John McGahern, letter to Michael McLaverty, 19 June 1961, *Dear Mr McLaverty*, p. 24.
85. John McGahern, letter to Michael McLaverty, 8 August 1965, *Dear Mr McLaverty*, p. 42.
86. Uncut tape recording of an interview with Mike Murphy, recorded 10 September 2000. Private collection. A shorter, edited version of the recording was broadcast on RTÉ Radio 1, and published in Ní Anluain (ed.), *Reading the Future*, pp. 136–55.
87. I am grateful to Matthew Francis, editor of W.S. Graham's *New Collected Poems* (London: Faber & Faber, 2004), for verifying this for me.
88. Ian Jack, 'Saving Grace', *The Guardian*, 8 April 2006, Saturday Review, p. 21.

Chapter 4: The Limits of Realism

1. See Denis Sampson, *Young John McGahern: becoming a novelist* (Oxford: Oxford University Press, 2012), pp. 91–2.
2. Eamon Maher, for example, comments on the tension of what remains unwritten in the Father Gerald chapters of *The Dark*: 'One is left wondering what is the nature of the relationship between Fr Gerald and the young fifteen-year-old boy who keeps house for him. Certainly, it is not a situation that could be countenanced today.' Maher, *John McGahern: from the local to the universal* (Dublin: Liffey, 2003), p. 25.

3. In a letter from 22 August 1959 to Michael McLaverty, McGahern wrote that 'Some years ago I read *Resurrection* and an Oxford [University] Press selection of his tales ... Now I am reading through his novels.' *Dear Mr McLaverty: the literary correspondence of John McGahern and Michael McLaverty 1959–1980*, ed. John Killen (Belfast: Linen Hall Library, 2006), p. 18.
4. Leo Tolstoy, *Anna Karenina* [1873–77], trans. Richard Pevear and Larissa Volokhonsky (London: Penguin, 2003), pp. 21–2.
5. F.R. Leavis, *Anna Karenina and Other Essays* (London: Chatto & Windus, 1973), pp. 13–14.
6. James Joyce, *Giacomo Joyce*, ed. Richard Ellmann (London: Faber & Faber, 1983), p. 16, quoted by McGahern in Justine McCarthy, 'I'm Not a Hero ... I'm Just a Clerk' (interview), *Irish Independent*, 27 August 2005, Weekend Review, pp. 2–4, at p. 3.
7. John McGahern, 'Summer at Strandhill', *New Yorker*, 21 September 1963, pp. 43–8, at p. 43.
8. James Joyce, *Dubliners* [1914] (Harmondsworth: Penguin, 1992), p. 12.
9. John McGahern, untitled typescript: NUIG, P71/1321 (p. 7).
10. See Sampson, *Young John McGahern*, p. 1.
11. Joe Jackson, 'Tales from the Darkside' (interview), *Hot Press*, 14 November 1991, pp. 18–20, at p. 19; Richard Robinson, 'An Umbrella, a Pair of Boots, and a "Spacious Nothing": McGahern and Beckett', *Irish University Review*, vol. 44, no. 2 (autumn/winter 2014), pp. 323–40, at p. 330.
12. See chapter one, note 6.
13. Gerd Kampen, *Zwischen Welt und Text: narratologische Studien zum irischen Gegenwartsroman am Beispiel von John McGahern und John Banville* (Trier: Wissenschaftlicher Verlag Trier, 2002), p. 356 (my translation).
14. Roland Barthes, *The Rustle of Language*, trans. Richard Howard (Oxford: Blackwell, 1986), p. 148.
15. Alain Robbe-Grillet, *For a New Novel: essays on fiction* [1963], trans. Richard Howard (New York: Grove, 1965), p. 16.
16. Seamus Perry, email to the present author, 7 January 2012.
17. Jackson, 'Tales from the Darkside', p. 19.
18. James Joyce, *Stephen Hero*, ed. Theodore Spencer, with John J. Slocum and Herbert Cahoon (New York: New Directions, 1963), pp. 77–8.
19. See also chapter three.
20. Fyodor Dostoevsky, *Crime and Punishment* [1866], trans. David McDuff (London: Penguin, 2003), pp. 329–31.
21. Roland Barthes, *Image Music Text*, trans. Stephen Heath (London: Fontana, 1977), p. 96.
22. Richard Pine enumerates 'domestic interiors (in every sense of the word)' among the major themes of *The Barracks* and *The Dark*. Pine, 'John McGahern' (obituary), *The Guardian*, 31 March 2006.
23. Paolo Vivante, 'McGahern and the Homeric Moment', *Canadian Journal of Irish Studies*, vol. 17, no. 1 (July 1991), pp. 53–6, at pp. 55, 54.
24. Aaron Kelly, *Twentieth-century Irish Literature: a reader's guide to essential criticism* (Basingstoke: Palgrave Macmillan, 2008), p. 127; Robinson, 'An Umbrella', p. 330.
25. John McGahern, letter to Patrick Swift, n.d. [*c.* 1961]: The *X* Mss, Lilly Library, Indiana University.
26. John McGahern, letter to Brian Friel, n.d.: The Brian Friel Papers, National Library of Ireland, MS 37,259.
27. Marcel Proust, *By Way of Sainte-Beuve*, trans. Sylvia Townsend Warner (London: Chatto & Windus, 1958), p. 127.
28. See for example Harry E. Shaw, *Narrating Reality: Austen, Scott, Eliot* (Ithaca: Cornell University Press, 1999), especially chapter two (at pp. 38–89).

29. See Stanley van der Ziel, '"All This Talk and Struggle": John McGahern's *The Dark*', *Irish University Review*, vol. 35, no. 1 (spring/summer 2005), pp. 104–20.
30. *Selected Letters of James Joyce*, ed. Richard Ellmann (London: Faber & Faber, 1975), p. 90. See Vicki Mahaffey, '*Dubliners*: surprised by chance', in Richard Brown (ed.), *A Companion to James Joyce* (Malden and Oxford: Wiley–Blackwell, 2011), pp. 19–33, at p. 21.
31. James Joyce, *Ulysses* [1922]: annotated students' edition (Harmondsworth: Penguin, 1992), p. 6.
32. The quote is from Joyce's *Ulysses*, p. 28.
33. William Shakespeare, *Hamlet*, ed. T.J.B. Spencer (Harmondsworth: Penguin, 1996), III. ii.21–2.
34. *Complete Works of Oscar Wilde*: centenary edition (Glasgow: HarperCollins, 1999), p. 17.
35. Gustave Flaubert, *Madame Bovary* [1857], trans. Geoffrey Wall (London: Penguin, 2003), p. 21.
36. Ibid., p. 21.
37. McGahern's remark is quoted on p. 102 above.
38. Stendhal, *Scarlet and Black: a chronicle of the nineteenth century* [1830], trans. Margaret R.B. Shaw (Harmondsworth: Penguin, 1953), p. 93. Stendhal was one of the French writers whose work McGahern first read in English translation during his time as a student at St Patrick's College, Drumcondra. That McGahern had read Stendhal early on is clear from the list of titles invoked in his memory of the conversations about literature with Patrick Swift during the formative summer of 1960 in 'The Bird Swift' (*LW*, p. 74).
39. Frank O'Connor, *The Mirror in the Roadway: a study of the modern novel* (London: Hamish Hamilton, 1957), p. 15.
40. *Letters of Anton Chekhov*, sel. and ed. Avrahm Yarmolinsky (London: Cape, 1974), p. 37.
41. Anton Chekhov, *Plays*, trans. Elisaveta Fen (Harmondsworth: Penguin, 1959), p. 177.
42. Michael McLaverty, letter to John McGahern, 23 March 1961, *Dear Mr McLaverty*, p. 22.
43. Quoted, in French translation, in the translator's preface in John McGahern, *Lignes de Fond, précédé de L'Image*, trans. Pierre Leyris (Paris: Mercure de France, 1971), pp. 9–14, at p. 9.
44. W.B. Yeats, *Essays and Introductions* (London: Macmillan, 1961), p. 102.
45. *The Letters of Gustave Flaubert 1830–1857*, sel., ed. and trans. Francis Steegmuller (Cambridge, MA: Harvard University Press, 1980), p. 191.
46. *The Letters of Gustave Flaubert 1857–1880*, sel., ed. and trans. Francis Steegmuller (Cambridge, MA: Harvard University Press, 1982), p. 231. The passage was quoted by McGahern in his essay on *Dubliners* (*LW*, p. 204).
47. Eamon Maher, 'Catholicism and National Identity in the Works of John McGahern: interview', *Studies*, vol. 90, no. 357 (spring 2001), pp. 70–83, at p. 80; cf. *The Letters of Gustave Flaubert 1857–1880*, p. 231.
48. Cf. *Complete Works of Oscar Wilde*, p. 1153.
49. Julia Carlson (ed.), *Banned in Ireland: censorship and the Irish writer* (London: Routledge, 1990), pp. 53–67, at p. 67.
50. *Complete Works of Oscar Wilde*, p. 17. In his essay on *Dubliners*, McGahern quotes both Henry James' summary in one of his letters of the position of the Flaubert circle towards the relationship between morality and art: 'The only duty of a novel was to be well written; that merit included every other of which it was capable' (*LW*, p. 202), and Flaubert's letter to George Sand containing the statement that 'Even obscene books are immoral only if they lack truth' (*LW*, p. 204). Cf. *The Letters of Gustave Flaubert 1857–1880*, pp. 225, 231.
51. Joe Kennedy, 'McGahern, "Art Is a Luxury": an interview with the author of *The Dark*', *Evening Herald*, 11 November 1970, p. 7.
52. Lord Byron, *Selected Letters and Journals*, ed. Leslie A. Marchand (Cambridge, MA: Harvard University Press, 1982), p. 328. A reference in a letter to Michael McLaverty from

9 March 1960 shows that McGahern had read Byron's letters early on: *Dear Mr McLaverty*, p. 21.

53. Leo Tolstoy, quoted in Donna Tussing Orwin (ed.), *The Cambridge Companion to Tolstoy* (Cambridge: Cambridge University Press, 2002), p. 80.
54. *Selected Letters of James Joyce*, p. 329. Joyce's remark about Thomas Hardy is reminiscent of Stephen Dedalus' fear of 'those big words . . . which make us so unhappy' in the Nestor episode of *Ulysses* (p. 38). The latter phrase was quoted by McGahern in a 2002 *Guardian* interview: Nicholas Wroe, 'Ireland's Rural Elegist' (profile), *The Guardian*, 5 January 2002, Saturday Review, pp. 6–7, at p. 7. He had already echoed the same phrase in 'Korea' more than thirty years earlier. The narrator of that story is as 'wary of the big words' spoken by his father about economic woe and emigration to the land of opportunity as Joyce's Stephen is of Mr Deasy's prudent financial advice (*N*, p. 88).
55. Fintan O'Toole, 'The Family as Independent Republic' (profile), *Irish Times*, 13 October 1990, Weekend, p. 2.
56. John McGahern, at a reading from his own work at St Patrick's College, Drumcondra, 9 April 2003.
57. Michael McLaverty, letter to John McGahern, 23 May 1965, *Dear Mr McLaverty*, p. 39.
58. Augustine Martin, *Bearing Witness: essays on Anglo-Irish literature*, ed. Anthony Roche (Dublin: University College Dublin Press, 1996), p. 89. It is certain that Martin was aware of McGahern's admiration of this aspect of Joyce's aesthetic: McGahern's essay on *Dubliners* originally appeared in a 1990 book edited by him.
59. See Maria DiBattista, 'Joyce's Ghost: the bogey of realism in John McGahern's *Amongst Women*', in Karen R. Lawrence (ed.), *Transcultural Joyce* (Cambridge: Cambridge Unversity Press, 1998), pp. 21–36, at p. 25.
60. Denis Sampson, 'The "Rich Whole": John McGahern's *Collected Stories* as autobiography', *Journal of the Short Story in English*, no. 34 (spring 2000), pp. 21–30, at p. 27. Presumably the reference Sampson intended is that to 'the odour of ashpits and old weeds and offal [which] hangs round my stories'. *Selected Letters of James Joyce*, pp. 89–90.
61. *Letters of Anton Chekhov*, p. 41.
62. Eileen Kennedy, 'Q.&A. with John McGahern', *Irish Literary Supplement*, vol. 3, no. 1 (spring 1984), p. 40.
63. W.B. Yeats, *The Poems*, ed. Richard J. Finneran (London: Macmillan, 1984), p. 328.
64. *Letters of Anton Chekhov*, p. 88. Chekhov used the same legal analogy to explain the nature of good writing on a number of occasions. See also for example another letter written earlier in the same year (p. 71).
65. John McGahern, quoted in Eugene Moloney, 'Lift-off for the Party's Opener', *Irish Independent*, 18 July 1991, p. 11.
66. Uncut tape recording of an interview with Mike Murphy, recorded 10 September 2000. Private collection. In the published version, this quotation is mistranscribed to such an extent that its meaning is significantly altered: see Clíodhna Ní Anluain (ed.), *Reading the Future: Irish writers in conversation with Mike Murphy* (Dublin: Lilliput, 2000), pp. 137–55, at p. 139. Compare also a comment he made in an essay: 'I have always felt that self-expression is the opposite of creativity' (*LW*, p. 14).
67. *The Letters of Gustave Flaubert 1830–1857*, p. 202.
68. See chapter one, note 17.
69. *The Letters of Gustave Flaubert 1830–1857*, p. 173. See also another letter, written five years later, which contains an all but identical sentence: 'The artist in his work must be like God in his creation — invisible and all-powerful: he must be everywhere felt, but never seen' (p. 230).

70. James Joyce, *A Portrait of the Artist as a Young Man* [1914–15] (Harmondsworth: Penguin, 1992), p. 233.
71. *The Letters of Gustave Flaubert 1857–1880*, p. 94.
72. Joyce, *A Portrait*, p. 233. On the Reegan children at bedtime, see p. 44 above.
73. Samuel Beckett, *Molloy/Malone Dies/The Unnamable* [1950–52] (London: Calder, 1997), p. 26.
74. Luigi Pirandello, *The Late Mattia Pascal* [1904], trans. William Weaver (London: André Deutsch, 1993), p. 145.
75. See John McGahern, letter to Tony Whelan, 16 July 1958, *John McGahern Yearbook*, vol. 2 (2009), pp. 32–3.
76. Sean O'Hagan, 'A Family Touched with Madness', *The Observer*, 28 August 2005, Review, p. 9.
77. John McGahern, letter to Patrick Swift, 5 September [1961?]: The *X* Mss, Lilly Library, Indiana University.
78. John McGahern, letter to C.M. Newman, 16 February 1963, quoted in Sampson, *Young John McGahern*, p. 60.
79. W.B. Yeats, *Autobiographies* (London: Macmillan, 1955), p. 279; Yeats, *Essays and Introductions*, p. 101. See Denis Sampson, *Outstaring Nature's Eye: the fiction of John McGahern* (Washington, DC: Catholic University of America Press, 1993), p. 143 n. 9.
80. Forrest Reid, *Brian Westby* (London: Faber & Faber, 1934), pp. 165–6.
81. *Some Like It Hot*, dir. Billy Wilder (Metro Goldwyn Mayer, 1959).
82. See Mikhail Bakhtin, *The Dialogic Imagination: four essays*, ed. Michael Holquist, trans. Caryl Emerson and Michael Holquist (Austin: University of Texas Press, 1981), p. 32.
83. Cf. 'To lose one parent may be regarded as a misfortune... to lose both seems like carelessness.' *Complete Works of Oscar Wilde*, p. 369.
84. Ibid., p. 376.
85. Ibid., p. 1120.
86. Cf. also the final line of Old Mr Moroney's speech in an unpublished dramatic fragment: NUIG, P71/1279. Quoted on pp. 231–2 below.
87. Denis Sampson, 'A Conversation with John McGahern', *Canadian Journal of Irish Studies*, vol. 17, no. 1 (July 1991), pp. 13–18, at p. 15.
88. Such theoretical concerns notwithstanding, the question of what exactly *is* or *is not* believable, either in real life or in the plot of a novel, is a matter of judgement that varies for each individual reader. McGahern was well aware of this subjectivity. It formed the basis of a comic anecdote he told about his relationship with Michael McLaverty. In an essay he recalls how he had told McLaverty a story he considered too strange for fiction, only to find that not only did McLaverty '[find] the story believable, but was so delighted by it that he worked it into the fabric of his last novel' (*LW*, pp. 76–7).
89. Charles Dickens, *Nicholas Nickleby* [1839], ed. Mark Ford (London: Penguin, 2003), p. 4.
90. Luigi Pirandello, *Six Characters in Search of an Author and Other Plays*, trans. Mark Musa (Harmondsworth: Penguin, 1995), p. 12. McGahern talks about his memory of seeing that play in Ní Anluain (ed.), *Reading the Future*, p. 151.
91. Cf. 'It is fortunate for us ... that Nature is so imperfect, as otherwise we should have no art at all.' 'The Decay of Lying', *Complete Works of Oscar Wilde*, p. 1071.
92. Mark Twain, *Following the Equator* [1897], quoted in Forrest G. Robinson (ed.), *The Cambridge Companion to Mark Twain* (Cambridge: Cambridge University Press, 1995), p. 43.
93. John McGahern, 'Three Answers to an Interview', typescript. Private collection.
94. *Complete Works of Oscar Wilde*, pp. 1086–7.

95. F.S.L. Lyons, *Ireland since the Famine* (London: Weidenfeld & Nicolson, 1971), p. 551. McGahern may have been reminded of Lyons shortly before he wrote 'From a Glorious Dream to Wink and Nod' by J.J. Lee's newly published *Ireland 1912–1985: politics and society* (Cambridge: Cambridge University Press, 1989), which uses the phrase 'Plato's cave' as a heading in the chapter about the 1940s (p. 258). McGahern cited Lee's book in another newspaper article at the end of the decade (*LW*, p. 129); we can only speculate whether he read it before writing 'From a Glorious Dream' in 1991.

Chapter 5: A Modernist Mind I: Proustian Thought and Forms

1. Marcel Proust, *In Search of Lost Time* [1913–27], gen. ed. Christopher Prendergast, 6 vols (London: Allen Lane, 2002), vol. iii, p. 393 (*The Guermantes Way*, trans. Mark Treharne).
2. [Joyce Andrews], 'John McGahern' (profile), in Daniel Murphy (dir. of research), *Education and the Arts: the educational autobiographies of contemporary Irish poets, novelists, dramatists, musicians, painters and sculptors: a research report* (Dublin: Trinity College Department of Higher Education, 1987), pp. 129–43, at pp. 139–40.
3. On the significance of classical poetry for McGahern, see the section on 'Reading, writing and tradition' in the introduction.
4. See the handwritten draft of an elegiac essay on Ó Céileachair which he started to write at that time: NUIG, P71/1319. See also Denis Sampson, *Young John McGahern: becoming a novelist* (Oxford: Oxford University Press, 2012), pp. 38–9.
5. Andrews, 'John McGahern', p. 139.
6. John McGahern, letter to Stanley van der Ziel, 14 February 2006. Private collection.
7. Sampson, *Young John McGahern*, pp. 46–7.
8. See ibid., p. 53; and Stanley van der Ziel, 'An Interview with John McGahern', appendix ii in van der Ziel, 'Medusa's Mirror: art, style, vision and tradition in the fiction of John McGahern', PhD dissertation, University College, Dublin, 2008, pp. 361–81, at p. 372.
9. Ibid., pp. 371–2.
10. Colm Tóibín, 'Out of the Dark: a profile of John McGahern' [1985], *The Trials of the Generals: selected journalism 1980–1990* (Dublin: Raven Arts, 1990), pp. 94–102, at p. 98.
11. Linda Collinge and Emmanuel Vernadakis, 'John McGahern' (interview), *Journal of the Short Story in English*, no. 41 (autumn 2003), pp. 123–41, at p. 130. McGahern mentions Thomas Mann's *The Magic Mountain* and *Felix Krull* in two letters to Michael McLaverty, dated 22 August 1959 and 9 March 1960 respectively: *Dear Mr McLaverty: the literary correspondence of John McGahern and Michael McLaverty 1959–1980*, ed. John Killen (Belfast: Linen Hall Library, 2006), pp. 18, 21. A letter to Patrick Swift also refers to an unspecified book by Thomas Mann which McGahern owned. John McGahern, letter to Patrick Swift, n.d. [*c.* 1961]: The *X* Mss, Lilly Library, Indiana University.
12. Collinge and Vernadakis, 'John McGahern', p. 127. On McGahern's early reading of Yeats, see p. 190 below.
13. Virginia Woolf, 'The Mark on the Wall', *Selected Short Stories*, ed. Sandra Kemp (London: Penguin, 2000), p. 53.
14. James Joyce, *Ulysses* [1922]: annotated students' edition (Harmondsworth: Penguin, 1992), p. 28; T.S. Eliot, 'The Waste Land', *Collected Poems 1909–1962* (London: Faber & Faber, 2002), p. 53.
15. Eliot, *Collected Poems*, p. 53.
16. Proust, *In Search of Lost Time*, vol. ii, pp. 124–5 (*In the Shadow of Young Girls in Flower*, trans. James Grieve); Marcel Proust, *By Way of Sainte-Beuve*, trans. Sylvia Townsend Warner (London: Chatto & Windus, 1958), p. 127.

17. Cf. Marcel Proust, *On Reading* [1905], trans. and ed. Jean Autret and William Burford (London: Souvenir, 1972), p. 3.
18. Denis Sampson, 'A Conversation with John McGahern', *Canadian Journal of Irish Studies*, vol. 17, no. 1 (July 1991), pp. 13–18, at p. 16.
19. Proust, *In Search of Lost Time*, vol. v, p. 88 (*The Prisoner and The Fugitive*, trans. Carol Clark and Peter Collier).
20. John McGahern, letter to Michael McLaverty, 22 August 1959, *Dear Mr McLaverty*, p. 18.
21. Samuel Beckett, *Proust and Three Dialogues with Georges Duthuit* (London: Calder, 1965), pp. 19, 13–14.
22. See Denis Sampson, 'The Lost Image: some notes on McGahern and Proust', *Canadian Journal of Irish Studies*, vol. 17, no. 1 (July 1991), pp. 57–68; and Stanley van der Ziel, '"All This Talk and Struggle": John McGahern's *The Dark*', *Irish University Review*, vol. 35, no. 1 (spring/summer 2005), pp. 104–20.
23. James Joyce, *Dubliners* [1914] (Harmondsworth: Penguin, 1992), p. 20.
24. Proust, *In Search of Lost Time*, vol. iii, p. 393. Contemporaneous with his first reading of Proust in the mid-1950s, McGahern had probably also come across the same misgivings about intellectual, rather than physical, intimacy in another key modernist novelist. The eponymous Lady Chatterley 'had always feared' the 'yearning adoration' she feels for her lover, lest 'if she adored him too much, then she would lose herself, become effaced'. D.H. Lawrence, *Lady Chatterley's Lover* [1928], ed. Michael Squires (London: Penguin, 2006), p. 135.
25. Beckett, *Proust*, p. 66; cf. Proust, *In Search of Lost Time*, vol. v, p. 418.
26. Sampson, 'A Conversation with John McGahern', p. 16; Joe Jackson, 'Tales from the Darkside' (interview), *Hot Press*, 14 November 1991, pp. 18–20, at p. 19.
27. Note, however, that characters in all of these and other works can also sometimes momentarily go against their usual Proustian instinct for separateness and solitariness. The fathers in both *The End or the Beginning of Love* and *The Dark* express the concern that 'We're too cooped up in ourselves here' (McGahern, 'The End or the Beginning of Love: episodes from a novel', *X: a quarterly review*, vol. 2, no. 1 [April 1961], pp. 36–46, at p. 37; *D*, p. 19), and that they 'need an outing… It'd take us out of ourselves' (*D*, p. 19). Equally, Moran in *Amongst Women* tells his family in the fields that 'Alone we might be nothing. Together we can do anything' (*AW*, p. 84) — a statement which McGahern attributed to his own father's 'courting' of his estranged son in the proof copies of *Memoir* that were distributed to reviewers prior to publication. See John McGahern, *Memoir*, uncorrected proofs (London: Faber & Faber, 2005), p. 220. In the final published text of *Memoir*, his father's statement survives only in free indirect speech (*M*, p. 214).
28. Cf. Thomas De Quincey, *Recollections of the Lakes and the Lake Poets* [1862], ed. David Wright (Harmondsworth: Penguin, 1970), p. 361.
29. Beckett, *Proust*, p. 46.
30. St Augustine, *Confessions*, trans. R.S. Pine-Coffin (Harmondsworth: Penguin, 1961), p. 55.
31. See Stanley van der Ziel, editor's preface in McGahern, *Love of the World*, p. xliv n. 15.
32. See p. 124 above.
33. Proust, *In Search of Lost Time*, vol. ii, p. 492 (emphasis added).
34. The phrase 'we can only love what we know' which is remembered by the narrator of *The Leavetaking* occurs both in E.M. Forster's 1941 essay 'Tolerance', *Two Cheers for Democracy* [1951] (Harmondsworth: Penguin, 1976), p. 45; and in Aldous Huxley's *The Perennial Philosophy* (London: Chatto & Windus, 1946), p. 95. McGahern had used the same phrase in his notes (probably written *c.* 1967) on Melville's 'Bartleby, the Scrivener': see p. 95 above.
35. On McGahern's deliberately 'bad' prose in *The Leavetaking*, see Marianne (Koenig) Mays, '"Ravished and Exasperated": the evolution of John McGahern's plain style', *Canadian Journal of Irish Studies*, vol. 17, no. 1 (July 1991), pp. 38–52.

36. Matthew Arnold, *Poetical Works*, ed. C.B. Tinker and H.F. Lowry (London: Oxford University Press, 1961), p. 211.
37. See Eamon Maher, 'An Interview with John McGahern', appendix in Maher, *John McGahern: from the local to the universal* (Dublin: Liffey, 2003), pp. 143–61, at p. 156; and Nicholas Wroe, 'Ireland's Rural Elegist' (profile), *The Guardian*, 5 January 2002, Saturday Review, pp. 6–7, at p. 7, respectively.
38. Evelyn Waugh, *Brideshead Revisited: the sacred and profane memories of Captain Charles Ryder* [1945] (London: Penguin, 2003), p. 32. The lovers' conundrum in 'Along the Edges' that 'They would have to know that they could know nothing', like the priest's remark in 'The Wine Breath' (published in the same volume) that 'I know one thing... *I know that I know nothing*' (*GT*, p. 105, emphasis added), also obviously echoes a line commonly (but erroneously) attributed to Plato's recollections of the life of Socrates. See Gail Fine, 'Does Socrates Claim to Know that He Knows Nothing?', *Oxford Studies in Ancient Philosophy*, vol. 35 (winter 2008), pp. 49–88.
39. John McGahern, 'The White Boat', in A.S. Byatt and Peter Porter (eds), *New Writing 6: an anthology* (London: Vintage, 1997), pp. 342–72, at p. 350.
40. McGahern borrowed that line from *The Importance of Being Earnest* in his review of Peter Parker's biography of J.R. Ackerley (*LW*, p. 350); cf. *Complete Works of Oscar Wilde*: centenary edition (Glasgow: HarperCollins, 1999), p. 362.
41. Lawrence, *Lady Chatterley's Lover*, p. 145.
42. John Williams, *Augustus* [1972], with an introduction by John McGahern (London: Vintage, 2003), pp. 304–5.
43. See Maher, 'An Interview with John McGahern', p. 148. For a lengthy treatment of the theme of 'the Self and the Other' which includes extended references to the significance of John Williams' various works, see Stanley van der Ziel, 'Medusa's Mirror: art, style, vision and tradition in the fiction of John McGahern', PhD dissertation, University College, Dublin, 2008, pp. 157–64.
44. F. Scott Fitzgerald, *Tender Is the Night* [1934] (London: Penguin, 1997), pp. 40, 148.
45. Samuel Beckett, *Complete Dramatic Works* (London: Faber & Faber, 1986), p. 160.
46. That a specifically Yeatsean allusion (as opposed to a more generalised reference to the Gaelic myth) is intended is strongly suggested by the inclusion of a reference to Yeats' theatrical collaborator Florence Farr on the preceding page. Noting a lack of unusual sexual props or practices in the story the pornographer has delivered, Maloney remarks: 'A pity. "We are nothing if not advanced," Miss Florence Farr, the future Lady Brandon, said as far back as 1894' (*P*, p. 204). Both the quote (which originally referred to experimental *theatrical*, not *sexual*, practices) and the reference to 'the future Lady Brandon' are taken from Farr's 1894 interview with *The Sketch*; McGahern probably found it quoted in D.J. Gordon, *W.B. Yeats: images of a poet: my permanent or impermanent images*, with contributions by Ian Fletcher, Frank Kermode and Robin Skelton (Manchester: Manchester University Press, 1961), p. 58.
47. John McGahern, at a reading from his own work at St Patrick's College, Drumcondra, 9 April 2003.
48. See pp. 72–3 above.
49. William Shakespeare, *Twelfth Night*, ed. M.M. Mahood (London: Penguin, 2005), V.i.374.
50. John McGahern, seminar on Primo Levi, Modern Writing series, University College, Dublin, 7 April 1999 (see note 55 of the introduction).
51. See L.P. Hartley, *The Go-between* (London: Hamish Hamilton, 1953), p. 9.
52. The same idea is repeated later in the novel by Mary: 'People we know come and go in our minds whether they are here or in England or alive or dead' (*TRS*, p. 115). That matter-of-fact statement may echo Synge's dispassionate report of the news that greets his return to Inishmaan in *The Aran Islands*: 'Old Pat Dirane is dead, and several of my friends have gone

to America; that is all the news they have to give me after an absence of many months.' J.M. Synge, *Collected Works*, gen. ed. Robin Skelton, 4 vols (London: Oxford University Press, 1962–68), vol. ii, p. 106.

53. John McGahern, seminar on Alistair MacLeod, Modern Writing series, University College, Dublin, 24 February 1999 (see note 55 of the introduction).
54. Eliot, *Collected Poems*, p. 177.
55. Clíodhna Ní Anluain (ed.), *Reading the Future: Irish writers in conversation with Mike Murphy* (Dublin: Lilliput, 2000), pp. 137–55, at p. 138.
56. Gordon, *W.B. Yeats: images of a poet*, p. 43. A set of McGahern's handwritten notes on W.B. Yeats begins with a quotation from Gordon's book on Yeats: 'From the tension of opposites he makes his art that abolishes time and establishes memory.' NUIG, P71/1291. McGahern described that sentence as 'One of my favourite descriptions of art' in Maher, 'An Interview with John McGahern', p. 146.
57. W.B. Yeats, 'The Municipal Gallery Re-visited', *The Poems*, ed. Richard J. Finneran (London: Macmillan, 1984), p. 320.
58. The phrase is Patrick Kavanagh's, from his sonnet 'The Chest Hospital'. See also p. 95 above.
59. Vivian Mercier, *The New Novel: from Queneau to Pinget* (New York: Farrar, Straus & Giroux, 1966), p. 345.
60. Proust, *In Search of Lost Time*, vol. ii, p. 395.
61. *Complete Poetical Works of Thomas Hardy*, ed. Samuel Hynes, 5 vols (Oxford: Clarendon, 1982–95), vol. ii, p. 45.
62. McGahern first read *The Death of Ivan Ilych* in 1959, following a tip from Michael McLaverty. It is clear from his letter of 22 August 1959 to McLaverty that its discovery was important to him: *Dear Mr McLaverty*, p. 18. McGahern cited both *The Death of Ivan Ilych* and Thomas Hardy's 'Under the Waterfall' as kindred texts to *In Search of Lost Time* in van der Ziel, 'An Interview with John McGahern', p. 373.
63. Denis Sampson, *Outstaring Nature's Eye: the fiction of John McGahern* (Washington, DC: Catholic University of America Press, 1993), p. 17. See also ibid., pp. 175–6.
64. Proust, *In Search of Lost Time*, vol. i, p. 9 (*The Way by Swann's*, trans. Lydia Davis).
65. Bertrand Cardin, '"Absence does not cast a shadow": Yeats's shadowy presence in McGahern's "The Wine Breath"', *Journal of the Short Story in English*, no. 53 (autumn 2009), pp. 111–25, at p. 114.
66. Proust, *In Search of Lost Time*, vol. i, pp. 47, 46.
67. Sampson, *Outstaring Nature's Eye*, p. 128. McGahern mentions O'Malley's description of that technique in his essay on O'Malley (*LW*, p. 254). Cf. Ernie O'Malley, *On Another Man's Wound* [1936] (Dublin: Anvil, 2002), pp. 293–4.
68. See p. 109 above.
69. St Augustine, *Confessions*, pp. 226–7.
70. William Wordsworth, 'Composed upon Westminster Bridge, September 3, 1802', *Poetical Works*, ed. Thomas Hutchinson, rev. Ernest de Sélincourt (Oxford: Oxford University Press, 1973), p. 214.
71. See also the discussion of circular narratives in the section on 'The shapes of modern narrative' in chapter six.
72. See Proust, *In Search of Lost Time*, vol. i, pp. 180–2.
73. For an extended version of this argument, see Stanley van der Ziel, review of *Memoir*, *Irish University Review*, vol.35, no.2 (autumn/winter 2005), pp. 463–9, at pp. 467–8.
74. Declan Kiberd, 'Fallen Nobility: the world of John McGahern', *Irish University Review*, vol. 35, no. 1 (spring/summer 2005), pp. 164–74, at pp. 171–2.
75. Eamon Grennan, '"Only What Happens": mulling over McGahern', *Irish University Review*, vol. 35, no. 1 (spring/summer 2005), pp. 13–27, at p. 23.

76. William Shakespeare, *Hamlet*, ed. T.J.B. Spencer (Harmondsworth: Penguin, 1996), III.i.79.
77. Kate O'Brien, *The Ante-room* [1934] (London: Virago, 1988), p. 213. McGahern's handwritten notes on *The Ante-room* (probably taken for his Modern Writing seminars in the 1990s: see note 55 of the introduction) can be found on the first page of a notepad marked 'Notes on reading Primo Levi': NUIG, P71/1490.
78. Proust, *In Search of Lost Time*, vol. ii, p. 395.
79. See p. 115 above.
80. See also McGahern's rambling but useful comment in a later interview: 'it seems to me that we live in days ... There's a book I like very much called *The Greeks and the Irrational* by [E.R.] Dodds ... and a wonderful book, *The Homeric Imagination* [by Paolo Vivante], and the unit of time in Greek — and that's echoed in a great Gaelic classic, *The Islandman* ... [in which] again the unit of time is the day, which probably goes back to their religious experience, and I actually see them as people immersed in time; and of course, it's very exciting to come across that in Proust as well. But I mean, we do live in days, and one gets the sense, especially in Homer and in [*The Islandman*] ... the sense of a man's life being made up of a succession of single days.' Liliane Louvel, Gilles Ménégaldo and Claudine Verley, 'John McGahern — 17 November 1993' (interview), *La Licorne*, no. 32 (1995), pp. 19–31, at p. 23.
81. See John Cronin, 'John McGahern's *Amongst Women*: retrenchment and renewal', *Irish University Review*, vol. 22, no. 1 (spring/summer 1992), pp. 168–76, at pp. 170–1; and Sampson, *Outstaring Nature's Eye*, p. 221. See also p. 82 above.
82. John McGahern, seminar on Primo Levi, Modern Writing series, University College, Dublin, 7 April 1999 (see note 55 of the introduction).
83. Primo Levi, *The Drowned and the Saved* [1986], trans. Raymond Rosenthal (London: Abacus, 2002), p. 56.
84. Joe Joyce, 'Fiction Farmer' (interview), *The Guardian*, 26 April 1990, p. 25.
85. Primo Levi, *If This Is a Man and The Truce* [1958/1963], trans. Stuart Woolf (London: Abacus, 1987), p. 80.
86. William Shakespeare, *The Tempest*, ed. Martin Butler (London: Penguin, 2007), II.ii.56, 71; Beckett, *Complete Dramatic Works*, p. 83.
87. William Shakespeare, *The Sonnets and A Lover's Complaint*, ed. John Kerrigan (Harmondsworth: Penguin, 1986), pp. 91, 130 (emphasis added).

Chapter 6: A Modernist Mind II: After Yeats and Joyce

1. See W.R. Rodgers (ed.), *Irish Literary Portraits* (London: British Broadcasting Corporation, 1972), p. 19.
2. On McGahern's relationship to the latter group of writers, see my forthcoming essay on 'McGahern, Post-Revival Literature and Irish Cultural Criticism', in Adam Bargroff, Raymond Mullen and Tom Walker (eds), *John McGahern: ways of seeing*.
3. Julia Carlson (ed.), *Banned in Ireland: censorship and the Irish writer* (London: Routledge, 1990), pp. 53–67, at p. 64.
4. Roberta Gefter Wondrich, 'Exilic Returns: self and history outside Ireland in recent Irish fiction', *Irish University Review*, vol. 30, no. 1 (spring/summer 2000), pp. 1–16, at p. 12.
5. Vincent Hurley, 'Recent Fictional Perspectives on Provincial Ireland', *Colby Quarterly*, vol. 31, no. 1 (March 1995), pp. 23–9.
6. Derek Mahon, 'Is There No Escape?' (rev. of *Nightlines*), *The Times*, 12 November 1970, p. 14.
7. Audrey L. Lynch, 'An Interview with John McGahern', *Books Ireland*, no. 88 (November 1984), p. 213. For 'scrupulous meanness', see *Selected Letters of James Joyce*, ed. Richard Ellmann (London: Faber & Faber, 1975), p. 83.

8. Harold Bloom, *The Anxiety of Influence: a theory of poetry* [1973], 2nd edn (Oxford: Oxford University Press, 1997).
9. See Fergal Casey, 'Competing Philosophies in John McGahern's *That They May Face the Rising Sun*', *Irish University Review*, vol. 43, no. 2 (autumn/winter 2013), pp. 414–28, at p. 418, for an alternative reading of that line in a very different literary-philosophical context.
10. James Joyce, *A Portrait of the Artist as a Young Man* [1914–15] (Harmondsworth: Penguin, 1992), p. 233.
11. See for example Maria DiBattista, 'Joyce's Ghost: the bogey of realism in John McGahern's *Amongst Women*', in Karen R. Lawrence (ed.), *Transcultural Joyce* (Cambridge: Cambridge University Press, 1998), pp. 21–36, at p. 26; and Eamon Wall, 'The Living Stream: John McGahern's *Amongst Women* and Irish writing in the 1990s', *Studies*, vol. 88, no. 351 (autumn 1999), pp. 305–14, at pp. 307–8.
12. See the concluding paragraphs of the section on 'using the imagination on behalf of others' in chapter two.
13. John McGahern, letter to Michael McLaverty, 21 September 1960, *Dear Mr McLaverty: the literary correspondence of John McGahern and Michael McLaverty 1959–1980*, ed. John Killen (Belfast: Linen Hall Library, 2006), p. 21. Cf. James Joyce, *Ulysses* [1922]: annotated students' edition (Harmondsworth: Penguin, 1992), p. 24.
14. See also Stanley van der Ziel, 'Learning to Read', *John McGahern Yearbook*, vol. 4 (2011), pp. 20–9, at pp. 22–3.
15. John McGahern, letter to Declan Kiberd, *c.* December 2001. Private collection. Cf. Joyce's comment, quoted in Richard Ellmann, *James Joyce* [1959], rev. edn, with corrections (Oxford: Oxford University Press, 1983), p. 530.
16. Joyce, *A Portrait*, p. 180. This connection was first made by John Cronin, 'John McGahern: a new image?', in Jacqueline Genet and Wynne Hellegouarc'h (eds), *Irish Writers and Their Creative Process* (Gerrards Cross: Colin Smythe, 1996), pp. 110–17, at p. 112.
17. Joyce, *A Portrait*, p. 261.
18. Terence Brown, 'Redeeming the Time: the novels of John McGahern and John Banville', in James Acheson (ed.), *The British and Irish Novel since 1960* (New York: St Martin's, 1991), pp. 159–73, at p. 164.
19. Cf. also the narrator's thought in 'Wheels' about 'trembling between timidity and the edges of violence as the rest of your race' (*N*, p. 14).
20. James Joyce, *Poems and Exiles*, ed. J.C.C. Mays (Harmondsworth: Penguin, 1992), p. 107.
21. James Joyce, *Stephen Hero*, ed. Theodore Spencer, with John J. Slocum and Herbert Cahoon (New York: New Directions, 1963), p. 54.
22. James Joyce, *Finnegans Wake* [1939] (London: Faber & Faber, 1975), p. 214. See also Frank Shovlin, *Journey Westward: Joyce,* Dubliners *and the Literary Revival* (Liverpool: Liverpool University Press, 2012), pp. 51–2. The resonance of Maloney's obscene aphorism extends beyond Joyce. The structure of the three sentences in which it appears also exactly replicates a famous piece of Patrick Pearse's nationalist rhetoric from the 1910s: 'Ireland as we of to-day would surely have her: not free merely, but Gaelic as well; not Gaelic merely, but free as well.' *Collected Works of Padraic H. Pearse: political writings and speeches* (Dublin: Maunsel & Roberts, 1922), p. 135.
23. See especially the chapter on *Nightlines* in Denis Sampson, *Outstaring Nature's Eye: the fiction of John McGahern* (Washington, DC: Catholic University of America Press, 1993); and my own 'John McGahern: *Nightlines*', in Cheryl Alexander Malcolm and David Malcolm (eds), *A Companion to the British and Irish Short Story* (Malden and Oxford: Wiley–Blackwell, 2008), pp. 488–97.
24. John McGahern (screenplay), *The Sisters*, dir. Stephen Frears, prod. Gavin Millar and Melvyn Bragg, BBC 2, 17 February 1973. Typescripts of McGahern's adaptation are held at the BBC Written Archives Centre, Caversham Park, Reading: T51/188/1.

25. See my readings of that same opening paragraph on pp. 41 and 128–9, respectively.
26. James Joyce, *Dubliners* [1914] (Harmondsworth: Penguin, 1992), p. 29.
27. Ibid., pp. 1, 21.
28. Ibid., p. 102. McGahern mentions Maria's twice-sung verse in his essay on *Dubliners* (*LW*, p. 206).
29. Joyce, *A Portrait*, p. 220.
30. W.B. Yeats, *The Poems*, ed. Richard J. Finneran (London: Macmillan, 1984), p. 240.
31. Cf. ibid., p. 302.
32. John McGahern, letter to James (Jim) Rigney, 26 February 1963: NUIG, P71/item not yet catalogued.
33. The narrator's mother recites lines from Yeats' 'The Lover Pleads with His Friend for Old Friends' and 'Red Hanrahan's Song about Ireland', respectively (cf. Yeats, *The Poems*, pp. 71, 82). Her girlhood memory of being ridiculed for her love of poetry by a friend in the grounds of a Big House after a game of tennis on a summer's day (*L*, pp. 37–8) perhaps knowingly inverts the situation in the opening lines of Yeats' 'Adam's Curse', the lyric which immediately precedes 'Red Hanrahan' in Yeats' *Poems*: 'We sat together at one summer's end,/ That beautiful mild woman, your close friend,/ And you and I, and talked of poetry.' Yeats, *The Poems*, p. 80.
34. Denis Sampson, 'A Conversation with John McGahern', *Canadian Journal of Irish Studies*, vol. 17, no. 1 (July 1991), pp. 13–18, at p. 13.
35. W.B. Yeats, *Autobiographies* (London: Macmillan, 1955), p. 199.
36. Sampson, 'A Conversation with John McGahern', p. 13.
37. Ibid., pp. 13, 15.
38. Yeats, *The Poems*, p. 32.
39. Ibid., p. 81. On McGahern's earlier use of that same poem in his fiction, see note 33 of this chapter.
40. Ibid., p. 33.
41. Eamon Maher, 'Catholicism in the Writing of John McGahern', in Michael Böss and Eamon Maher (eds), *Engaging Modernity: readings of Irish politics, culture and literature at the turn of the century* (Dublin: Veritas, 2003), pp. 85–96, at p. 92.
42. Yeats, *Autobiographies*, p. 27. The echo was pointed out by Declan Kiberd, 'John McGahern's *Amongst Women*', in Maria Tymoczko and Colin Ireland (eds), *Language and Tradition in Ireland: continuities and displacements* (Amherst: University of Massachusetts Press, 2003), pp. 195–213, at p. 197.
43. Joyce, *A Portrait*, p. 178.
44. Ibid., pp. 178, 186.
45. Declan Kiberd, notes in Joyce, *Ulysses*, p. 1181.
46. See p. 210 below.
47. Cf. Joyce, *Ulysses*, p. 65.
48. *Letters on Poetry from W.B. Yeats to Dorothy Wellesley* (London: Oxford University Press, 1964), p. 183.
49. Cf. Yeats, *Autobiographies*, p. 482.
50. *Letters on Poetry from W.B. Yeats to Dorothy Wellesley*, p. 174.
51. See Brian Arkins, *Builders of My Soul: Greek and Roman themes in Yeats* (Gerrards Cross: Colin Smythe, 1990), p. 148. The quote is from Dryden's translation of Lucretius, which Yeats (and perhaps McGahern) knew.
52. Yeats, *The Poems*, pp. 216–17.
53. Joyce, *Ulysses*, p. 266. See also Karen Lawrence, 'Paternity, the Legal Fiction', in Robert D. Newman and Weldon Thornton (eds), *Joyce's* Ulysses*: the larger perspective* (Newark: University of Delaware Press, 1987), pp. 89–97.
54. Joyce, *Ulysses*, p. 30.

55. Andrew Gibson, *Joyce's Revenge: history, politics, and aesthetics in* Ulysses (Oxford: Oxford University Press, 2002), p. 38.
56. See my comments on *The Leavetaking* and historical revisionism on pp. 223–5 below. On Joyce, see Gibson's chapter on 'Stephen Dedalus, Ireland, and History' in *Joyce's Revenge*.
57. Nicholas Collins, '"[L]ike a shoal of fish moving within a net": *King Lear* and McGahern's family in *Amongst Women*', in Raymond Mullen, Adam Bargroff and Jennifer Mullen (eds), *John McGahern: critical essays* (Oxford: Peter Lang, 2014), pp. 113–36, at p. 134 n. 73.
58. W.B. Yeats, *A Vision* (London: Macmillan, 1937), p. 81.
59. Eamon Grennan, 'John McGahern: vision and revisionism', *Colby Quarterly*, vol. 31, no. 1 (March 1995), pp. 30–9, at p. 35. See also two more recent articles: Frank Shovlin, 'The Ghost of W.B. Yeats', *John McGahern Yearbook*, vol. 2 (2009), pp. 43–51; and Bertrand Cardin, '"Absence does not cast a shadow": Yeats's shadowy presence in McGahern's "The Wine Breath"', *Journal of the Short Story in English*, no. 53 (autumn 2009), pp. 111–25.
60. Yeats, *The Poems*, pp. 227–30.
61. Sampson, *Outstaring Nature's Eye*, p. 174. Cf. Yeats, *The Poems*, p. 243.
62. See my forthcoming essay on 'McGahern, Post-Revival Literature and Irish Cultural Criticism', in Adam Bargroff, Raymond Mullen and Tom Walker (eds), *John McGahern: ways of seeing*.
63. Yeats, *The Poems*, p. 134. See also Belinda McKeon, '"Robins Feeding with the Sparrows": the Protestant "Big House" in the fiction of John McGahern', *Irish University Review*, vol. 35, no. 1 (spring/summer 2005), pp. 72–89, at pp. 82–3; and Shovlin, 'The Ghost of W.B. Yeats', p. 50.
64. Yeats, *The Poems*, p. 216. See also Frank Shovlin, 'Four Ducks', *John McGahern Yearbook*, vol. 4 (2011), pp. 48–53, at pp. 52–3.
65. W.B. Yeats, *Mythologies* (London: Macmillan, 1959), p. 331. Denis Sampson suggests that 'so many echoes from [*Per Amica Silentia Lunae*] appear in McGahern's own prose that it is clear that he had sought it out and was deeply affected by it'. Sampson, *Young John McGahern: becoming a novelist* (Oxford: Oxford University Press, 2012), p. 71.
66. W.B. Yeats, *Essays and Introductions* (London: Macmillan, 1961), pp. 522–3.
67. See Stanley van der Ziel, editor's preface in McGahern, *Love of the World*, pp. xxxvii–xxxviii.
68. Evidently, the murder story was only of secondary interest to McGahern. He complained to the producer that the abridged version made for a BBC Radio 4 broadcast which foregrounded the violence of the murder plot 'read like a thriller'. Frances Byrnes, 'John McGahern' (obituary), *The Guardian*, 31 March 2006.
69. Madeline McGahern, in conversation with the present author, April 2008. See my editor's preface in McGahern, *Love of the World*, pp. xli–xlii.
70. Richard Ellmann, *Yeats: the man and the masks* (London: Faber & Faber, 1965), p. 201.
71. Yeats, *The Poems*, pp. 161–2 (emphasis added).
72. Ibid., p. 162.
73. Ibid., p. 161. One of the aphoristic artistic credos McGahern liked to repeat — that 'art is the opposite of self-expression' (see chapter four, note 66) — is precisely a reiteration of the Yeatsean doctrine of the anti-self as it is developed in 'Ego Dominus Tuus'.
74. Louis de Paor, '"Adhlachadh mo Mháthar", Seán Ó Riordáin', *Irish University Review*, vol. 39, no. 2 (autumn/winter 2009), pp. 172–81, at p. 175.
75. Samuel Beckett, *Molloy/Malone Dies/The Unnamable* [1950–52] (London: Calder, 1997), p. 418. On McGahern and the 'absurd', see the section on 'Post-war thought' in chapter seven.
76. W.B. Yeats, *Collected Plays* (London: Macmillan, 1963), p. 561.
77. St Augustine, *Confessions*, trans. R.S. Pine-Coffin (Harmondsworth: Penguin, 1961), p. 85.
78. See Liam Kelly, 'Homily Preached at the Funeral Mass of John McGahern', *Leitrim Guardian*, vol. 39 (2007), pp. 37–8.

79. Yeats, 'Two Songs from a Play', *The Poems*, p. 213.
80. Yeats, *Collected Plays*, p. 688.
81. Beckett, *Molloy/Malone Dies/The Unnamable*, p. 8.
82. John McGahern, 'The End or the Beginning of Love: episodes from a novel', *X: a quarterly review*, vol. 2, no. 1 (April 1961), pp. 36–46, at p. 41.
83. Frank Kermode, *The Sense of an Ending: studies in the theory of fiction* (London: Oxford University Press, 1966), pp. 44–6 and *passim*.
84. Ibid., p. 6.
85. Ephesians 3:21.
86. Patrick Kavanagh, *Collected Poems*, ed. Antoinette Quinn (London: Allen Lane, 2004), p. 63.
87. Joyce, *Finnegans Wake*, pp. 3, 628.
88. Roger Shattuck, *Proust's Way: a field guide to* In Search of Lost Time (Harmondsworth: Penguin, 2000), pp. 168–9.
89. Hermione Lee, 'Everything under the Sun' (rev. of *That They May Face the Rising Sun*), *The Observer*, 6 January 2002, Review, p. 16.
90. Sampson, 'A Conversation with John McGahern', p. 14.
91. *The Diary of Virginia Woolf*, ed. Anne Olivier Bell, 5 vols (Harmondsworth: Penguin, 1982), vol. iii, p. 312.
92. *The Letters of Virginia Woolf*, ed. Nigel Nicolson, 6 vols (London: Hogarth, 1975–80), vol. iv, p. 204.
93. Matthew Arnold, *Poetical Works*, ed. C.B. Tinker and H.F. Lowry (London: Oxford University Press, 1961), p. 211.
94. Cf. Yeats, *The Poems*, p. 181. The echo of 'Easter 1916' in *Amongst Women* has been remarked upon by a number of critics. They, like the present author, are all indebted to Denis Sampson, who first pointed it out in *Outstaring Nature's Eye*, p. 30 n. 65. NB that the same Yeatsean metaphor from 'Easter 1916' of the stone 'in the midst of it all' generating ripples in the stream of life is also recalled in *The Leavetaking*, in Isobel's description of the function of psychotherapy: 'The stone falling in the water throws out circles, it was the outer circle, the beginning of the journey from circle to inner circle, down to the stone in the mud in the river' (*L*, p. 132).
95. Arnold, 'Dover Beach', *Poetical Works*, p. 211.
96. Keith Hopper, recalling a meeting with McGahern during the 1990s: conversation with the present author, 26 July 2005.
97. Cf. 'Words alone are certain good.' Yeats, *The Poems*, p. 7; 'Ho, talk save us!' Joyce, *Finnegans Wake*, p. 215.
98. Samuel Beckett, *Complete Dramatic Works* (London: Faber & Faber, 1986), p. 58.
99. Declan Kiberd, *Irish Classics* (London: Granta, 2000), p. 40.
100. J.M. Synge, *Collected Works*, gen. ed. Robin Skelton, 4 vols (London: Oxford University Press, 1962–68), vol. iv, p. 173.
101. Beckett, *Molloy/Malone Dies/The Unnamable*, p. 7.
102. Ibid., p. 180.
103. Joyce, *A Portrait*, p. 262.
104. Yeats, *The Poems*, p. 337.
105. Emer Nolan, 'Modernism and the Irish Revival', in Joe Cleary and Claire Connolly (eds), *The Cambridge Companion to Modern Irish Culture* (Cambridge: Cambridge University Press, 2005), pp. 157–72, at p. 168.
106. See pp. 54 and 63 above.
107. Joyce, *Finnegans Wake*, pp. 196, 198.

108. Joyce, *Ulysses*, p. 38. On McGahern's use of that quote in interviews and works of fiction, see chapter four, note 54.
109. Cf. *The Letters of Virginia Woolf*, vol. v, p. 301.
110. See in particular Sam Phipps, 'The Curse of the Gab' (rev. of *That They May Face the Rising Sun*), *The Spectator*, 19 January 2002, p. 32.

Chapter 7: Post-war Philosophies

1. Albert Camus, *The Myth of Sisyphus* [1942], trans. Justin O'Brien (London: Penguin, 2000), p. 13.
2. The common critical fallacy that Ireland remained completely cut off from the wider world during the 'Emergency' (as the War was euphemistically known in Ireland), and that no references to the Second World War exist in the literature written during and immediately after that conflict because it was not pertinent to the imagination of Irish writers, has been comprehensively redressed in Clair Wills, *That Neutral Island: a cultural history of Ireland during the Second World War* (London: Faber & Faber, 2007).
3. Albert Camus, interview reprinted in *Lyrical and Critical Essays*, ed. Philip Thody, trans. Ellen Conroy Kennedy (London: Hamish Hamilton, 1967), p. 345.
4. Jean-Paul Sartre, *Being and Nothingness* [1943], trans. Hazel Barnes (London: Routledge, 1969), p. 619.
5. Clíodhna Ní Anluain (ed.), *Reading the Future: Irish writers in conversation with Mike Murphy* (Dublin: Lilliput, 2000), pp. 137–55, at p. 151.
6. Denis Sampson, *Outstaring Nature's Eye: the fiction of John McGahern* (Washington, DC: Catholic University of America Press, 1993), p. 35.
7. Camus, *The Myth of Sisyphus*, p. 111.
8. Ibid., p. xxi.
9. Ibid., p. xxi.
10. Albert Camus, *The Outsider* [1942], trans. Stuart Gilbert (Harmondsworth: Penguin, 1961), p. 120. See also Stanley van der Ziel, '"All This Talk and Struggle": John McGahern's *The Dark*', *Irish University Review*, vol. 35, no. 1 (spring/summer 2005), pp. 104–20, at pp. 113–16.
11. See p. 65 above.
12. For a lucid discussion of Irish historical revisionism, see for example the first three chapters of R.F. Foster, *The Irish Story: telling tales and making it up in Ireland* (London: Allen Lane, 2001).
13. Alun Munslow, *Deconstructing History*, 2nd edn (London: Routledge, 2006), p. 132.
14. McGahern may have been introduced to post-war French writers like Simon, Robbe-Grillet and Nathalie Sarraute through his friend Tony Whelan. McGahern had met Whelan during the summer holidays in 1954 in London, where the latter worked in a bookshop. During that time, Whelan kept McGahern abreast of new writers and new literary trends. See Denis Sampson, *Young John McGahern: becoming a novelist* (Oxford: Oxford University Press, 2012), p. 32. See also Tony Whelan, 'Working at the Mill', *John McGahern Yearbook*, vol. 2 (2009), pp. 28–41.
15. Claude Simon, *The Flanders Road* [1960], trans. Richard Howard (London: Cape, 1962), p. 140.
16. Ibid., p. 14 (ellipses in original).
17. John McGahern, letter to Michael McLaverty, 31 May 1965, *Dear Mr McLaverty: the literary correspondence of John McGahern and Michael McLaverty 1959–1980*, ed. John Killen (Belfast: Linen Hall Library, 2006), p. 40.

18. Cf. W.H. Auden, 'In Memory of W.B. Yeats', *Collected Poems*, ed. Edward Mendelson (London: Faber & Faber, 1994), p. 248.
19. Primo Levi, *If This Is a Man and The Truce* [1958/1963], trans. Stuart Woolf (London: Abacus, 1987), p. 93.
20. William Shakespeare, *King Lear*, ed. G.K. Hunter (London: Penguin, 2005), IV.i.27–8.
21. John McGahern, seminar on Primo Levi, Modern Writing series, University College, Dublin, 7 April 1999 (see note 55 of the introduction). See also a notepad marked 'Notes on reading Primo Levi' in which McGahern copied out a passage from *If This Is a Man* which reads: 'Sooner or later in life everyone discovers that perfect happiness is unrealizable, but there are few who pause to consider the antithesis: that perfect unhappiness is equally unattainable.' Levi, *If This Is a Man*, p. 23; cf. NUIG, P71/1490 (p. 2).
22. Samuel Beckett, *Complete Dramatic Works* (London: Faber & Faber, 1986), pp. 55–6, 229.
23. John McGahern, seminar on Primo Levi, Modern Writing series, University College, Dublin, 7 April 1999 (see note 55 of the introduction).
24. Ibid.
25. See p. 179 above.
26. Levi, *If This Is a Man*, p. 98.
27. See Sampson, *Young John McGahern*, p. 53.
28. Derek Hand, 'Saying Goodbye to John: or thank you for the day', John McGahern Irish Writing Commemorative Lecture, St Patrick's College, Drumcondra, 10 May 2007.
29. Hermione Lee, 'Readings & Conversations — John McGahern with Hermione Lee, 7 April 2004', www.lannan.org/docs/john-mcgahern-040407-trans-conv.pdf (accessed 19 January 2006), p. 6.
30. See my comment in chapter six (p. 203) on the presence of a Beckettian liminal bilingualism in some of McGahern's works.
31. McGahern refers to the 'lost generation' in Ní Anluain (ed.), *Reading the Future*, p. 149.
32. Ruttledge's comment may also specifically recall Elizabeth Bowen's infamous wish in her 'Notes on Eire': 'that the English kept history in mind more, that the Irish kept it in mind less'. Quoted in R.F. Foster, *Paddy and Mr Punch: connections in Irish and English history* (London: Allen Lane, 1993), p. 113.
33. Samuel Beckett, *Molloy/Malone Dies/The Unnamable* [1950–52] (London: Calder, 1997), p. 36. See also p. 43 above.
34. John McGahern, 'Sinclair', *The Listener*, 18 November 1971, pp. 690–2; Beckett, *Complete Dramatic Works*, pp. 192, 195–6.
35. John McGahern, incomplete manuscript draft of a dramatic work: NUIG, P71/1279 (p. 3).
36. Linda Collinge and Emmanuel Vernadakis, 'John McGahern' (interview), *Journal of the Short Story in English*, no. 41 (autumn 2003), pp. 123–41, at p. 129.
37. See James Knowlson, *Damned to Fame: the life of Samuel Beckett* (London: Bloomsbury, 1996), pp. 122–4.
38. Joe Jackson, 'Tales from the Darkside' (interview), *Hot Press*, 14 November 1991, pp. 18–20, at p. 20.
39. Beckett, *Molloy/Malone Dies/The Unnamable*, pp. 162, 304; Samuel Beckett, *How It Is* [1964] (London: Calder, 1996), p. 128; Samuel Beckett, *Worstward Ho* (London: Calder, 1983), p. 7.
40. Cathy Herbert, 'Window on the World' (interview), *Magill*, vol. 10, no. 13 (October 1987), pp. 56–62, at p. 60.
41. Beckett, *Complete Dramatic Works*, p. 11.
42. John McGahern, at a reading from his own work at St Patrick's College, Drumcondra, 9 April 2003.

43. Vivian Mercier, *Beckett/Beckett* (Oxford: Oxford University Press, 1977), p. xii.
44. Clare Boylan, 'John McGahern: evicting the ghosts from his imagination on to the pages of his stories' (interview), *Sunday Tribune*, 31 October 1993, People, p. 11.
45. See Nicole Ollier, 'Step by Step through *The Barracks* with John McGahern' (interview), *La Licorne*, no. 32 (1995), pp. 55–86, at p. 60.
46. Derek Mahon, 'A Disused Shed in Co. Wexford', *New Collected Poems* (Oldcastle: Gallery, 2011), p. 81.
47. Samuel Beckett, *Proust and Three Dialogues with Georges Duthuit* (London: Calder, 1965), p. 19.
48. Ibid., p. 20; Beckett, *Complete Dramatic Works*, p. 84.
49. For George O'Brien, 'the Metropole ... is not only a well-known Dublin venue from years gone by but a symbol of the chance encounter, the artificial atmosphere and the syncopated rhythms of the city'. O'Brien, *The Irish Novel 1960–2010* (Cork: Cork University Press, 2012), p. 68.
50. See John McGahern, 'Waiting', *Threshold*, no. 17 (1962), pp. 10–16; and McGahern, 'Waiting', *Transatlantic Review*, no. 12 (spring 1963), pp. 5–15.
51. Beckett, *Complete Dramatic Works*, p. 46.
52. Beckett, *Molloy/Malone Dies/The Unnamable*, p. 180.
53. Samuel Beckett, *Watt* [1953] (London: Calder, 1976), p. 24. I am indebted for the reading of the porter in *Watt* as a Sisyphus figure to C.J. Ackerley and S.E. Gontarski (eds), *The Faber Companion to Samuel Beckett: a reader's guide to his works, life, and thought* (London: Faber & Faber, 2006), p. 529.
54. See Walter Benjamin, *Charles Baudelaire: a lyric poet in the era of high capitalism*, trans. Harry Zohn (London: NLB, 1973), p. 75.
55. McGahern confirmed in general terms that he always took care over the ordering of the individual stories within each of his short-story collections, and specifically that he deliberately placed 'Wheels' at the head of *Nightlines*, in Stanley van der Ziel, 'An Interview with John McGahern', appendix ii in van der Ziel, 'Medusa's Mirror: art, style, vision and tradition in the fiction of John McGahern', PhD dissertation, University College, Dublin, 2008, pp. 361–81, at p. 378.
56. Denis Sampson has also drawn attention to the Beckettian significance of waiting in *The Barracks* in general, and made a comparison with *Malone Dies* in particular, in his *Young John McGahern*, pp. 86–7.
57. Mercier, *Beckett/Beckett*, p. 53.
58. Beckett, *Complete Dramatic Works*, p. 41.

Epilogue

1. Quoted in Michael C. Prusse, 'John McGahern', in Meritt Moseley (ed.), *British and Irish Short Story Writers 1945–2000*: vol. 231 of *Dictionary of Literary Biography* (Detroit: Gale, 2001), pp. 135–45, at p. 136.
2. See Mike McCormack, '*Nightlines*', *John McGahern Yearbook*, vol. 1 (2008), p. 129. On Claire Keegan's debt to McGahern, see James Ryan, 'Acknowledging a Debt to the Master', *John McGahern Yearbook*, vol. 1 (2008), pp. 111–13.
3. Joseph O'Connor, 'John McGahern', in Anthony Roche (ed.), *The UCD Aesthetic: celebrating 150 years of UCD writers* (Dublin: New Island, 2005), pp. 183–9.
4. Joseph O'Connor, 'Approaching the Silence' (rev. of *Creatures of the Earth*), *The Guardian*, 23 December 2006, Saturday Review, p. 14.

5. See Denis Sampson, *Young John McGahern: becoming a novelist* (Oxford: Oxford University Press, 2012), p. 55.
6. Clíodhna Ní Anluain (ed.), *Reading the Future: Irish writers in conversation with Mike Murphy* (Dublin: Lilliput, 2000), pp. 137–55, at p. 144.
7. W.B. Yeats, *The Poems*, ed. Richard J. Finneran (London: Macmillan, 1984), p. 348.
8. For the chronology of the different French and English versions of that play, see Ruby Cohn, *A Beckett Canon* (Ann Arbor: University of Michigan Press, 2001), p. 236.
9. Samuel Beckett, *Complete Dramatic Works* (London: Faber & Faber, 1986), p. 231 (emphasis added).
10. Samuel Beckett, 'The Gloaming', MS dated January 1956: The Beckett Collection, University of Reading Library, MS 1396/4/6 (p. 9). I am indebted to Mark Nixon at the University of Reading for helping me procure a copy of a transcript (BC MS 5030).
11. Samuel Beckett, 'Fragment de théatre', *Minuit*, no. 8 (March 1974), pp. 65–72, at p. 69.
12. See James Knowlson and John Pilling, *Frescoes of the Skull: the later prose and drama of Samuel Beckett* (London: Calder, 1979), p. 229; and C.J. Ackerley and S.E. Gontarski (eds), *The Faber Companion to Samuel Beckett: a reader's guide to his works, life, and thought* (London: Faber & Faber, 2006), p. 524.

Selected Bibliography

I. By John McGahern

Fiction

'The End or the Beginning of Love: episodes from a novel', *X: a quarterly review*, vol. 2, no. 1 (April 1961), pp. 36–46

'A Barrack Evening' (extract from *The Barracks*), in Thomas Kinsella and John Montague (eds), *The Dolmen Miscellany of Irish Writing* (Dublin: Dolmen, 1962), pp. 84–94

'Waiting' (extract from *The Barracks*), *Threshold*, no. 17 (1962), pp. 10–16

'Waiting' (extract from *The Barracks*), *Transatlantic Review*, no. 12 (spring 1963), pp. 5–15

The Barracks (London: Faber & Faber, 1963)

'Summer at Strandhill', *New Yorker*, 21 September 1963, pp. 43–8

The Dark (London: Faber & Faber, 1965)

Nightlines (London: Faber & Faber, 1970)

The Leavetaking (London: Faber & Faber, 1974)

Getting Through (London: Faber & Faber, 1978)

The Pornographer (London: Faber & Faber, 1979)

The Leavetaking, rev. 2nd edn (London: Faber & Faber, 1984)

High Ground (London: Faber & Faber, 1985)

Amongst Women (London: Faber & Faber, 1990)

Collected Stories (London: Faber & Faber, 1992)

'The White Boat', in A.S. Byatt and Peter Porter (eds), *New Writing 6: an anthology* (London: Vintage, 1997), pp. 342–72

That They May Face the Rising Sun (London: Faber & Faber, 2002)

'Evening: an extract from a short story', in Terence Brown and Gerald Dawe (eds), *The Writer Fellow: an anthology* (Dublin: Trinity College School of English, 2004), pp. 59–64

Creatures of the Earth: new and selected stories (London: Faber & Faber, 2006)

Dramatic writings

'Sinclair', *The Listener*, 18 November 1971, pp. 690–2
The Power of Darkness (London: Faber & Faber, 1991)

Non-fiction

'An tOileánach/The Islandman', *Canadian Journal of Irish Studies*, vol. 13, no. 1 (June 1987), pp. 7–15
'A Note on the Stories', in the programme for the touring production of *My Love, My Umbrella: a new opera by Kevin O'Connell and James Conway, based on John McGahern's short stories* (Opera Theatre Company, Ireland, 1997), pp. 12–13
Memoir (London: Faber & Faber, 2005)
Love of the World: essays, ed. Stanley van der Ziel (London: Faber & Faber, 2009)

Published correspondence

Dear Mr McLaverty: the literary correspondence of John McGahern and Michael McLaverty 1959–1980, ed. John Killen (Belfast: Linen Hall Library, 2006)
Letter to Tony Whelan, 16 July 1959, *John McGahern Yearbook*, vol. 2 (2009), pp. 32–3

II. About John McGahern

Interviews, profiles and recollections

[Andrews, Joyce], 'John McGahern', in Daniel Murphy (dir. of research), *Education and the Arts: the educational autobiographies of contemporary Irish poets, novelists, dramatists, musicians, painters and sculptors: a research report* (Dublin: Trinity College Department of Higher Education, 1987), pp. 129–43
Boylan, Clare, 'John McGahern: evicting the ghosts from his imagination on to the pages of his stories', *Sunday Tribune*, 31 October 1993, People, p. 11
Burch, Simon, 'The Perfectionist', *Cara*, vol. 35, no. 2 (March 2002), pp. 42–6
Byrnes, Frances, 'John McGahern' (obituary), *The Guardian*, 31 March 2006
Carlson, Julia (ed.), *Banned in Ireland: censorship and the Irish writer* (London: Routledge, 1990), pp. 53–67
Carthy, Ciaran, 'Out of the Dark', *Sunday Tribune*, 6 September 1987, p. 18
—, 'Sex, Ignorance and the Irish', *Sunday Tribune*, 29 September 1991, p. 27
Clements, Paul, 'The Book and Magazine Collector Interview: John McGahern', *Book and Magazine Collector*, no. 208 (July 2001), pp. 80–9
Collinge, Linda and Emmanuel Vernadakis, 'John McGahern', *Journal of the Short Story in English*, no. 41 (autumn 2003), pp. 123–41
Collins, Pat (dir.), *John McGahern: a private world*, Arts Lives documentary, RTÉ 1 television, 11 January 2005

Cronin, John, 'Interviewing John McGahern', in Laura P.Z. Izarra and Beatriz Kopschitz X. Bastos (eds), *A New Ireland in Brazil* (São Paulo: Humanitas, 2008), pp. 231–6

Dungan, Myles, Interview with John McGahern at Vicar Street, Dublin, RTÉ Radio 1, 8 June 2002

González, Rosa, 'An Interview with John McGahern', in Jacqueline Hurtley, Rosa González, Inés Praga and Esther Aliaga (eds), *Ireland in Writing: interviews with writers and academics* (Amsterdam: Rodopi, 1998), pp. 37–50

Grant, Linda, 'Private Isle', *Independent on Sunday*, 11 October 1992

Heneghan, Grace, 'In the Family: novel experiences', *Garda Journal*, November 1995, pp. 34–8

Herbert, Cathy, 'Window on the World', *Magill*, vol. 10, no. 13 (October 1987), pp. 56–62

Jack, Ian, 'Saving Grace', *The Guardian*, 8 April 2006, Saturday Review, p. 21

Jackson, Joe, 'Tales from the Darkside', *Hot Press*, 14 November 1991, pp. 18–22

Johnston, Fred, 'John McGahern at Fifty', *Irish Times*, 13 August 1985, p. 10

Joyce, Joe, 'Fiction Farmer', *The Guardian*, 26 April 1990, p. 25

Kampen, Gerd, 'An Interview with John McGahern', appendix in Kampen, *Zwischen Welt und Text: narratologische Studien zum irischen Gegenwartsroman am Beispiel von John McGahern und John Banville* (Trier: Wissenschaftlicher Verlag Trier, 2002), pp. 336–42

Kelly, Shirley, 'The Writing Keeps the Cattle in High Style', *Books Ireland*, no. 246 (February 2002), pp. 5–6

Kennedy, Eileen, 'Q.&A. with John McGahern', *Irish Literary Supplement*, vol. 3, no. 1 (spring 1984), p. 40

Kennedy, Joe, 'McGahern, "Art Is a Luxury": an interview with the author of *The Dark*', *Evening Herald*, 11 November 1970, p. 7

Lavery, Brian, 'From Rural Ireland, Prose Carved with Precise Simplicity', *New York Times*, 1 May 2003, E1, p. 6

Lee, Hermione, 'Readings & Conversations — John McGahern with Hermione Lee, 7 April 2004', www.lannan.org/docs/john-mcgahern-040407-trans-conv.pdf (accessed 19 January 2006)

Louvel, Liliane, Gilles Ménégaldo and Claudine Verley, 'John McGahern — 17 November 1993', *La Licorne*, no. 32 (1995), pp. 19–31

Lynch, Audrey L., 'An Interview with John McGahern', *Books Ireland*, no. 88 (November 1984), p. 213

Maher, Eamon, 'Catholicism and National Identity in the Works of John McGahern: interview', *Studies*, vol. 90, no. 357 (spring 2001), pp. 70–83

—, 'An Interview with John McGahern', appendix in Maher, *John McGahern: from the local to the universal* (Dublin: Liffey, 2003), pp. 143–61

—, 'Drawing from a Life of Fugitive Days', *Irish Book Review*, vol. 1, no. 2 (autumn 2005), pp. 12–13

McCarthy, Justine, 'Why John McGahern Would Never Tell a Lie', *Irish Independent*, 22 December 2001, Review, p. 9

—, 'I'm Not a Hero . . . I'm Just a Clerk' (interview), *Irish Independent*, 27 August 2005, Weekend Review, pp. 2–4

McCrum, Robert, 'The Books Interview: John McGahern', *The Observer*, 6 January 2002, Review, p. 16

McKay, Susan, 'Ordinary Man', *Sunday Tribune*, 6 January 2002, ArtLife, p. 1

Murphy, Colin, 'The Calm Journey through the Day', *Village*, 16–22 September 2005, pp. 32–3

Ní Anluain, Clíodhna (ed.), *Reading the Future: Irish writers in conversation with Mike Murphy* (Dublin: Lilliput, 2000), pp. 137–55

O'Hagan, Sean, 'A Family Touched with Madness', *The Observer*, 28 August 2005, Review, p. 9

Ollier, Nicole, 'Step by Step through *The Barracks* with John McGahern', *La Licorne*, no. 32 (1995), pp. 55–86

O'Toole, Fintan, 'The Family as Independent Republic', *Irish Times*, 13 October 1990, Weekend, p. 2

Pine, Richard, 'John McGahern' (obituary), *The Guardian*, 31 March 2006

Sampson, Denis, 'A Conversation with John McGahern', *Canadian Journal of Irish Studies*, vol. 17, no. 1 (July 1991), pp. 13–18

Tóibín, Colm, 'Out of the Dark: a profile of John McGahern' [1985], *The Trials of the Generals: selected journalism 1980–1990* (Dublin: Raven Arts, 1990), pp. 94–102

Wallace, Arminta, 'Out of the Dark', *Irish Times*, 28 April 1990, Weekend, p. 5

Whelan, Tony, 'Working at the Mill', *John McGahern Yearbook*, vol. 2 (2009), pp. 28–41

Whyte, James, 'An Interview with John McGahern', appendix in Whyte, *History, Myth, and Ritual in the Fiction of John McGahern: strategies of transcendence* (Lewiston: Edwin Mellen, 2002), pp. 227–35

Wroe, Nicholas, 'Ireland's Rural Elegist', *The Guardian*, 5 January 2002: Saturday Review, pp. 6–7

Ziel, Stanley van der, 'An Interview with John McGahern', appendix ii in van der Ziel, 'Medusa's Mirror: art, style, vision and tradition in the fiction of John McGahern' (PhD dissertation, University College, Dublin, 2008), pp. 361–81

Criticism and commentary

Banville, John, 'To Have Is to Hold, and Hate' (rev. of *Amongst Women*), *The Observer*, 6 May 1990, p. 61

Brannigan, John (ed.), *Irish University Review*, vol. 35, no. 1 (spring/summer 2005): special issue on John McGahern

Brihault, Jean and Liliane Louvel (eds), *La Licorne*, no. 32 (1995): special issue on John McGahern

Brown, Terence, 'John McGahern's *Nightlines*: tone, technique and symbolism', in Patrick Rafroidi and Terence Brown (eds), *The Irish Short Story* (Gerrards Cross: Colin Smythe, 1979), pp. 289–301

—, 'Redeeming the Time: the novels of John McGahern and John Banville', in James Acheson (ed.), *The British and Irish Novel since 1960* (New York: St Martin's, 1991), pp. 159–73

Caleshu, Anthony, 'How McGahern Did It', *Dublin Review*, no. 37 (winter 2009–10), pp. 70–6

Cardin, Bertrand, 'Figures of Silence: ellipses and eclipses in John McGahern's *Collected Stories*', *Journal of the Short Story in English*, no. 40 (spring 2003), pp. 57–68

—, '"Absence does not cast a shadow": Yeats's shadowy presence in McGahern's "The Wine Breath"', *Journal of the Short Story in English*, no. 53 (autumn 2009), pp. 111–25

Casey, Fergal, 'Competing Philosophies in John McGahern's *That They May Face the Rising Sun*', *Irish University Review*, vol. 43, no. 2 (autumn/winter 2013), pp. 414–28

Collinge, Linda and Emmanuel Vernadakis (eds), *Journal of the Short Story in English*, no. 53 (autumn 2009): special issue on the short stories of John McGahern

Collins, Nicholas, '"[L]ike a shoal of fish moving within a net": *King Lear* and McGahern's family in *Amongst Women*', in Raymond Mullen, Adam Bargroff and Jennifer Mullen (eds), *John McGahern: critical essays* (Oxford: Peter Lang, 2014), pp. 113–36

Cowie, Douglas, '"Korea" by John McGahern', *Journal of the Short Story in English*, no. 53 (autumn 2009), pp. 237–48

[Cronin, Anthony], 'Swotting out of the Farm' (rev. of *The Dark*), *Times Literary Supplement*, 13 May 1965, p. 365

Cronin, John, 'Art and the Failure of Love: the fiction of John McGahern', *Studies*, vol. 77, no. 306 (summer 1988), pp. 201–17

—, 'John McGahern's *Amongst Women*: retrenchment and renewal', *Irish University Review*, vol. 22, no. 1 (spring/summer 1992), pp. 168–76

—, 'John McGahern: a new image?', in Jacqueline Genet and Wynne Hellegouarc'h (eds), *Irish Writers and Their Creative Process* (Gerrards Cross: Colin Smythe, 1996), pp. 110–17

Deane, Seamus, 'A New Dawn' (rev. of *That They May Face the Rising Sun*), *The Guardian*, 12 January 2002, Saturday Review, p. 9

Devine, Paul, 'Style and Structure in John McGahern's *The Dark*', *Critique*, vol. 21, no. 1 (spring 1979), pp. 49–58

DiBattista, Maria, 'Joyce's Ghost: the bogey of realism in John McGahern's *Amongst Women*', in Karen R. Lawrence (ed.), *Transcultural Joyce* (Cambridge: Cambridge University Press, 1998), pp. 21–36

Fahey, Fergus, 'Reinvented, Reimagined and Somehow Dislocated', *Journal of the Short Story in English*, no. 53 (autumn 2009), pp. 39–51

Fierobe, Claude (ed.), *Études sur* The Barracks *de John McGahern*, special issue of *Études Irlandaises* (October 1994)

Forkner, Ben (ed.), *Journal of the Short Story in English*, no. 34 (spring 2000), pp. 13–85: special issue section on the art of John McGahern's short fiction

Fournier, Suzanne J., 'Structure and Theme in John McGahern's *The Pornographer*', *Éire–Ireland*, vol. 22, no. 1 (spring 1987), pp. 130–50

Goarzin, Anne, *John McGahern: reflets d'Irlande* (Rennes: Presses Universitaires de Rennes, 2002)

—, '"A Crack in the Concrete": objects in the works of John McGahern', *Irish University Review*, vol. 35, no. 1 (spring/summer 2005), pp. 28–41

Görtschacher, Wolfgang, 'The Real Experiment Is a Constant Experiment: John McGahern's "Strandhill, the Sea"', in Wolfgang Görtschacher and Holger Klein (eds), *Tale, Novella, Short Story: currents in short fiction* (Tübingen: Stauffenburg, 2004), pp. 239–48

Grennan, Eamon, 'John McGahern: vision and revisionism', *Colby Quarterly*, vol. 31, no. 1 (March 1995), pp. 30–9

—, 'Presence, Absence, Amputations: post-Catholic McGahern', *Facing the Music: Irish poetry in the twentieth century* (Omaha, NE: Creighton University Press, 1999), pp. 119–30

—, '"Only What Happens": mulling over McGahern', *Irish University Review*, vol. 35, no. 1 (spring/summer 2005), pp. 13–27

Hand, Derek, *A History of the Irish Novel* (Cambridge: Cambridge University Press, 2011): inter ch. 8: 'John McGahern's *That They May Face the Rising Sun*: saying the very last things', pp. 284–9

Harte, Liam, *Reading the Contemporary Irish Novel 1987–2007* (Malden and Oxford: Wiley–Blackwell, 2014): ch. 2: 'House Arrest: John McGahern's *Amongst Women*', pp. 51–74

Heaney, Seamus, 'Shedding the Skin of Youth' (rev. of *The Leavetaking*), *Sunday Independent*, 26 January 1975, p. 9

Holland, Siobhán, 'Re-citing the Rosary: women, Catholicism and agency in Brian Moore's *Cold Heaven* and John McGahern's *Amongst Women*', in Liam Harte and Michael Parker (eds), *Contemporary Irish Fiction: themes, tropes, theories* (London: Macmillan, 2000), pp. 56–78

—, '"Hel-lo . . . Hel-lo . . . Hel-lo": the uncertain voice of patriarchy in John McGahern's fictions of the War of Independence', *Moving Worlds*, vol. 3, no. 1 (2003), pp. 87–100

—, 'Marvellous Fathers in the Fiction of John McGahern', *Yearbook of English Studies*, vol. 35 (2005), pp. 186–98

Hughes, Eamonn, '"All That Surrounds Our Life": time, sex, and death in *That They May Face the Rising Sun*', *Irish University Review*, vol. 35, no. 1 (spring/summer 2005), pp. 147–63

Hurley, Vincent, 'Recent Fictional Perspectives on Provincial Ireland', *Colby Quarterly*, vol. 31, no. 1 (March 1995), pp. 23–9

Kampen, Gerd, *Zwischen Welt und Text: narratologische Studien zum irischen Gegenwartsroman am Beispiel von John McGahern und John Banville* (Trier: Wissenschaftlicher Verlag Trier, 2002)

Kearney, Richard, 'A Crisis of Imagination (an analysis of a counter-tradition in the Irish novel)', *Crane Bag*, vol. 3, no. 1 (1979), pp. 58–70

Kennedy, Eileen, 'The Novels of John McGahern: the road away becomes the road back', in James D. Brophy and Raymond J. Porter (eds), *Contemporary Irish Writing* (Boston: Twayne, 1983), pp. 115–26

—, 'Sons and Fathers in John McGahern's Short Stories', in James D. Brophy and Eamon Grennan (eds), *New Irish Writing* (Boston: Twayne, 1989), pp. 65–74

Kenny, John (ed.), *John McGahern Yearbook*, vol. 1– (2008–)

Kiberd, Declan, 'John McGahern's *Amongst Women*', in Maria Tymoczko and Colin Ireland (eds), *Language and Tradition in Ireland: continuities and displacements* (Amherst: University of Massachusetts Press, 2003), pp. 195–213

—, 'Fallen Nobility: the world of John McGahern', *Irish University Review*, vol. 35, no. 1 (spring/summer 2005), pp. 164–74

—, 'Forms of Life', *John McGahern Yearbook*, vol. 1 (2008), pp. 20–9

Killeen, Terence, 'Versions of Exile: a reading of *The Leavetaking*', *Canadian Journal of Irish Studies*, vol. 17, no. 1 (July 1991), pp. 69–78

King, Sophia Hillan, '"Quiet Desperation": variations on a theme in the writings of Daniel Corkery, Michael McLaverty and John McGahern', in Myrtle Hill and Sarah Barber (eds), *Aspects of Irish Studies* (Belfast: Institute of Irish Studies, Queen's University, 1990), pp. 39–43

Lanters, José, '"It Fills Many a Vacuum": food and hunger in the early novels of John McGahern', *Canadian Journal of Irish Studies*, vol. 20, no. 1 (July 1994), pp. 30–40

Lee, Hermione, 'Everything under the Sun' (rev. of *That They May Face the Rising Sun*), *The Observer*, 6 January 2002, Review, p. 16

Louvel, Liliane, 'Reading John McGahern's "Love of the World": a fistful of images', *Journal of the Short Story in English*, no. 53 (autumn 2009), pp. 53–67

Maher, Eamon, 'John McGahern, a Writer in Tune with His Time', *Crosscurrents and Confluences: echoes of religion in twentieth-century fiction* (Dublin: Veritas, 2000), pp. 139–54

—, 'Catholicism in the Writings of John McGahern', in Michael Böss and Eamon Maher (eds), *Engaging Modernity: readings of Irish politics, culture and literature at the turn of the century* (Dublin: Veritas, 2003), pp. 85–96

—, *John McGahern: from the local to the universal* (Dublin: Liffey, 2003)

—, 'Circles and Circularity in the Writings of John McGahern', *Nordic Irish Studies*, vol. 4 (2005), pp. 157–66

—, *'The Church and Its Spire': John McGahern and the Catholic question* (Blackrock: Columba, 2011)

Maher, Eamon and Declan Kiberd, 'John McGahern: writer, stylist, seeker of a lost world', *Doctrine & Life*, vol. 52, no. 2 (February 2002), pp. 82–97

Mahon, Derek, 'Is There No Escape?' (rev. of *Nightlines*), *The Times*, 12 November 1970, p. 14

Malcolm, David, '"All Is True"?: the functions of auto/biographical materials in John McGahern's fiction', in Sabine Coelsch-Foisner and Wolfgang Görtschacher (eds), *Fiction and Autobiography: modes and models of interaction* (Frankfurt: Peter Lang, 2006), pp. 181–93

—, *Understanding John McGahern* (Columbia: University of South Carolina Press, 2007)

Mays, Marianne (Koenig), '"Ravished and Exasperated": the evolution of John McGahern's plain style', *Canadian Journal of Irish Studies*, vol. 17, no. 1 (July 1991), pp. 38–52

McCarthy, Dermot, *John McGahern and the Art of Memory* (Oxford: Peter Lang, 2010)

McCormack, Mike, '*Nightlines*', *John McGahern Yearbook*, vol. 1 (2008), p. 129

McKeon, Belinda, '"Robins Feeding with the Sparrows": the Protestant "Big House" in the fiction of John McGahern', *Irish University Review*, vol. 35, no. 1 (spring/summer 2005), pp. 72–89

McWilliams, Ellen, *Women and Exile in Contemporary Irish Fiction* (Basingstoke: Palgrave Macmillan, 2013): ch. 4: 'Relative Visibility: women, exile and censorship in John McGahern's *The Leavetaking* and *Amongst Women*', pp. 93–125

Mercier, Vivian, 'Growing up in Ireland' (rev. of *The Dark*), *New York Times Book Review*, 6 March 1966, p. 50

Montague, John, 'John McGahern', in D.L. Kirkpatrick (ed.), *Contemporary Novelists*, 4th edn (Chicago: St James, 1986), pp. 592–3

Mullen, Raymond, '"The womb and the grave": living, loving and dying in John McGahern's *The Pornographer* and Albert Camus' *L'Étranger*', in Eamon Maher, Eugene O'Brien and Grace Neville (eds), *Reinventing Ireland through a French Prism* (Frankfurt: Peter Lang, 2007), pp. 229–43

Mullen, Raymond, Adam Bargroff and Jennifer Mullen (eds), *John McGahern: critical essays* (Oxford: Peter Lang, 2014)

Murray, Christopher, 'The "fallen world" of *The Power of Darkness*', *John McGahern Yearbook*, vol. 2 (2009), pp. 78–90

O'Brien, George, 'Going Inland' (rev. of *Memoir*), *Dublin Review*, no. 22 (spring 2006), pp. 36–46

—, *The Irish Novel 1960–2010* (Cork: Cork University Press, 2012): ch.: 'John McGahern: *The Pornographer*', pp. 67–70

O'Connor, Joseph, 'John McGahern', in Anthony Roche (ed.), *The UCD Aesthetic: celebrating 150 years of UCD writers* (Dublin: New Island, 2005), pp. 183–9

—, 'Approaching the Silence' (rev. of *Creatures of the Earth*), *The Guardian*, 23 December 2006, Saturday Review, p. 14

Paccaud-Huguet, Josiane, 'A Strangely Polished Looking-glass: John McGahern's peculiar realism', *Q/W/E/R/T/Y*, vol. 4 (October 1994), pp. 315–24

Phipps, Sam, 'The Curse of the Gab' (rev. of *That They May Face the Rising Sun*), *The Spectator*, 19 January 2002, p. 32

Pierce, David, *Light, Freedom and Song: a cultural history of modern Irish writing* (New Haven: Yale University Press, 2005): ch. 9: 'John McGahern: a parting glass', pp. 280–7

Price, Graham, 'Impure and Complicated Truth: Brian Friel's *Faith Healer* and John McGahern's "The Country Funeral"', *New Hibernia Review*, vol. 16, no. 4 (winter 2012), pp. 95–109.

—, 'The Fact Is a Fiction: representations of memory, place and modernity in Friel and McGahern's short stories', in Raymond Mullen, Adam Bargroff and Jennifer Mullen (eds), *John McGahern: critical essays* (Oxford: Peter Lang, 2014), pp. 155–72

Prusse, Michael C., 'John McGahern', in Meritt Moseley (ed.), *British and Irish Short Story Writers 1945–2000*: vol. 231 of *Dictionary of Literary Biography* (Detroit: Gale, 2001), pp. 135–45

—, 'Symmetry Matters: John McGahern's "Korea" as hypertext of Ernest Hemingway's "Indian Camp"', in Georges Letissier (ed.), *Rewritting/Reprising* (Newcastle: Cambridge Scholars, 2009), pp. 22–39

—, 'Repetition, Difference and Chiasmus in John McGahern's Narratives', *Language and Literature*, vol. 21, no. 4 (November 2012), pp. 363–80

Quinn, Antoinette, 'Varieties of Disenchantment: narrative technique in John McGahern's short stories', *Journal of the Short Story in English*, no. 13 (autumn 1989), pp. 77–89

—, 'A Prayer for My Daughter: patriarchy in *Amongst Women*', *Canadian Journal of Irish Studies*, vol. 17, no. 1 (July 1991), pp. 79–90

Raban, Jonathan, 'Exiles — new fiction' (rev. of *The Leavetaking*), *Encounter*, vol. 44, no. 6 (June 1975), pp. 77–9

Robinson, Richard, 'An Umbrella, a Pair of Boots, and a "Spacious Nothing": McGahern and Beckett', *Irish University Review*, vol. 44, no. 2 (autumn/winter 2014), pp. 323–40

Rogers, Lori, *Feminine Nation: performance, gender and resistance in the works of John McGahern and Neil Jordan* (Lanham: University Press of America, 1998)

Ryan, James, 'Acknowledging a Debt to the Master', *John McGahern Yearbook*, vol. 1 (2008), pp. 111–13

Sampson, Denis (ed.), *Canadian Journal of Irish Studies*, vol. 17, no. 1 (July 1991): special issue on John McGahern

—, 'The Lost Image: some notes on McGahern and Proust', *Canadian Journal of Irish Studies*, vol. 17, no. 1 (July 1991), pp. 57–68

—, 'John McGahern: a preliminary checklist', *Canadian Journal of Irish Studies*, vol. 17, no. 1 (July 1991), pp. 93–101

—, *Outstaring Nature's Eye: the fiction of John McGahern* (Washington, DC: Catholic University of America Press, 1993)

—, 'The "Rich Whole": John McGahern's *Collected Stories* as autobiography', *Journal of the Short Story in English*, no. 34 (spring 2000), pp. 21–30

—, '"Open to the World": a reading of John McGahern's *That They May Face the Rising Sun*', *Irish University Review*, vol. 35, no. 1 (spring/summer 2005), pp. 136–46

—, 'The "sacred weather" of County Leitrim: John McGahern's *Memoir*', *Irish Review*, no. 36/37 (winter 2007), pp. 120–8

—, '"The Day Set Alight in the Mind": notes on John McGahern's late style', *Irish University Review*, vol. 39, no. 1 (spring/summer 2009), pp. 122–8

—, *Young John McGahern: becoming a novelist* (Oxford: Oxford University Press, 2012)

Schwartz, Karlheinz, 'John McGahern's Point of View', *Éire–Ireland*, vol. 19, no. 3 (autumn 1984), pp. 92–110

Sheridan, John D., 'Classic Tragedy in the Barracks' (rev. of *The Barracks*), *Irish Independent*, 16 March 1963, p. 10

Shovlin, Frank, 'The Ghost of W.B. Yeats', *John McGahern Yearbook*, vol. 2 (2009), pp. 43–51

—, 'Four Ducks', *John McGahern Yearbook*, vol. 4 (2011), pp. 48–53

Toolan, Michael J., 'John McGahern: the historian and the pornographer', *Canadian Journal of Irish Studies*, vol. 7, no. 2 (December 1981), pp. 39–55

Tosser, Yvon, 'Théorie de l'image, sensibilité absurd et aspects de la pratique textuelle dans *Nightlines*', *Cahiers du Centre d'Études Irlandaises*, no. 4 (1979), pp. 7–31

Vivante, Paolo, 'McGahern and the Homeric Moment', *Canadian Journal of Irish Studies*, vol. 17, no. 1 (July 1991), pp. 53–6

Wall, Eamon, 'The Living Stream: John McGahern's *Amongst Women* and Irish writing in the 1990s', *Studies*, vol. 88, no. 351 (autumn 1999), pp. 305–14

Whyte, James, *History, Myth, and Ritual in the Fiction of John McGahern: strategies of transcendence* (Lewiston: Edwin Mellen, 2002)

Wondrich, Roberta Gefter, 'Exilic Returns: self and history outside Ireland in recent Irish fiction', *Irish University Review*, vol. 30, no. 1 (spring/summer 2000), pp. 1–16

Ziel, Stanley van der, 'The Aesthetics of Redemption: John McGahern's *That They May Face the Rising Sun*', *Studies*, vol. 93, no. 372 (winter 2004), pp. 473–86

—, '"All This Talk and Struggle": John McGahern's *The Dark*', *Irish University Review*, vol. 35, no. 1 (spring/summer 2005), pp. 104–20

—, 'John McGahern — an annotated bibliography', *Irish University Review*, vol. 35, no. 1 (spring/summer 2005), pp. 175–202

—, 'Fionn and Oisin in the Land of Wink and Nod: heroes, history, and the creative imagination in John McGahern's *Amongst Women*', *Canadian Journal of Irish Studies*, vol. 31, no. 2 (autumn 2005), pp. 10–18

—, Review of *Memoir*, *Irish University Review*, vol. 35, no. 2 (autumn/winter 2005), pp. 463–9

—, 'John McGahern: *Nightlines*', in Cheryl Alexander Malcolm and David Malcolm (eds), *A Companion to the British and Irish Short Story* (Malden and Oxford: Wiley–Blackwell, 2008), pp. 488–97

—, 'Learning to Read', *John McGahern Yearbook*, vol. 4 (2011), pp. 20–9

—, 'McGahern, Austen and the Aesthetics of Good Manners', *Essays in Criticism*, vol. 63, no. 2 (April 2013), pp. 203–22

Index